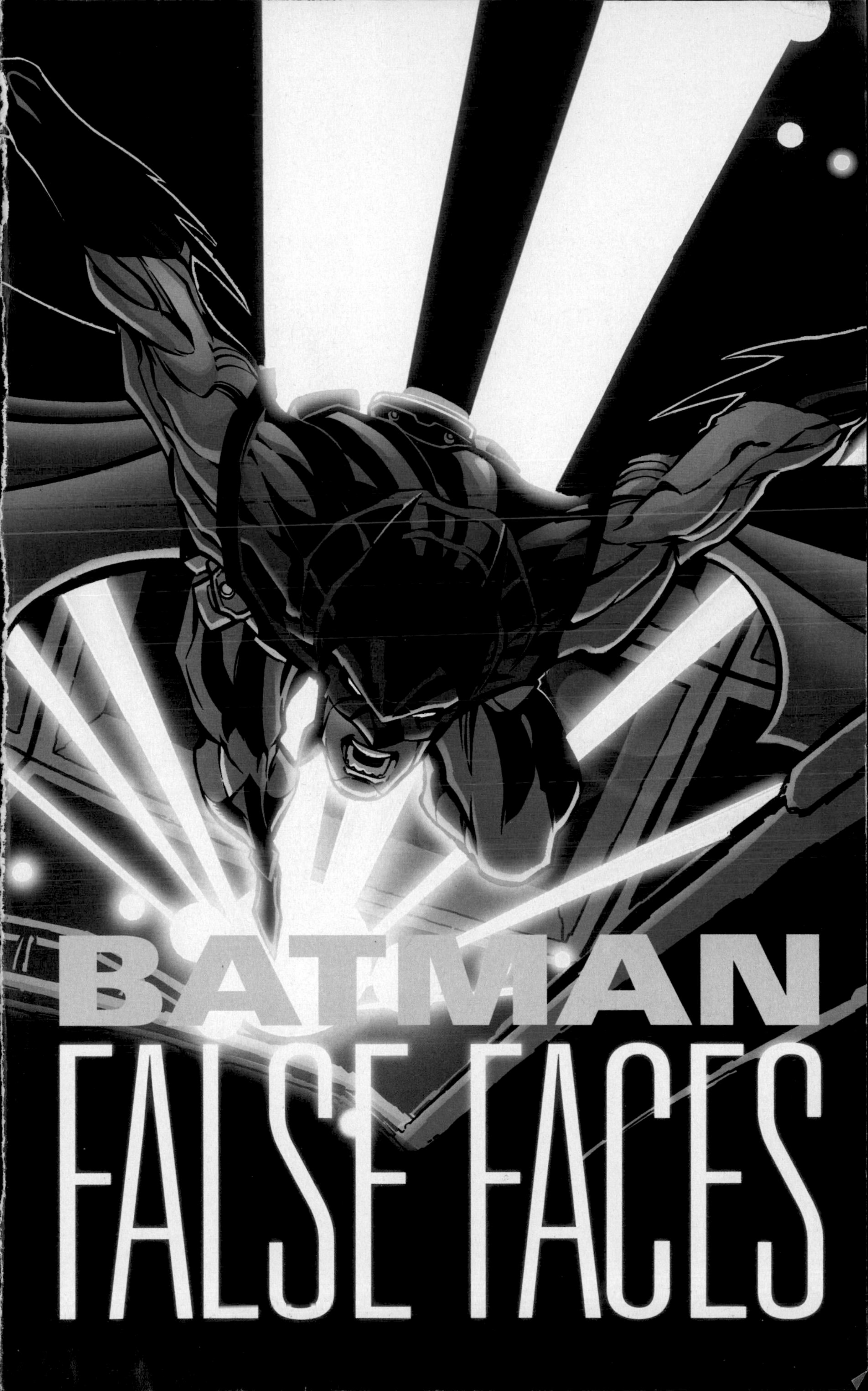
BATMAN
FALSE FACES

ALL STORIES WRITTEN BY **BRIAN K. VAUGHAN**

CLOSE BEFORE STRIKING

SCOTT McDANIEL Penciller
KARL STORY Inker
ROBERTA TEWES Colorist
JOHN COSTANZA Letterer

MIMSY WERE THE BOROGOVES

RICK BURCHETT Penciller
JOHN LOWE Inker
JASON WRIGHT Colorist
JOHN COSTANZA Letterer

A PIECE OF YOU

SCOTT KOLINS Penciller
DAN PANOSIAN / DREW GERACI Inkers
PAM RAMBO Colorist
JOHN COSTANZA Letterer

SKULLDUGGERY

MARCOS MARTIN Penciller
MARK PENNINGTON Inker
TOM McCRAW Colorist
TIM HARKINS Letterer

BATMAN CREATED BY **BOB KANE**
WONDER WOMAN CREATED BY **WILLIAM MOULTON MARSTON**

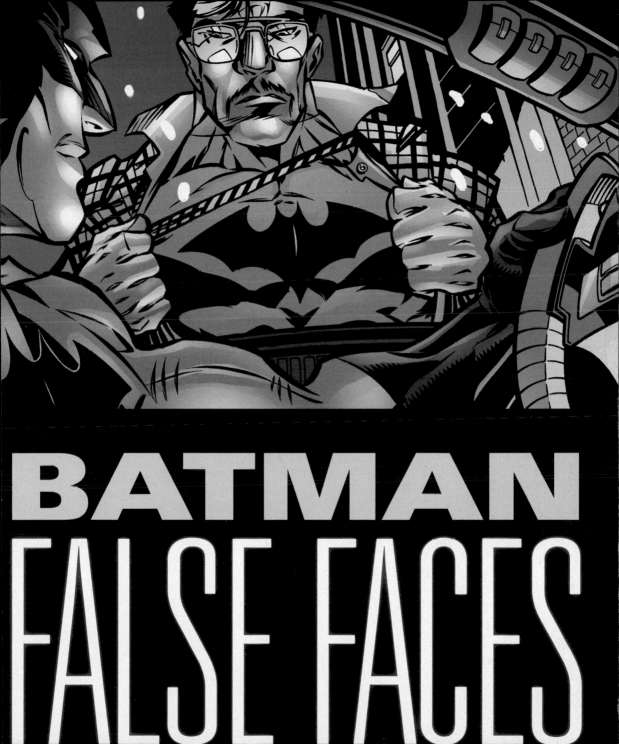

BATMAN
FALSE FACES

DAN DIDIO Senior VP-Executive Editor

BOB SCHRECK / MAUREEN McTIGUE / TONY BEDARD Editors-original series

MICHAEL WRIGHT Associate Editor-original series

BOB HARRAS Editor-collected edition

ROBBIN BROSTERMAN Senior Art Director

PAUL LEVITZ President & Publisher

GEORG BREWER VP-Design & DC Direct Creative

RICHARD BRUNING Senior VP-Creative Director

PATRICK CALDON Executive VP-Finance & Operations

CHRIS CARAMALIS VP-Finance

JOHN CUNNINGHAM VP-Marketing

TERRI CUNNINGHAM VP-Managing Editor

ALISON GILL VP-Manufacturing

DAVID HYDE VP-Publicity

HANK KANALZ VP-General Manager, WildStorm

JIM LEE Editorial Director-WildStorm

PAULA LOWITT Senior VP-Business & Legal Affairs

MARYELLEN McLAUGHLIN VP-Advertising & Custom Publishing

JOHN NEE Senior VP-Business Development

GREGORY NOVECK Senior VP-Creative Affairs

SUE POHJA VP-Book Trade Sales

STEVE ROTTERDAM Senior VP- Sales & Marketing

CHERYL RUBIN Senior VP-Brand Management

JEFF TROJAN VP-Business Development, DC Direct

BOB WAYNE VP-Sales

Cover by Scott McDaniel and Andy Owens.
Cover colored by Guy Major.
Publication design by Amelia Grohman.

BATMAN: FALSE FACES

Published by DC Comics.
Cover, introduction and compilation copyright
© 2008 DC Comics. All Rights Reserved.

Originally published in single magazine form in WONDER WOMAN
160, 161, BATMAN: GOTHAM CITY SECRET FILES 1, BATMAN 588-590,
DETECTIVE COMICS 787 Copyright © 2000, 2001, 2003 DC Comics.
All Rights Reserved. All characters, their distinctive likenesses and related
elements featured in this publication are trademarks of DC Comics.
The stories, characters and incidents featured in this publication are
entirely fictional. DC Comics does not read or accept unsolicited
submissions of ideas, stories or artwork.

DC Comics, 1700 Broadway, New York, NY 10019
A Warner Bros. Entertainment Company
Printed in Canada. First Printing.
ISBN: 978-1-4012-1640-5

This is all Kurt Busiek's fault.

We were signing next to each other at a convention in rainy Bristol a few months back, and Kurt (whose knowledge of all things comic rivals that of any other carbon-based life form) turned to me and said that DC should really reprint those Batman and Wonder Woman stories I did several years ago, and call the collection "False Faces."

I swear that I didn't even remember writing some of the stories that Kurt mentioned, but a nearby DC staffer scribbled a quick note, and the next thing I know...

Lo, the Power of Busiek.

At first, I have to admit that I was kind of horrified by the thought of some of my earliest writing being dragged back into the harsh light of day. On the off chance that people know who I am at all, I've found that they often think of me as an "overnight success." That illusion is aces with me, but I actually started toiling away in comics more than a decade ago as a nineteen-year-old kid, way back when I still had hair (a little).

The book you're now weighing in your sweaty paws doesn't contain all of my superhero stories for DC (bargain hunters and masochists can track down my old JLA ANNUAL that introduced the world's first Turkish superheroine), but I'm pleased to say that these are the ones I'm most proud of, all of which I was surprised to find deal in some capacity with the concept of identity.

There are definitely some clunky beats here and there, and you can really see me awkwardly growing up in public as a writer in places, but rereading these issues for the first time in years, I was more horrified by the parts that I loved, as they seem to confirm my darkest fears that I peaked way back when and have been spiraling into mediocrity ever since.

Chronologically, I think I wrote the Wonder Woman two-parter first, and it's probably the least developed of the stories in here in terms of my meager skills, though my patient editors and fantastic artist Scott Kolins did some heroic work to smooth out the rougher edges. But anyone who thinks that pitting a character made of magical clay against friggin' Clayface isn't a totally awesome idea is a dirty communist.

Next up came "Skullduggery," a short story that I did for GOTHAM SECRET FILES with the great Marcos Martin (my recent collaborator on Marvel's *Doctor Strange: The Oath*), who became a dear friend despite the overwhelming amount of pink captions I used to cover his lovely artwork here. We thought it would be cool to create a new villain with an intimate connection to Bruce Wayne, but the character never really caught on, so his true identity remains a secret to this day. I still get the occasional e-mail about the Skeleton, so maybe I'll unmask him (or her?) to the first person who finds the obscenely juvenile punchline that I hid somewhere in the story.

It was about a year later that I wrote the three-part Matches Malone storyline in BATMAN, and I like to think that's when I started to hit my stride, having finally crapped out my proverbial 9,999th page of garbage after several years of writing ten pages every single day. I remember getting Scott McDaniel's glorious artwork over my antiquated fax machine, and being so creatively reinvigorated by the way his kinetic storytelling elevated my simple script.

That arc was my audition for the regular writing assignment on BATMAN, a gig that ultimately ended up going to the infinitely more deserving Ed Brubaker. At the time, I was pretty crestfallen, but I channeled my renewed love for the medium into developing a dumb idea I had about a boy and his monkey. So things shook out okay.

My final contribution to the DCU was a DETECTIVE COMICS one-shot that I wrote as an "inventory issue," an old-school practice of having a relatively continuity-free stand-alone story on hand in case of deadline emergencies. It remained in a drawer for years, so I was thrilled when it was finally published since it's a real favorite, thanks both to the elegant linework of the incomparable Rick Burchett, and the obvious debt the story owes to my old day job at the psychiatric ward of St. Vincent's Hospital, where I was still working to support myself while writing these very stories.

At this stage of my life, I've decided to concentrate more or less exclusively on new comics of my own creation, but it's not because of any snobbish disdain for these wonderful old characters. Every writer worth her or his salt has one good Batman or Wonder Woman story in them, but it takes a much more talented creator than I to make a career out of breathing new life into icons who've been an important part of the cultural landscape for generations.

I'm in awe of writers like Mark Waid, Devin Grayson, Mark Millar, Brian Michael Bendis, Geoff Johns, and Kurt Busiek, all of whom have greatly added to the tapestry of shared universes while also creating amazing new concepts of their own. These industry legends were particularly supportive of me as I was breaking in, and if anything in this book is worth dedicating, I'd like to dedicate it to them, as well as to the many collaborators who made me look good, and the editors who bravely and/or foolishly gave work to the couch-surfing bald guy who nervously pitched them outside the DC offices.

Most of all, thanks to you, especially those of you who read these humble efforts the first time around. For those of you who've never before checked out some of my "formative work," I hope you'll find at least one small thing to enjoy in these pages. If not, Busiek will be more than happy to give you a refund.

Brian K. Vaughan
Los Angeles 2007

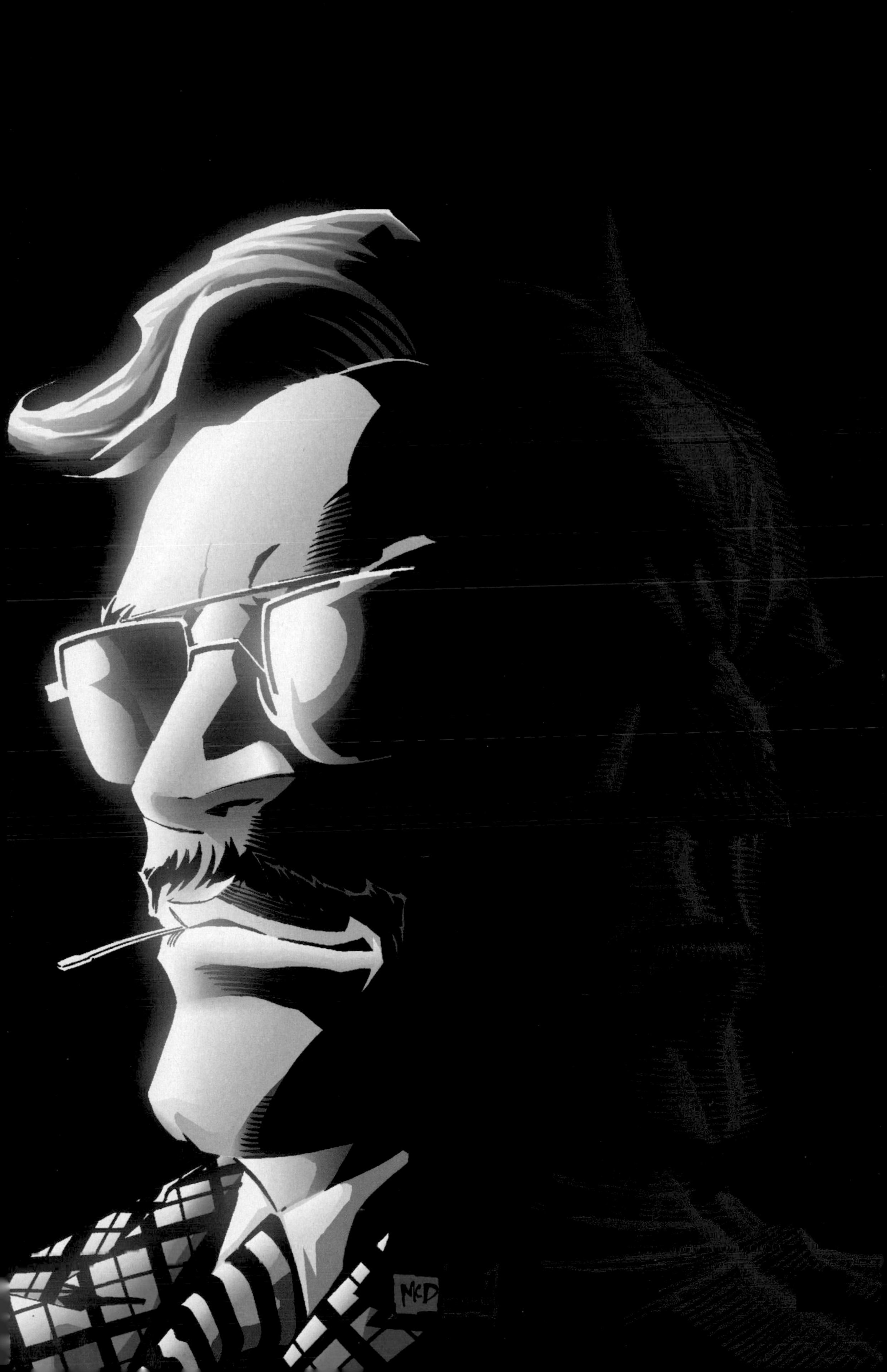
McD

CLOSE BEFORE STRIKING **CHAPTER ONE**

cover art by **SCOTT McDANIEL**   *colored by* **PATRICK MARTIN**

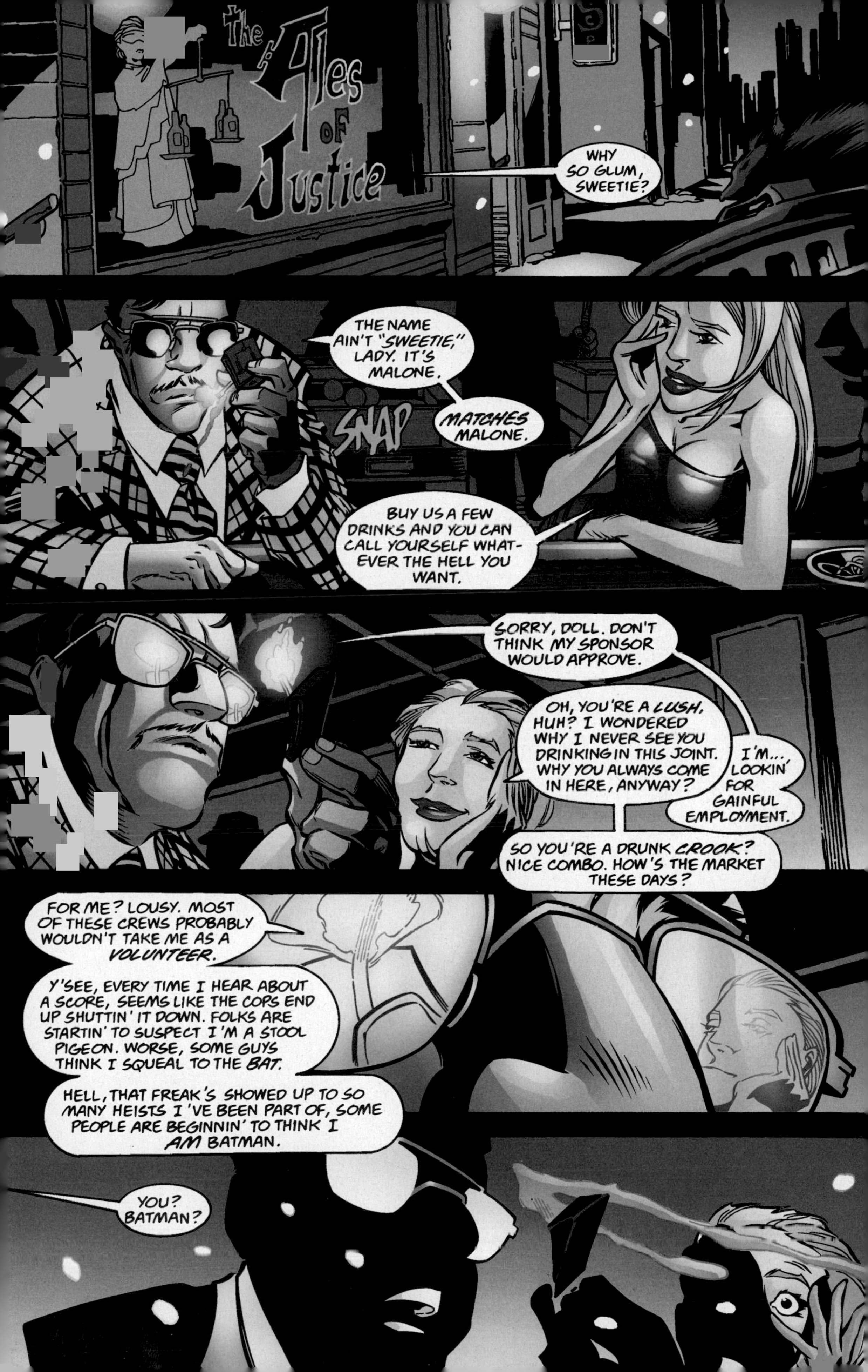
The Ales of Justice
WHY SO GLUM, SWEETIE?
THE NAME AIN'T "SWEETIE," LADY. IT'S MALONE.
SNAP
MATCHES MALONE.
BUY US A FEW DRINKS AND YOU CAN CALL YOURSELF WHAT-EVER THE HELL YOU WANT.
SORRY, DOLL. DON'T THINK MY SPONSOR WOULD APPROVE.
OH, YOU'RE A LUSH, HUH? I WONDERED WHY I NEVER SEE YOU DRINKING IN THIS JOINT. WHY YOU ALWAYS COME IN HERE, ANYWAY?
I'M... LOOKIN' FOR GAINFUL EMPLOYMENT.
SO YOU'RE A DRUNK CROOK? NICE COMBO. HOW'S THE MARKET THESE DAYS?
FOR ME? LOUSY. MOST OF THESE CREWS PROBABLY WOULDN'T TAKE ME AS A VOLUNTEER.
Y'SEE, EVERY TIME I HEAR ABOUT A SCORE, SEEMS LIKE THE COPS END UP SHUTTIN' IT DOWN. FOLKS ARE STARTIN' TO SUSPECT I'M A STOOL PIGEON. WORSE, SOME GUYS THINK I SQUEAL TO THE BAT.
HELL, THAT FREAK'S SHOWED UP TO SO MANY HEISTS I'VE BEEN PART OF, SOME PEOPLE ARE BEGINNIN' TO THINK I AM BATMAN.
YOU? BATMAN?

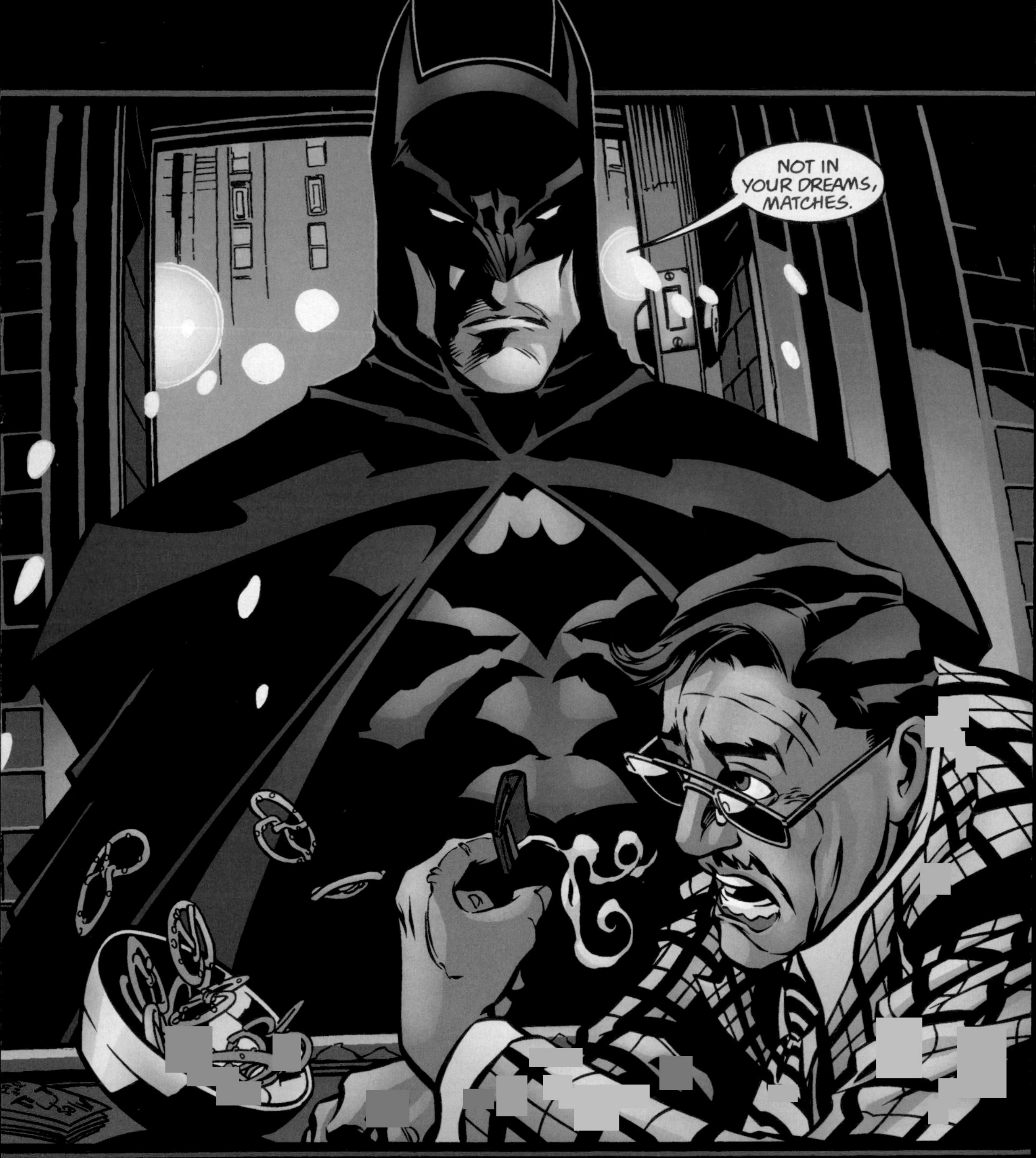
NOT IN YOUR DREAMS, MATCHES.

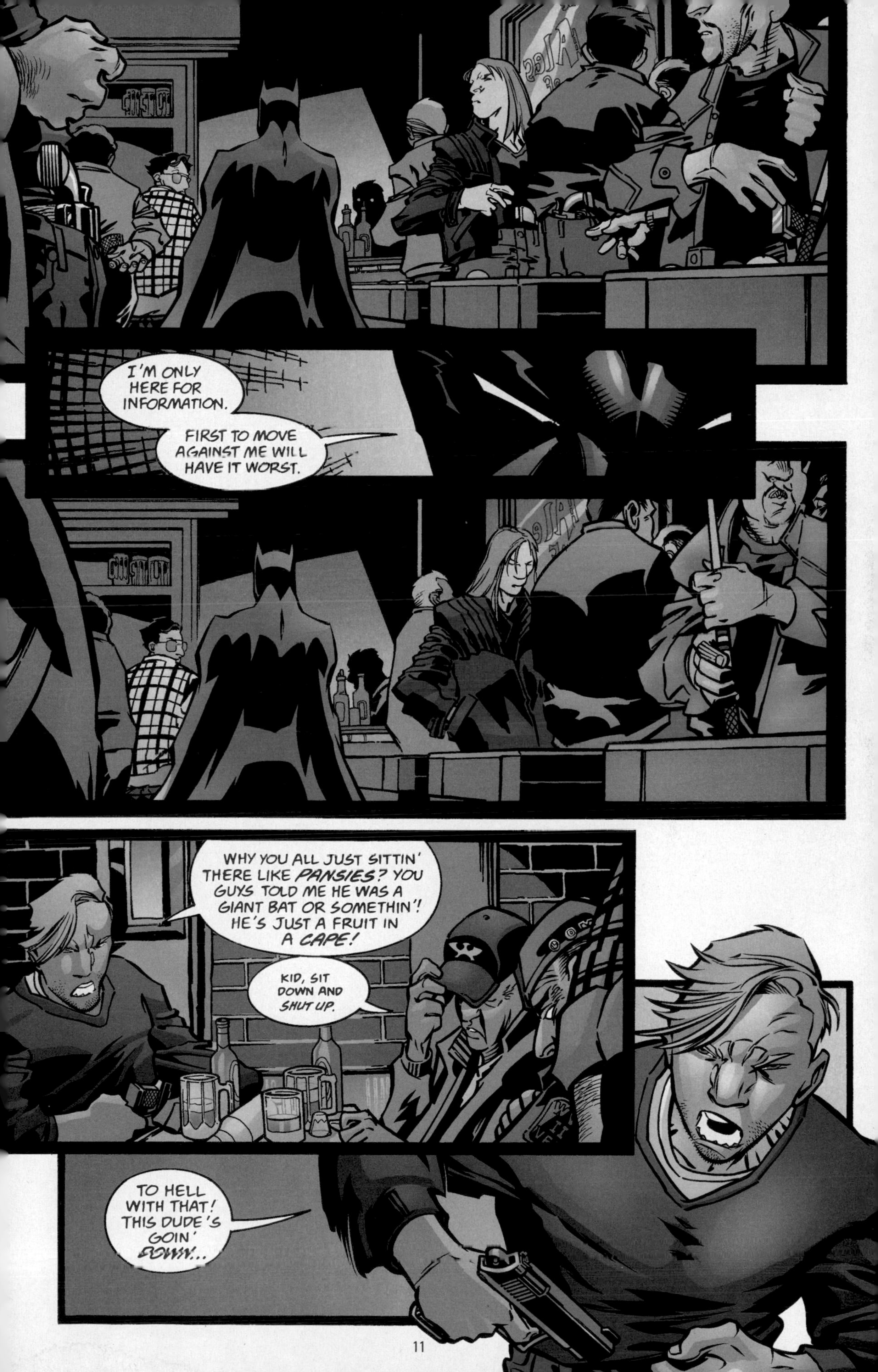

I'M ONLY HERE FOR INFORMATION.
FIRST TO MOVE AGAINST ME WILL HAVE IT WORST.
WHY YOU ALL JUST SITTIN' THERE LIKE PANSIES? YOU GUYS TOLD ME HE WAS A GIANT BAT OR SOMETHIN'! HE'S JUST A FRUIT IN A CAPE!
KID, SIT DOWN AND SHUT UP.
TO HELL WITH THAT! THIS DUDE'S GOIN'

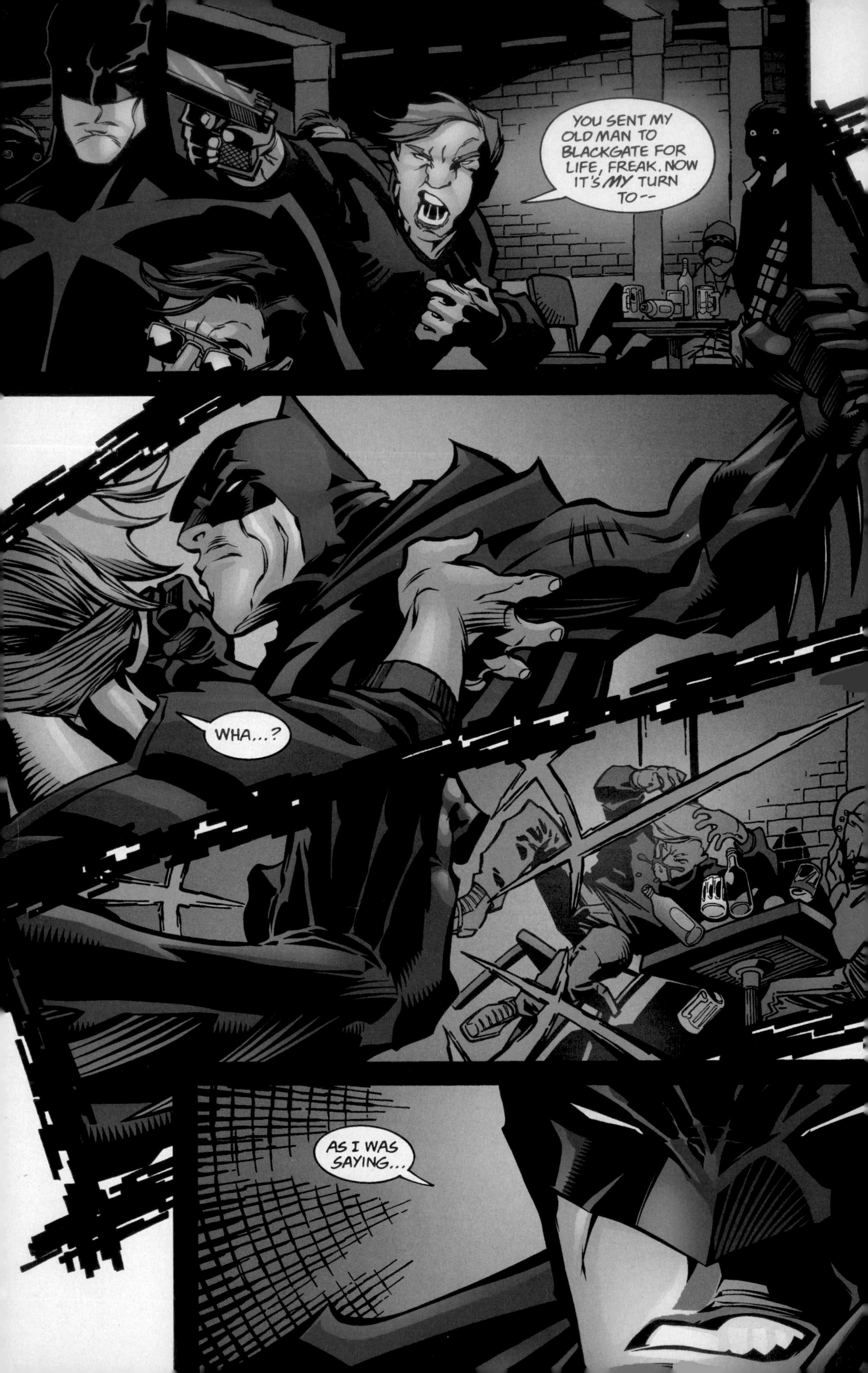
YOU SENT MY OLD MAN TO BLACKGATE FOR LIFE, FREAK. NOW IT'S MY TURN TO--
WHA...?
AS I WAS SAYING...

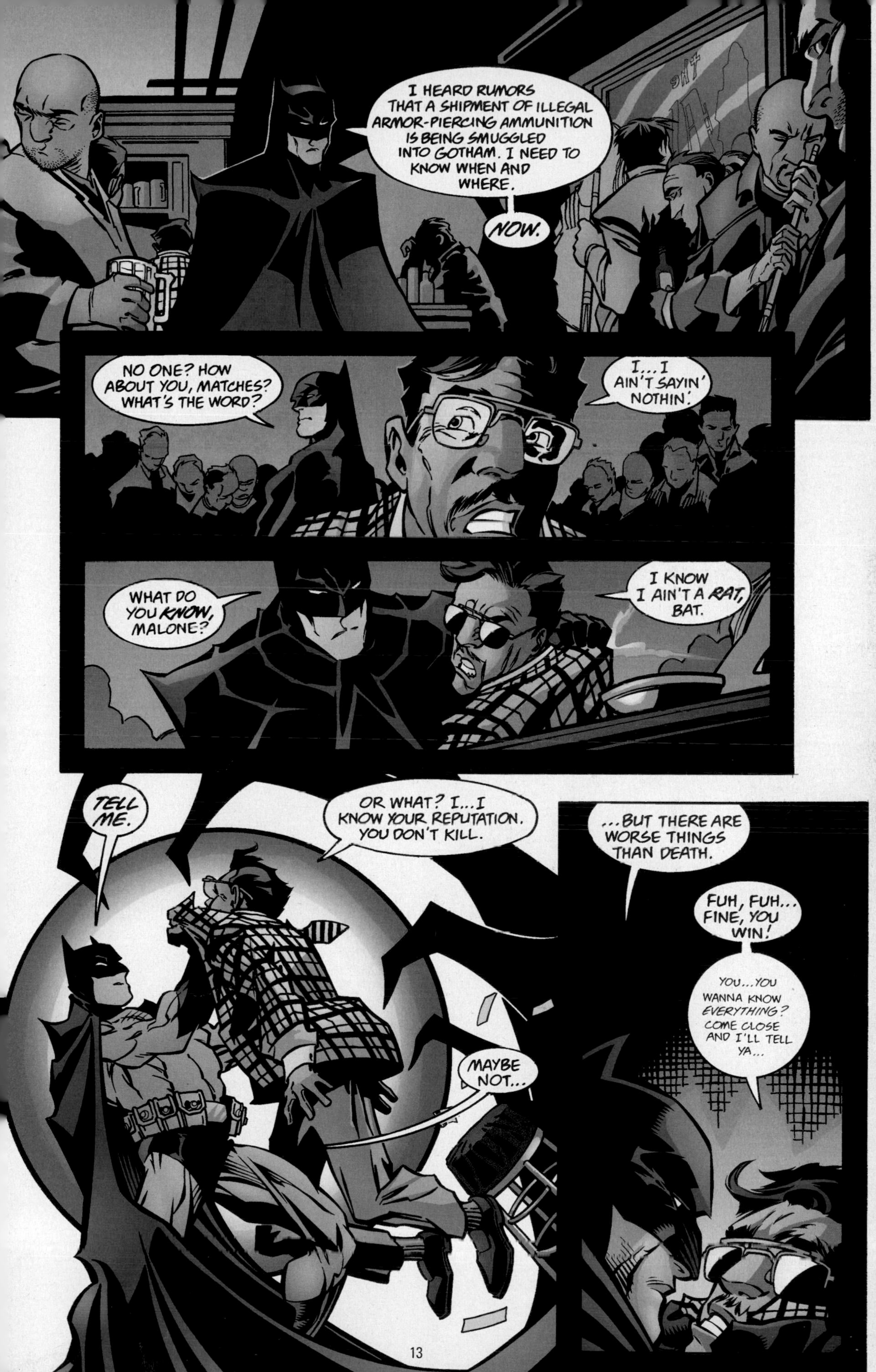
I HEARD RUMORS THAT A SHIPMENT OF ILLEGAL ARMOR-PIERCING AMMUNITION IS BEING SMUGGLED INTO GOTHAM. I NEED TO KNOW WHEN AND WHERE.
NOW.
NO ONE? HOW ABOUT YOU, MATCHES? WHAT'S THE WORD?
I...I AIN'T SAYIN' NOTHIN'.
WHAT DO YOU KNOW, MALONE?
I KNOW I AIN'T A RAT, BAT.
TELL ME.
OR WHAT? I...I KNOW YOUR REPUTATION. YOU DON'T KILL.
MAYBE NOT...
...BUT THERE ARE WORSE THINGS THAN DEATH.
FUH, FUH... FINE, YOU WIN!
YOU...YOU WANNA KNOW EVERYTHING? COME CLOSE AND I'LL TELL YA...

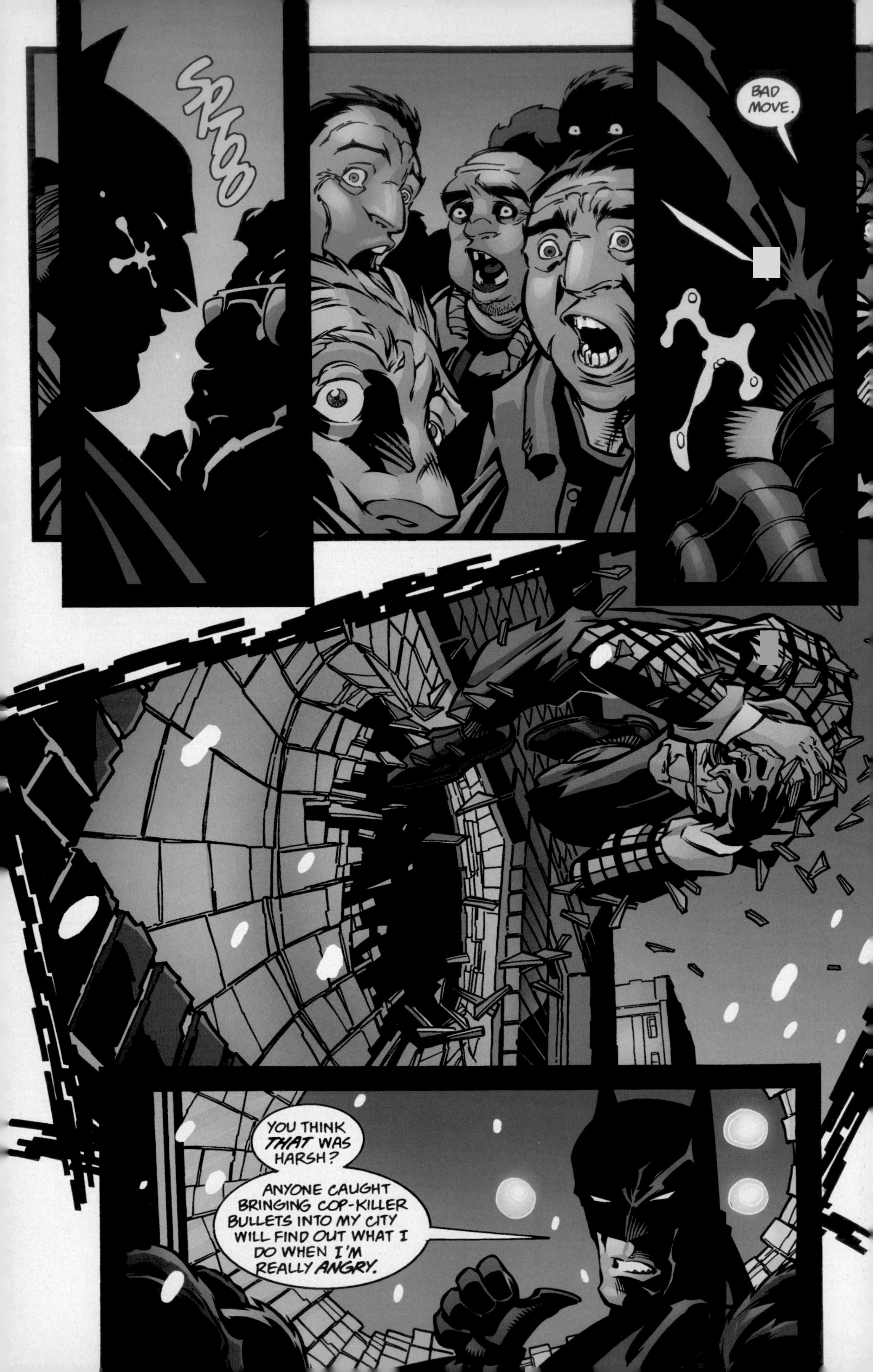
SPTOO
BAD MOVE.
YOU THINK THAT WAS HARSH?
ANYONE CAUGHT BRINGING COP-KILLER BULLETS INTO MY CITY WILL FIND OUT WHAT I DO WHEN I'M REALLY ANGRY.

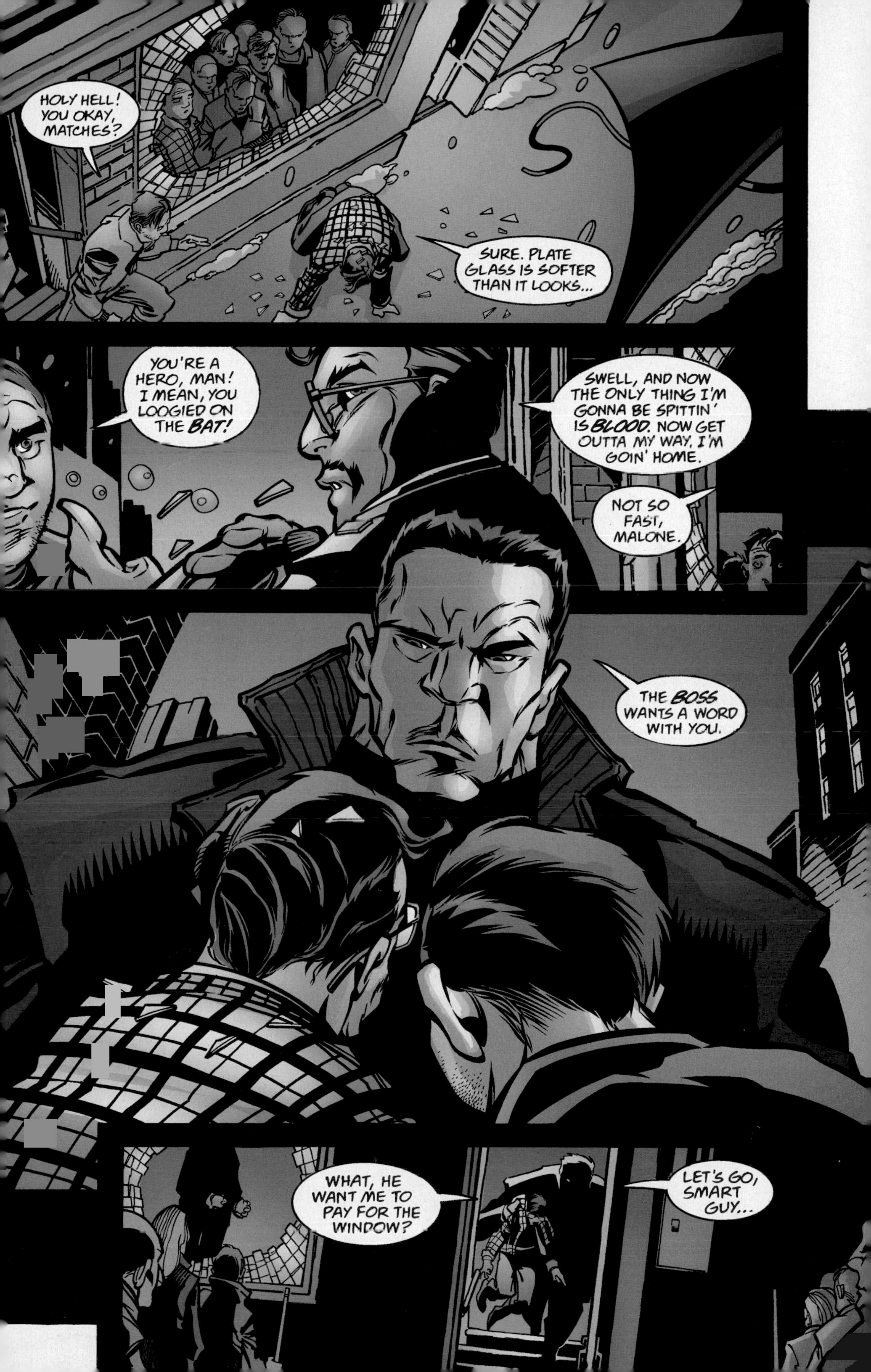

HOLY HELL! YOU OKAY, MATCHES?
SURE. PLATE GLASS IS SOFTER THAN IT LOOKS...
YOU'RE A HERO, MAN! I MEAN, YOU LOOGIED ON THE BAT!
SWELL, AND NOW THE ONLY THING I'M GONNA BE SPITTIN' IS BLOOD. NOW GET OUTTA MY WAY, I'M GOIN' HOME.
NOT SO FAST, MALONE.
THE BOSS WANTS A WORD WITH YOU.
WHAT, HE WANT ME TO PAY FOR THE WINDOW?
LET'S GO, SMART GUY...

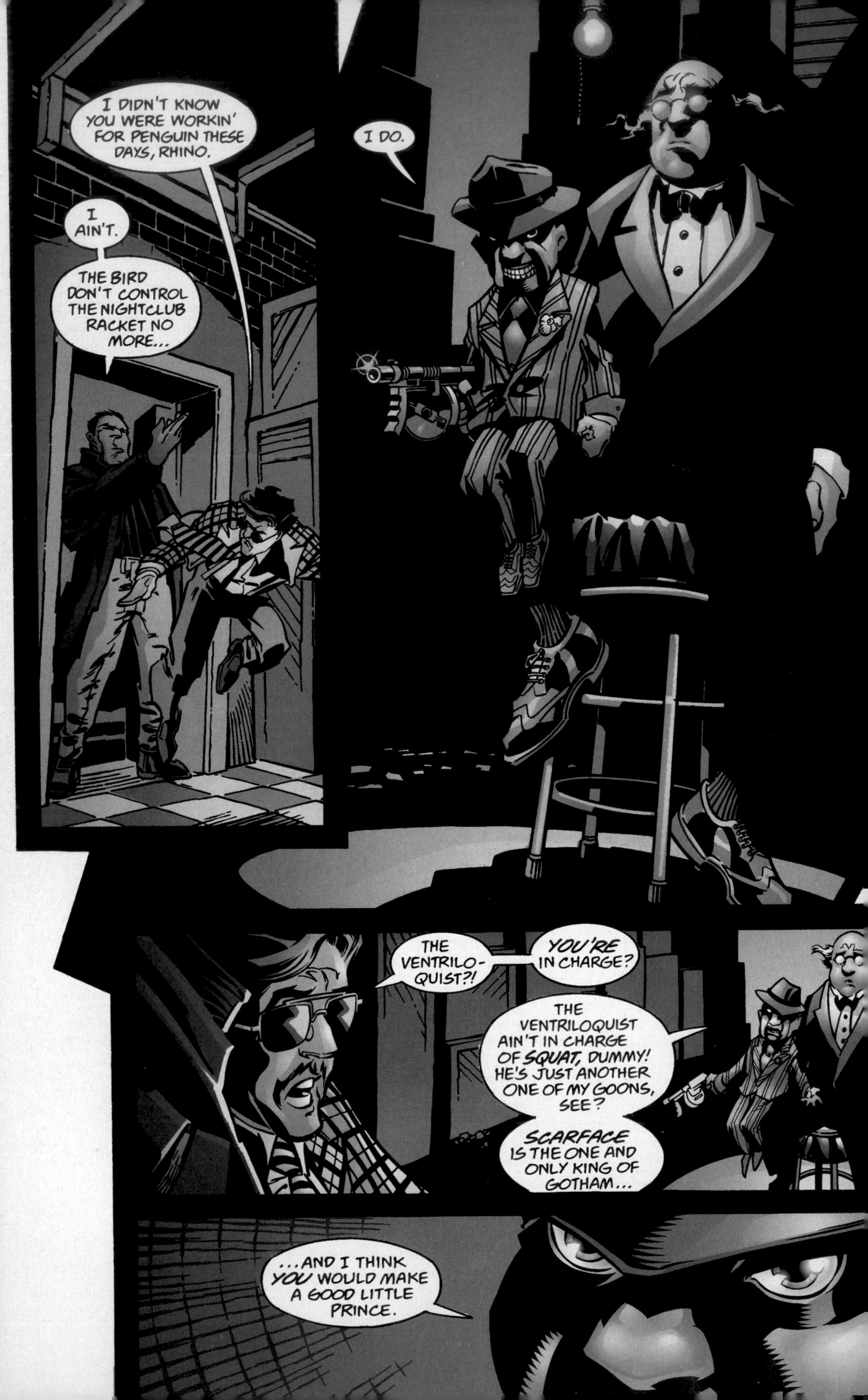
I DIDN'T KNOW YOU WERE WORKIN' FOR PENGUIN THESE DAYS, RHINO.
I AIN'T.
THE BIRD DON'T CONTROL THE NIGHTCLUB RACKET NO MORE...
I DO.
THE VENTRILOQUIST?!
YOU'RE IN CHARGE?
THE VENTRILOQUIST AIN'T IN CHARGE OF SQUAT, DUMMY! HE'S JUST ANOTHER ONE OF MY GOONS, SEE?
SCARFACE IS THE ONE AND ONLY KING OF GOTHAM...
...AND I THINK YOU WOULD MAKE A GOOD LITTLE PRINCE.

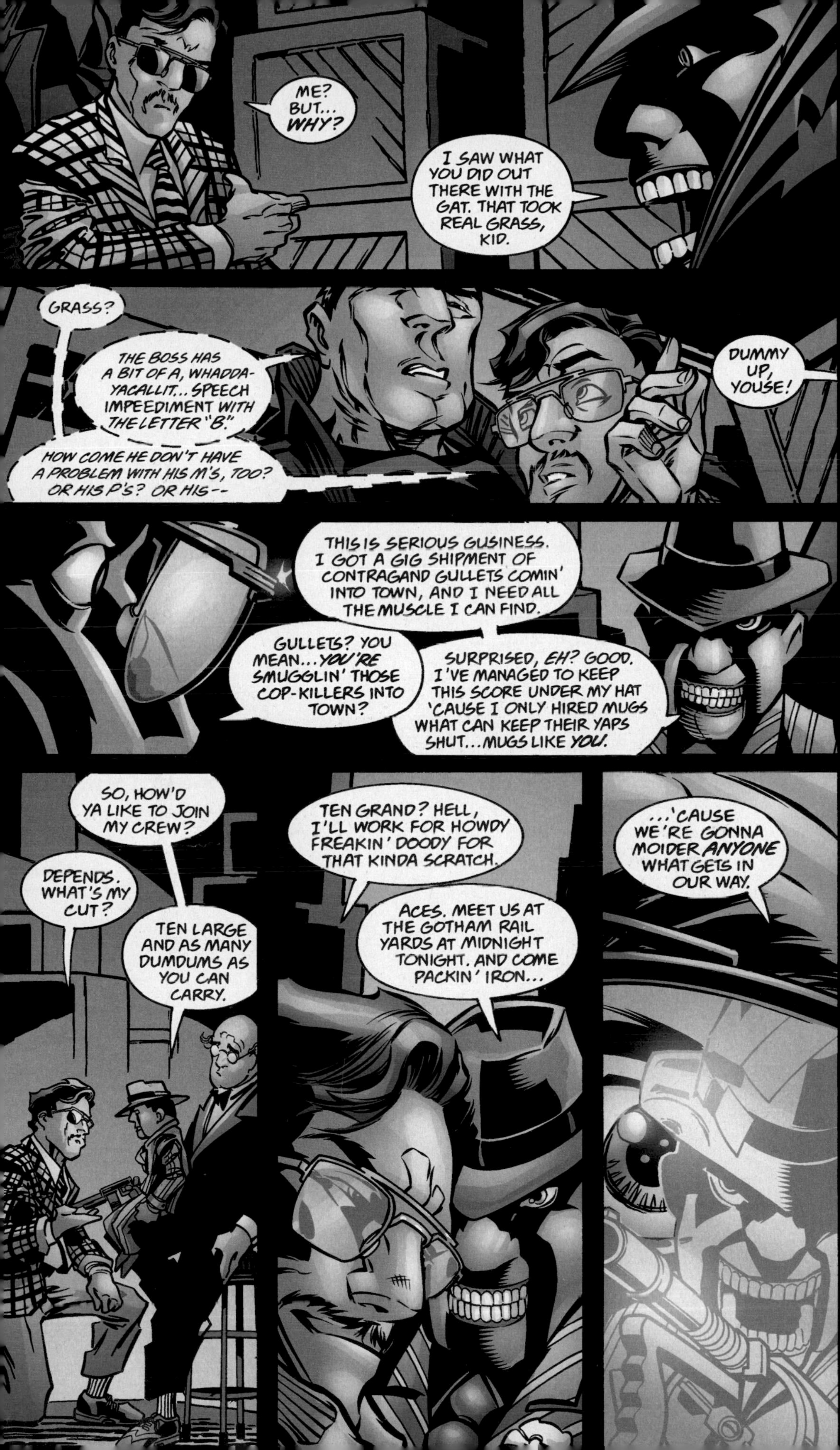
ME? BUT... WHY?
I SAW WHAT YOU DID OUT THERE WITH THE GAT. THAT TOOK REAL GRASS, KID.
GRASS?
THE BOSS HAS A BIT OF A, WHADDA-YACALLIT... SPEECH IMPEEDIMENT WITH THE LETTER "B."
HOW COME HE DON'T HAVE A PROBLEM WITH HIS M'S, TOO? OR HIS P'S? OR HIS--
DUMMY UP, YOUSE!
THIS IS SERIOUS GUSINESS. I GOT A GIG SHIPMENT OF CONTRAGAND GULLETS COMIN' INTO TOWN, AND I NEED ALL THE MUSCLE I CAN FIND.
GULLETS? YOU MEAN... YOU'RE SMUGGLIN' THOSE COP-KILLERS INTO TOWN?
SURPRISED, EH? GOOD. I'VE MANAGED TO KEEP THIS SCORE UNDER MY HAT 'CAUSE I ONLY HIRED MUGS WHAT CAN KEEP THEIR YAPS SHUT... MUGS LIKE YOU.
SO, HOW'D YA LIKE TO JOIN MY CREW?
DEPENDS. WHAT'S MY CUT?
TEN LARGE AND AS MANY DUMDUMS AS YOU CAN CARRY.
TEN GRAND? HELL, I'LL WORK FOR HOWDY FREAKIN' DOODY FOR THAT KINDA SCRATCH.
ACES. MEET US AT THE GOTHAM RAIL YARDS AT MIDNIGHT TONIGHT. AND COME PACKIN' IRON...
...'CAUSE WE'RE GONNA MOIDER ANYONE WHAT GETS IN OUR WAY.

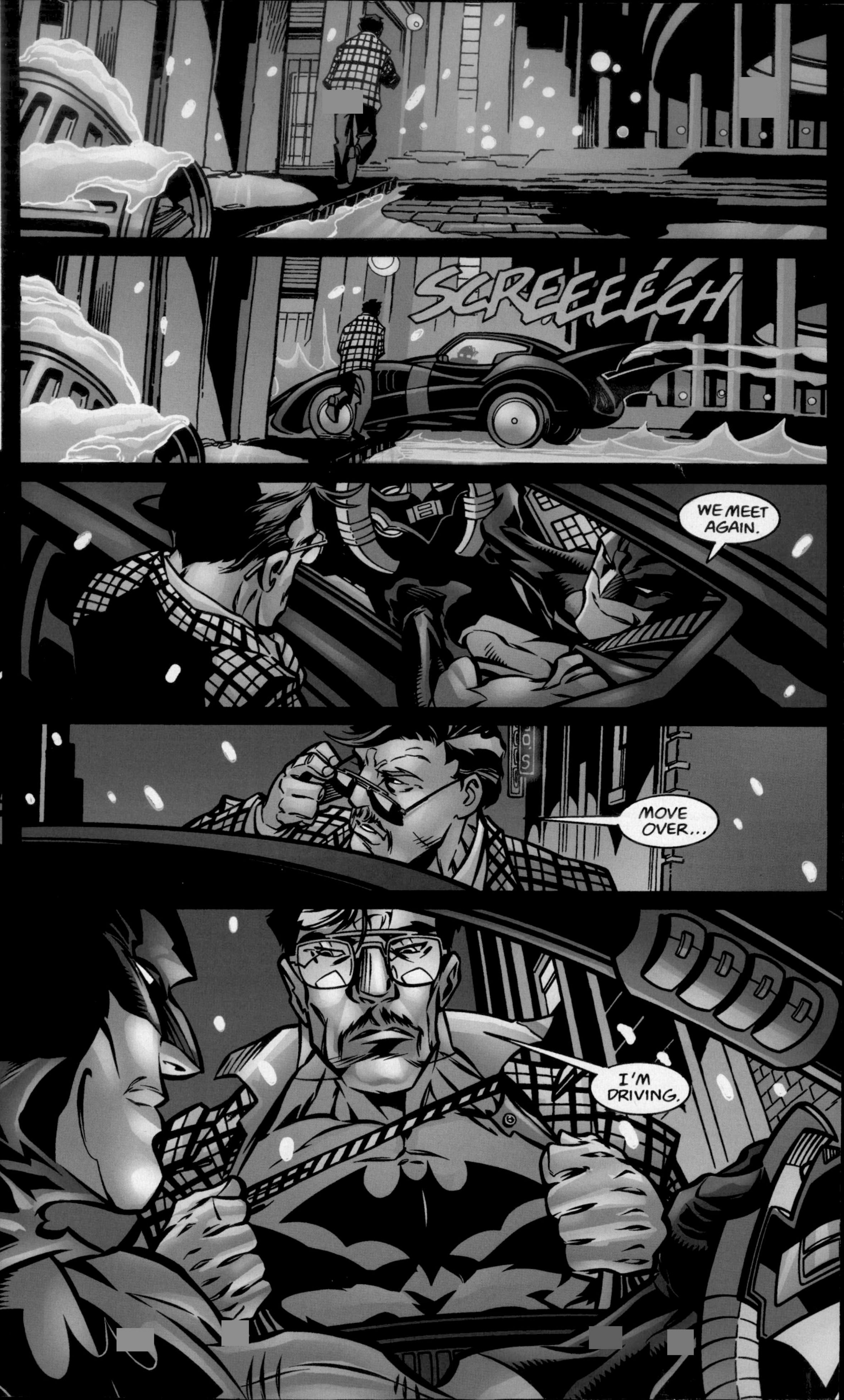
SCREEEECH
WE MEET AGAIN.
MOVE OVER...
I'M DRIVING.

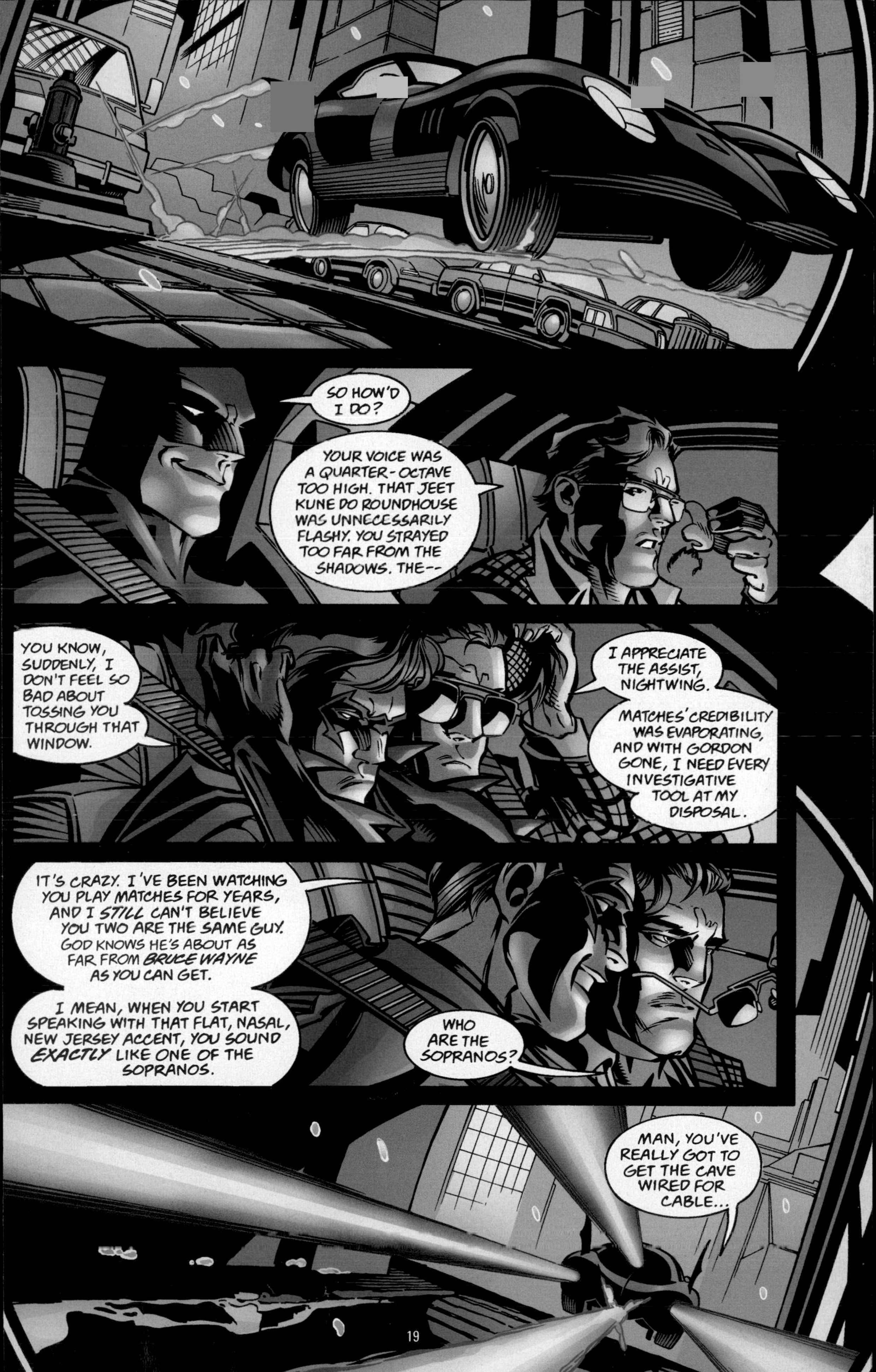

SO HOW'D I DO?
YOUR VOICE WAS A QUARTER-OCTAVE TOO HIGH. THAT JEET KUNE DO ROUNDHOUSE WAS UNNECESSARILY FLASHY. YOU STRAYED TOO FAR FROM THE SHADOWS. THE--
YOU KNOW, SUDDENLY, I DON'T FEEL SO BAD ABOUT TOSSING YOU THROUGH THAT WINDOW.
I APPRECIATE THE ASSIST, NIGHTWING.
MATCHES' CREDIBILITY WAS EVAPORATING, AND WITH GORDON GONE, I NEED EVERY INVESTIGATIVE TOOL AT MY DISPOSAL.
IT'S CRAZY. I'VE BEEN WATCHING YOU PLAY MATCHES FOR YEARS, AND I *STILL* CAN'T BELIEVE YOU TWO ARE THE *SAME GUY*. GOD KNOWS HE'S ABOUT AS FAR FROM *BRUCE WAYNE* AS YOU CAN GET.
I MEAN, WHEN YOU START SPEAKING WITH THAT FLAT, NASAL, NEW JERSEY ACCENT, YOU SOUND *EXACTLY* LIKE ONE OF THE SOPRANOS.
WHO ARE THE SOPRANOS?
MAN, YOU'VE REALLY GOT TO GET THE CAVE WIRED FOR CABLE...

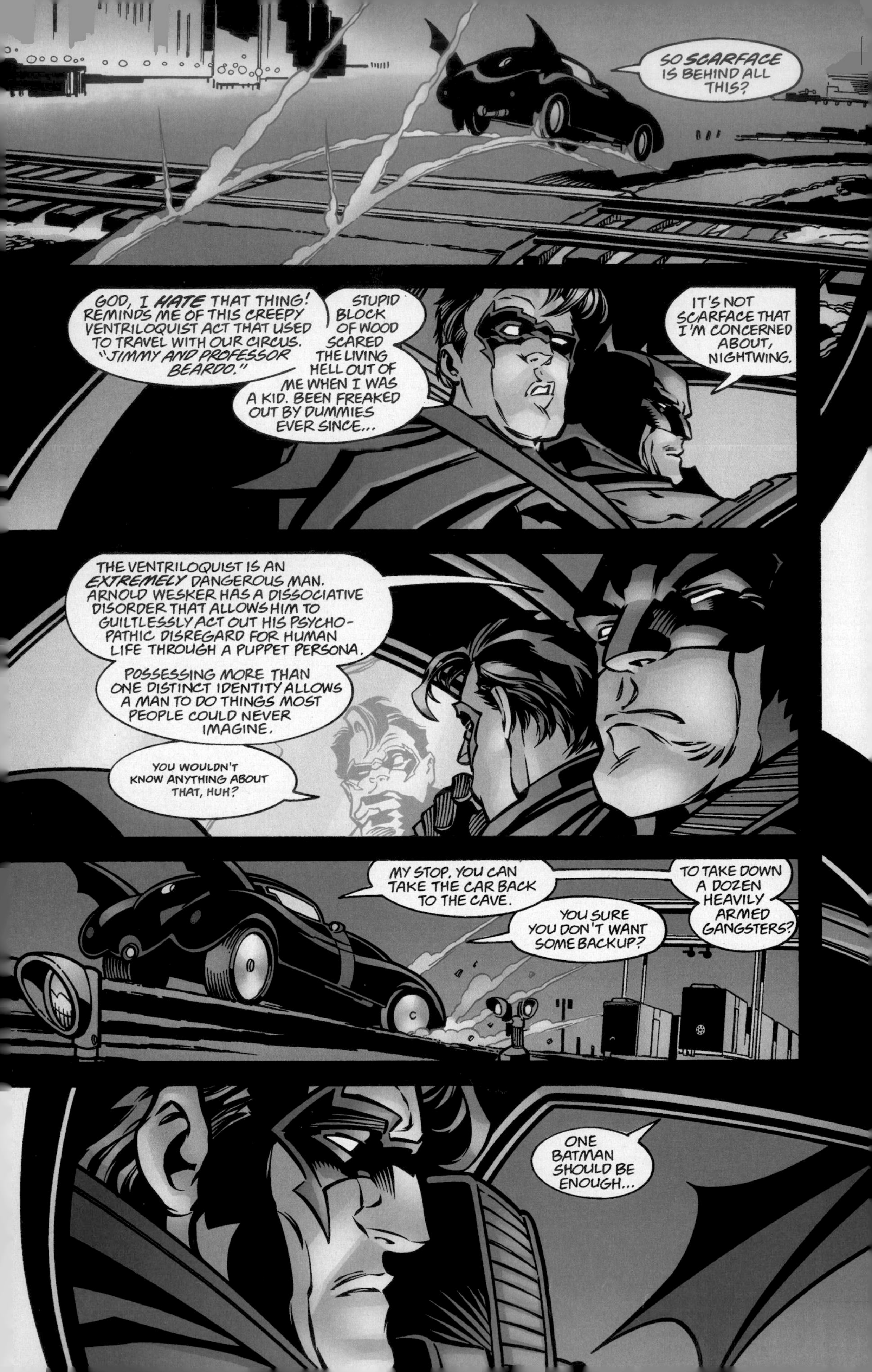
SO SCARFACE IS BEHIND ALL THIS?
GOD, I HATE THAT THING! REMINDS ME OF THIS CREEPY VENTRILOQUIST ACT THAT USED TO TRAVEL WITH OUR CIRCUS. "JIMMY AND PROFESSOR BEARDO."
STUPID BLOCK OF WOOD SCARED THE LIVING HELL OUT OF ME WHEN I WAS A KID. BEEN FREAKED OUT BY DUMMIES EVER SINCE...
IT'S NOT SCARFACE THAT I'M CONCERNED ABOUT, NIGHTWING.
THE VENTRILOQUIST IS AN EXTREMELY DANGEROUS MAN. ARNOLD WESKER HAS A DISSOCIATIVE DISORDER THAT ALLOWS HIM TO GUILTLESSLY ACT OUT HIS PSYCHOPATHIC DISREGARD FOR HUMAN LIFE THROUGH A PUPPET PERSONA.
POSSESSING MORE THAN ONE DISTINCT IDENTITY ALLOWS A MAN TO DO THINGS MOST PEOPLE COULD NEVER IMAGINE.
YOU WOULDN'T KNOW ANYTHING ABOUT THAT, HUH?
MY STOP. YOU CAN TAKE THE CAR BACK TO THE CAVE.
YOU SURE YOU DON'T WANT SOME BACKUP?
TO TAKE DOWN A DOZEN HEAVILY ARMED GANGSTERS?
ONE BATMAN SHOULD BE ENOUGH...

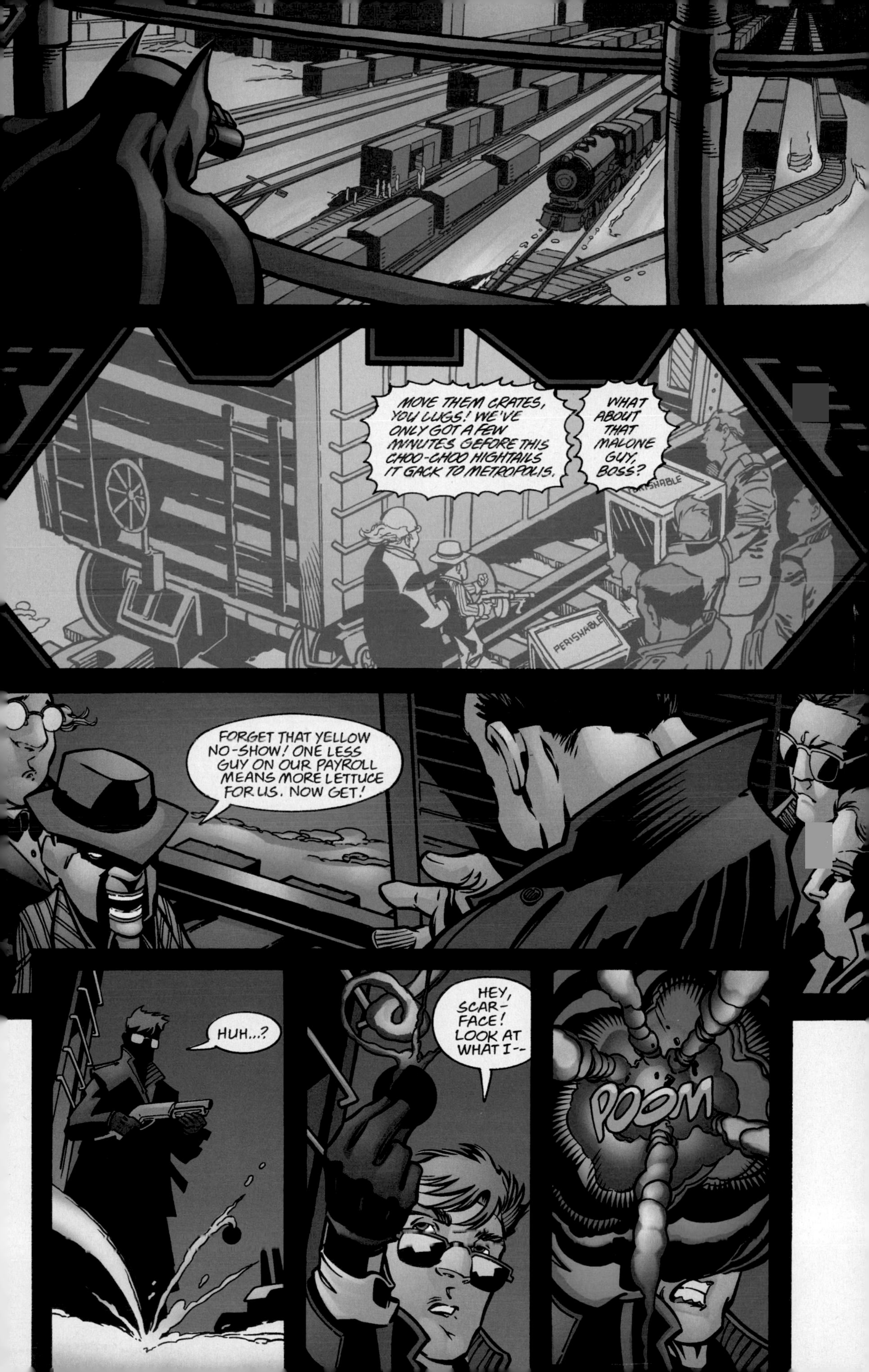
MOVE THEM CRATES, YOU LUGS! WE'VE ONLY GOT A FEW MINUTES BEFORE THIS CHOO-CHOO HIGHTAILS IT BACK TO METROPOLIS.
WHAT ABOUT THAT MALONE GUY, BOSS?
PERISHABLE
PERISHABLE
FORGET THAT YELLOW NO-SHOW! ONE LESS GUY ON OUR PAYROLL MEANS MORE LETTUCE FOR US. NOW GET!
HUH...?
HEY, SCAR-FACE! LOOK AT WHAT I--
POOM

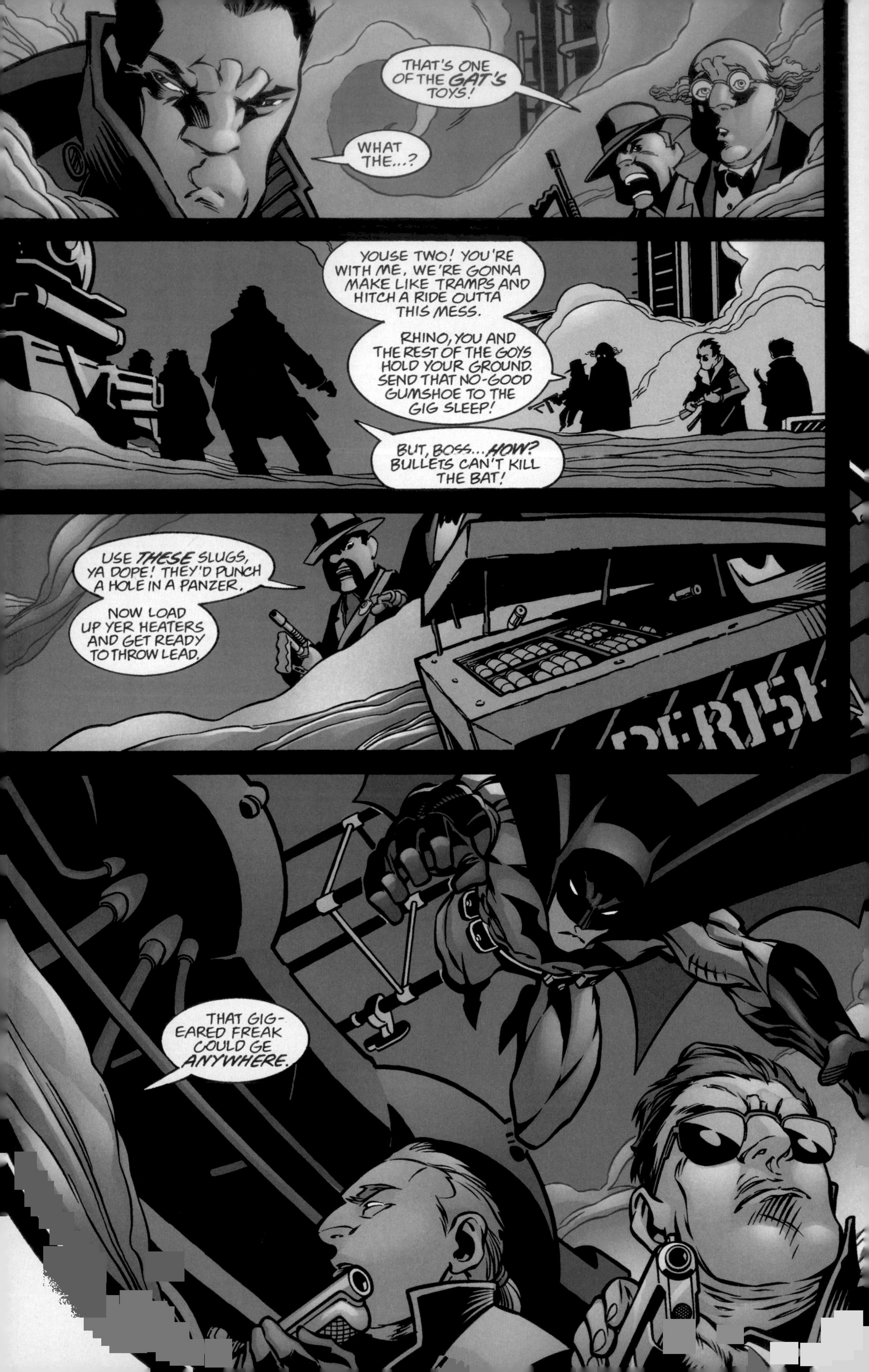
THAT'S ONE OF THE GAT'S TOYS!
WHAT THE...?
YOUSE TWO! YOU'RE WITH ME. WE'RE GONNA MAKE LIKE TRAMPS AND HITCH A RIDE OUTTA THIS MESS.
RHINO, YOU AND THE REST OF THE GOYS HOLD YOUR GROUND. SEND THAT NO-GOOD GUMSHOE TO THE GIG SLEEP!
BUT, BOSS... HOW? BULLETS CAN'T KILL THE BAT!
USE THESE SLUGS, YA DOPE! THEY'D PUNCH A HOLE IN A PANZER.
NOW LOAD UP YER HEATERS AND GET READY TO THROW LEAD.
THAT GIG-EARED FREAK COULD GE ANYWHERE.

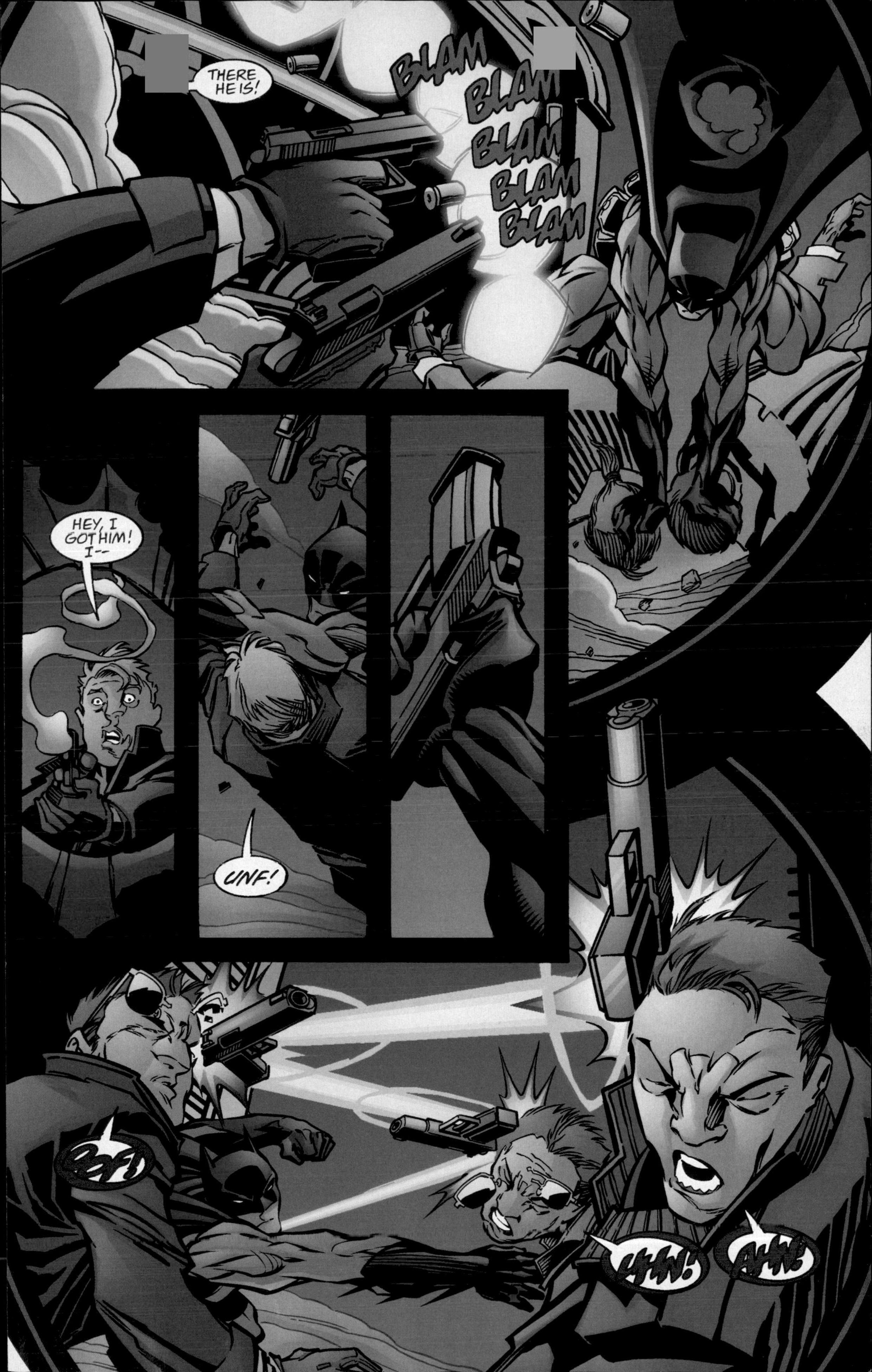
THERE HE IS!
BLAM
BLAM
BLAM
BLAM
BLAM
HEY, I GOT HIM! I--
UNF!
OOF!
UHN!
AHN!

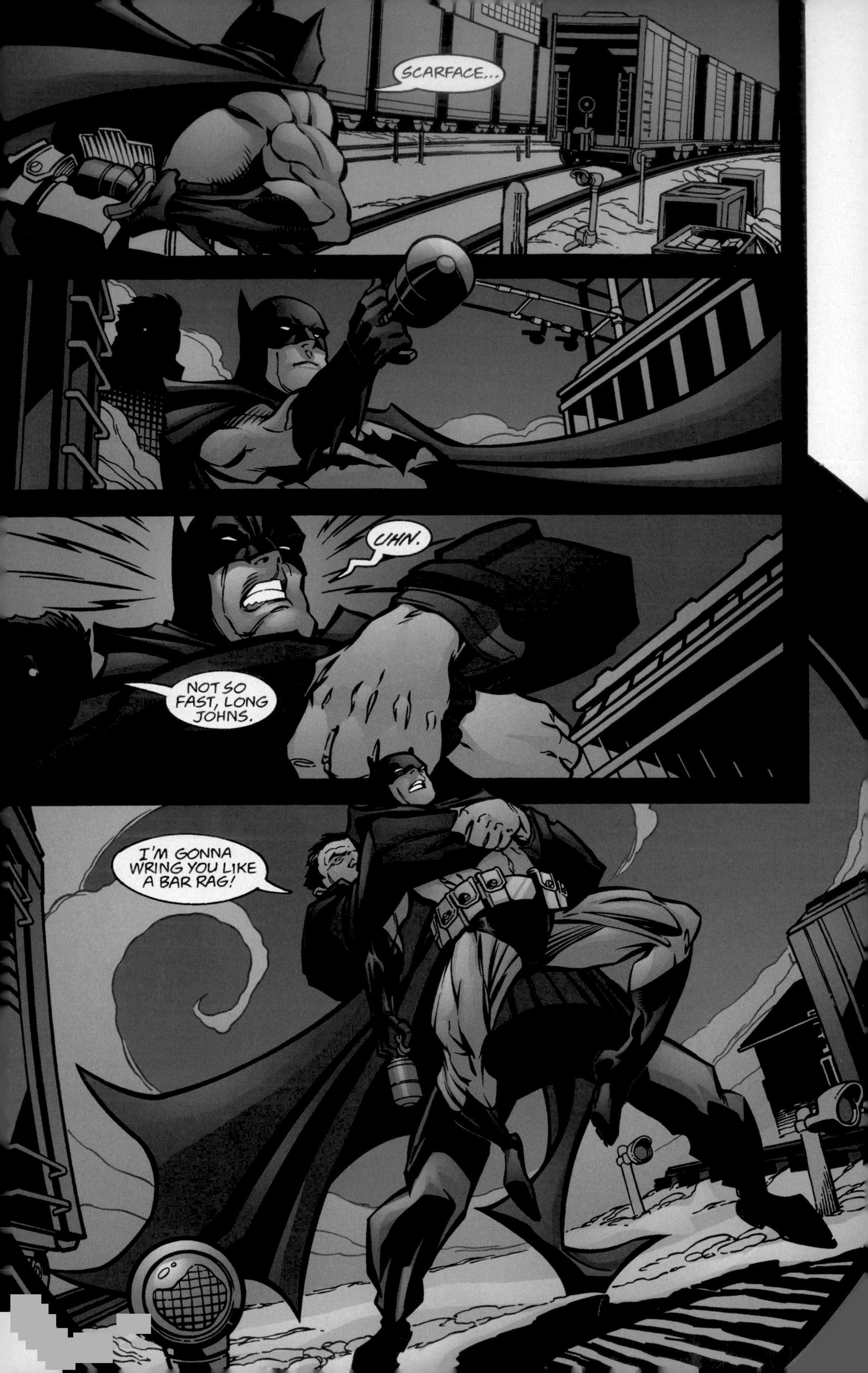
SCARFACE...
UHN.
NOT SO FAST, LONG JOHNS.
I'M GONNA WRING YOU LIKE A BAR RAG!

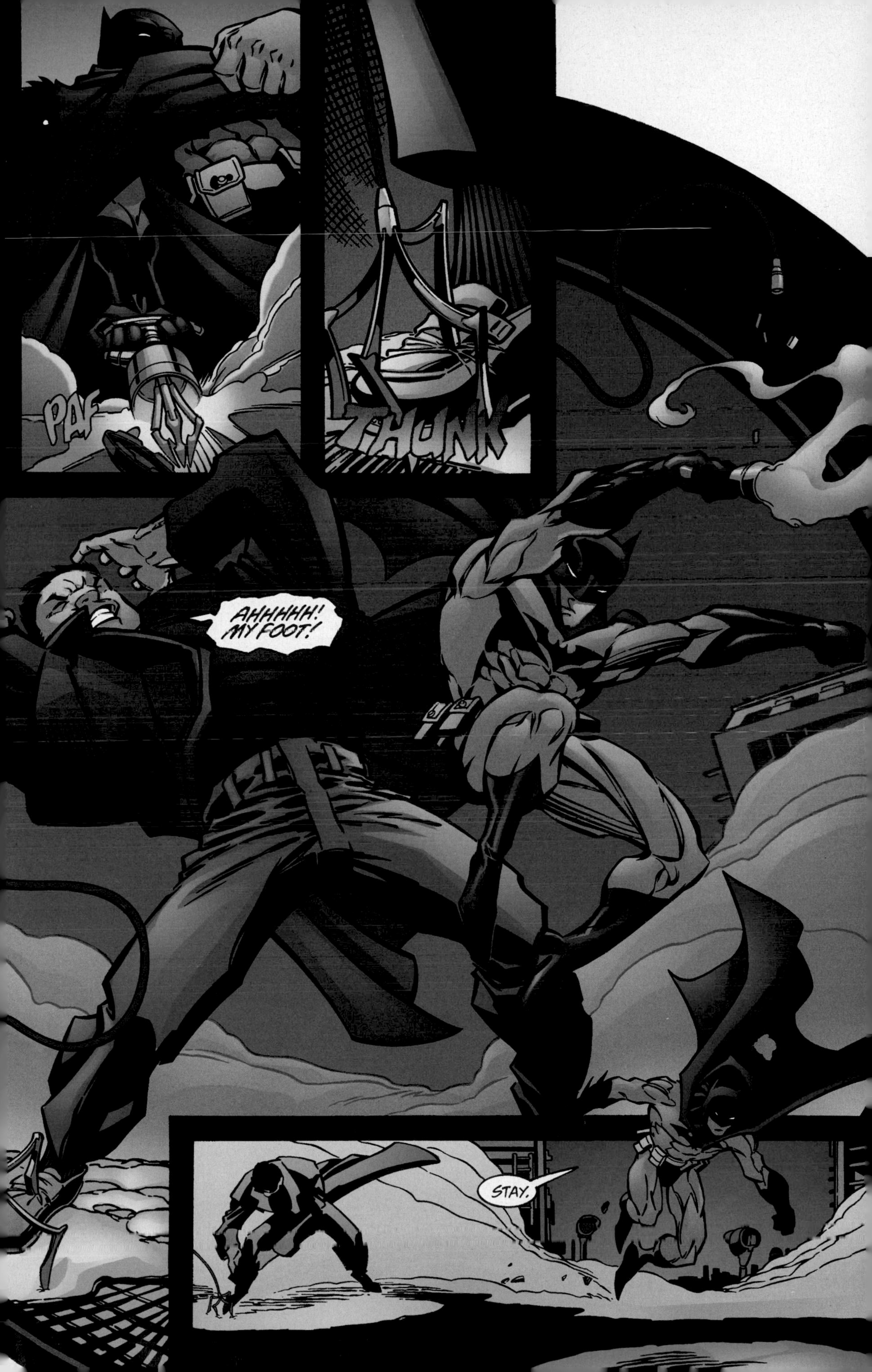
PAF
THUNK
AHHHHH! MY FOOT!
STAY.

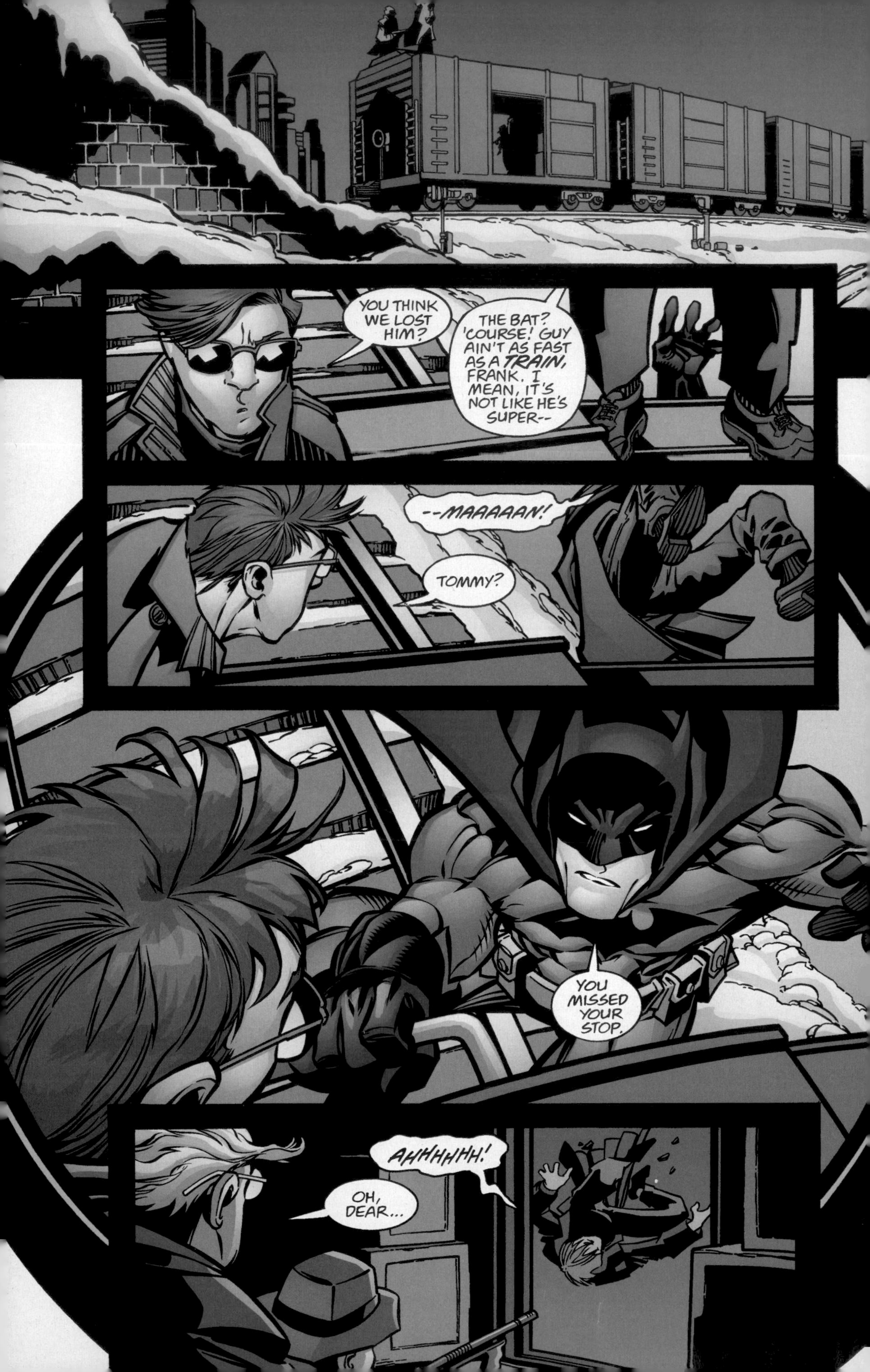

YOU THINK WE LOST HIM?
THE BAT? 'COURSE! GUY AIN'T AS FAST AS A TRAIN, FRANK. I MEAN, IT'S NOT LIKE HE'S SUPER--
--MAAAAAN!
TOMMY?
YOU MISSED YOUR STOP.
AHHHHHH!
OH, DEAR...

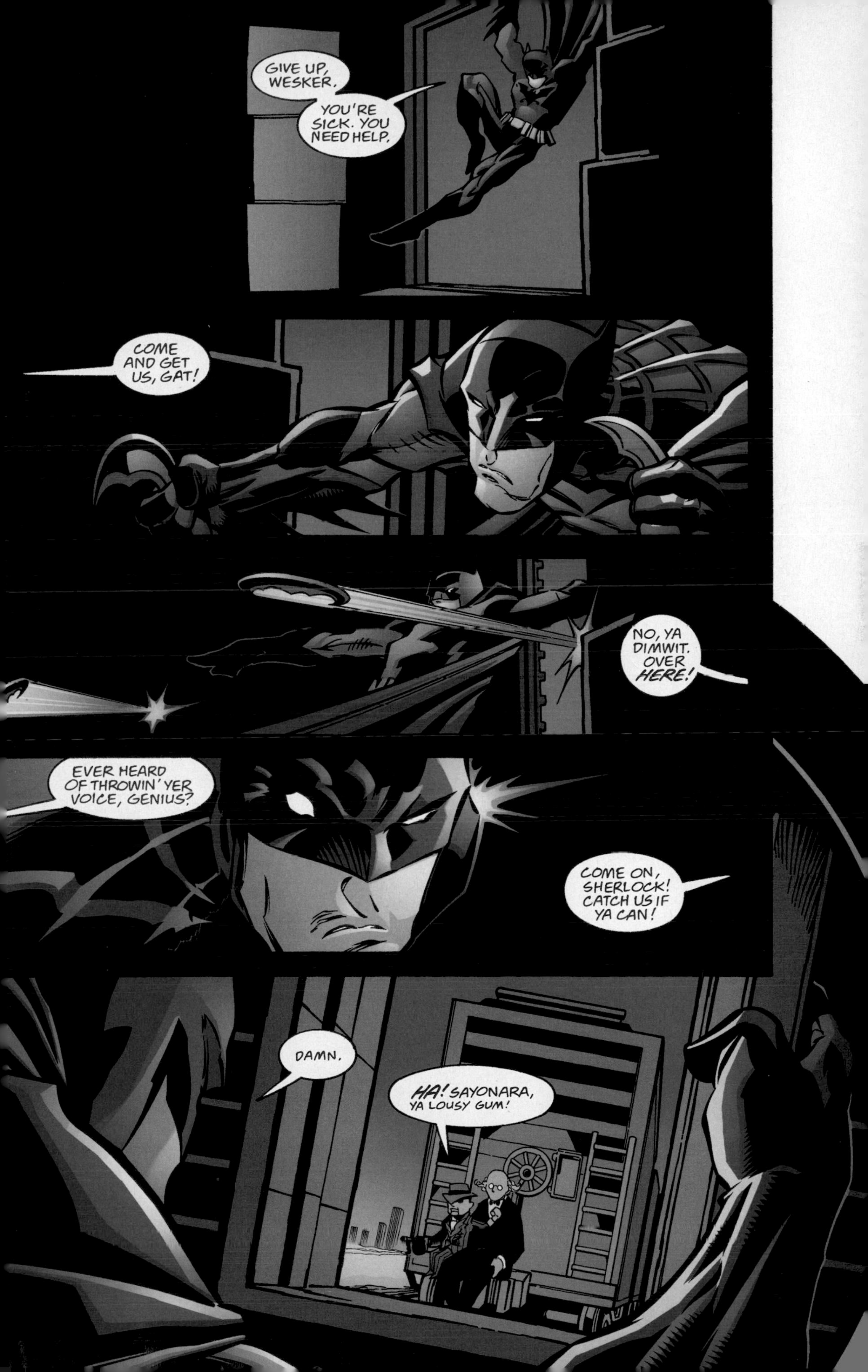
GIVE UP, WESKER.
YOU'RE SICK. YOU NEED HELP.
COME AND GET US, GAT!
NO, YA DIMWIT. OVER HERE!
EVER HEARD OF THROWIN' YER VOICE, GENIUS?
COME ON, SHERLOCK! CATCH US IF YA CAN!
DAMN.
HA! SAYONARA, YA LOUSY GUM!

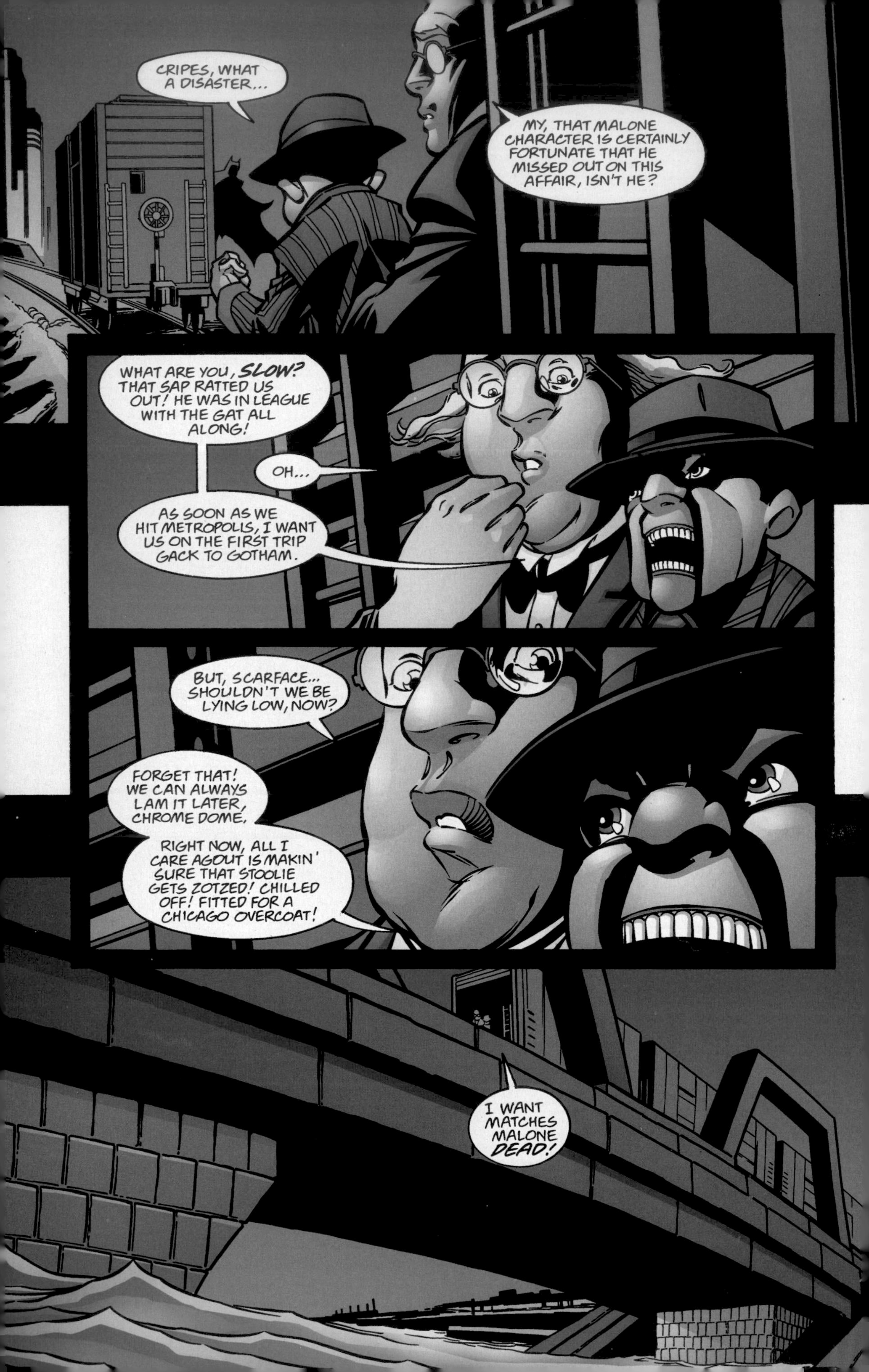
CRIPES, WHAT A DISASTER...
MY, THAT MALONE CHARACTER IS CERTAINLY FORTUNATE THAT HE MISSED OUT ON THIS AFFAIR, ISN'T HE?
WHAT ARE YOU, SLOW? THAT SAP RATTED US OUT! HE WAS IN LEAGUE WITH THE GAT ALL ALONG!
OH...
AS SOON AS WE HIT METROPOLIS, I WANT US ON THE FIRST TRIP GACK TO GOTHAM.
BUT, SCARFACE... SHOULDN'T WE BE LYING LOW, NOW?
FORGET THAT! WE CAN ALWAYS LAM IT LATER, CHROME DOME.
RIGHT NOW, ALL I CARE AGOUT IS MAKIN' SURE THAT STOOLIE GETS ZOTZED! CHILLED OFF! FITTED FOR A CHICAGO OVERCOAT!
I WANT MATCHES MALONE DEAD!

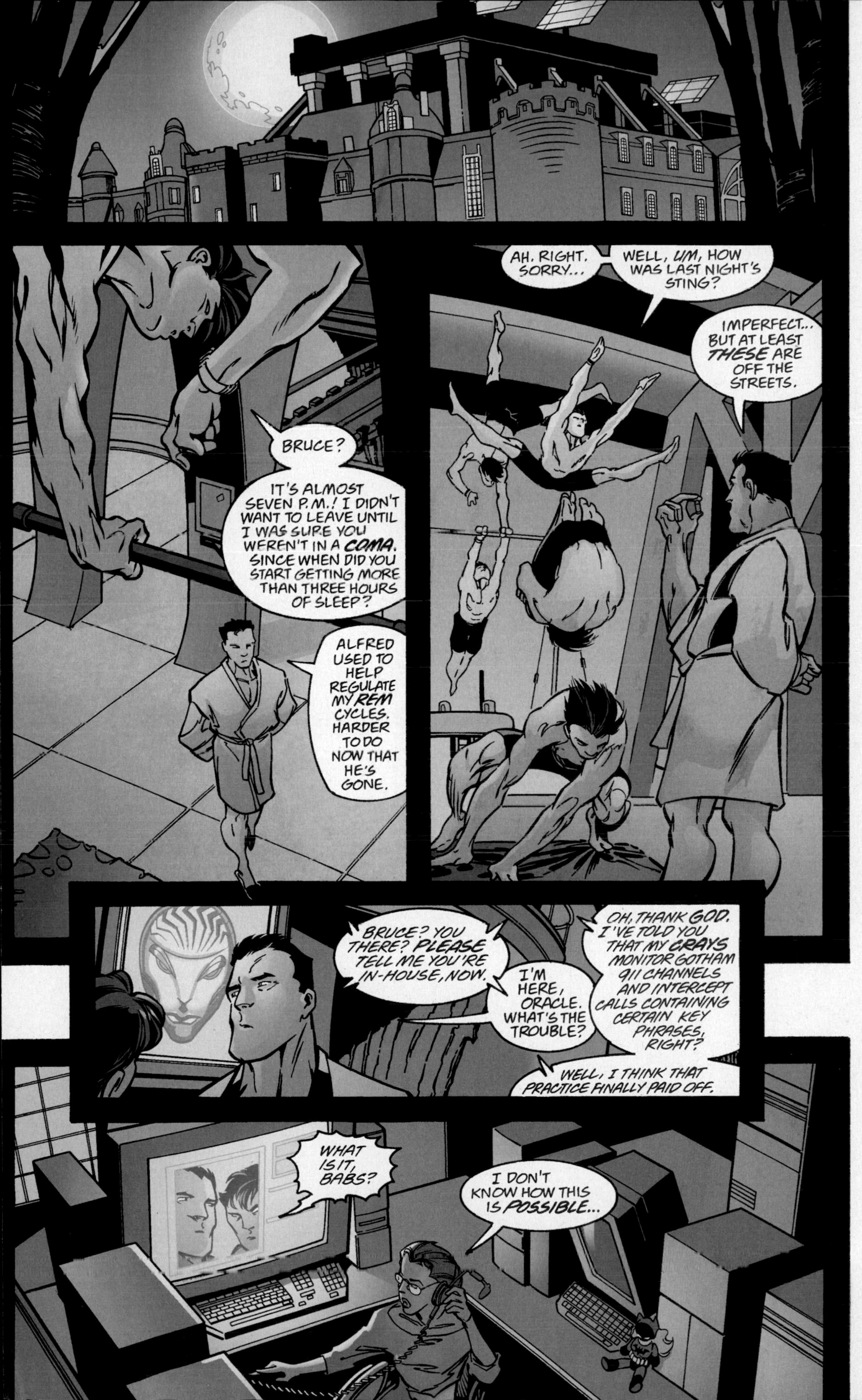
BRUCE?
IT'S ALMOST SEVEN P.M.! I DIDN'T WANT TO LEAVE UNTIL I WAS SURE YOU WEREN'T IN A COMA. SINCE WHEN DID YOU START GETTING MORE THAN THREE HOURS OF SLEEP?
ALFRED USED TO HELP REGULATE MY REM CYCLES. HARDER TO DO NOW THAT HE'S GONE.
AH. RIGHT. SORRY...
WELL, UM, HOW WAS LAST NIGHT'S STING?
IMPERFECT... BUT AT LEAST THESE ARE OFF THE STREETS.
BRUCE? YOU THERE? PLEASE TELL ME YOU'RE IN-HOUSE, NOW.
I'M HERE, ORACLE. WHAT'S THE TROUBLE?
OH, THANK GOD. I'VE TOLD YOU THAT MY CRAYS MONITOR GOTHAM 911 CHANNELS AND INTERCEPT CALLS CONTAINING CERTAIN KEY PHRASES, RIGHT?
WELL, I THINK THAT PRACTICE FINALLY PAID OFF.
WHAT IS IT, BABS?
I DON'T KNOW HOW THIS IS POSSIBLE...

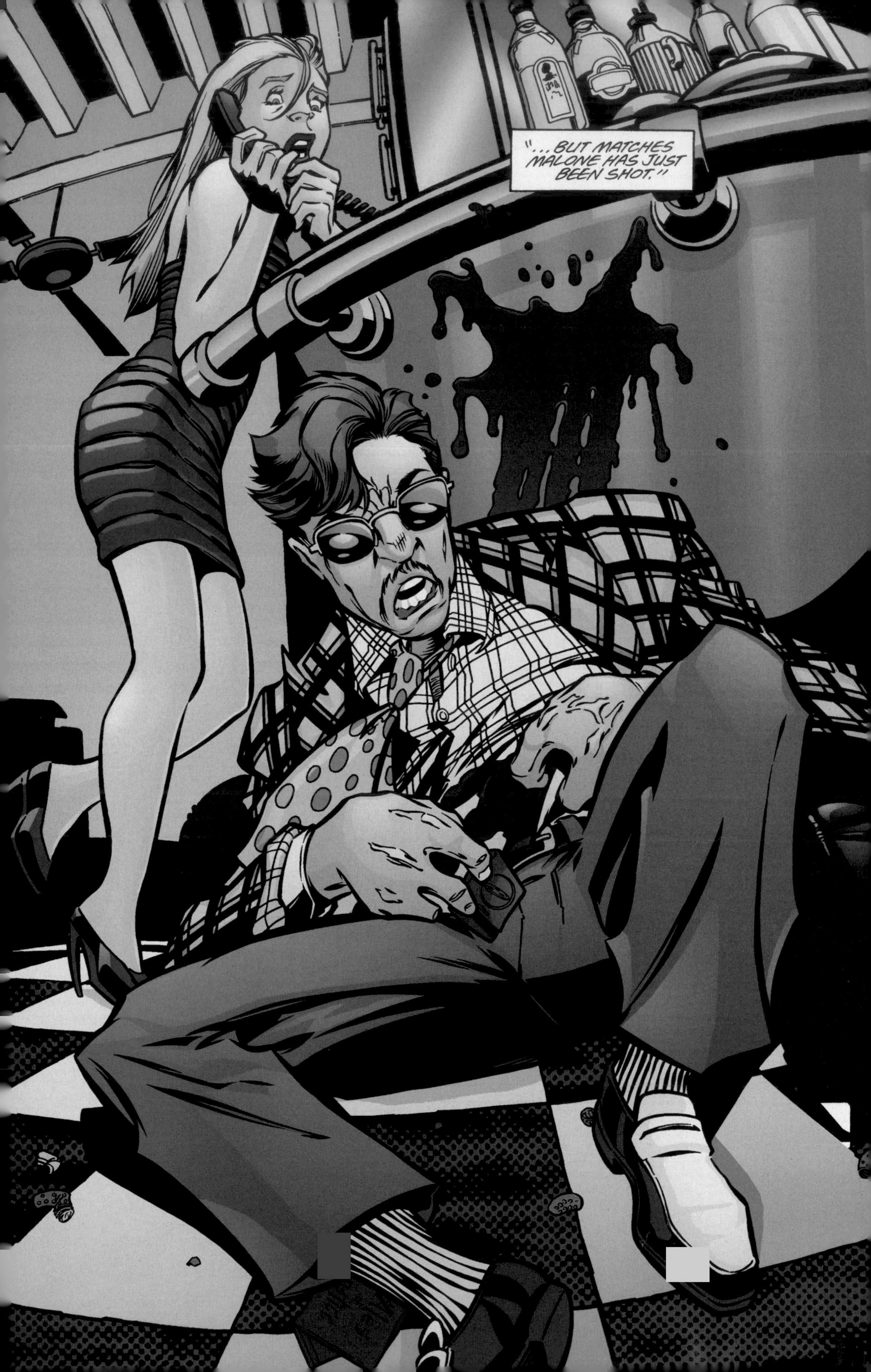
"...BUT MATCHES MALONE HAS JUST BEEN SHOT."

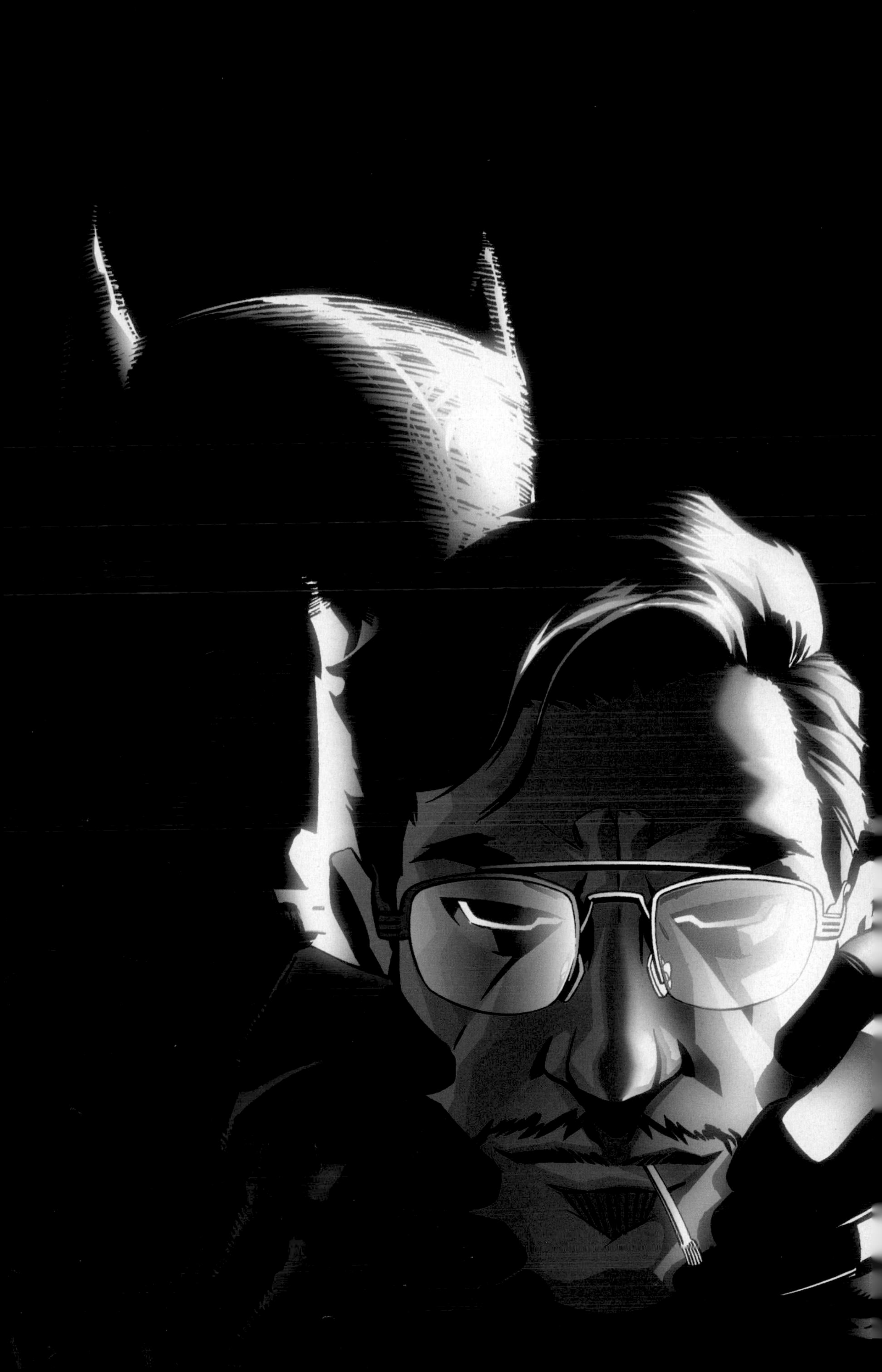

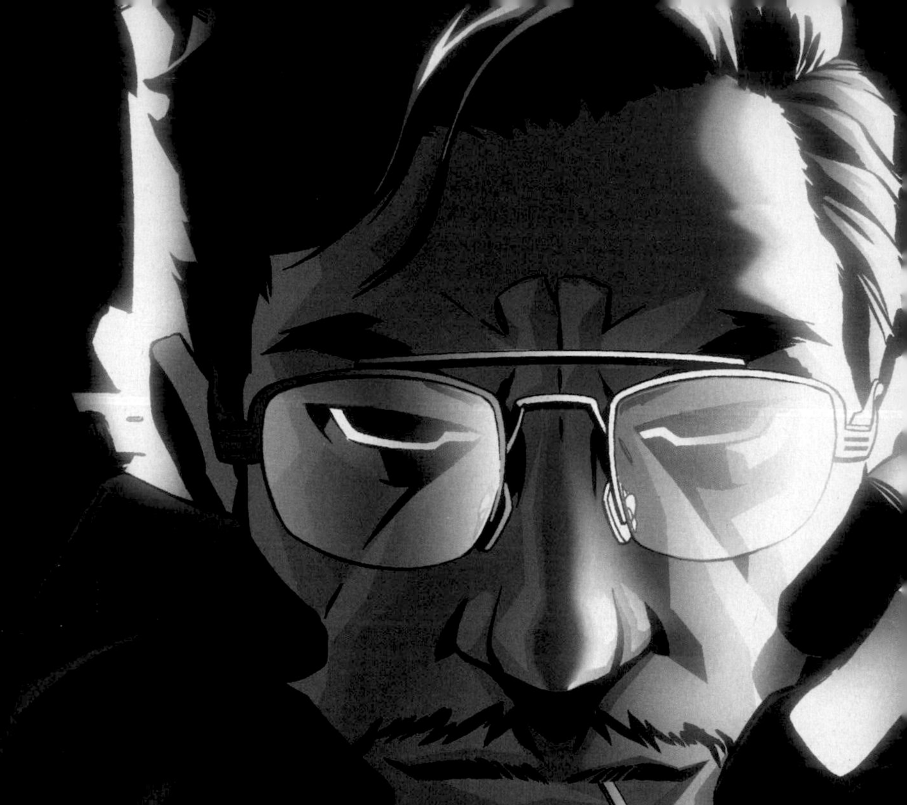

CLOSE BEFORE STRIKING CHAPTER TWO

cover art by **SCOTT McDANIEL** colored by **PATRICK MARTIN**

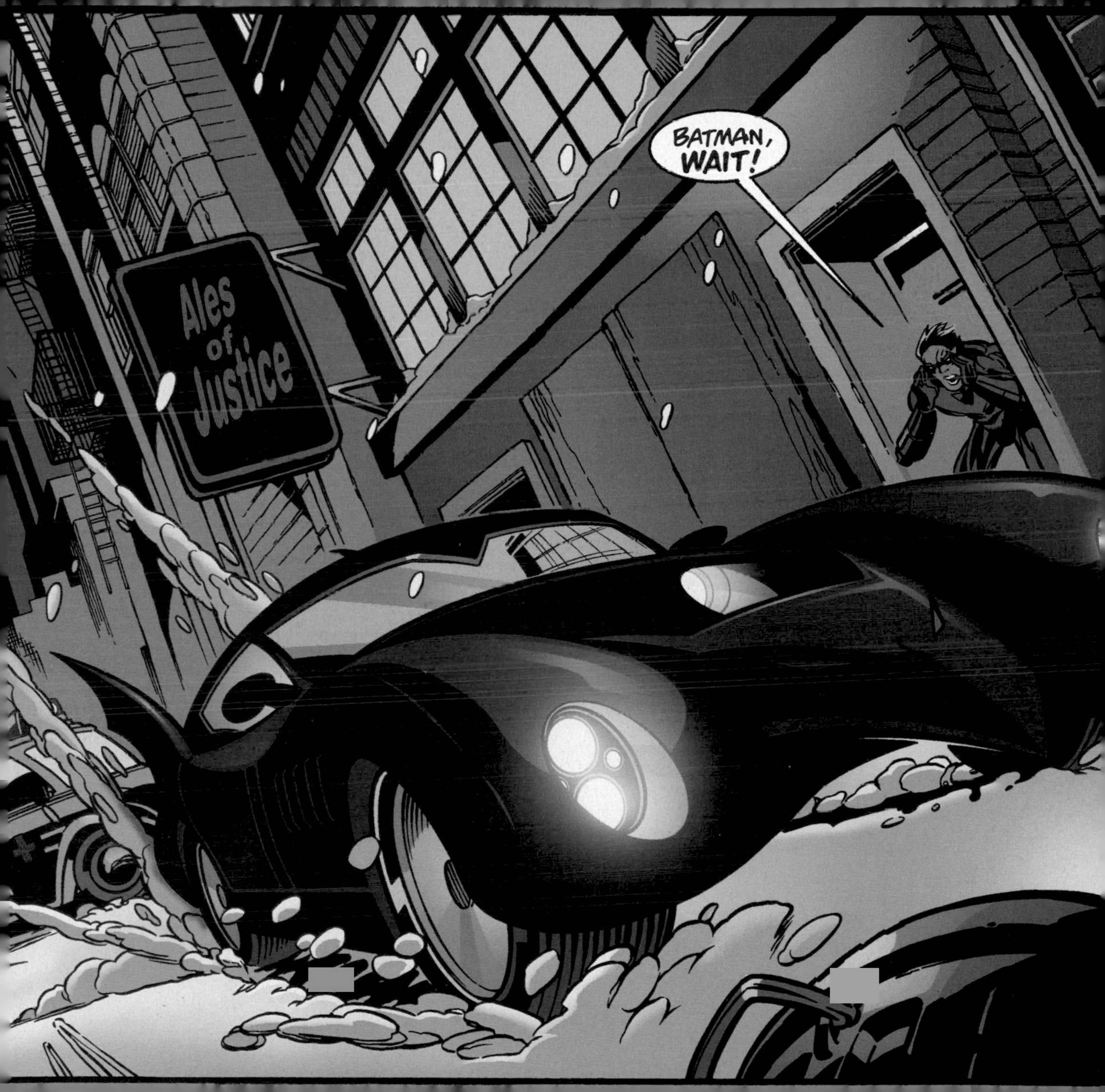
Ales of Justice
BATMAN, WAIT!

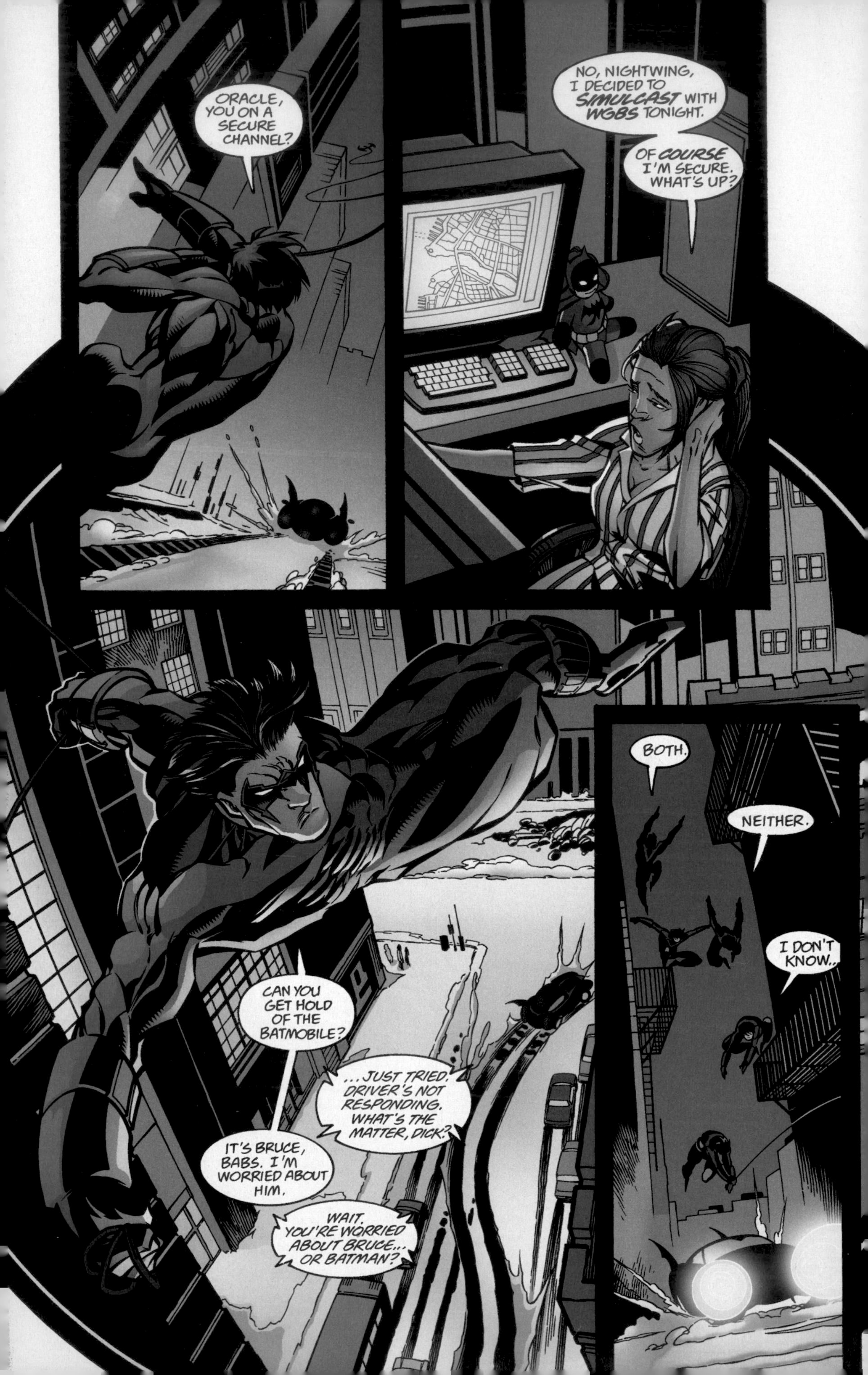
ORACLE, YOU ON A SECURE CHANNEL?
NO, NIGHTWING, I DECIDED TO SIMULCAST WITH WGBS TONIGHT.
OF COURSE I'M SECURE. WHAT'S UP?
CAN YOU GET HOLD OF THE BATMOBILE?
...JUST TRIED. DRIVER'S NOT RESPONDING. WHAT'S THE MATTER, DICK?
IT'S BRUCE, BABS. I'M WORRIED ABOUT HIM.
WAIT. YOU'RE WORRIED ABOUT BRUCE... OR BATMAN?
BOTH.
NEITHER.
I DON'T KNOW...

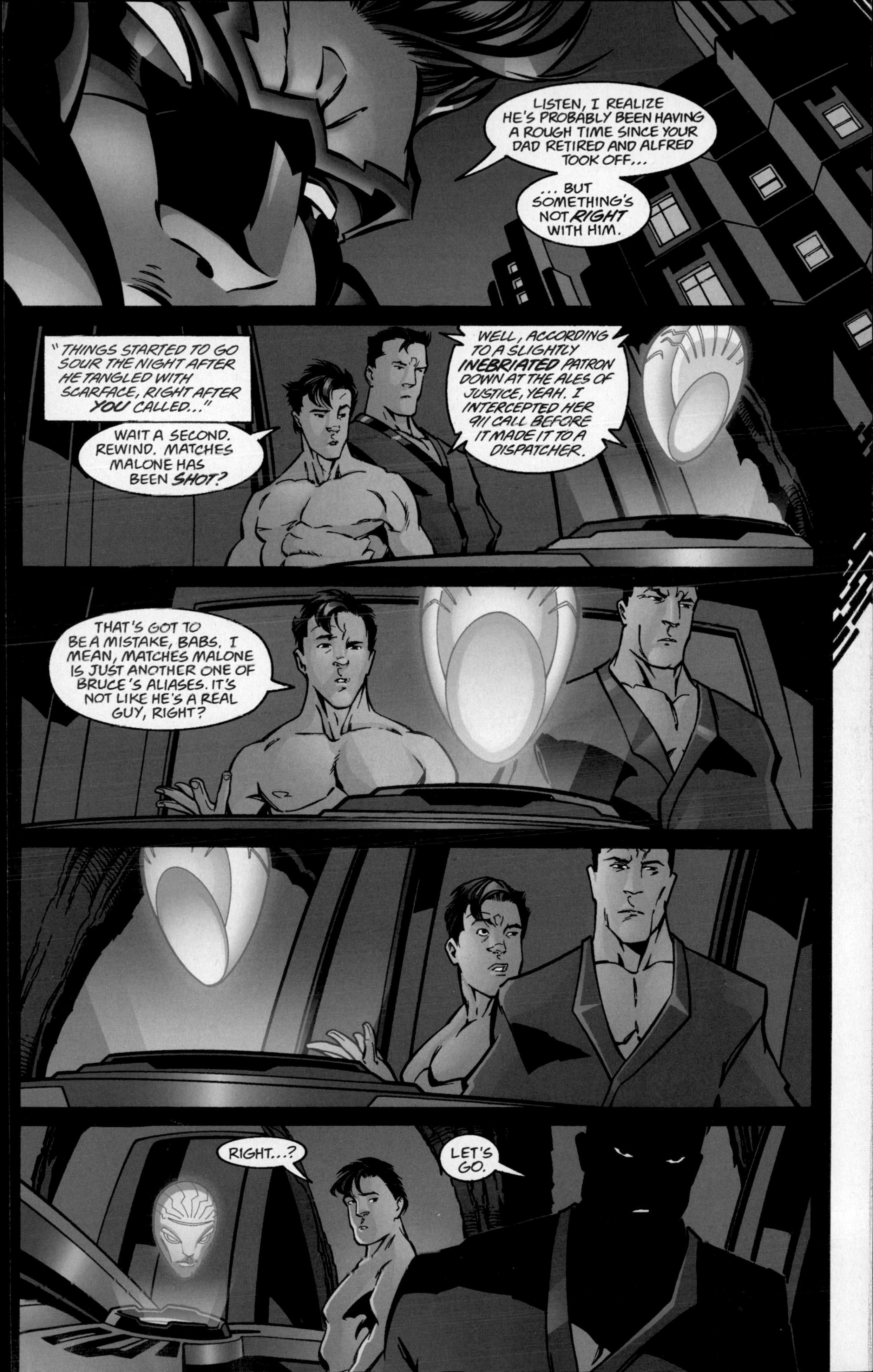
LISTEN, I REALIZE HE'S PROBABLY BEEN HAVING A ROUGH TIME SINCE YOUR DAD RETIRED AND ALFRED TOOK OFF...
... BUT SOMETHING'S NOT RIGHT WITH HIM.
"THINGS STARTED TO GO SOUR THE NIGHT AFTER HE TANGLED WITH SCARFACE, RIGHT AFTER YOU CALLED..."
WAIT A SECOND. REWIND. MATCHES MALONE HAS BEEN SHOT?
WELL, ACCORDING TO A SLIGHTLY INEBRIATED PATRON DOWN AT THE ALES OF JUSTICE, YEAH. I INTERCEPTED HER 911 CALL BEFORE IT MADE IT TO A DISPATCHER.
THAT'S GOT TO BE A MISTAKE, BABS. I MEAN, MATCHES MALONE IS JUST ANOTHER ONE OF BRUCE'S ALIASES. IT'S NOT LIKE HE'S A REAL GUY, RIGHT?
RIGHT...?
LET'S GO.

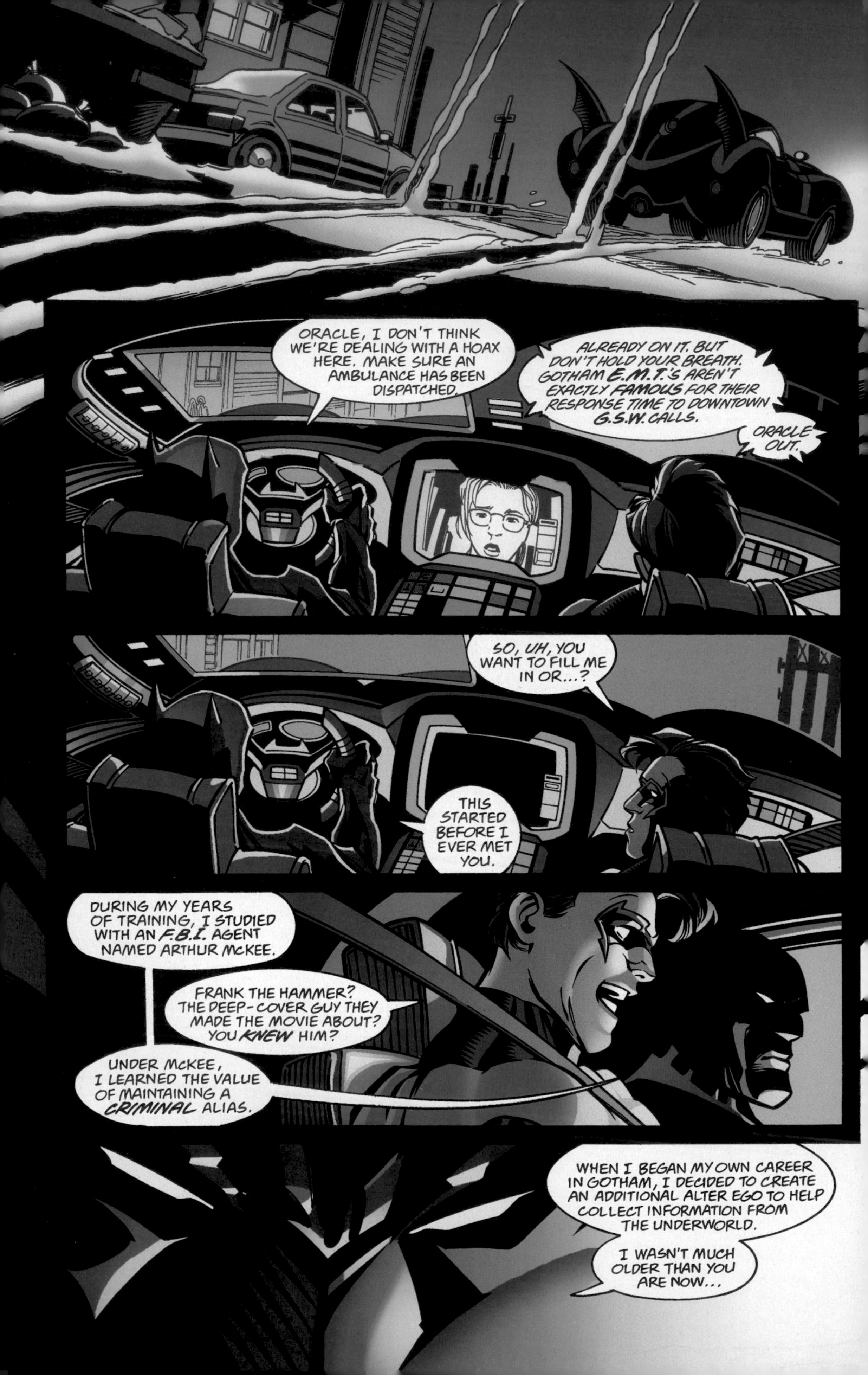
ORACLE, I DON'T THINK WE'RE DEALING WITH A HOAX HERE. MAKE SURE AN AMBULANCE HAS BEEN DISPATCHED.
ALREADY ON IT. BUT DON'T HOLD YOUR BREATH. GOTHAM E.M.T.'S AREN'T EXACTLY FAMOUS FOR THEIR RESPONSE TIME TO DOWNTOWN G.S.W. CALLS.
ORACLE OUT.
SO, UH, YOU WANT TO FILL ME IN OR...?
THIS STARTED BEFORE I EVER MET YOU.
DURING MY YEARS OF TRAINING, I STUDIED WITH AN F.B.I. AGENT NAMED ARTHUR MCKEE.
FRANK THE HAMMER? THE DEEP-COVER GUY THEY MADE THE MOVIE ABOUT? YOU KNEW HIM?
UNDER MCKEE, I LEARNED THE VALUE OF MAINTAINING A CRIMINAL ALIAS.
WHEN I BEGAN MY OWN CAREER IN GOTHAM, I DECIDED TO CREATE AN ADDITIONAL ALTER EGO TO HELP COLLECT INFORMATION FROM THE UNDERWORLD.
I WASN'T MUCH OLDER THAN YOU ARE NOW...

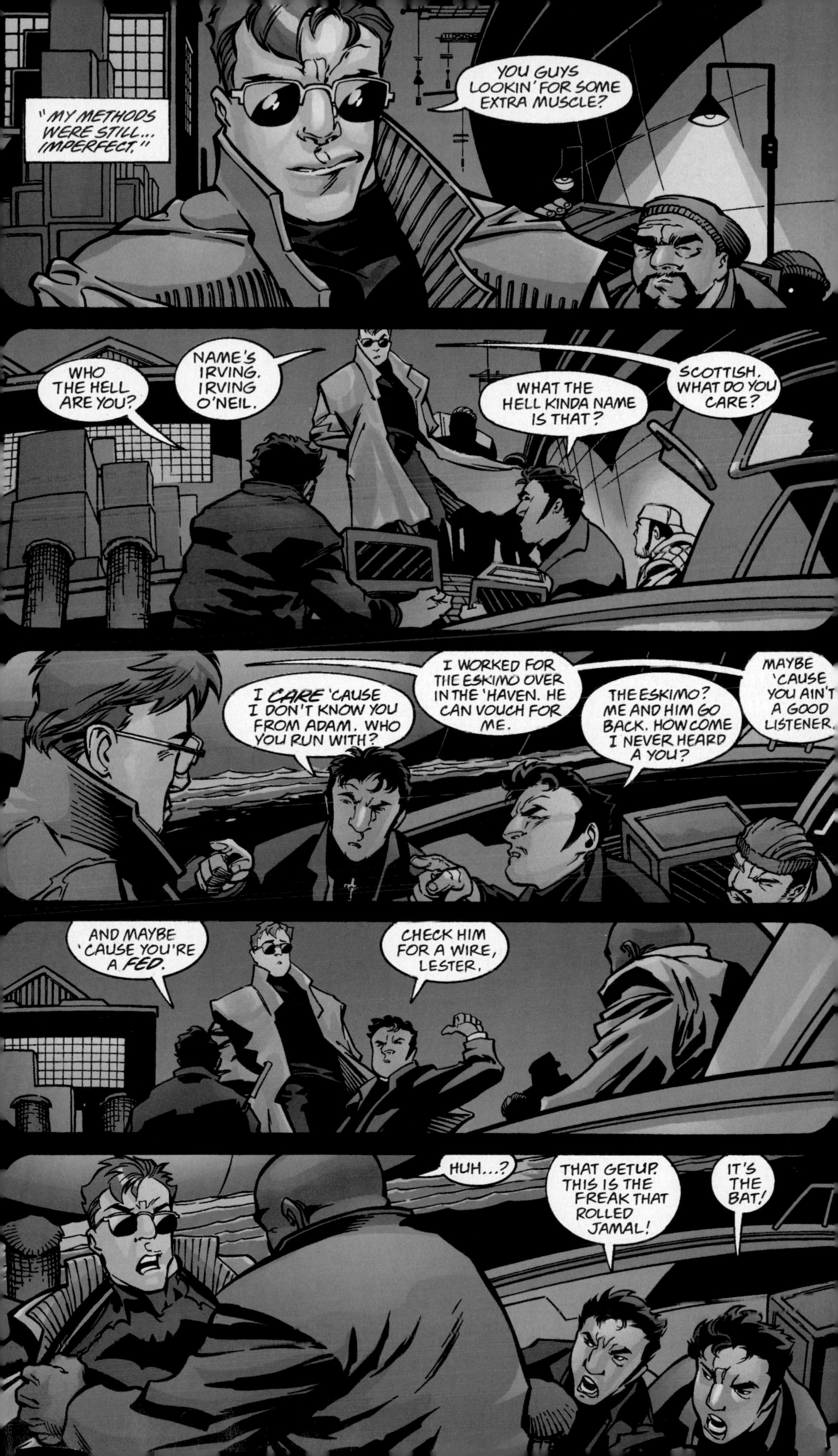
"MY METHODS WERE STILL... IMPERFECT."
YOU GUYS LOOKIN' FOR SOME EXTRA MUSCLE?
WHO THE HELL ARE YOU?
NAME'S IRVING. IRVING O'NEIL.
WHAT THE HELL KINDA NAME IS THAT?
SCOTTISH. WHAT DO YOU CARE?
I CARE 'CAUSE I DON'T KNOW YOU FROM ADAM. WHO YOU RUN WITH?
I WORKED FOR THE ESKIMO OVER IN THE 'HAVEN. HE CAN VOUCH FOR ME.
THE ESKIMO? ME AND HIM GO BACK. HOW COME I NEVER HEARD A YOU?
MAYBE 'CAUSE YOU AIN'T A GOOD LISTENER.
AND MAYBE 'CAUSE YOU'RE A FED.
CHECK HIM FOR A WIRE, LESTER.
HUH...?
THAT GETUP. THIS IS THE FREAK THAT ROLLED JAMAL!
IT'S THE BAT!

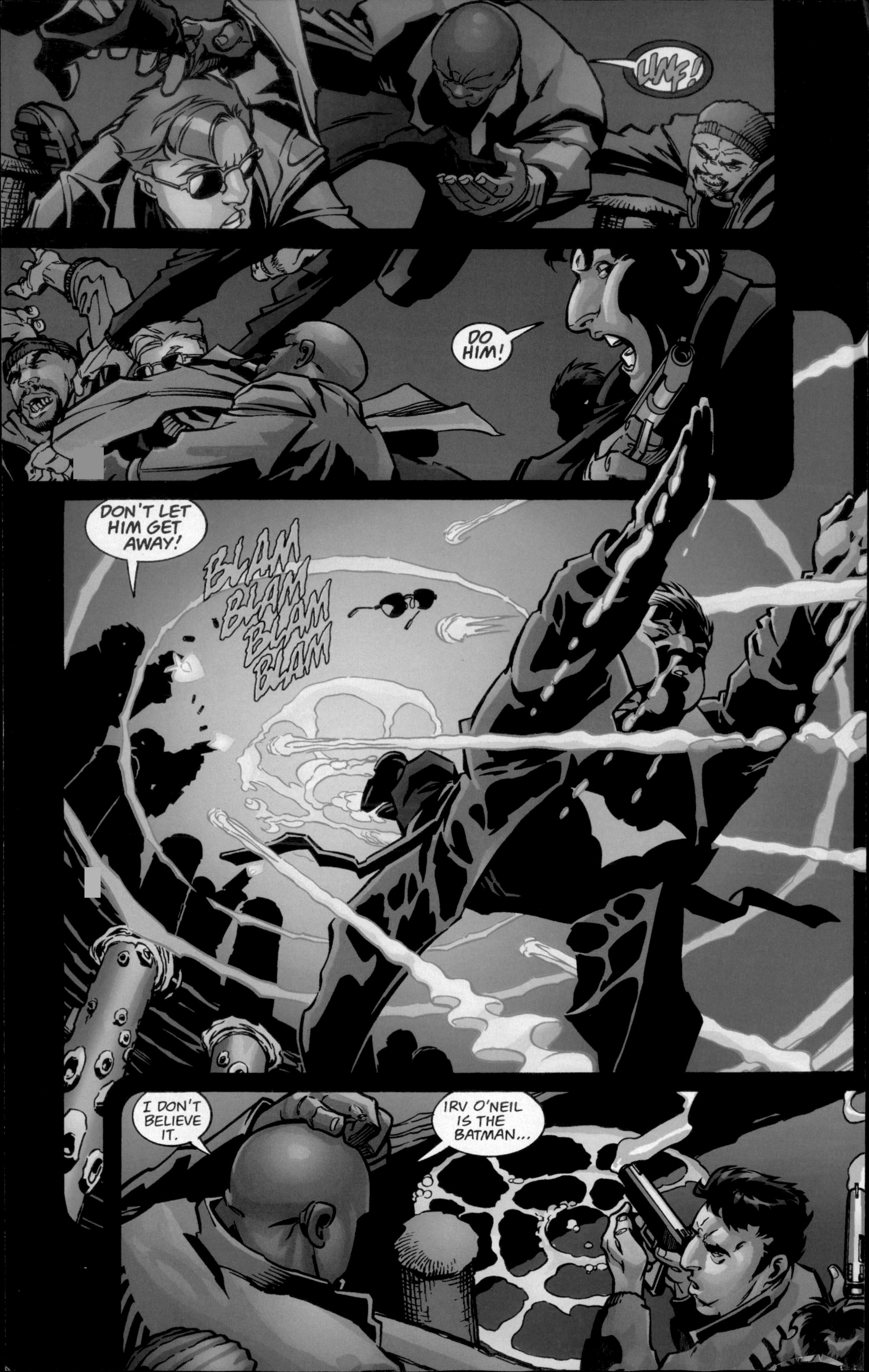
UMF!
DO HIM!
DON'T LET HIM GET AWAY!
BLAM BLAM BLAM BLAM BLAM
I DON'T BELIEVE IT.
IRV O'NEIL IS THE BATMAN...

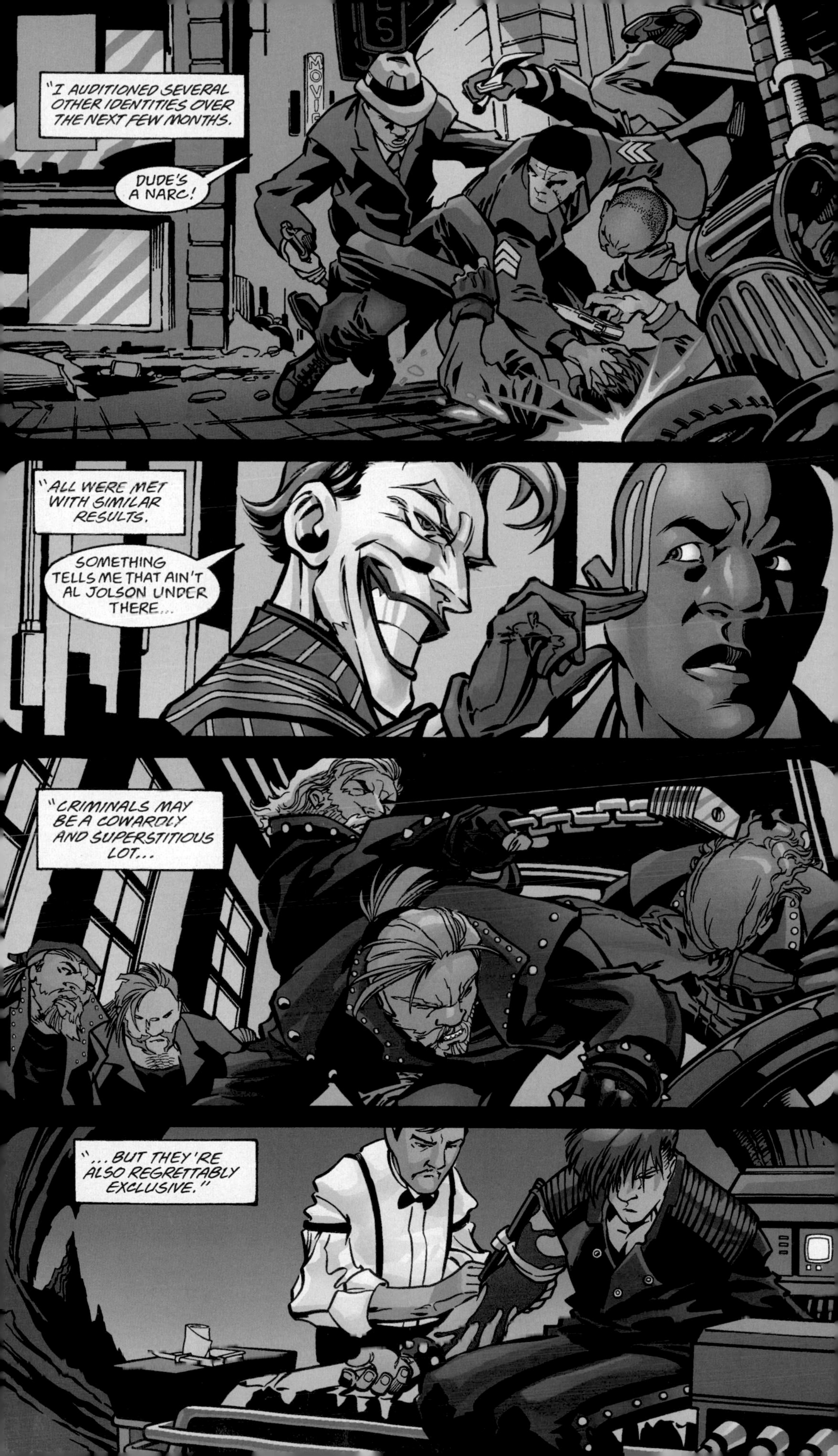
"I AUDITIONED SEVERAL OTHER IDENTITIES OVER THE NEXT FEW MONTHS.
DUDE'S A NARC!
"ALL WERE MET WITH SIMILAR RESULTS.
SOMETHING TELLS ME THAT AIN'T AL JOLSON UNDER THERE...
"CRIMINALS MAY BE A COWARDLY AND SUPERSTITIOUS LOT...
"...BUT THEY'RE ALSO REGRETTABLY EXCLUSIVE."

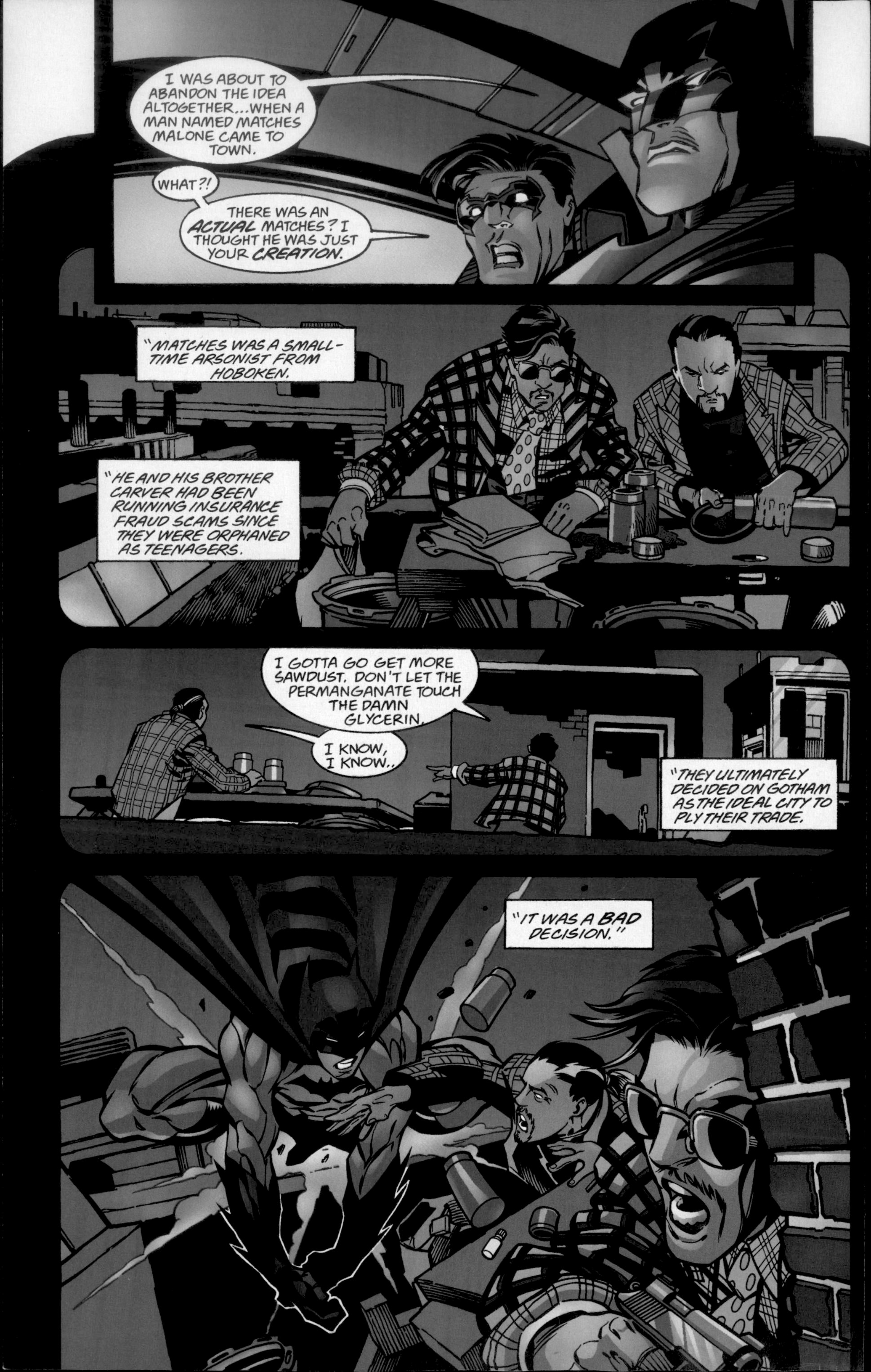
I WAS ABOUT TO ABANDON THE IDEA ALTOGETHER...WHEN A MAN NAMED MATCHES MALONE CAME TO TOWN.
WHAT?!
THERE WAS AN ACTUAL MATCHES? I THOUGHT HE WAS JUST YOUR CREATION.
"MATCHES WAS A SMALL-TIME ARSONIST FROM HOBOKEN.
"HE AND HIS BROTHER CARVER HAD BEEN RUNNING INSURANCE FRAUD SCAMS SINCE THEY WERE ORPHANED AS TEENAGERS.
I GOTTA GO GET MORE SAWDUST. DON'T LET THE PERMANGANATE TOUCH THE DAMN GLYCERIN.
I KNOW, I KNOW..
"THEY ULTIMATELY DECIDED ON GOTHAM AS THE IDEAL CITY TO PLY THEIR TRADE.
"IT WAS A BAD DECISION."

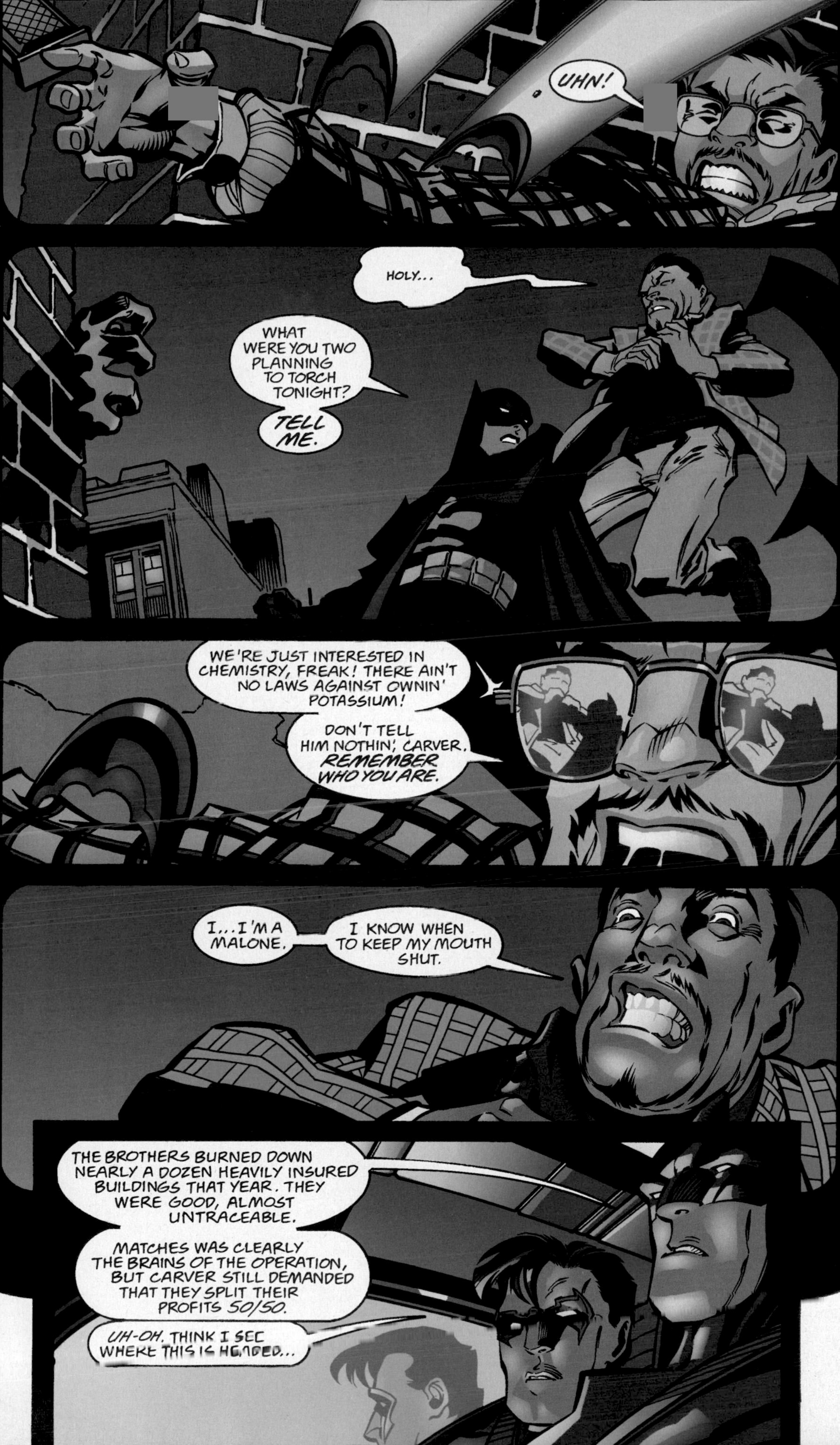
UHN!
HOLY...
WHAT WERE YOU TWO PLANNING TO TORCH TONIGHT?
TELL ME.
WE'RE JUST INTERESTED IN CHEMISTRY, FREAK! THERE AIN'T NO LAWS AGAINST OWNIN' POTASSIUM!
DON'T TELL HIM NOTHIN', CARVER. REMEMBER WHO YOU ARE.
I...I'M A MALONE.
I KNOW WHEN TO KEEP MY MOUTH SHUT.
THE BROTHERS BURNED DOWN NEARLY A DOZEN HEAVILY INSURED BUILDINGS THAT YEAR. THEY WERE GOOD, ALMOST UNTRACEABLE.
MATCHES WAS CLEARLY THE BRAINS OF THE OPERATION, BUT CARVER STILL DEMANDED THAT THEY SPLIT THEIR PROFITS 50/50.
UH-OH. THINK I SEE WHERE THIS IS HEADED...

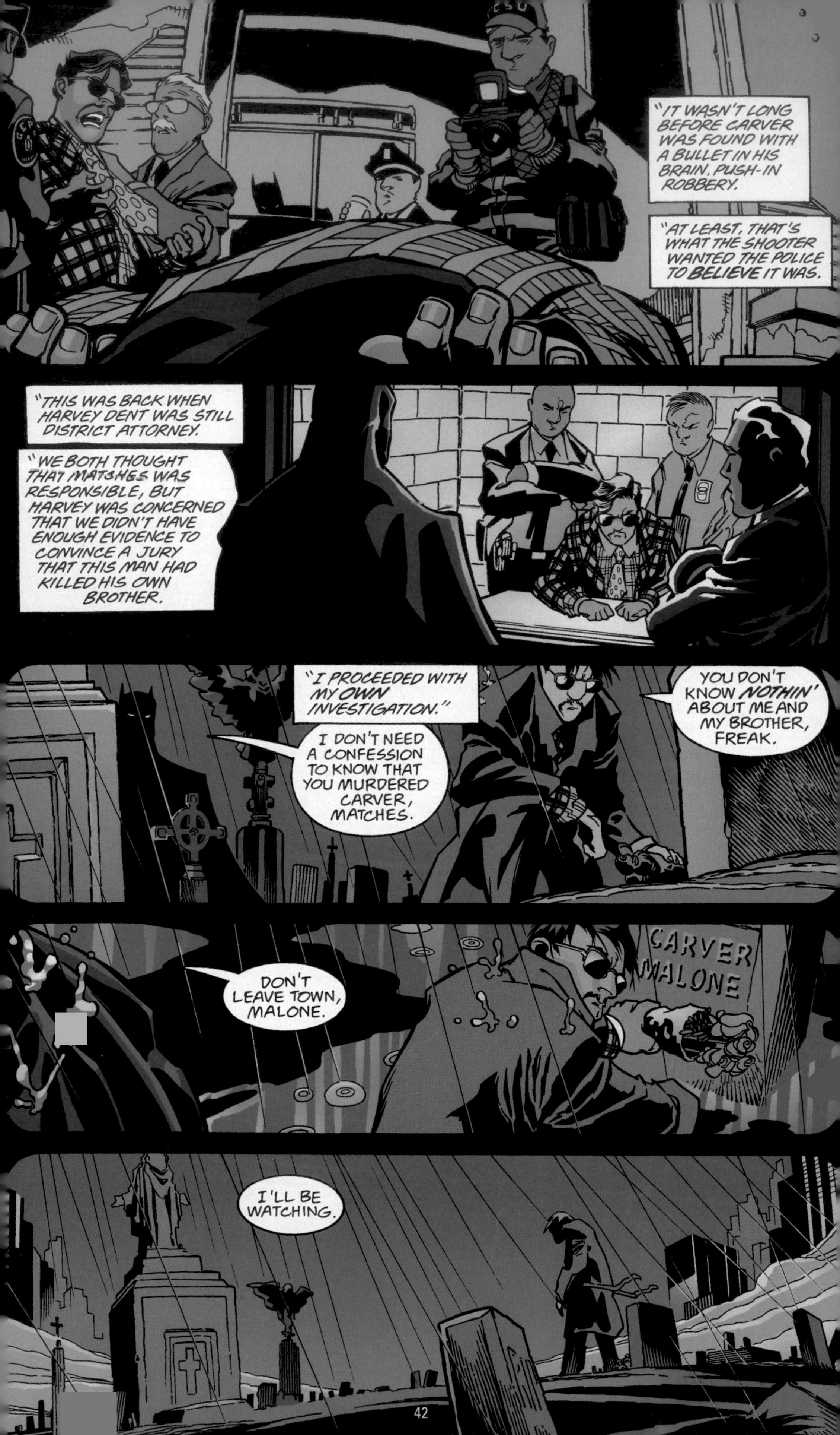
"IT WASN'T LONG BEFORE CARVER WAS FOUND WITH A BULLET IN HIS BRAIN. PUSH-IN ROBBERY.
"AT LEAST, THAT'S WHAT THE SHOOTER WANTED THE POLICE TO BELIEVE IT WAS.
"THIS WAS BACK WHEN HARVEY DENT WAS STILL DISTRICT ATTORNEY.
"WE BOTH THOUGHT THAT MATCHES WAS RESPONSIBLE, BUT HARVEY WAS CONCERNED THAT WE DIDN'T HAVE ENOUGH EVIDENCE TO CONVINCE A JURY THAT THIS MAN HAD KILLED HIS OWN BROTHER.
"I PROCEEDED WITH MY OWN INVESTIGATION."
I DON'T NEED A CONFESSION TO KNOW THAT YOU MURDERED CARVER, MATCHES.
YOU DON'T KNOW NOTHIN' ABOUT ME AND MY BROTHER, FREAK.
DON'T LEAVE TOWN, MALONE.
CARVER MALONE
I'LL BE WATCHING.

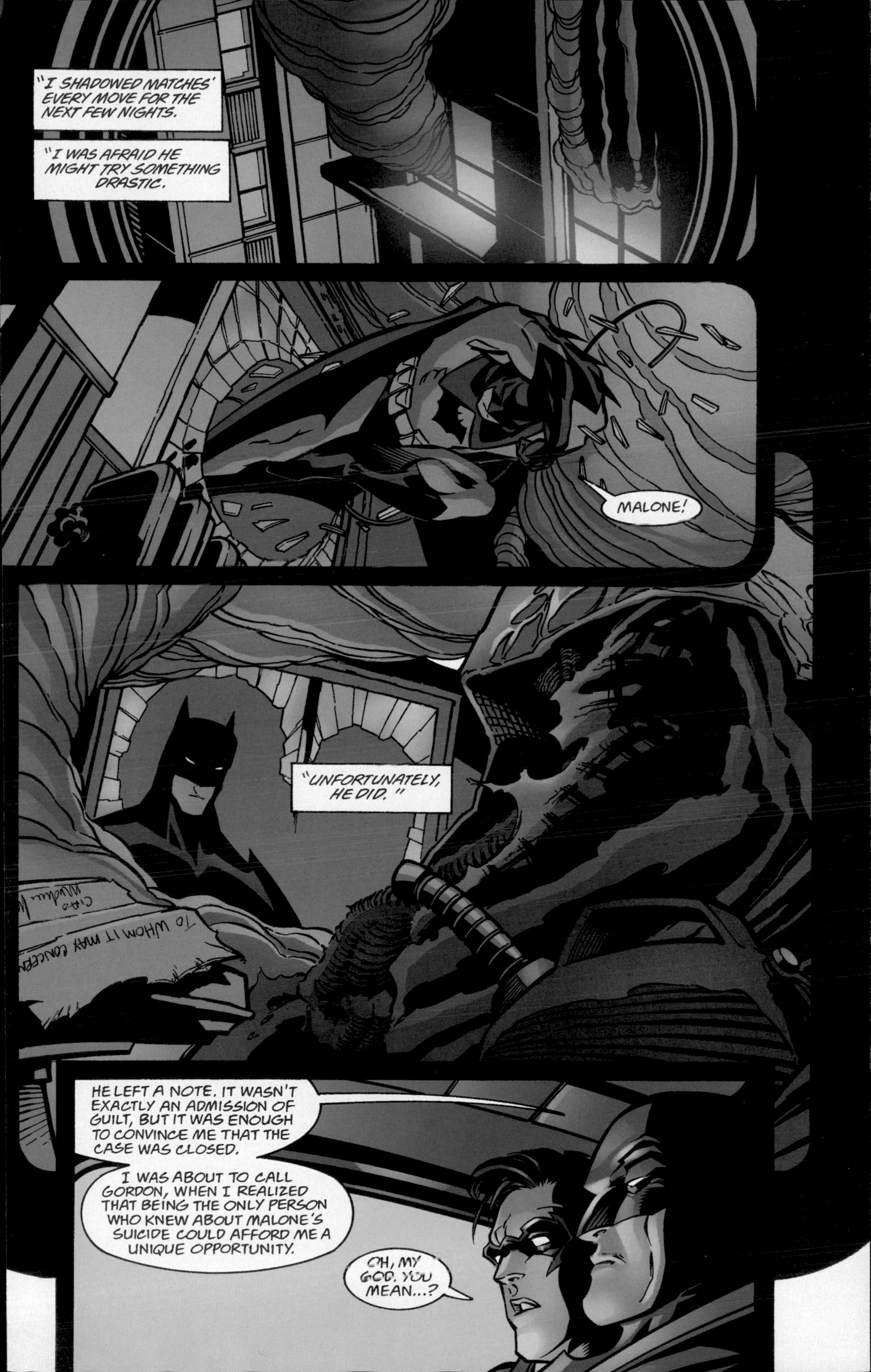
"I SHADOWED MATCHES' EVERY MOVE FOR THE NEXT FEW NIGHTS.
"I WAS AFRAID HE MIGHT TRY SOMETHING DRASTIC.
MALONE!
"UNFORTUNATELY, HE DID."
TO WHOM IT MAY CONCERN
HE LEFT A NOTE. IT WASN'T EXACTLY AN ADMISSION OF GUILT, BUT IT WAS ENOUGH TO CONVINCE ME THAT THE CASE WAS CLOSED.
I WAS ABOUT TO CALL GORDON, WHEN I REALIZED THAT BEING THE ONLY PERSON WHO KNEW ABOUT MALONE'S SUICIDE COULD AFFORD ME A UNIQUE OPPORTUNITY.
OH, MY GOD. YOU MEAN...?

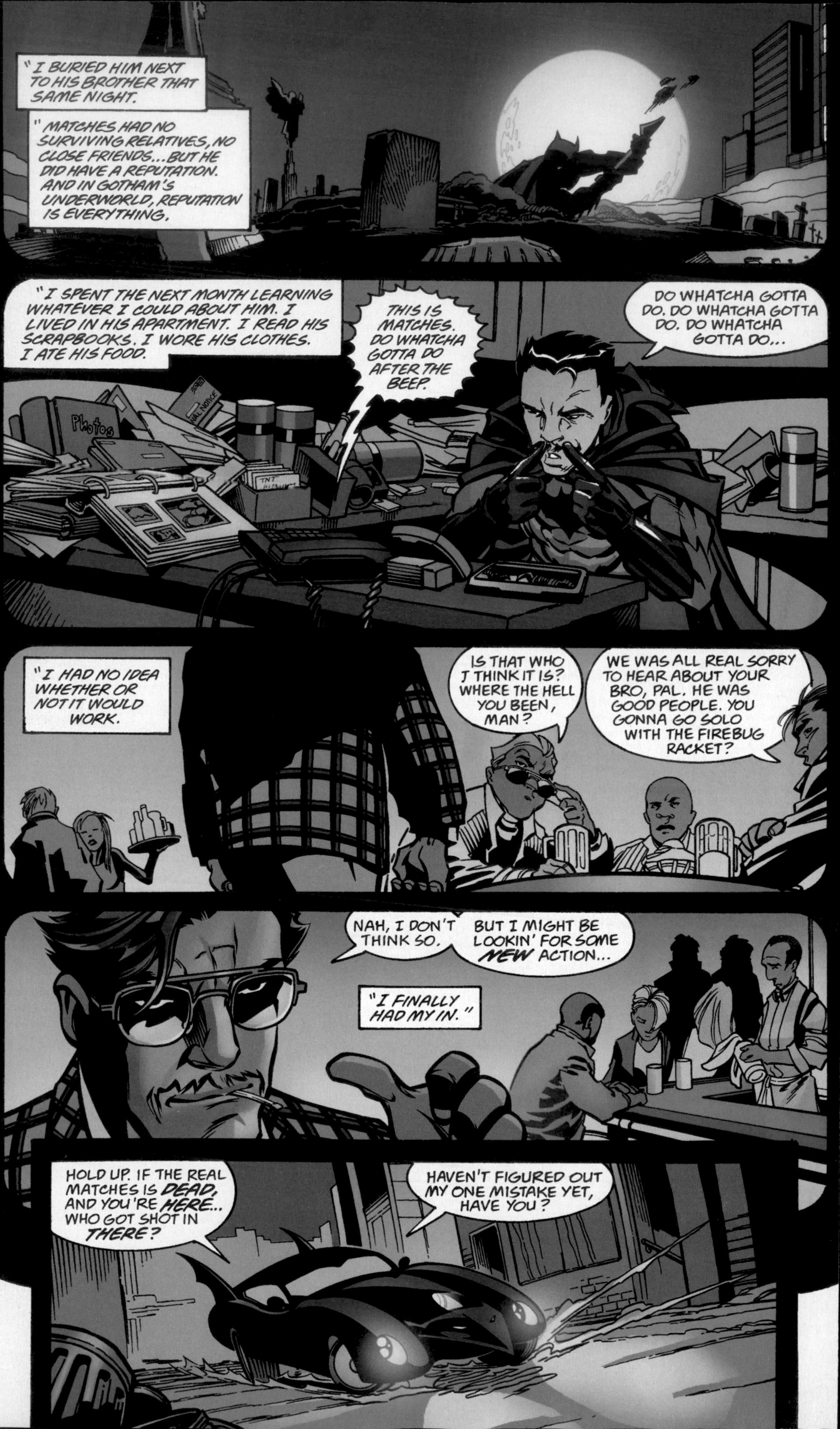
"I BURIED HIM NEXT TO HIS BROTHER THAT SAME NIGHT.
"MATCHES HAD NO SURVIVING RELATIVES, NO CLOSE FRIENDS... BUT HE DID HAVE A REPUTATION. AND IN GOTHAM'S UNDERWORLD, REPUTATION IS EVERYTHING.
"I SPENT THE NEXT MONTH LEARNING WHATEVER I COULD ABOUT HIM. I LIVED IN HIS APARTMENT. I READ HIS SCRAPBOOKS. I WORE HIS CLOTHES. I ATE HIS FOOD.
THIS IS MATCHES. DO WHATCHA GOTTA DO AFTER THE BEEP.
DO WHATCHA GOTTA DO. DO WHATCHA GOTTA DO. DO WHATCHA GOTTA DO...
Photos
"I HAD NO IDEA WHETHER OR NOT IT WOULD WORK.
IS THAT WHO I THINK IT IS? WHERE THE HELL YOU BEEN, MAN?
WE WAS ALL REAL SORRY TO HEAR ABOUT YOUR BRO, PAL. HE WAS GOOD PEOPLE. YOU GONNA GO SOLO WITH THE FIREBUG RACKET?
NAH, I DON'T THINK SO.
BUT I MIGHT BE LOOKIN' FOR SOME NEW ACTION...
"I FINALLY HAD MY IN."
HOLD UP. IF THE REAL MATCHES IS DEAD, AND YOU'RE HERE... WHO GOT SHOT IN THERE?
HAVEN'T FIGURED OUT MY ONE MISTAKE YET, HAVE YOU?

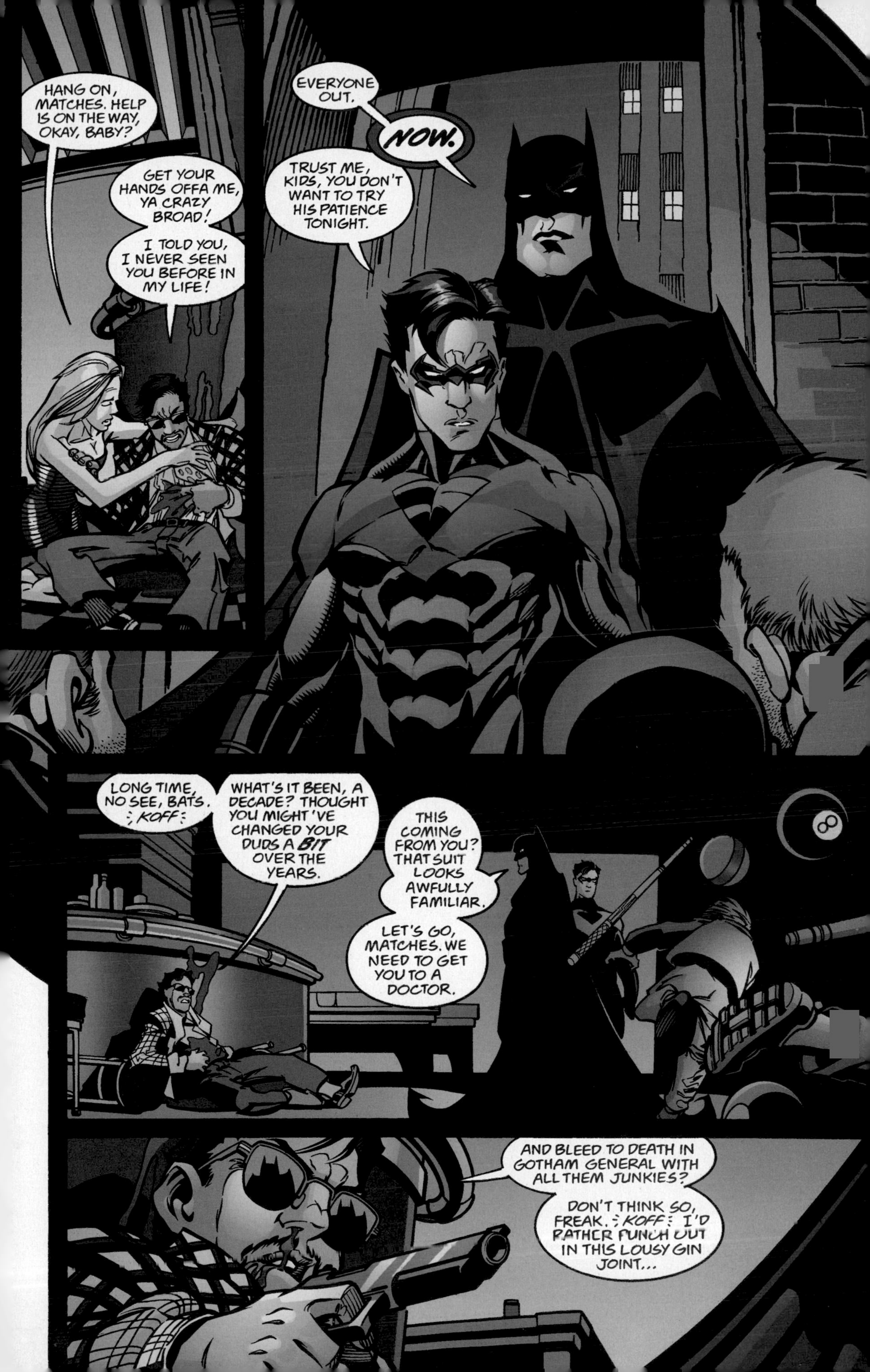
HANG ON, MATCHES. HELP IS ON THE WAY, OKAY, BABY?
GET YOUR HANDS OFFA ME, YA CRAZY BROAD!
I TOLD YOU, I NEVER SEEN YOU BEFORE IN MY LIFE!
EVERYONE OUT.
NOW.
TRUST ME, KIDS, YOU DON'T WANT TO TRY HIS PATIENCE TONIGHT.
LONG TIME, NO SEE, BATS. KOFF
WHAT'S IT BEEN, A DECADE? THOUGHT YOU MIGHT'VE CHANGED YOUR DUDS A BIT OVER THE YEARS.
THIS COMING FROM YOU? THAT SUIT LOOKS AWFULLY FAMILIAR.
LET'S GO, MATCHES. WE NEED TO GET YOU TO A DOCTOR.
AND BLEED TO DEATH IN GOTHAM GENERAL WITH ALL THEM JUNKIES?
DON'T THINK SO, FREAK. KOFF I'D RATHER PUNCH OUT IN THIS LOUSY GIN JOINT...

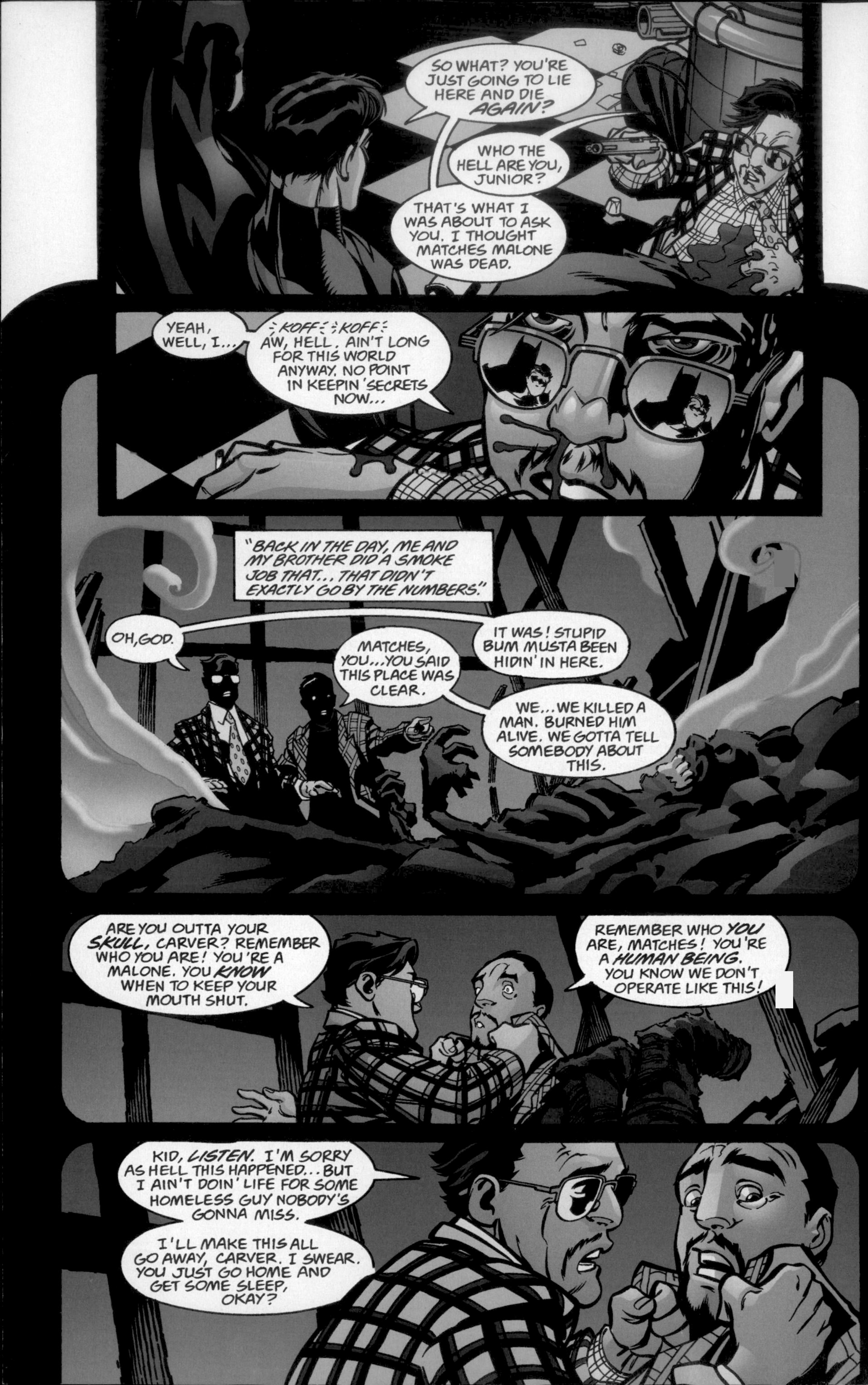
SO WHAT? YOU'RE JUST GOING TO LIE HERE AND DIE AGAIN?
WHO THE HELL ARE YOU, JUNIOR?
THAT'S WHAT I WAS ABOUT TO ASK YOU. I THOUGHT MATCHES MALONE WAS DEAD.
YEAH, WELL, I...
KOFF KOFF AW, HELL. AIN'T LONG FOR THIS WORLD ANYWAY. NO POINT IN KEEPIN' SECRETS NOW...
"BACK IN THE DAY, ME AND MY BROTHER DID A SMOKE JOB THAT... THAT DIDN'T EXACTLY GO BY THE NUMBERS."
OH, GOD.
MATCHES, YOU... YOU SAID THIS PLACE WAS CLEAR.
IT WAS! STUPID BUM MUSTA BEEN HIDIN' IN HERE.
WE... WE KILLED A MAN. BURNED HIM ALIVE. WE GOTTA TELL SOMEBODY ABOUT THIS.
ARE YOU OUTTA YOUR SKULL, CARVER? REMEMBER WHO YOU ARE! YOU'RE A MALONE. YOU KNOW WHEN TO KEEP YOUR MOUTH SHUT.
REMEMBER WHO YOU ARE, MATCHES! YOU'RE A HUMAN BEING. YOU KNOW WE DON'T OPERATE LIKE THIS!
KID, LISTEN. I'M SORRY AS HELL THIS HAPPENED... BUT I AIN'T DOIN' LIFE FOR SOME HOMELESS GUY NOBODY'S GONNA MISS.
I'LL MAKE THIS ALL GO AWAY, CARVER. I SWEAR. YOU JUST GO HOME AND GET SOME SLEEP, OKAY?

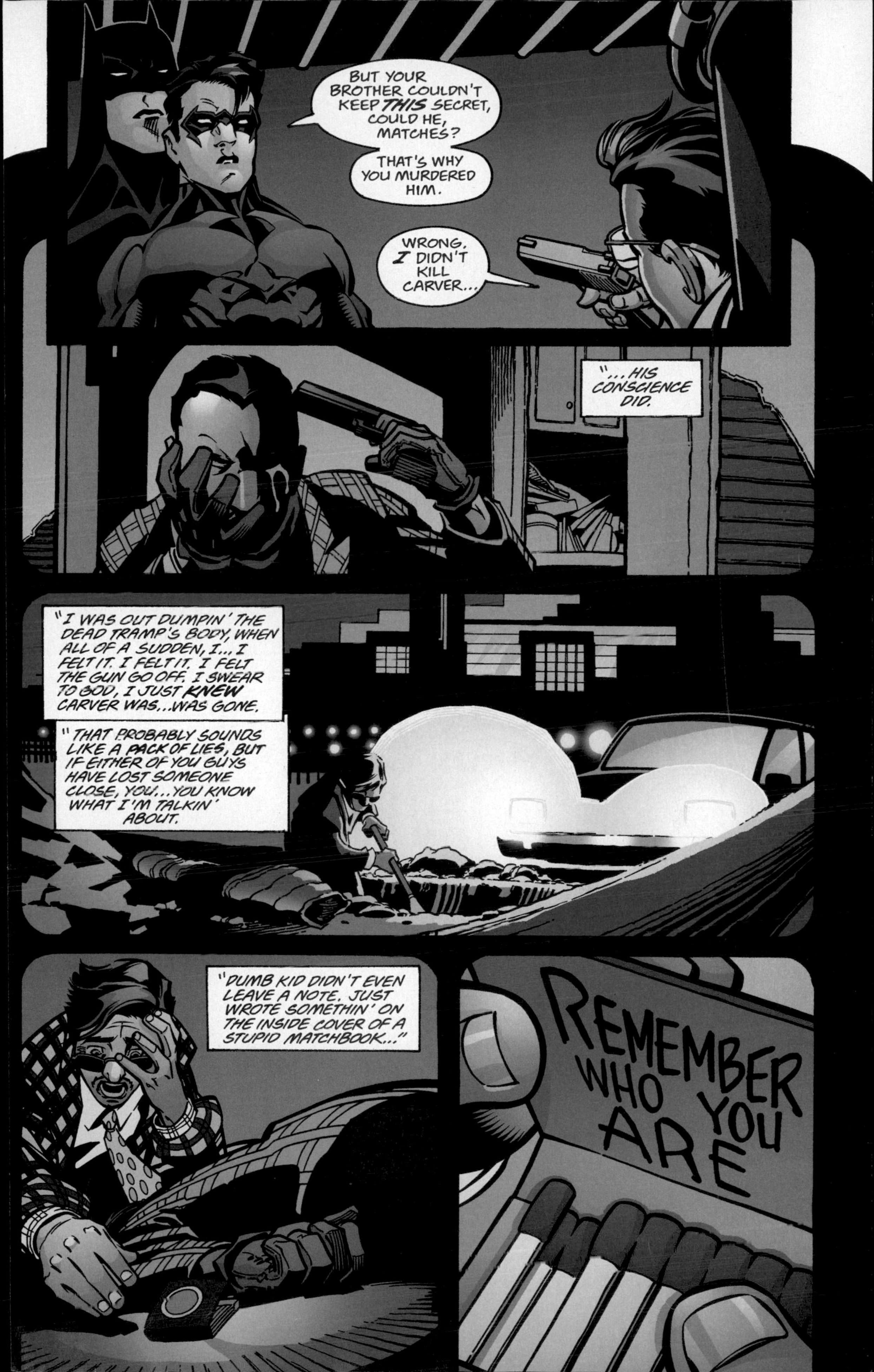
BUT YOUR BROTHER COULDN'T KEEP THIS SECRET, COULD HE, MATCHES?
THAT'S WHY YOU MURDERED HIM.
WRONG. I DIDN'T KILL CARVER...
"...HIS CONSCIENCE DID.
"I WAS OUT DUMPIN' THE DEAD TRAMP'S BODY, WHEN ALL OF A SUDDEN, I... I FELT IT. I FELT IT. I FELT THE GUN GO OFF. I SWEAR TO GOD, I JUST KNEW CARVER WAS... WAS GONE.
"THAT PROBABLY SOUNDS LIKE A PACK OF LIES, BUT IF EITHER OF YOU GUYS HAVE LOST SOMEONE CLOSE, YOU... YOU KNOW WHAT I'M TALKIN' ABOUT.
"DUMB KID DIDN'T EVEN LEAVE A NOTE. JUST WROTE SOMETHIN' ON THE INSIDE COVER OF A STUPID MATCHBOOK..."
REMEMBER WHO YOU ARE

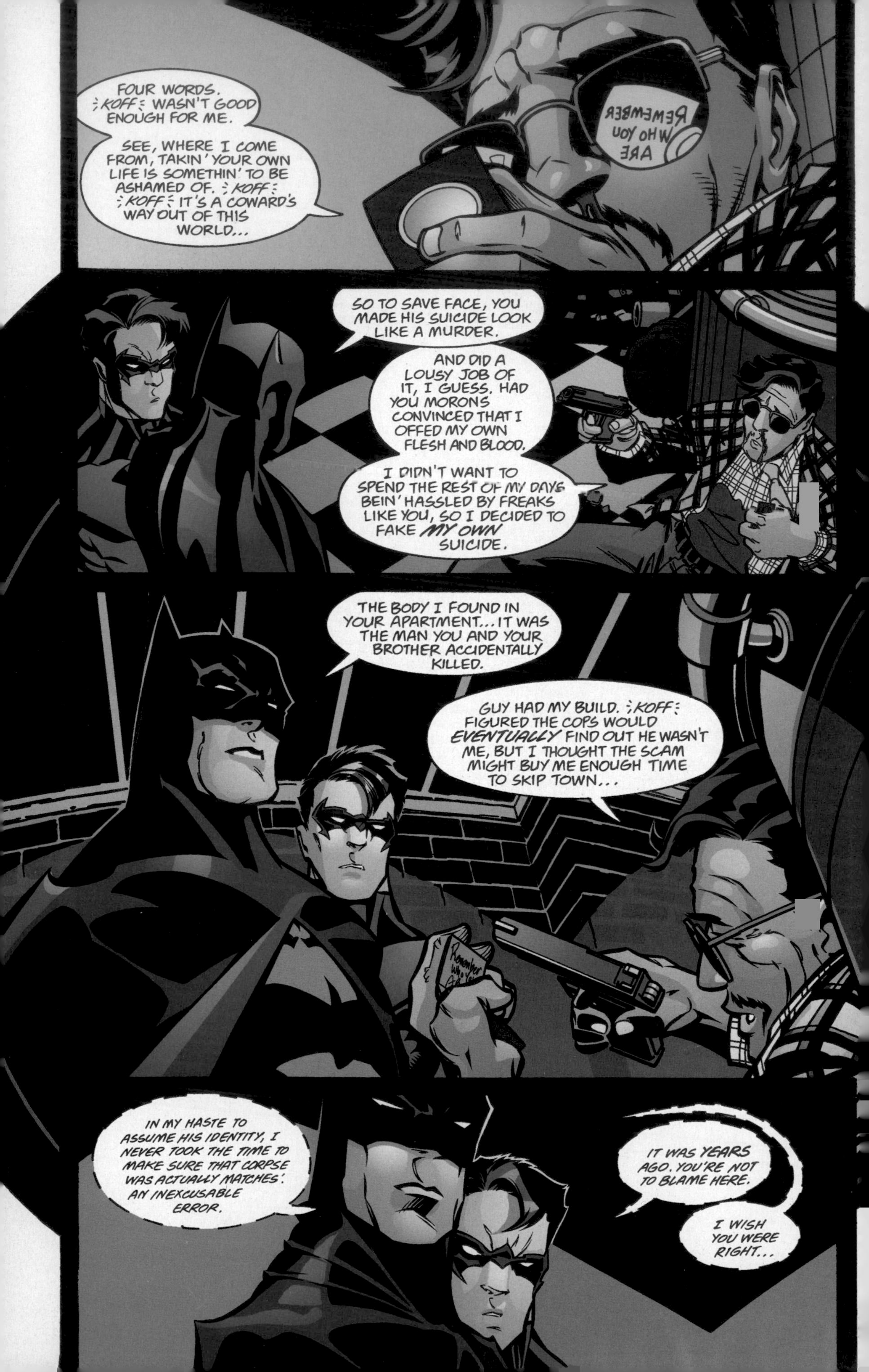
FOUR WORDS. ⁏KOFF⁏ WASN'T GOOD ENOUGH FOR ME.
SEE, WHERE I COME FROM, TAKIN' YOUR OWN LIFE IS SOMETHIN' TO BE ASHAMED OF. ⁏KOFF⁏ ⁏KOFF⁏ IT'S A COWARD'S WAY OUT OF THIS WORLD...
REMEMBER WHO YOU ARE
SO TO SAVE FACE, YOU MADE HIS SUICIDE LOOK LIKE A MURDER.
AND DID A LOUSY JOB OF IT, I GUESS. HAD YOU MORONS CONVINCED THAT I OFFED MY OWN FLESH AND BLOOD.
I DIDN'T WANT TO SPEND THE REST OF MY DAYS BEIN' HASSLED BY FREAKS LIKE YOU, SO I DECIDED TO FAKE MY OWN SUICIDE.
THE BODY I FOUND IN YOUR APARTMENT... IT WAS THE MAN YOU AND YOUR BROTHER ACCIDENTALLY KILLED.
GUY HAD MY BUILD. ⁏KOFF⁏ FIGURED THE COPS WOULD EVENTUALLY FIND OUT HE WASN'T ME, BUT I THOUGHT THE SCAM MIGHT BUY ME ENOUGH TIME TO SKIP TOWN...
IN MY HASTE TO ASSUME HIS IDENTITY, I NEVER TOOK THE TIME TO MAKE SURE THAT CORPSE WAS ACTUALLY MATCHES'. AN INEXCUSABLE ERROR.
IT WAS YEARS AGO. YOU'RE NOT TO BLAME HERE.
I WISH YOU WERE RIGHT...

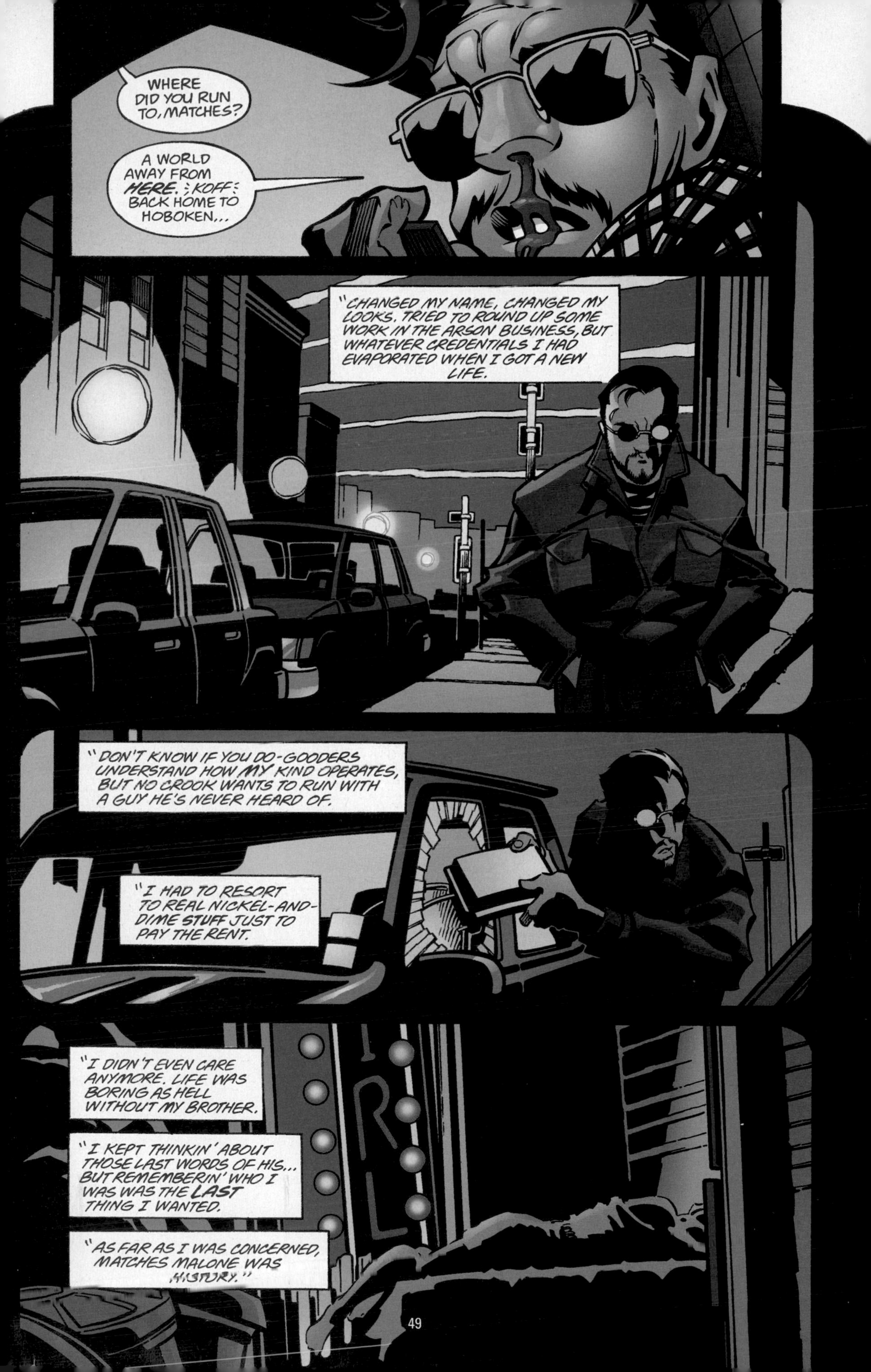
WHERE DID YOU RUN TO, MATCHES?
A WORLD AWAY FROM HERE. :KOFF: BACK HOME TO HOBOKEN...
"CHANGED MY NAME, CHANGED MY LOOKS. TRIED TO ROUND UP SOME WORK IN THE ARSON BUSINESS, BUT WHATEVER CREDENTIALS I HAD EVAPORATED WHEN I GOT A NEW LIFE.
"DON'T KNOW IF YOU DO-GOODERS UNDERSTAND HOW MY KIND OPERATES, BUT NO CROOK WANTS TO RUN WITH A GUY HE'S NEVER HEARD OF.
"I HAD TO RESORT TO REAL NICKEL-AND-DIME STUFF JUST TO PAY THE RENT.
"I DIDN'T EVEN CARE ANYMORE. LIFE WAS BORING AS HELL WITHOUT MY BROTHER.
"I KEPT THINKIN' ABOUT THOSE LAST WORDS OF HIS... BUT REMEMBERIN' WHO I WAS WAS THE LAST THING I WANTED.
"AS FAR AS I WAS CONCERNED, MATCHES MALONE WAS HISTORY."

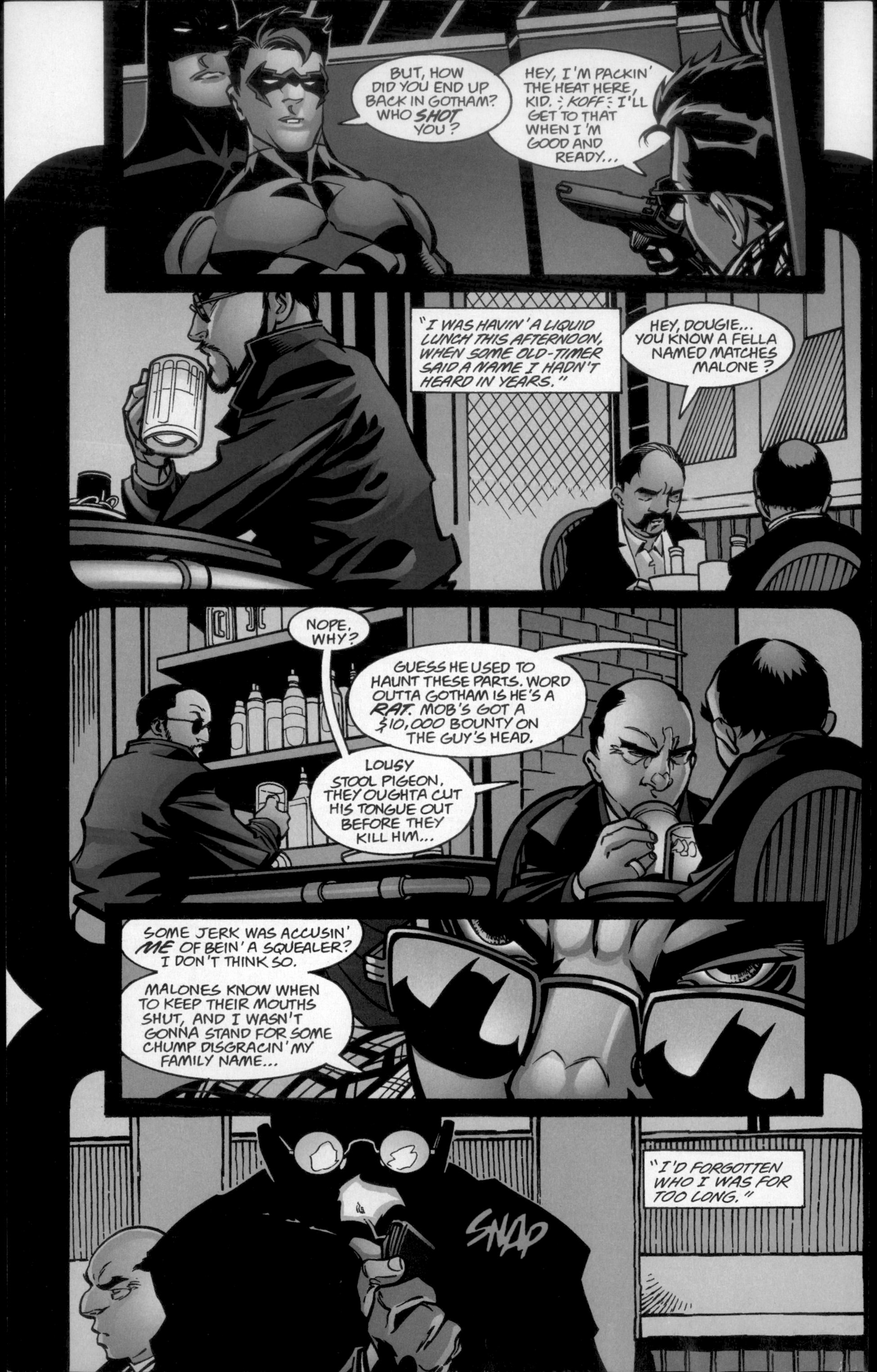
BUT, HOW DID YOU END UP BACK IN GOTHAM? WHO SHOT YOU?
HEY, I'M PACKIN' THE HEAT HERE, KID. :KOFF: I'LL GET TO THAT WHEN I'M GOOD AND READY...
"I WAS HAVIN' A LIQUID LUNCH THIS AFTERNOON, WHEN SOME OLD-TIMER SAID A NAME I HADN'T HEARD IN YEARS."
HEY, DOUGIE... YOU KNOW A FELLA NAMED MATCHES MALONE?
NOPE, WHY?
GUESS HE USED TO HAUNT THESE PARTS. WORD OUTTA GOTHAM IS HE'S A RAT. MOB'S GOT A $10,000 BOUNTY ON THE GUY'S HEAD.
LOUSY STOOL PIGEON. THEY OUGHTA CUT HIS TONGUE OUT BEFORE THEY KILL HIM...
SOME JERK WAS ACCUSIN' ME OF BEIN' A SQUEALER? I DON'T THINK SO.
MALONES KNOW WHEN TO KEEP THEIR MOUTHS SHUT, AND I WASN'T GONNA STAND FOR SOME CHUMP DISGRACIN' MY FAMILY NAME...
SNAP
"I'D FORGOTTEN WHO I WAS FOR TOO LONG."

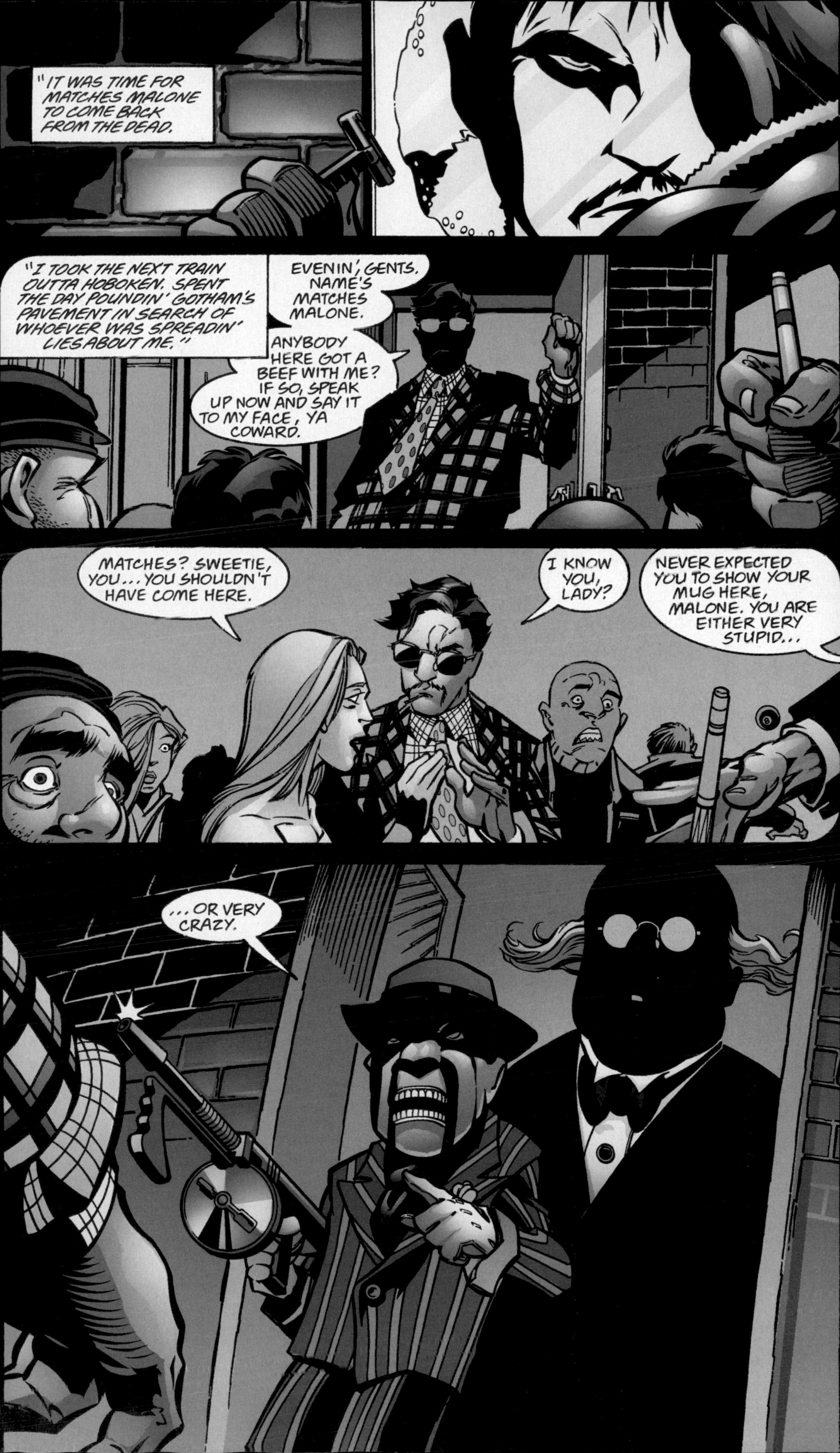
"IT WAS TIME FOR MATCHES MALONE TO COME BACK FROM THE DEAD.
"I TOOK THE NEXT TRAIN OUTTA HOBOKEN. SPENT THE DAY POUNDIN' GOTHAM'S PAVEMENT IN SEARCH OF WHOEVER WAS SPREADIN' LIES ABOUT ME."
EVENIN', GENTS. NAME'S MATCHES MALONE.
ANYBODY HERE GOT A BEEF WITH ME? IF SO, SPEAK UP NOW AND SAY IT TO MY FACE, YA COWARD.
MATCHES? SWEETIE, YOU... YOU SHOULDN'T HAVE COME HERE.
I KNOW YOU, LADY?
NEVER EXPECTED YOU TO SHOW YOUR MUG HERE, MALONE. YOU ARE EITHER VERY STUPID...
...OR VERY CRAZY.

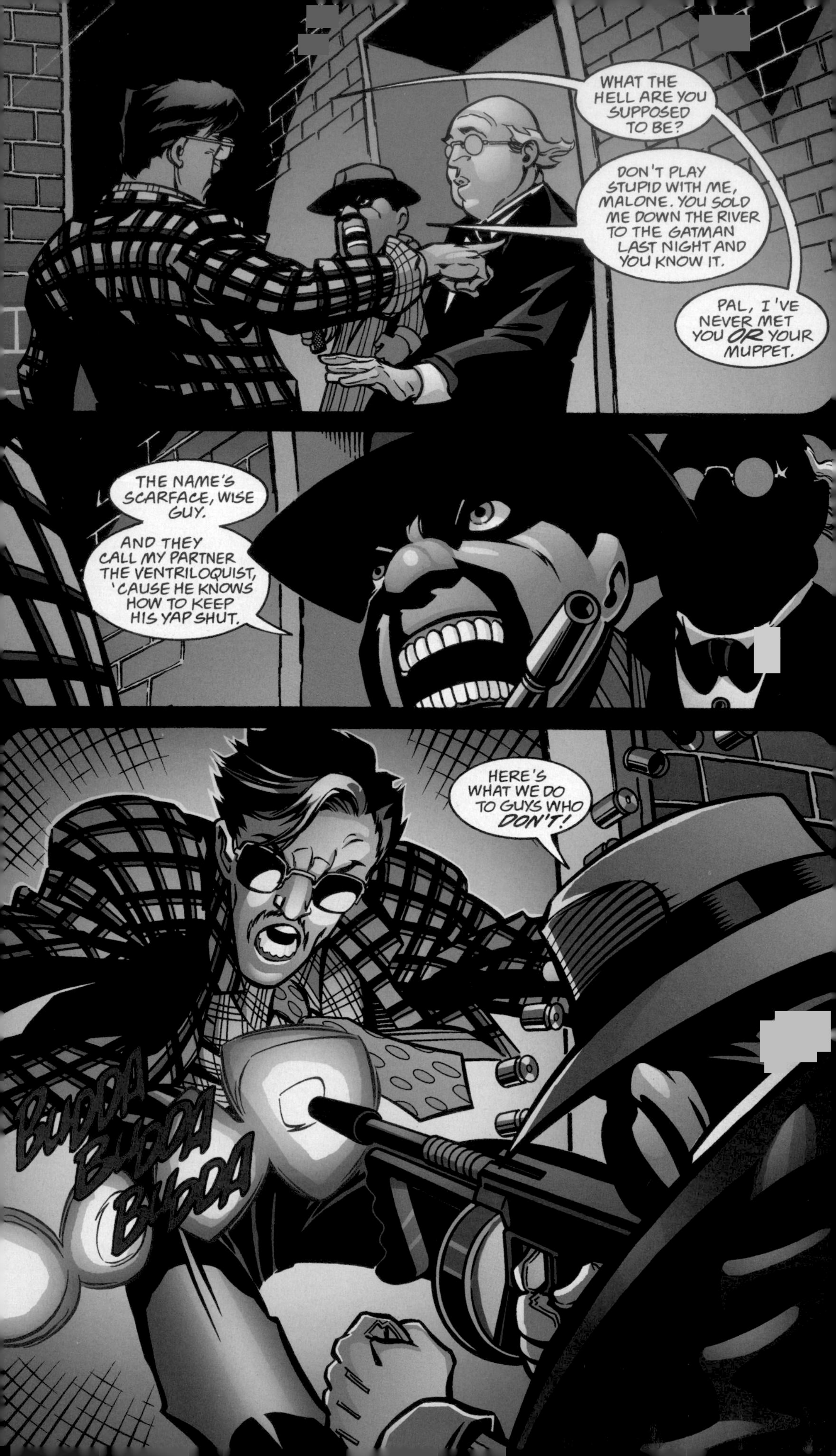
WHAT THE HELL ARE YOU SUPPOSED TO BE?
DON'T PLAY STUPID WITH ME, MALONE. YOU SOLD ME DOWN THE RIVER TO THE GATMAN LAST NIGHT AND YOU KNOW IT.
PAL, I'VE NEVER MET YOU OR YOUR MUPPET.
THE NAME'S SCARFACE, WISE GUY.
AND THEY CALL MY PARTNER THE VENTRILOQUIST, 'CAUSE HE KNOWS HOW TO KEEP HIS YAP SHUT.
HERE'S WHAT WE DO TO GUYS WHO DON'T!
BUDDA BUDDA BUDDA

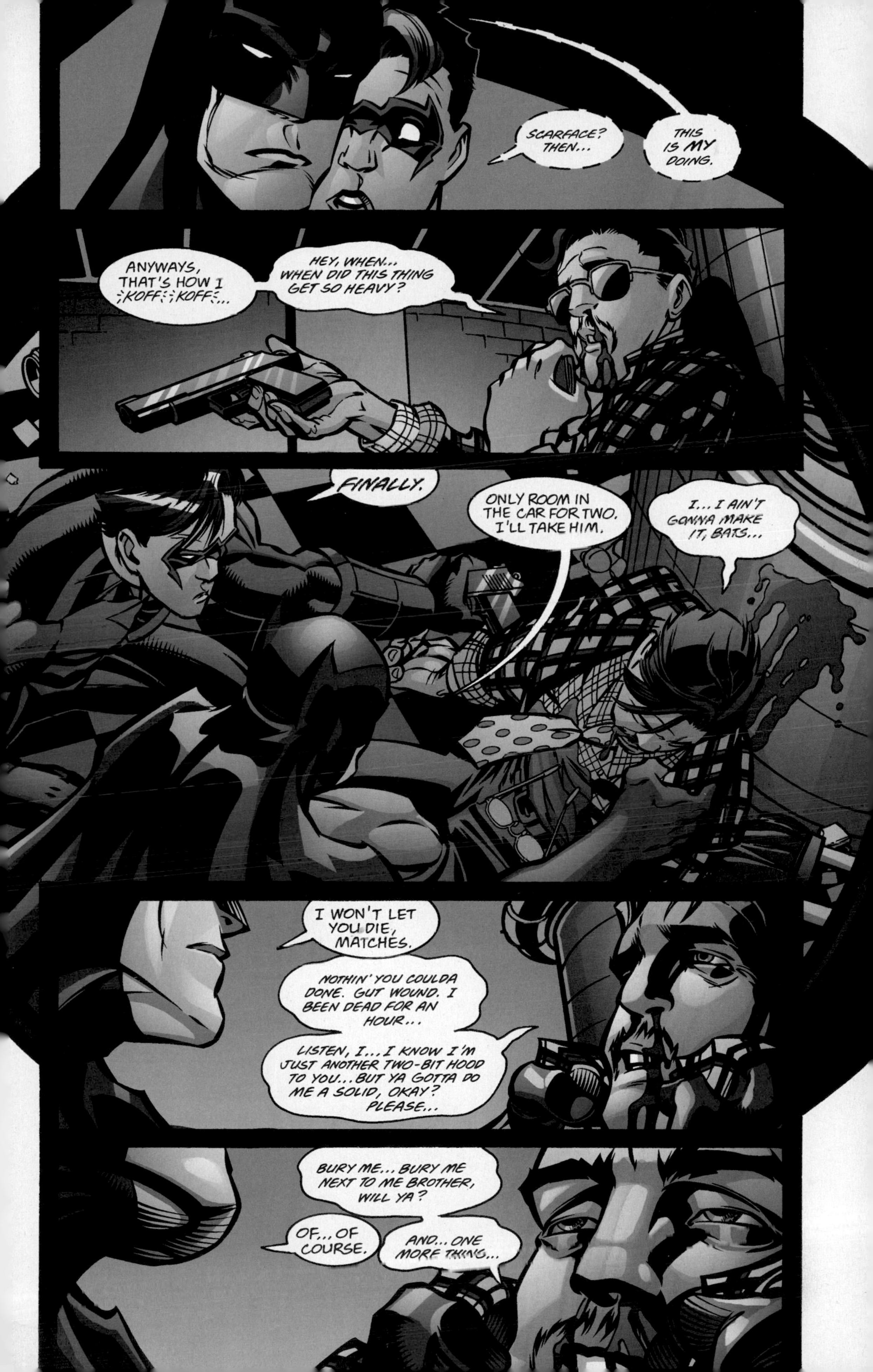
SCARFACE? THEN...
THIS IS MY DOING.
ANYWAYS, THAT'S HOW I ;KOFF;;KOFF;...
HEY, WHEN... WHEN DID THIS THING GET SO HEAVY?
FINALLY.
ONLY ROOM IN THE CAR FOR TWO. I'LL TAKE HIM.
I... I AIN'T GONNA MAKE IT, BATS...
I WON'T LET YOU DIE, MATCHES.
NOTHIN' YOU COULDA DONE. GUT WOUND. I BEEN DEAD FOR AN HOUR...
LISTEN, I... I KNOW I'M JUST ANOTHER TWO-BIT HOOD TO YOU... BUT YA GOTTA DO ME A SOLID, OKAY? PLEASE...
BURY ME... BURY ME NEXT TO ME BROTHER, WILL YA?
OF... OF COURSE.
AND... ONE MORE THING...

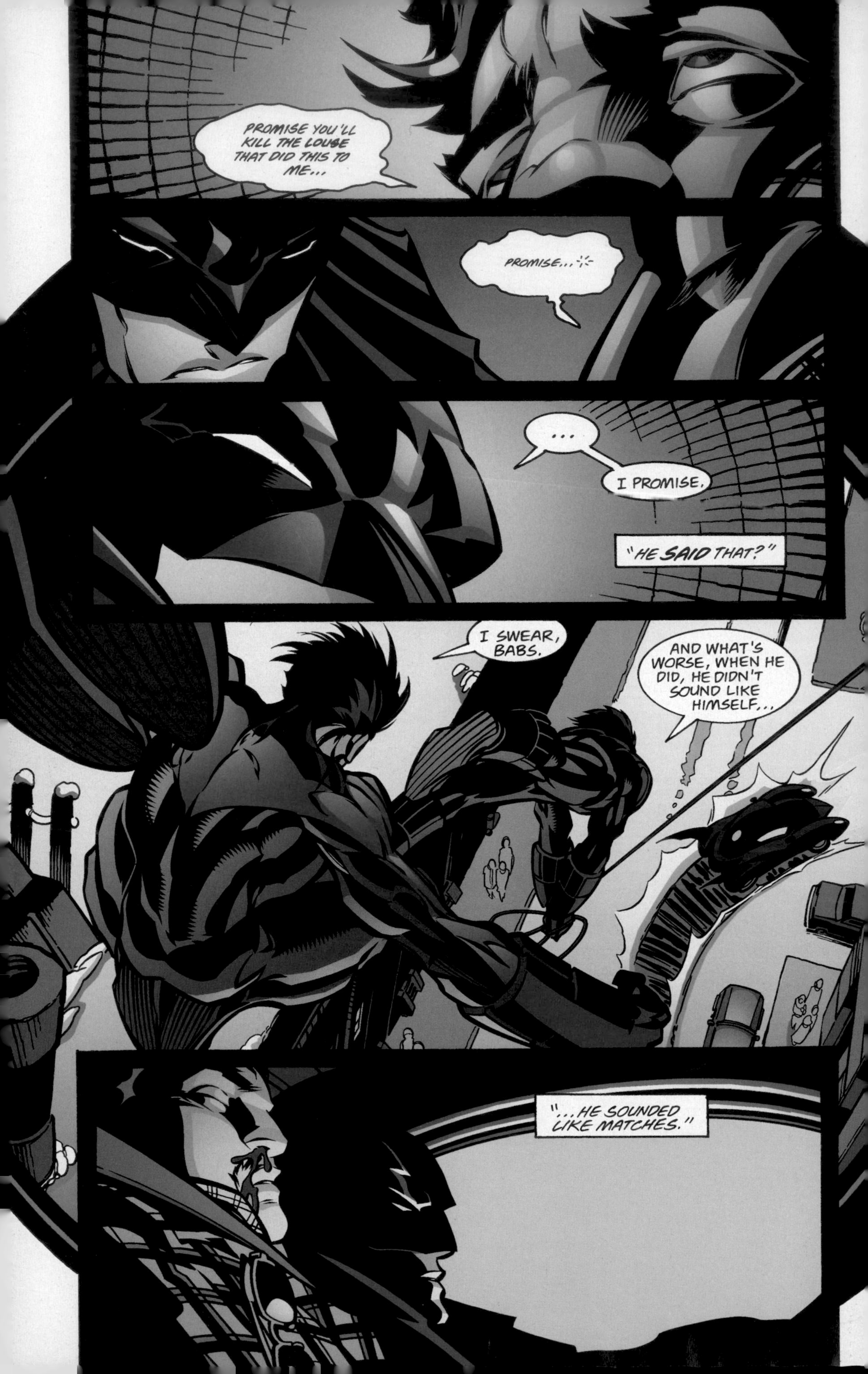
PROMISE YOU'LL KILL THE LOUSE THAT DID THIS TO ME...
PROMISE...
...
I PROMISE.
"HE SAID THAT?"
I SWEAR, BABS.
AND WHAT'S WORSE, WHEN HE DID, HE DIDN'T SOUND LIKE HIMSELF...
"...HE SOUNDED LIKE MATCHES."

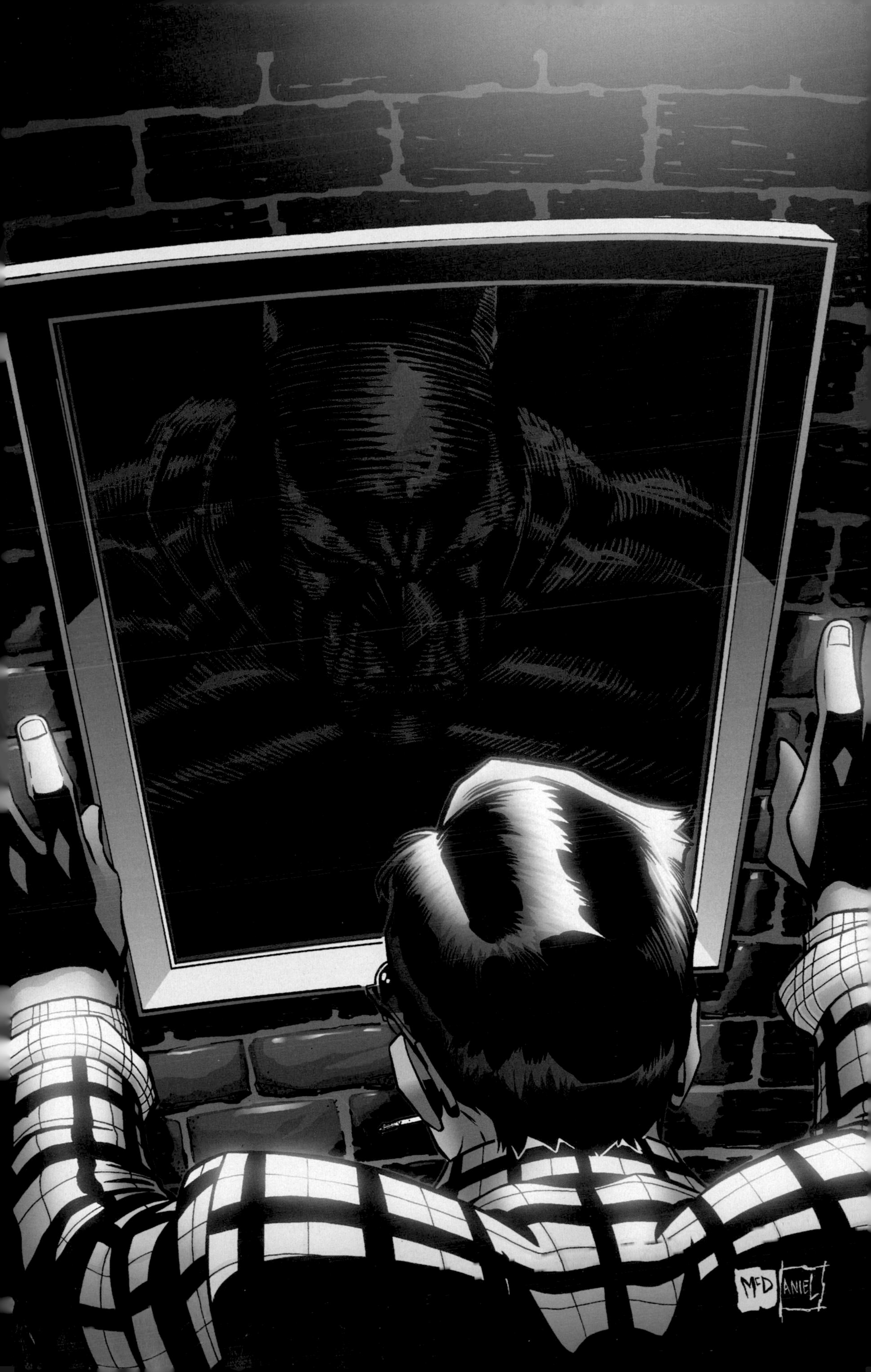

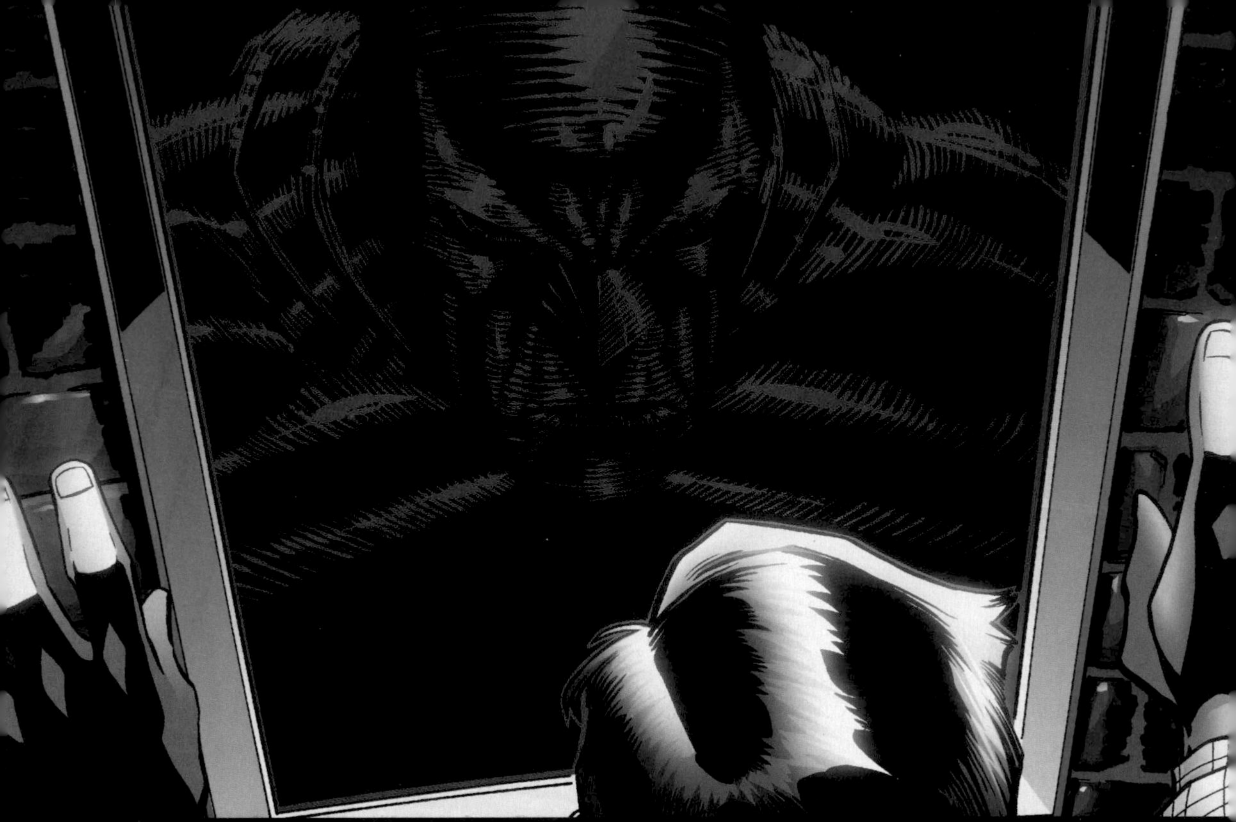

CLOSE BEFORE STRIKING CHAPTER THREE

cover art by **SCOTT McDANIEL** colored by **PATRICK MARTIN**

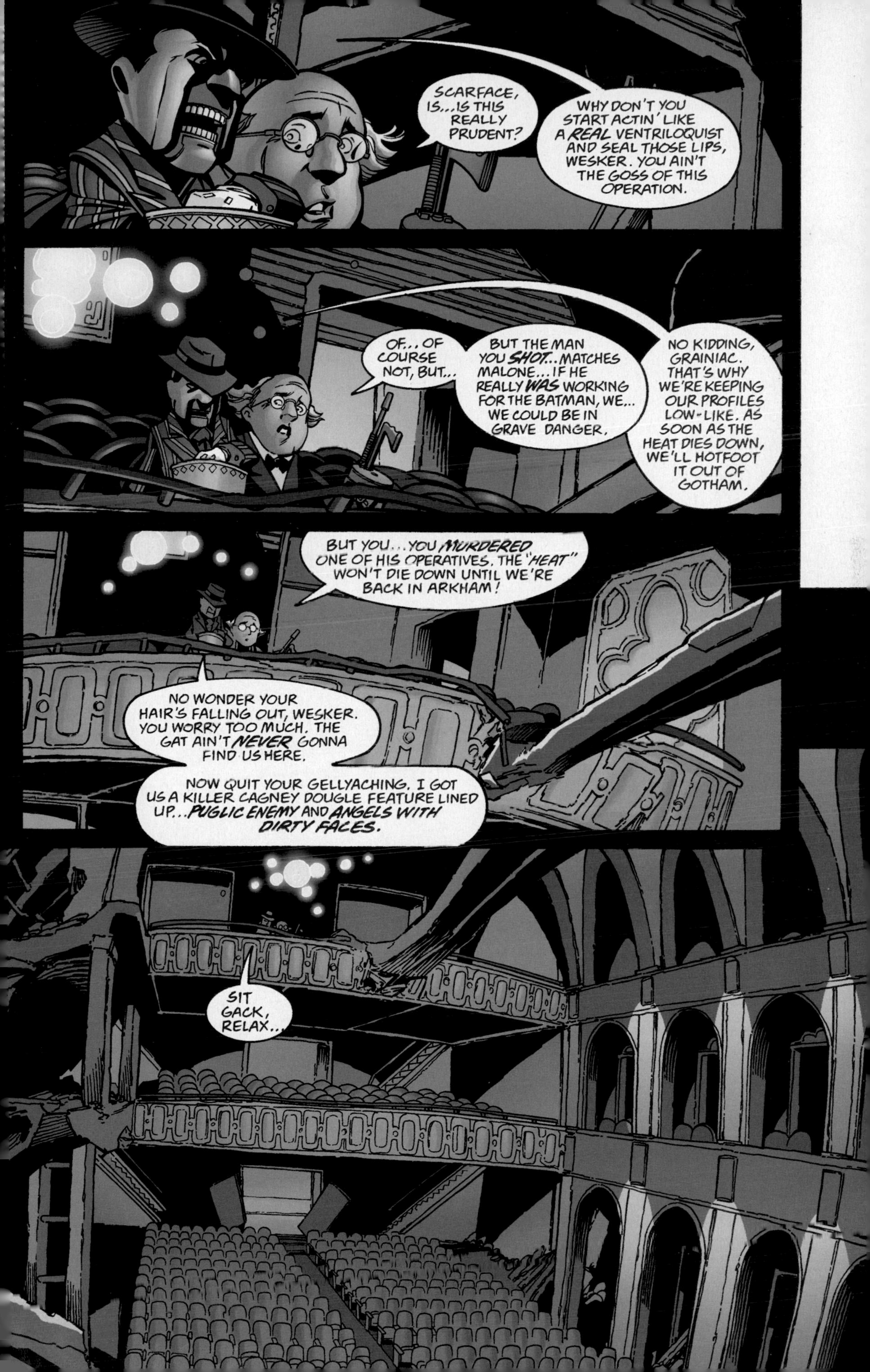
SCARFACE, IS... IS THIS REALLY PRUDENT?
WHY DON'T YOU START ACTIN' LIKE A REAL VENTRILOQUIST AND SEAL THOSE LIPS, WESKER. YOU AIN'T THE GOSS OF THIS OPERATION.
OF... OF COURSE NOT, BUT...
BUT THE MAN YOU SHOT... MATCHES MALONE... IF HE REALLY WAS WORKING FOR THE BATMAN, WE... WE COULD BE IN GRAVE DANGER.
NO KIDDING, GRAINIAC. THAT'S WHY WE'RE KEEPING OUR PROFILES LOW-LIKE. AS SOON AS THE HEAT DIES DOWN, WE'LL HOTFOOT IT OUT OF GOTHAM.
BUT YOU... YOU MURDERED ONE OF HIS OPERATIVES. THE "HEAT" WON'T DIE DOWN UNTIL WE'RE BACK IN ARKHAM!
NO WONDER YOUR HAIR'S FALLING OUT, WESKER. YOU WORRY TOO MUCH. THE GAT AIN'T NEVER GONNA FIND US HERE.
NOW QUIT YOUR GELLYACHING. I GOT US A KILLER CAGNEY DOUGLE FEATURE LINED UP... PUGLIC ENEMY AND ANGELS WITH DIRTY FACES.
SIT GACK, RELAX...

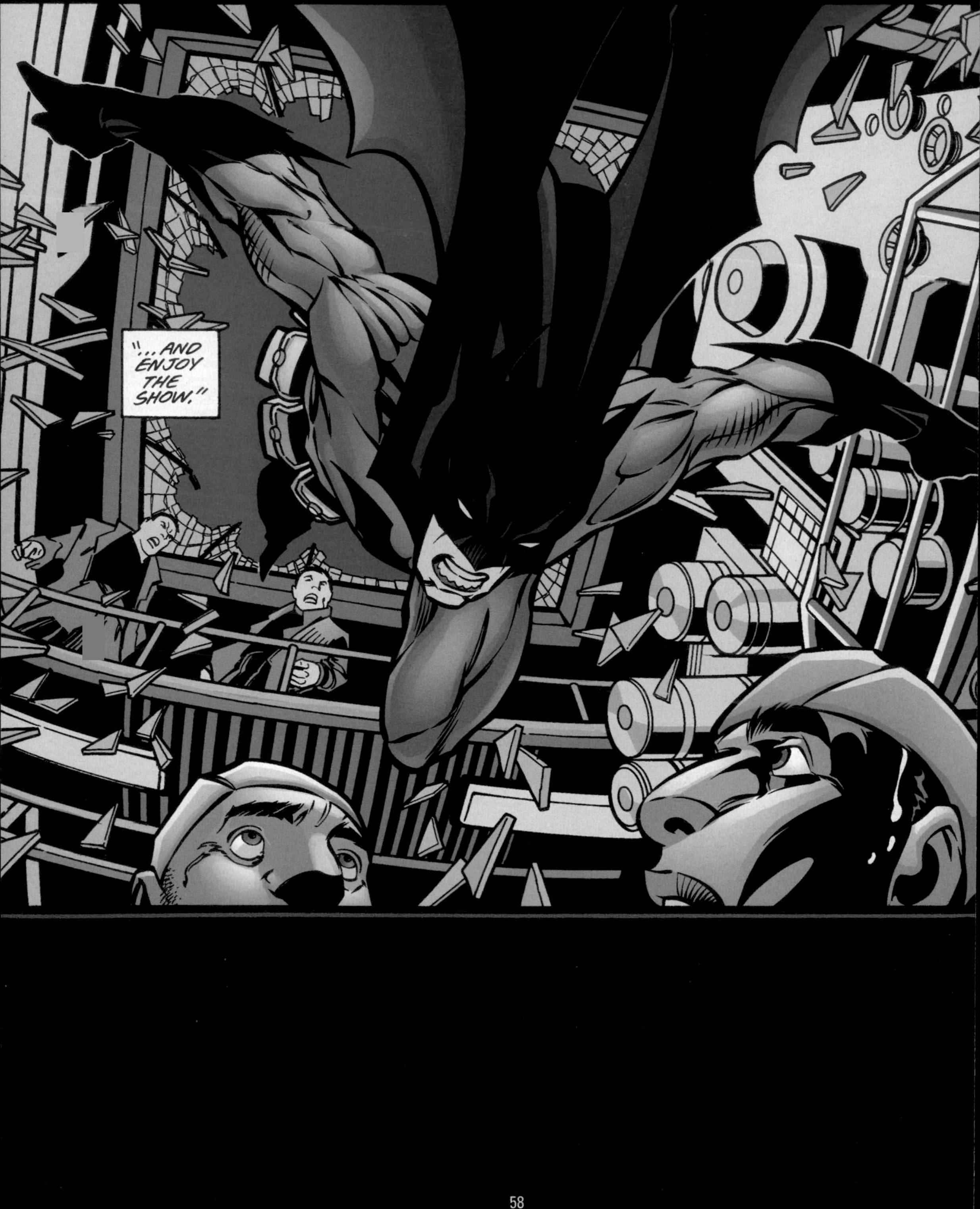
"...AND ENJOY THE SHOW."

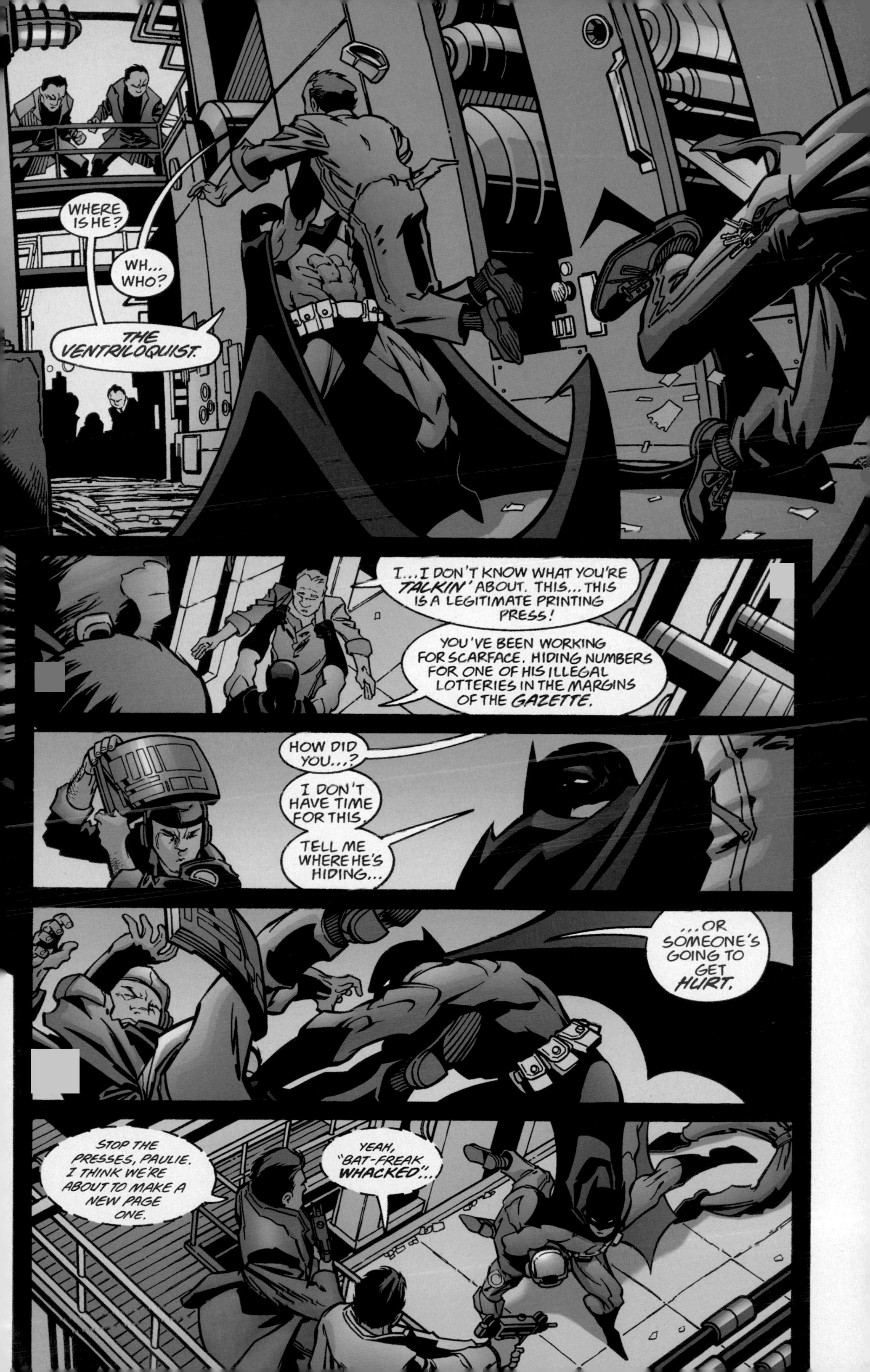
WHERE IS HE?
WH... WHO?
THE VENTRILOQUIST.
I...I DON'T KNOW WHAT YOU'RE TALKIN' ABOUT. THIS... THIS IS A LEGITIMATE PRINTING PRESS!
YOU'VE BEEN WORKING FOR SCARFACE, HIDING NUMBERS FOR ONE OF HIS ILLEGAL LOTTERIES IN THE MARGINS OF THE GAZETTE.
HOW DID YOU...?
I DON'T HAVE TIME FOR THIS.
TELL ME WHERE HE'S HIDING...
...OR SOMEONE'S GOING TO GET HURT.
STOP THE PRESSES, PAULIE. I THINK WE'RE ABOUT TO MAKE A NEW PAGE ONE.
YEAH, "BAT-FREAK WHACKED"...

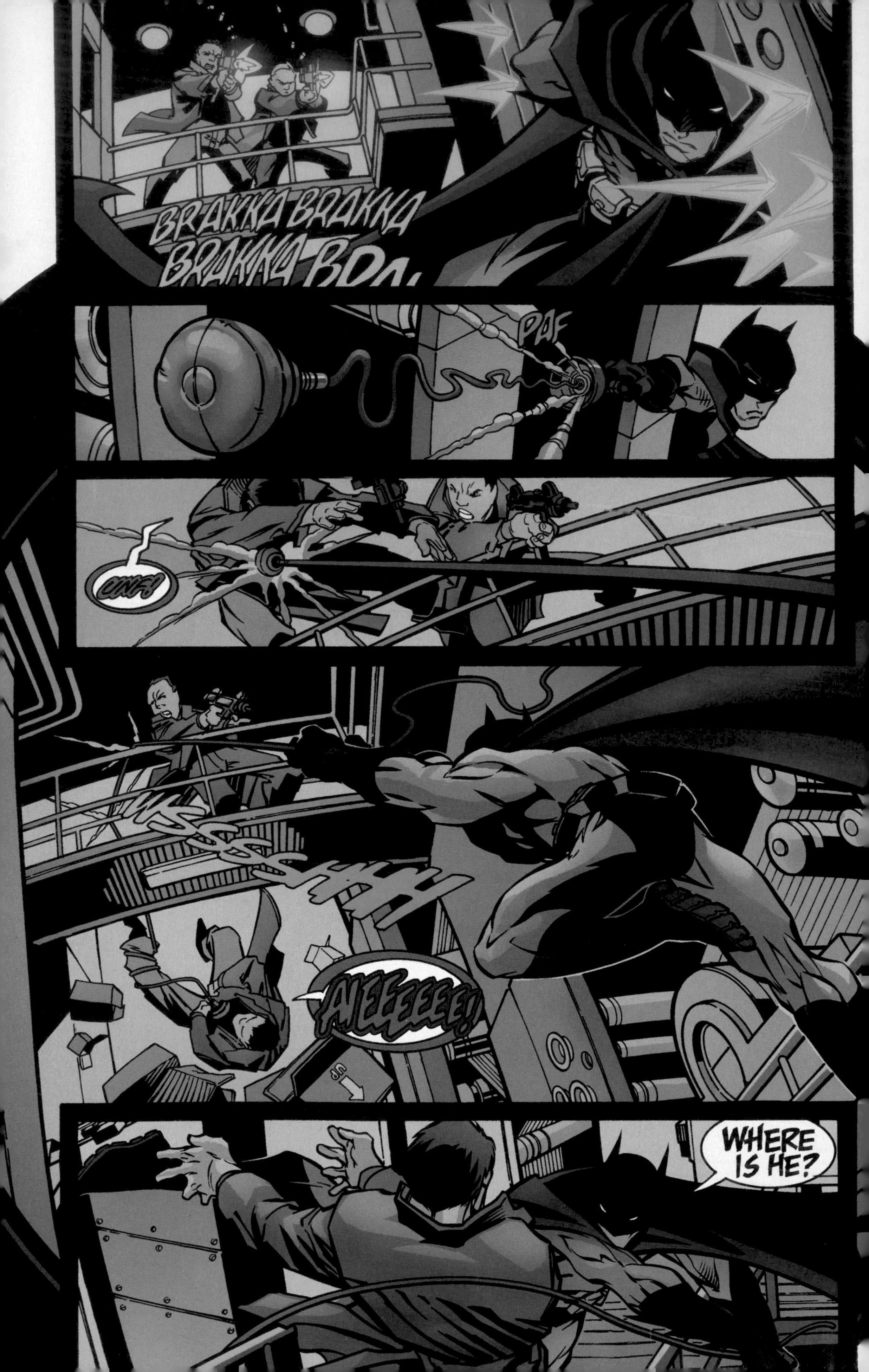
BRAKKA BRAKKA
BRAKKA BRA
PAF
UNF!
WSSSSHH
AIEEEEEE!
UP
WHERE IS HE?

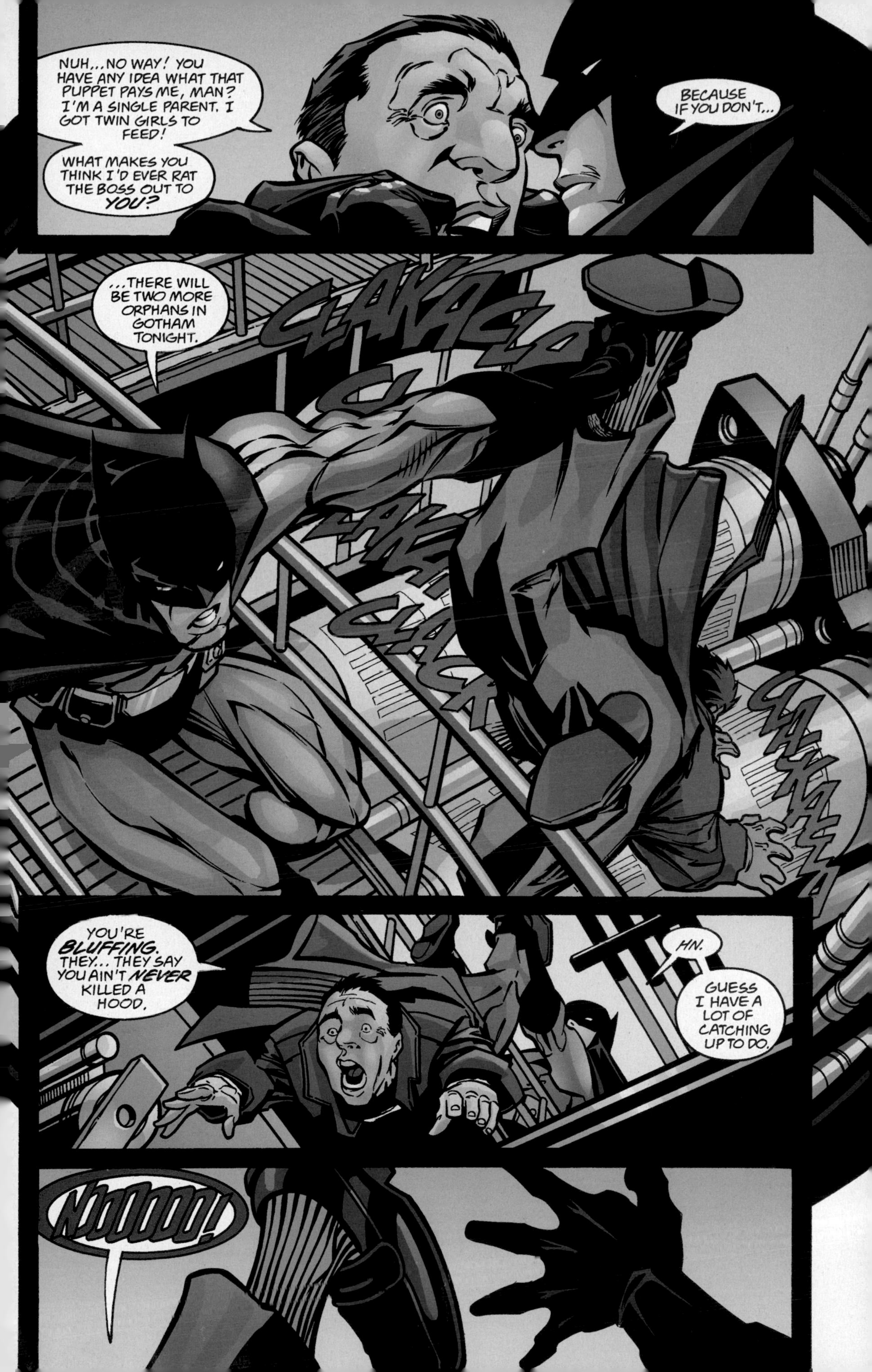
NUH,.. NO WAY! YOU HAVE ANY IDEA WHAT THAT PUPPET PAYS ME, MAN? I'M A SINGLE PARENT. I GOT TWIN GIRLS TO FEED!
WHAT MAKES YOU THINK I'D EVER RAT THE BOSS OUT TO YOU?
BECAUSE IF YOU DON'T...
...THERE WILL BE TWO MORE ORPHANS IN GOTHAM TONIGHT.
YOU'RE BLUFFING. THEY... THEY SAY YOU AIN'T NEVER KILLED A HOOD.
HN.
GUESS I HAVE A LOT OF CATCHING UP TO DO.
NOOOOO!

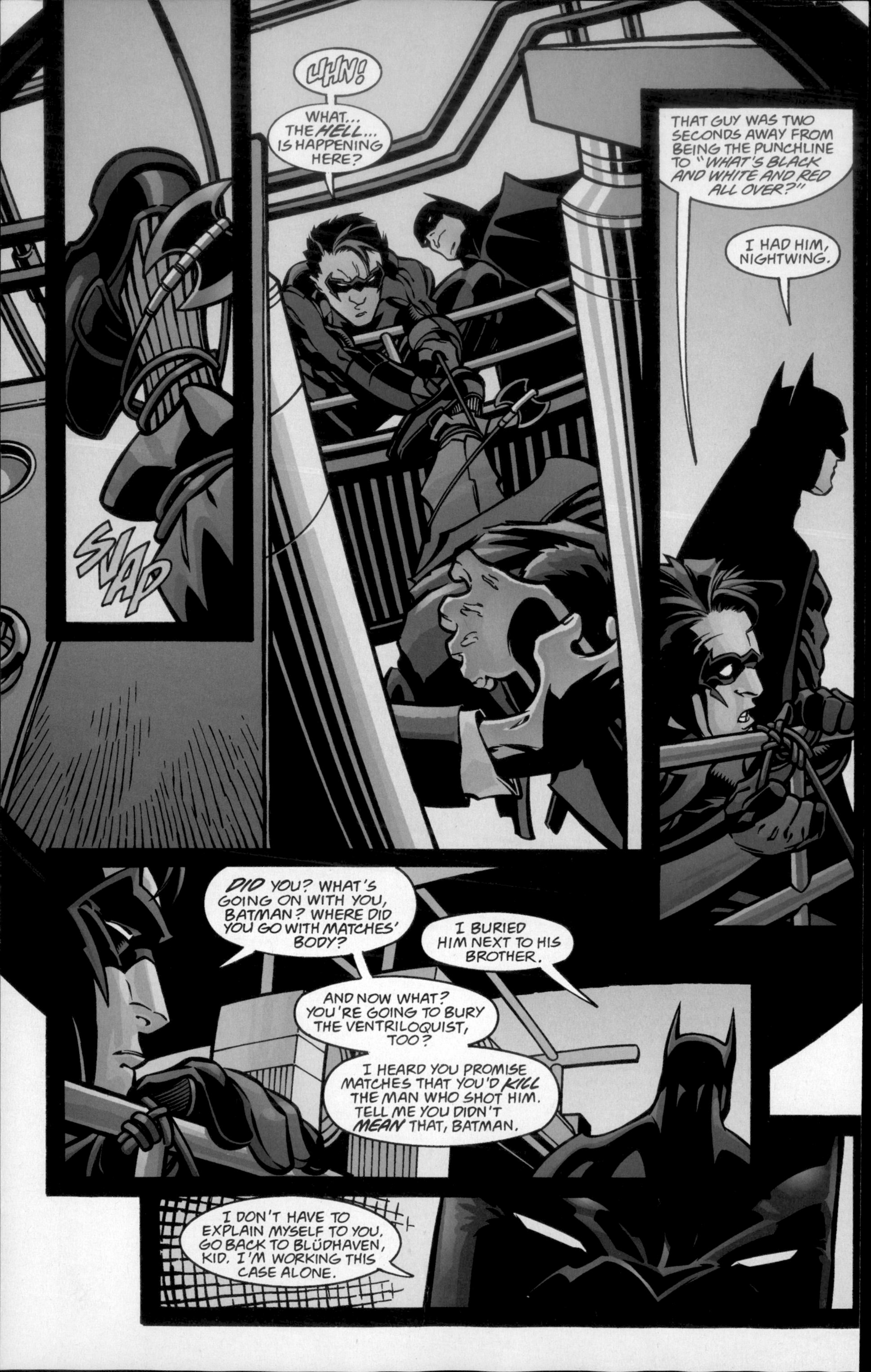
SNAP
UHN!
WHAT... THE HELL... IS HAPPENING HERE?
THAT GUY WAS TWO SECONDS AWAY FROM BEING THE PUNCHLINE TO "WHAT'S BLACK AND WHITE AND RED ALL OVER?"
I HAD HIM, NIGHTWING.
DID YOU? WHAT'S GOING ON WITH YOU, BATMAN? WHERE DID YOU GO WITH MATCHES' BODY?
I BURIED HIM NEXT TO HIS BROTHER.
AND NOW WHAT? YOU'RE GOING TO BURY THE VENTRILOQUIST, TOO?
I HEARD YOU PROMISE MATCHES THAT YOU'D KILL THE MAN WHO SHOT HIM. TELL ME YOU DIDN'T MEAN THAT, BATMAN.
I DON'T HAVE TO EXPLAIN MYSELF TO YOU. GO BACK TO BLÜDHAVEN, KID. I'M WORKING THIS CASE ALONE.

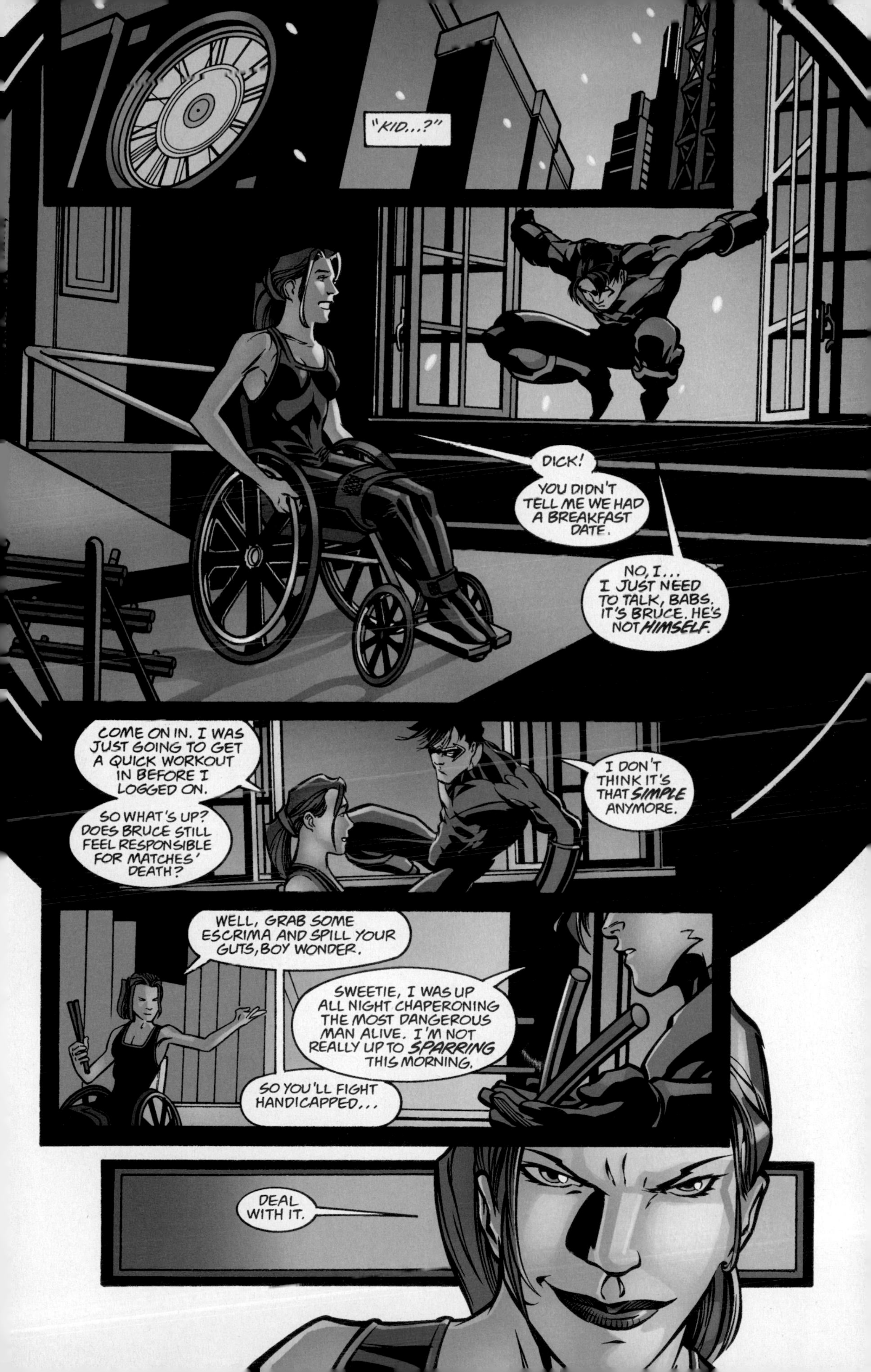
"KID...?"
DICK!
YOU DIDN'T TELL ME WE HAD A BREAKFAST DATE.
NO, I... I JUST NEED TO TALK, BABS. IT'S BRUCE. HE'S NOT HIMSELF.
COME ON IN. I WAS JUST GOING TO GET A QUICK WORKOUT IN BEFORE I LOGGED ON.
SO WHAT'S UP? DOES BRUCE STILL FEEL RESPONSIBLE FOR MATCHES' DEATH?
I DON'T THINK IT'S THAT SIMPLE ANYMORE.
WELL, GRAB SOME ESCRIMA AND SPILL YOUR GUTS, BOY WONDER.
SWEETIE, I WAS UP ALL NIGHT CHAPERONING THE MOST DANGEROUS MAN ALIVE. I'M NOT REALLY UP TO SPARRING THIS MORNING.
SO YOU'LL FIGHT HANDICAPPED...
DEAL WITH IT.

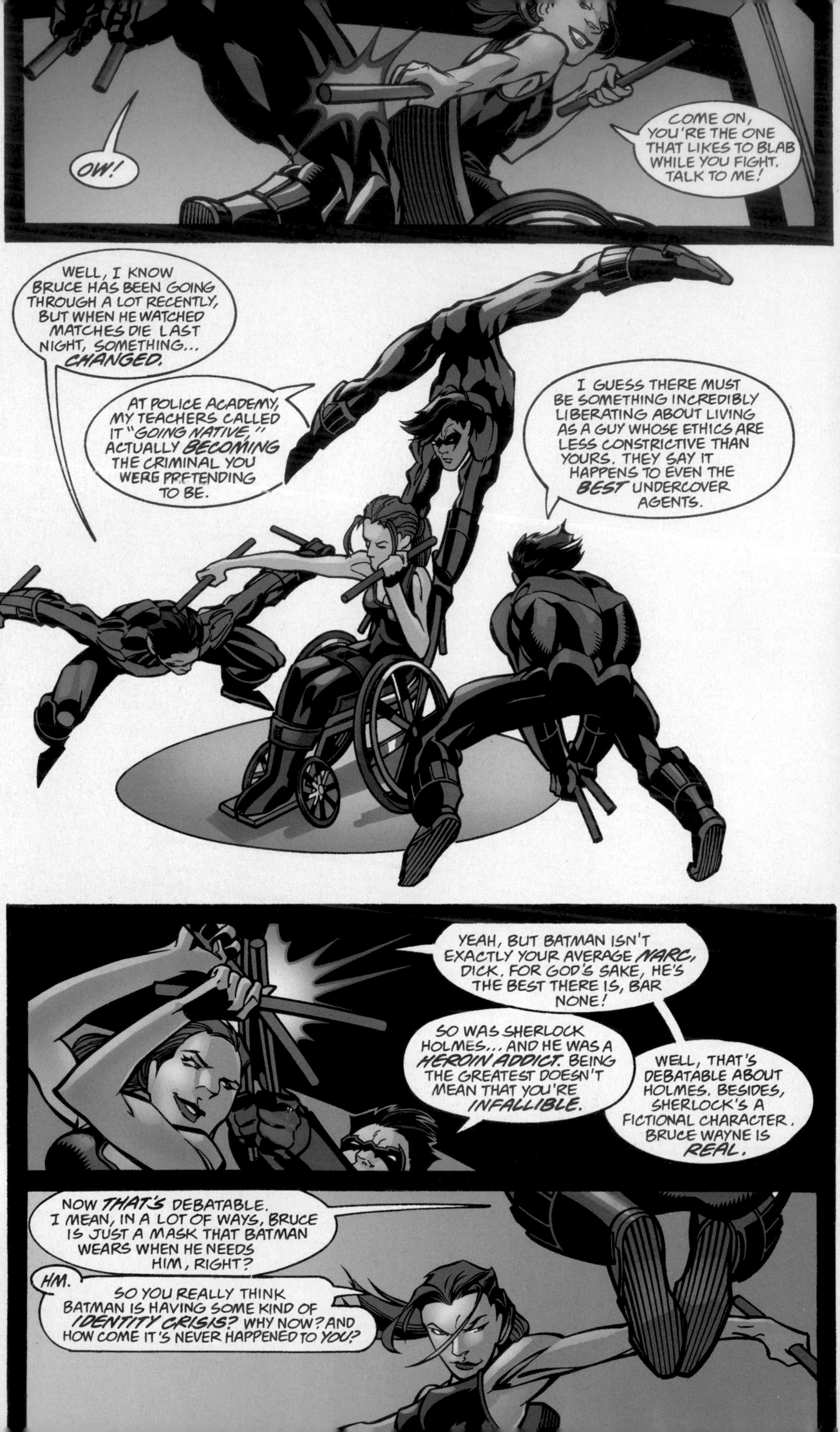
OW!
COME ON, YOU'RE THE ONE THAT LIKES TO BLAB WHILE YOU FIGHT. TALK TO ME!
WELL, I KNOW BRUCE HAS BEEN GOING THROUGH A LOT RECENTLY, BUT WHEN HE WATCHED MATCHES DIE LAST NIGHT, SOMETHING... CHANGED.
AT POLICE ACADEMY, MY TEACHERS CALLED IT "GOING NATIVE," ACTUALLY BECOMING THE CRIMINAL YOU WERE PRETENDING TO BE.
I GUESS THERE MUST BE SOMETHING INCREDIBLY LIBERATING ABOUT LIVING AS A GUY WHOSE ETHICS ARE LESS CONSTRICTIVE THAN YOURS. THEY SAY IT HAPPENS TO EVEN THE BEST UNDERCOVER AGENTS.
YEAH, BUT BATMAN ISN'T EXACTLY YOUR AVERAGE NARC, DICK. FOR GOD'S SAKE, HE'S THE BEST THERE IS, BAR NONE!
SO WAS SHERLOCK HOLMES... AND HE WAS A HEROIN ADDICT. BEING THE GREATEST DOESN'T MEAN THAT YOU'RE INFALLIBLE.
WELL, THAT'S DEBATABLE ABOUT HOLMES. BESIDES, SHERLOCK'S A FICTIONAL CHARACTER. BRUCE WAYNE IS REAL.
NOW THAT'S DEBATABLE. I MEAN, IN A LOT OF WAYS, BRUCE IS JUST A MASK THAT BATMAN WEARS WHEN HE NEEDS HIM, RIGHT?
HM.
SO YOU REALLY THINK BATMAN IS HAVING SOME KIND OF IDENTITY CRISIS? WHY NOW? AND HOW COME IT'S NEVER HAPPENED TO YOU?

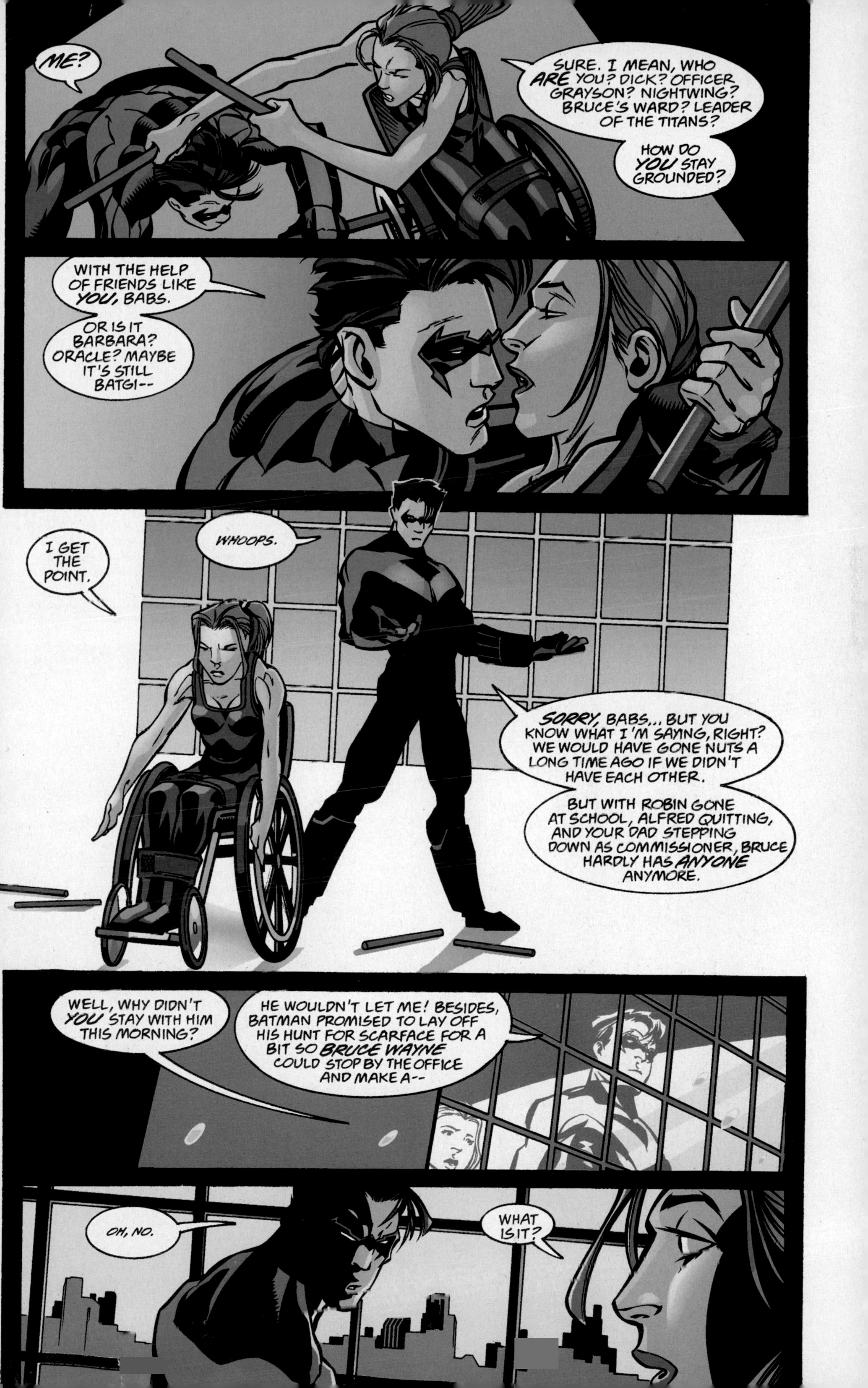

ME?
SURE. I MEAN, WHO ARE YOU? DICK? OFFICER GRAYSON? NIGHTWING? BRUCE'S WARD? LEADER OF THE TITANS?
HOW DO YOU STAY GROUNDED?
WITH THE HELP OF FRIENDS LIKE YOU, BABS.
OR IS IT BARBARA? ORACLE? MAYBE IT'S STILL BATGI--
I GET THE POINT.
WHOOPS.
SORRY, BABS... BUT YOU KNOW WHAT I'M SAYING, RIGHT? WE WOULD HAVE GONE NUTS A LONG TIME AGO IF WE DIDN'T HAVE EACH OTHER.
BUT WITH ROBIN GONE AT SCHOOL, ALFRED QUITTING, AND YOUR DAD STEPPING DOWN AS COMMISSIONER, BRUCE HARDLY HAS ANYONE ANYMORE.
WELL, WHY DIDN'T YOU STAY WITH HIM THIS MORNING?
HE WOULDN'T LET ME! BESIDES, BATMAN PROMISED TO LAY OFF HIS HUNT FOR SCARFACE FOR A BIT SO BRUCE WAYNE COULD STOP BY THE OFFICE AND MAKE A--
OH, NO.
WHAT IS IT?

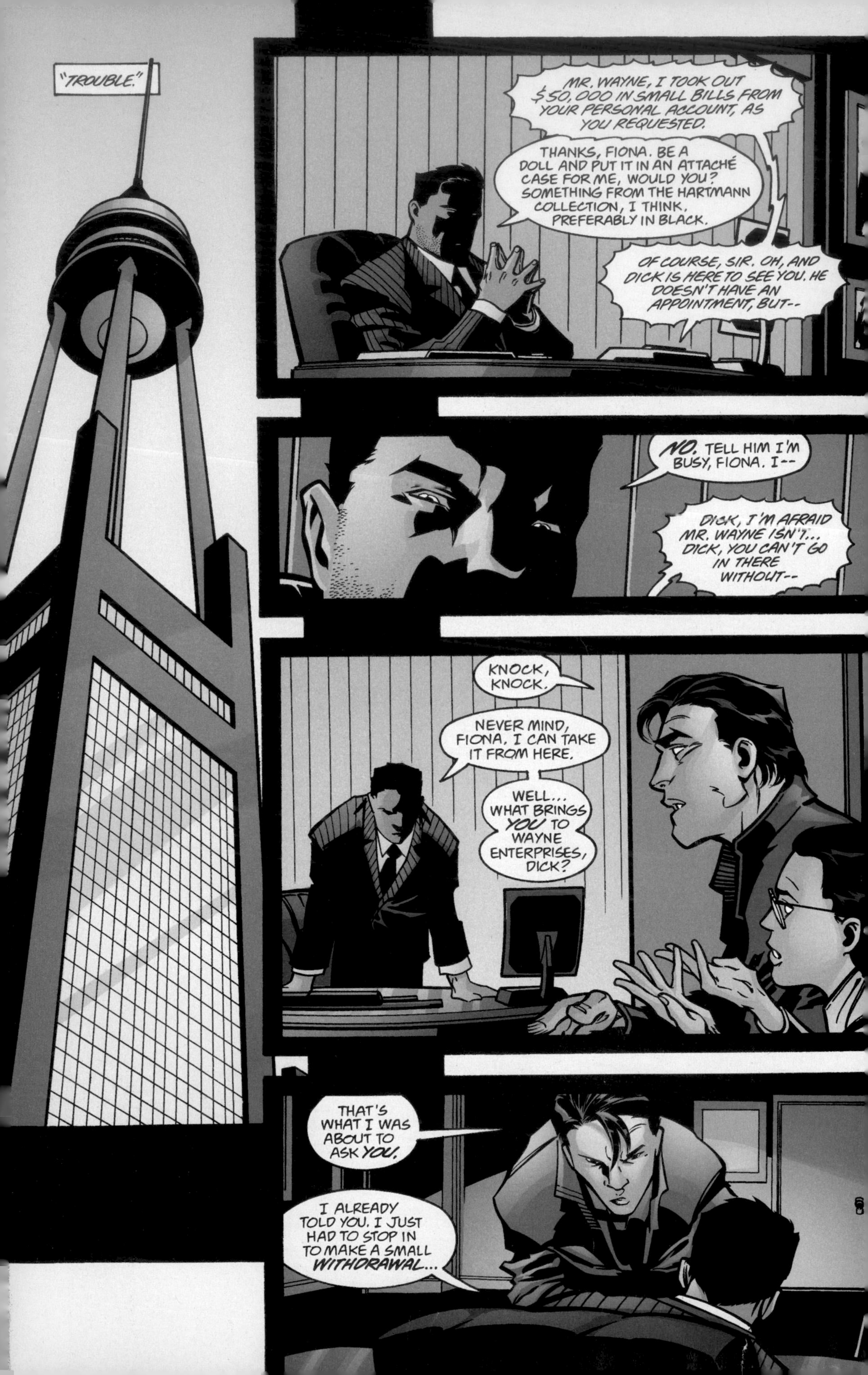
"TROUBLE."
MR. WAYNE, I TOOK OUT $50,000 IN SMALL BILLS FROM YOUR PERSONAL ACCOUNT, AS YOU REQUESTED.
THANKS, FIONA. BE A DOLL AND PUT IT IN AN ATTACHÉ CASE FOR ME, WOULD YOU? SOMETHING FROM THE HARTMANN COLLECTION, I THINK. PREFERABLY IN BLACK.
OF COURSE, SIR. OH, AND DICK IS HERE TO SEE YOU. HE DOESN'T HAVE AN APPOINTMENT, BUT--
NO. TELL HIM I'M BUSY, FIONA. I--
DICK, I'M AFRAID MR. WAYNE ISN'T... DICK, YOU CAN'T GO IN THERE WITHOUT--
KNOCK, KNOCK.
NEVER MIND, FIONA. I CAN TAKE IT FROM HERE.
WELL... WHAT BRINGS YOU TO WAYNE ENTERPRISES, DICK?
THAT'S WHAT I WAS ABOUT TO ASK YOU.
I ALREADY TOLD YOU. I JUST HAD TO STOP IN TO MAKE A SMALL WITHDRAWAL...

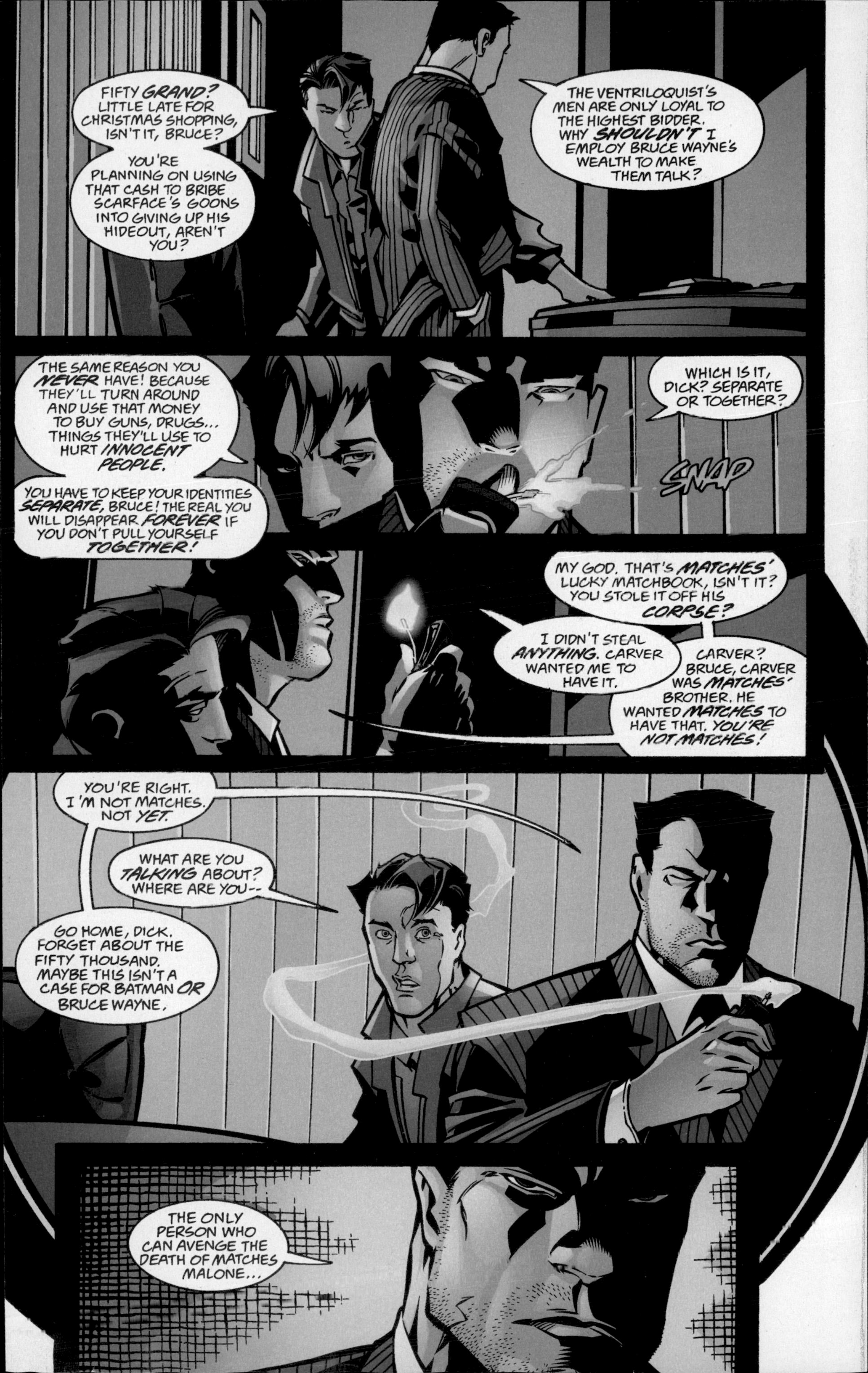

FIFTY GRAND? LITTLE LATE FOR CHRISTMAS SHOPPING, ISN'T IT, BRUCE?
YOU'RE PLANNING ON USING THAT CASH TO BRIBE SCARFACE'S GOONS INTO GIVING UP HIS HIDEOUT, AREN'T YOU?
THE VENTRILOQUIST'S MEN ARE ONLY LOYAL TO THE HIGHEST BIDDER. WHY SHOULDN'T I EMPLOY BRUCE WAYNE'S WEALTH TO MAKE THEM TALK?
THE SAME REASON YOU NEVER HAVE! BECAUSE THEY'LL TURN AROUND AND USE THAT MONEY TO BUY GUNS, DRUGS... THINGS THEY'LL USE TO HURT INNOCENT PEOPLE.
YOU HAVE TO KEEP YOUR IDENTITIES SEPARATE, BRUCE! THE REAL YOU WILL DISAPPEAR FOREVER IF YOU DON'T PULL YOURSELF TOGETHER!
WHICH IS IT, DICK? SEPARATE OR TOGETHER?
SNAP
MY GOD. THAT'S MATCHES' LUCKY MATCHBOOK, ISN'T IT? YOU STOLE IT OFF HIS CORPSE?
I DIDN'T STEAL ANYTHING. CARVER WANTED ME TO HAVE IT.
CARVER? BRUCE, CARVER WAS MATCHES' BROTHER. HE WANTED MATCHES TO HAVE THAT. YOU'RE NOT MATCHES!
YOU'RE RIGHT. I'M NOT MATCHES. NOT YET.
WHAT ARE YOU TALKING ABOUT? WHERE ARE YOU--
GO HOME, DICK. FORGET ABOUT THE FIFTY THOUSAND. MAYBE THIS ISN'T A CASE FOR BATMAN OR BRUCE WAYNE.
THE ONLY PERSON WHO CAN AVENGE THE DEATH OF MATCHES MALONE...

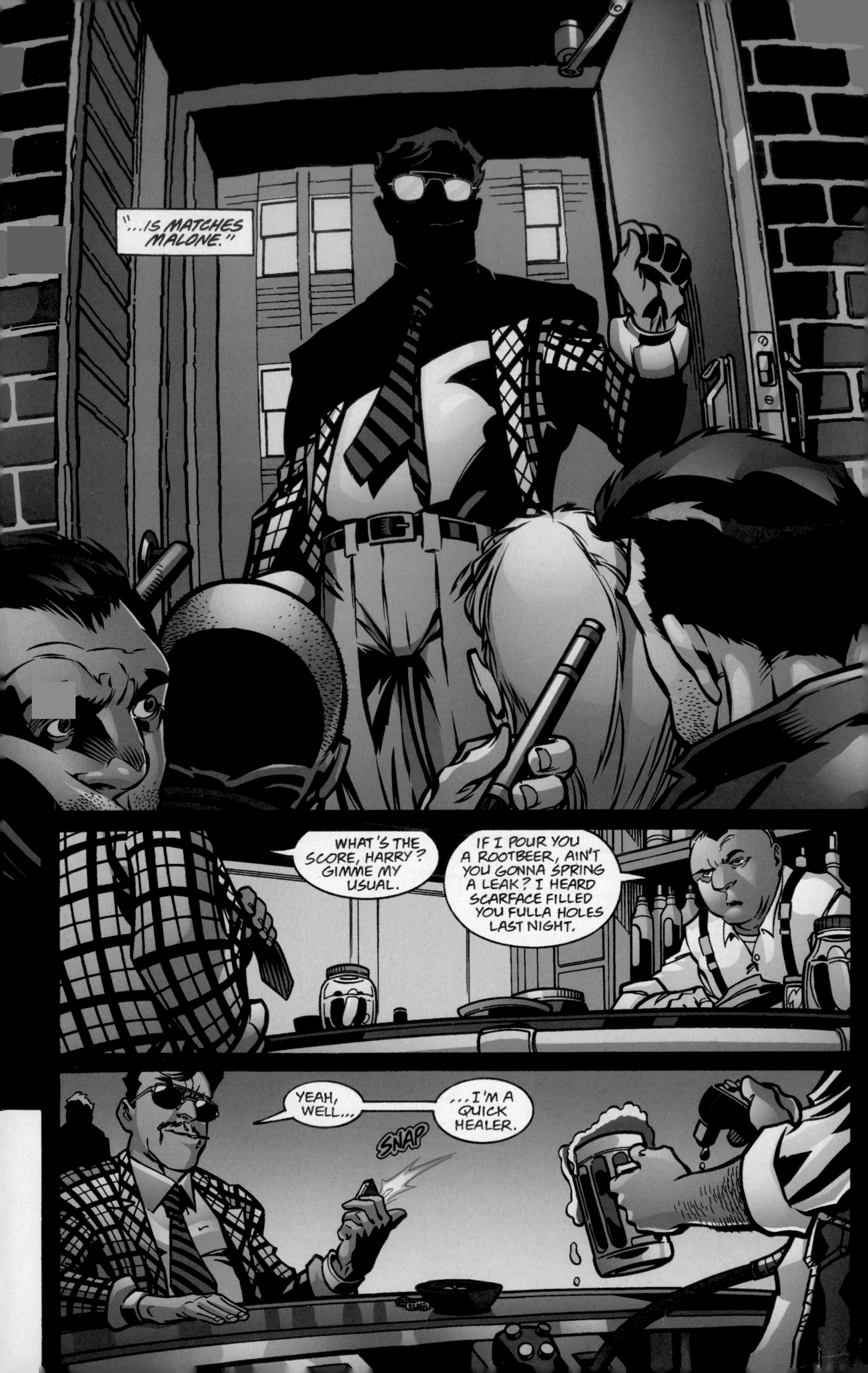
"...IS MATCHES MALONE."
WHAT'S THE SCORE, HARRY? GIMME MY USUAL.
IF I POUR YOU A ROOTBEER, AIN'T YOU GONNA SPRING A LEAK? I HEARD SCARFACE FILLED YOU FULLA HOLES LAST NIGHT.
YEAH, WELL...
...I'M A QUICK HEALER.
SNAP

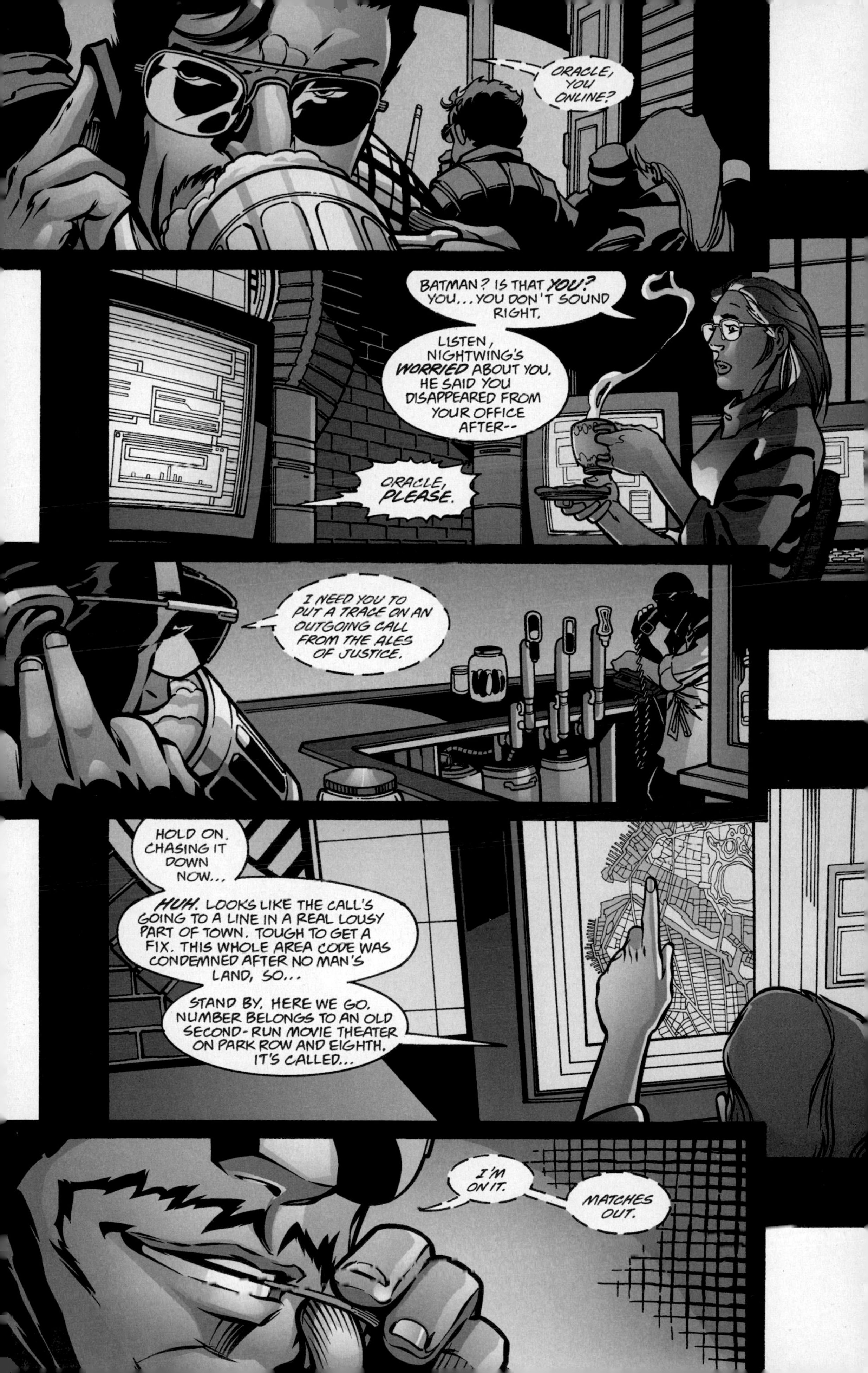

ORACLE, YOU ONLINE?
BATMAN? IS THAT YOU? YOU... YOU DON'T SOUND RIGHT.
LISTEN, NIGHTWING'S WORRIED ABOUT YOU. HE SAID YOU DISAPPEARED FROM YOUR OFFICE AFTER--
ORACLE, PLEASE.
I NEED YOU TO PUT A TRACE ON AN OUTGOING CALL FROM THE ALES OF JUSTICE.
HOLD ON. CHASING IT DOWN NOW...
HUH. LOOKS LIKE THE CALL'S GOING TO A LINE IN A REAL LOUSY PART OF TOWN. TOUGH TO GET A FIX. THIS WHOLE AREA CODE WAS CONDEMNED AFTER NO MAN'S LAND, SO...
STAND BY. HERE WE GO. NUMBER BELONGS TO AN OLD SECOND-RUN MOVIE THEATER ON PARK ROW AND EIGHTH. IT'S CALLED...
I'M ON IT.
MATCHES OUT.

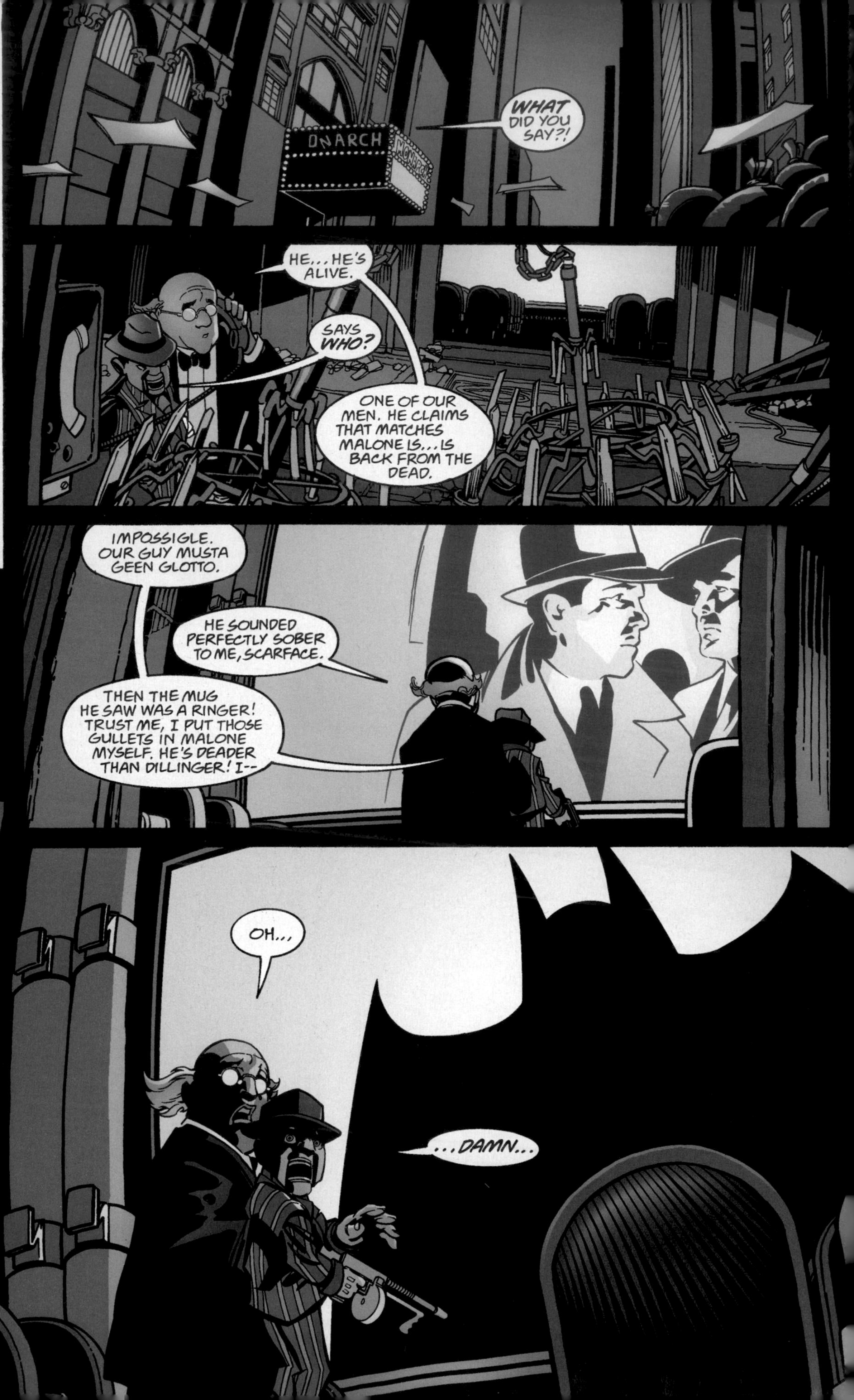
WHAT DID YOU SAY?!
HE... HE'S ALIVE.
SAYS WHO?
ONE OF OUR MEN. HE CLAIMS THAT MATCHES MALONE IS... IS BACK FROM THE DEAD.
IMPOSSIGLE. OUR GUY MUSTA GEEN GLOTTO.
HE SOUNDED PERFECTLY SOBER TO ME, SCARFACE.
THEN THE MUG HE SAW WAS A RINGER! TRUST ME, I PUT THOSE GULLETS IN MALONE MYSELF. HE'S DEADER THAN DILLINGER! I--
OH...
...DAMN...

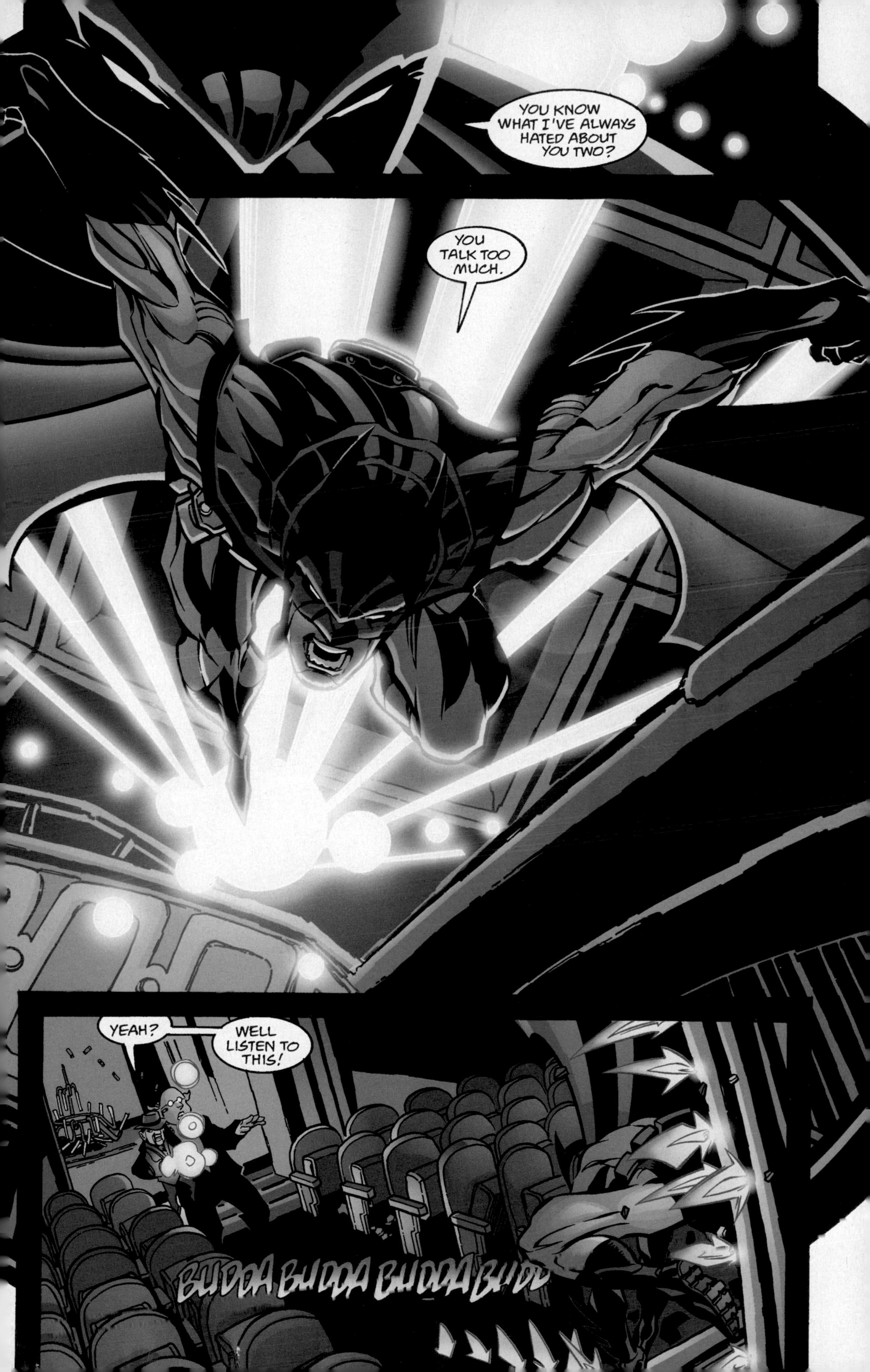
YOU KNOW WHAT I'VE ALWAYS HATED ABOUT YOU TWO?
YOU TALK TOO MUCH.
YEAH?
WELL LISTEN TO THIS!
BUDDA BUDDA BUDDA BUDD

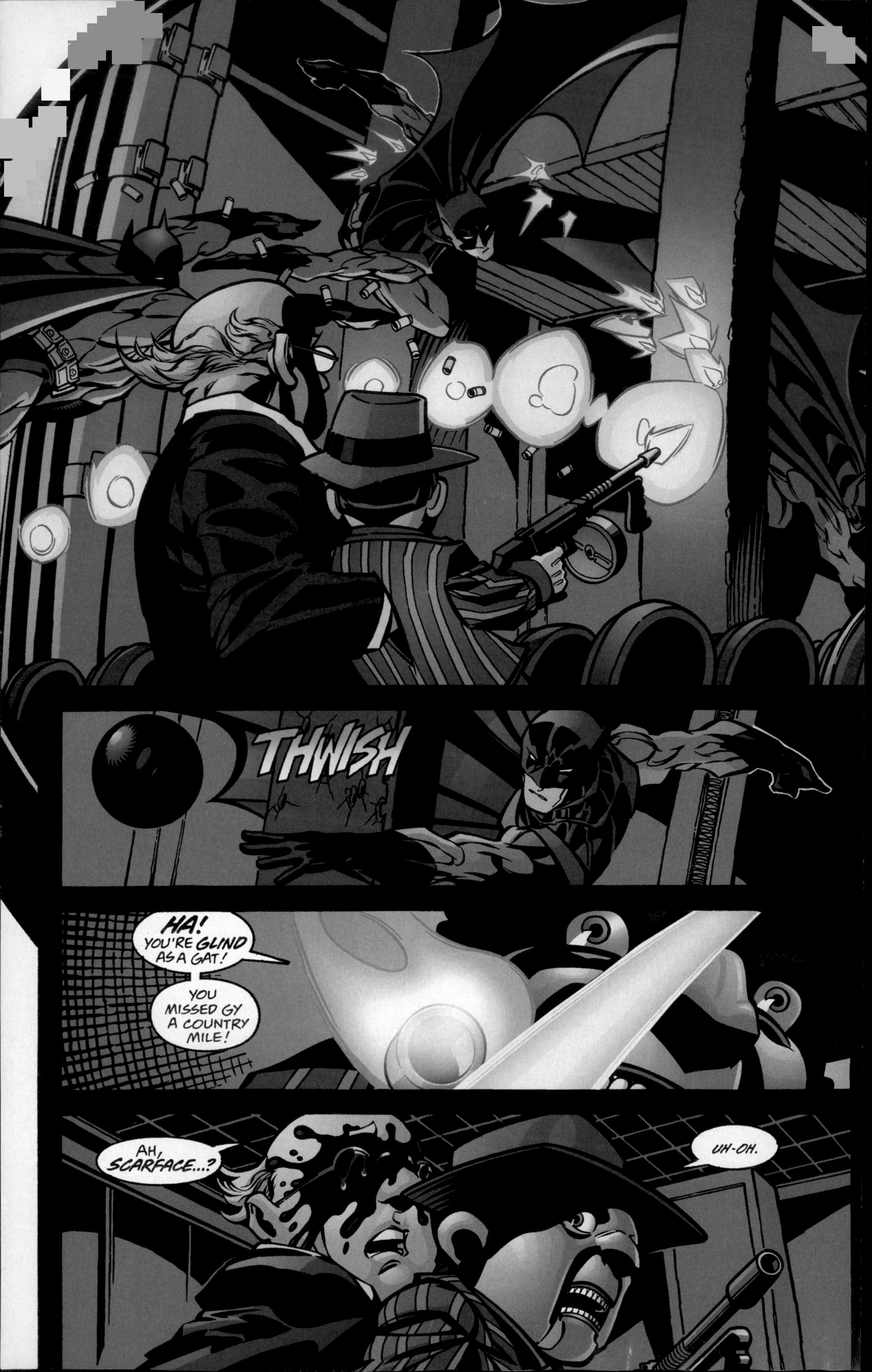
THWISH
HA! YOU'RE GLIND AS A GAT!
YOU MISSED GY A COUNTRY MILE!
AH, SCARFACE...?
UH-OH.

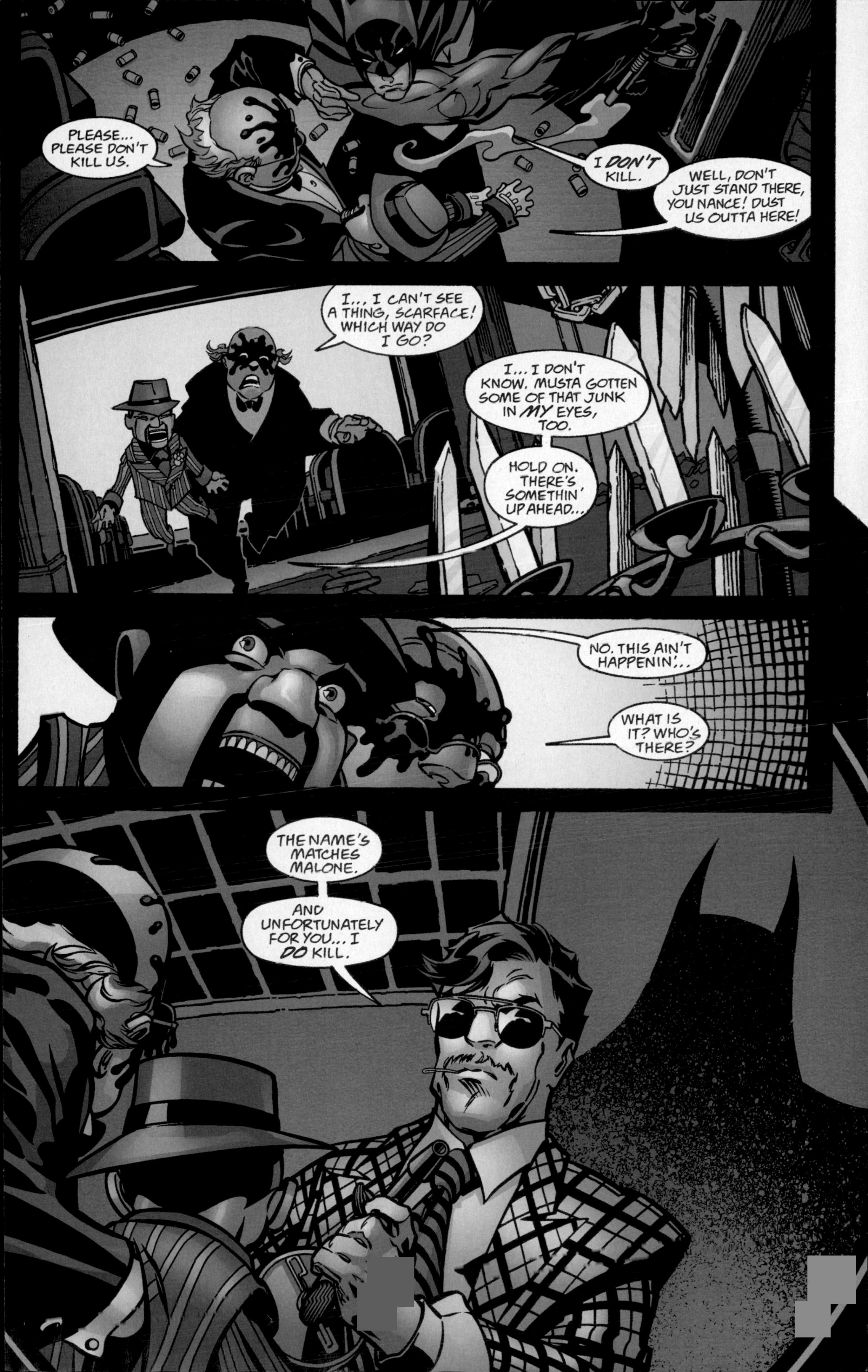
PLEASE... PLEASE DON'T KILL US.
I DON'T KILL.
WELL, DON'T JUST STAND THERE, YOU NANCE! DUST US OUTTA HERE!
I... I CAN'T SEE A THING, SCARFACE! WHICH WAY DO I GO?
I... I DON'T KNOW. MUSTA GOTTEN SOME OF THAT JUNK IN MY EYES, TOO.
HOLD ON. THERE'S SOMETHIN' UP AHEAD...
NO. THIS AIN'T HAPPENIN'...
WHAT IS IT? WHO'S THERE?
THE NAME'S MATCHES MALONE.
AND UNFORTUNATELY FOR YOU... I DO KILL.

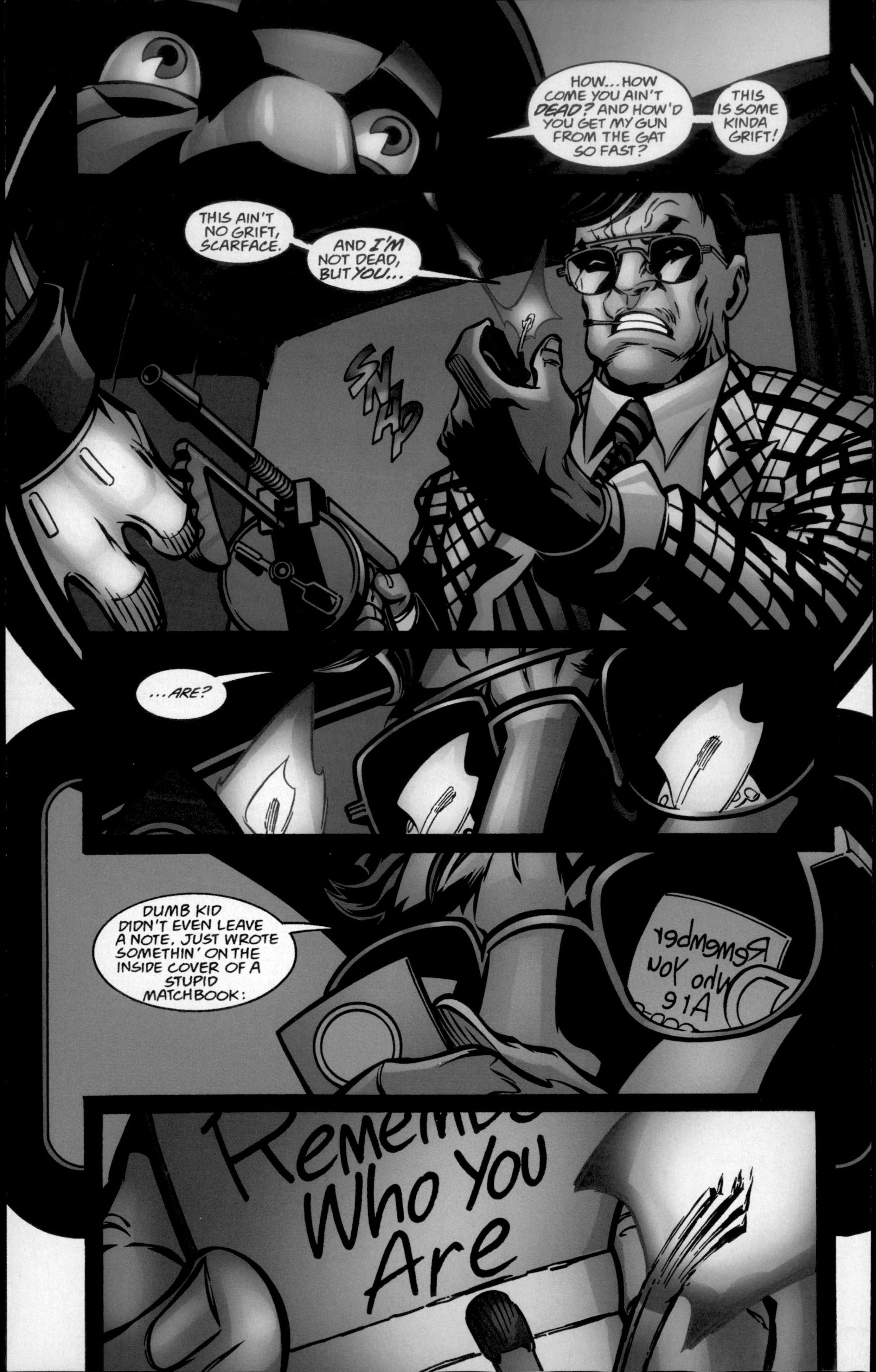

HOW... HOW COME YOU AIN'T DEAD? AND HOW'D YOU GET MY GUN FROM THE GAT SO FAST?
THIS IS SOME KINDA GRIFT!
THIS AIN'T NO GRIFT, SCARFACE.
AND I'M NOT DEAD, BUT YOU...
SNAP
...ARE?
DUMB KID DIDN'T EVEN LEAVE A NOTE. JUST WROTE SOMETHIN' ON THE INSIDE COVER OF A STUPID MATCHBOOK:
Who You Are

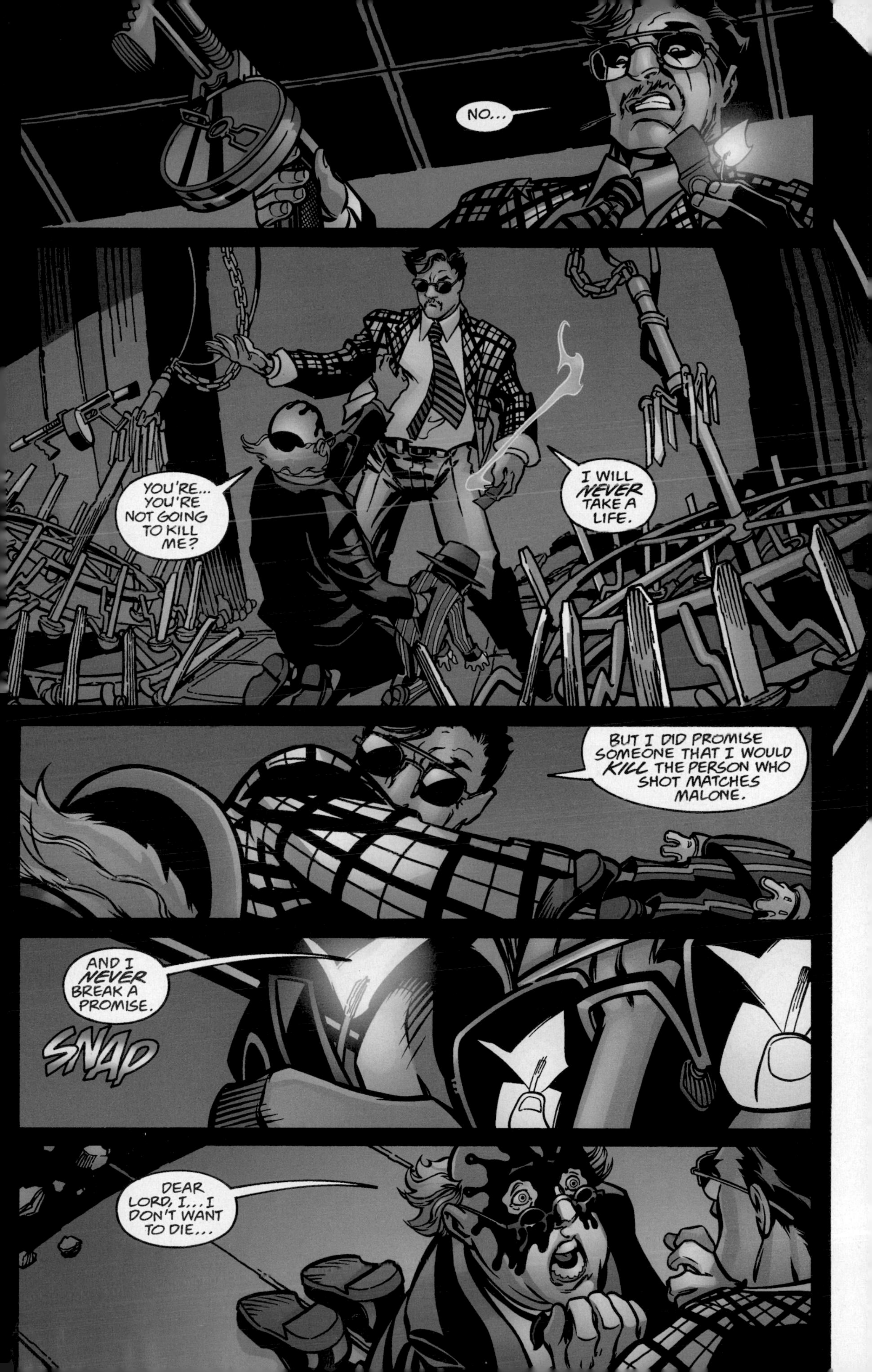
NO...
YOU'RE... YOU'RE NOT GOING TO KILL ME?
I WILL NEVER TAKE A LIFE.
BUT I DID PROMISE SOMEONE THAT I WOULD KILL THE PERSON WHO SHOT MATCHES MALONE.
AND I NEVER BREAK A PROMISE.
SNAP
DEAR LORD, I... I DON'T WANT TO DIE...

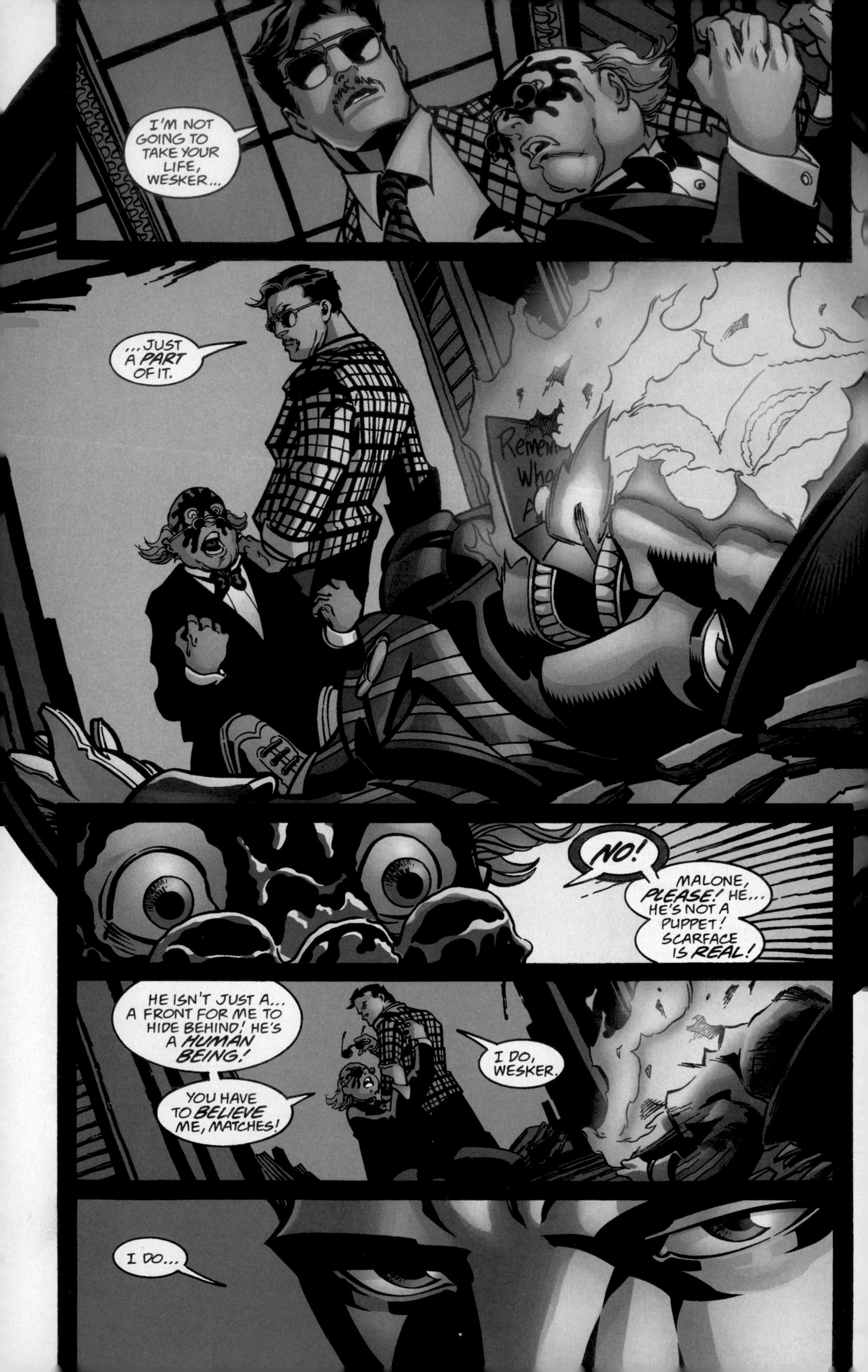
I'M NOT GOING TO TAKE YOUR LIFE, WESKER...
...JUST A PART OF IT.
Remem
Who
NO!
MALONE, PLEASE! HE... HE'S NOT A PUPPET! SCARFACE IS REAL!
HE ISN'T JUST A... A FRONT FOR ME TO HIDE BEHIND! HE'S A HUMAN BEING!
YOU HAVE TO BELIEVE ME, MATCHES!
I DO, WESKER.
I DO...

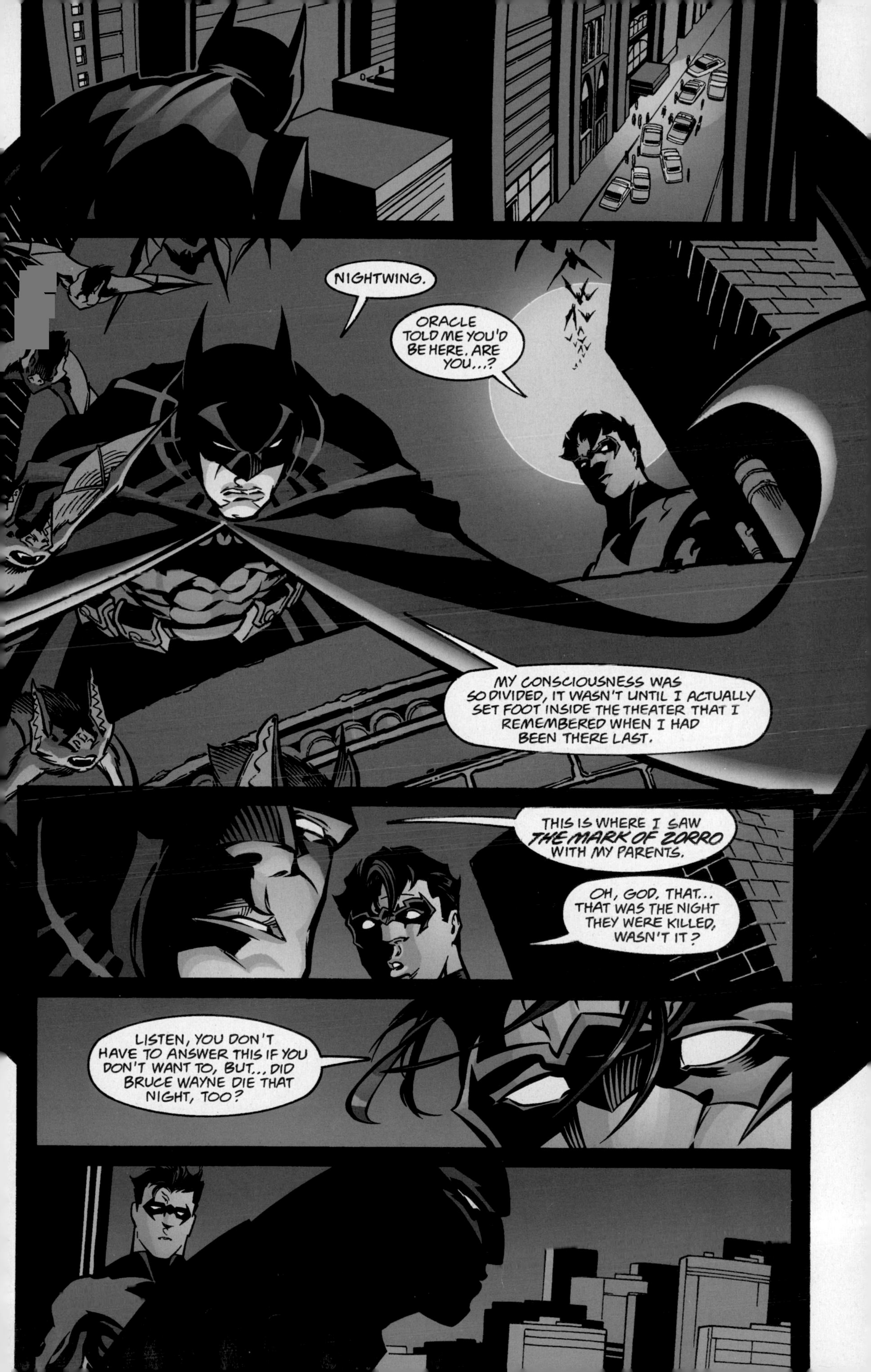
NIGHTWING.
ORACLE TOLD ME YOU'D BE HERE. ARE YOU...?
MY CONSCIOUSNESS WAS SO DIVIDED, IT WASN'T UNTIL I ACTUALLY SET FOOT INSIDE THE THEATER THAT I REMEMBERED WHEN I HAD BEEN THERE LAST.
THIS IS WHERE I SAW *THE MARK OF ZORRO* WITH MY PARENTS.
OH, GOD, THAT... THAT WAS THE NIGHT THEY WERE KILLED, WASN'T IT?
LISTEN, YOU DON'T HAVE TO ANSWER THIS IF YOU DON'T WANT TO, BUT... DID BRUCE WAYNE DIE THAT NIGHT, TOO?

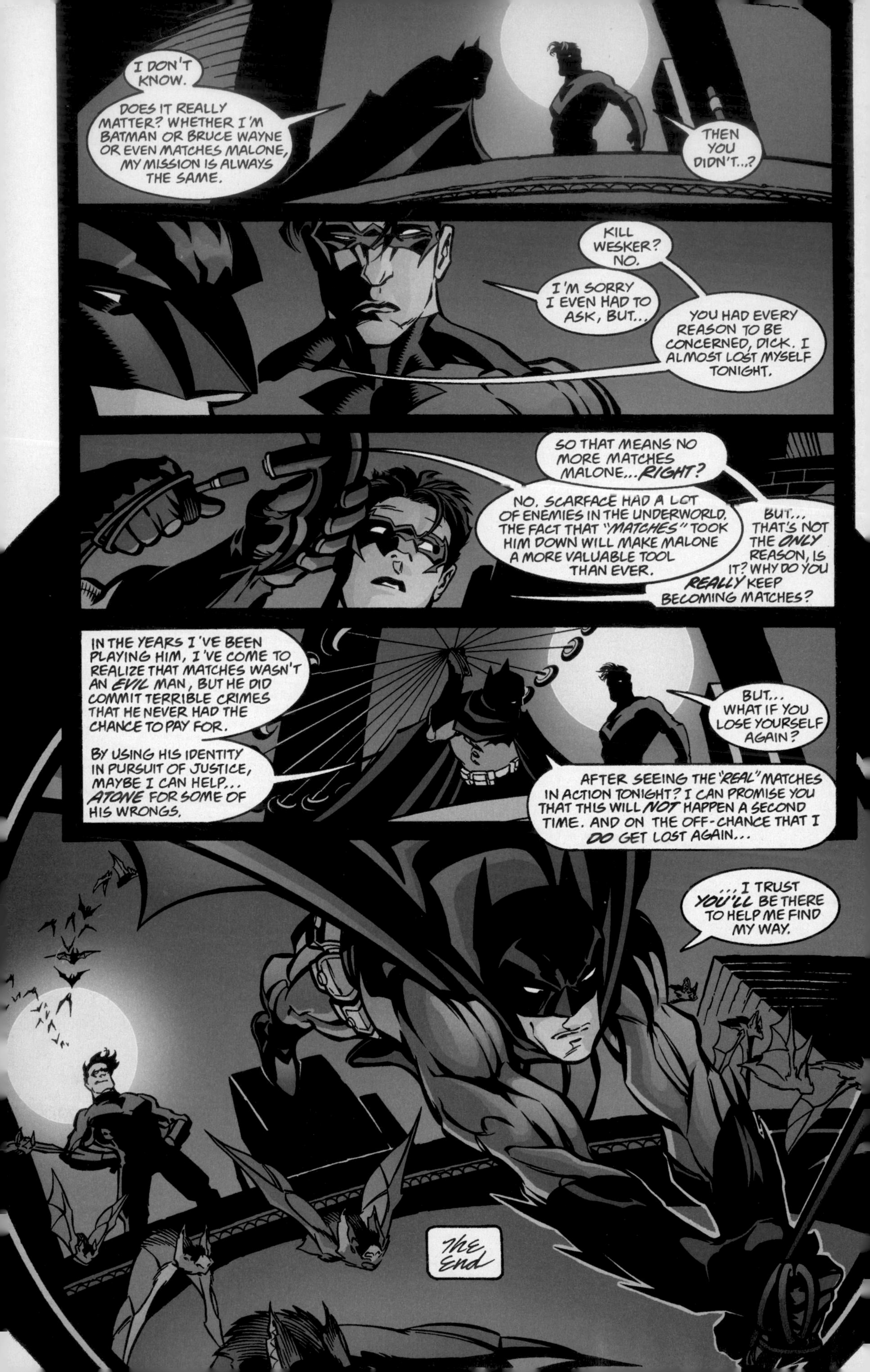

I DON'T KNOW.
DOES IT REALLY MATTER? WHETHER I'M BATMAN OR BRUCE WAYNE OR EVEN MATCHES MALONE, MY MISSION IS ALWAYS THE SAME.
THEN YOU DIDN'T...?
I'M SORRY I EVEN HAD TO ASK, BUT...
KILL WESKER? NO.
YOU HAD EVERY REASON TO BE CONCERNED, DICK. I ALMOST LOST MYSELF TONIGHT.
SO THAT MEANS NO MORE MATCHES MALONE... RIGHT?
NO. SCARFACE HAD A LOT OF ENEMIES IN THE UNDERWORLD. THE FACT THAT "MATCHES" TOOK HIM DOWN WILL MAKE MALONE A MORE VALUABLE TOOL THAN EVER.
BUT... THAT'S NOT THE ONLY REASON, IS IT? WHY DO YOU REALLY KEEP BECOMING MATCHES?
IN THE YEARS I'VE BEEN PLAYING HIM, I'VE COME TO REALIZE THAT MATCHES WASN'T AN EVIL MAN, BUT HE DID COMMIT TERRIBLE CRIMES THAT HE NEVER HAD THE CHANCE TO PAY FOR.
BY USING HIS IDENTITY IN PURSUIT OF JUSTICE, MAYBE I CAN HELP... ATONE FOR SOME OF HIS WRONGS.
BUT... WHAT IF YOU LOSE YOURSELF AGAIN?
AFTER SEEING THE "REAL" MATCHES IN ACTION TONIGHT? I CAN PROMISE YOU THAT THIS WILL NOT HAPPEN A SECOND TIME. AND ON THE OFF-CHANCE THAT I DO GET LOST AGAIN...
...I TRUST YOU'LL BE THERE TO HELP ME FIND MY WAY.
THE END

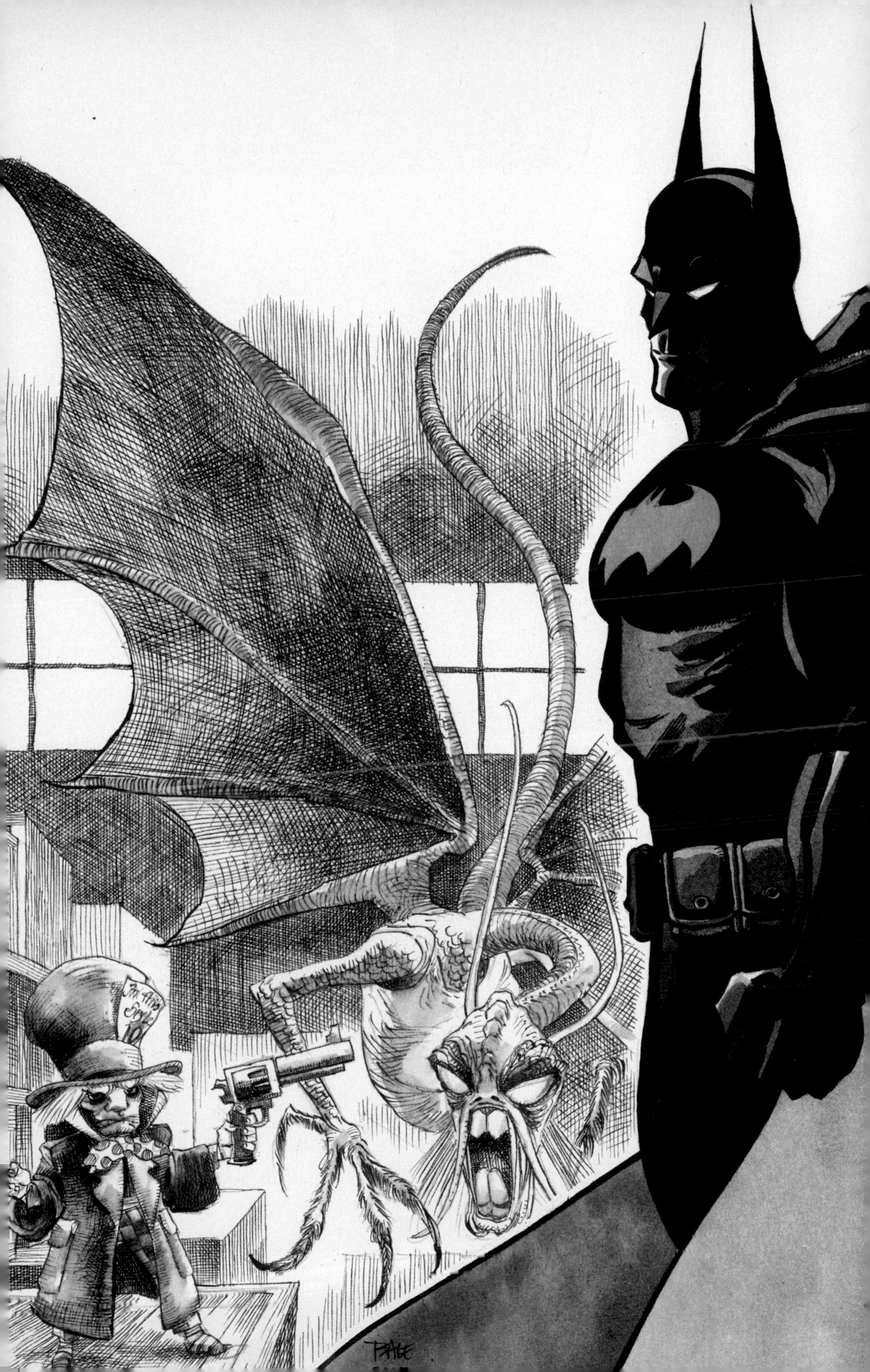

MIMSY WERE THE BOROGOVES

cover art by **TIM SALE**   colored by **MARK CHIARELLO**

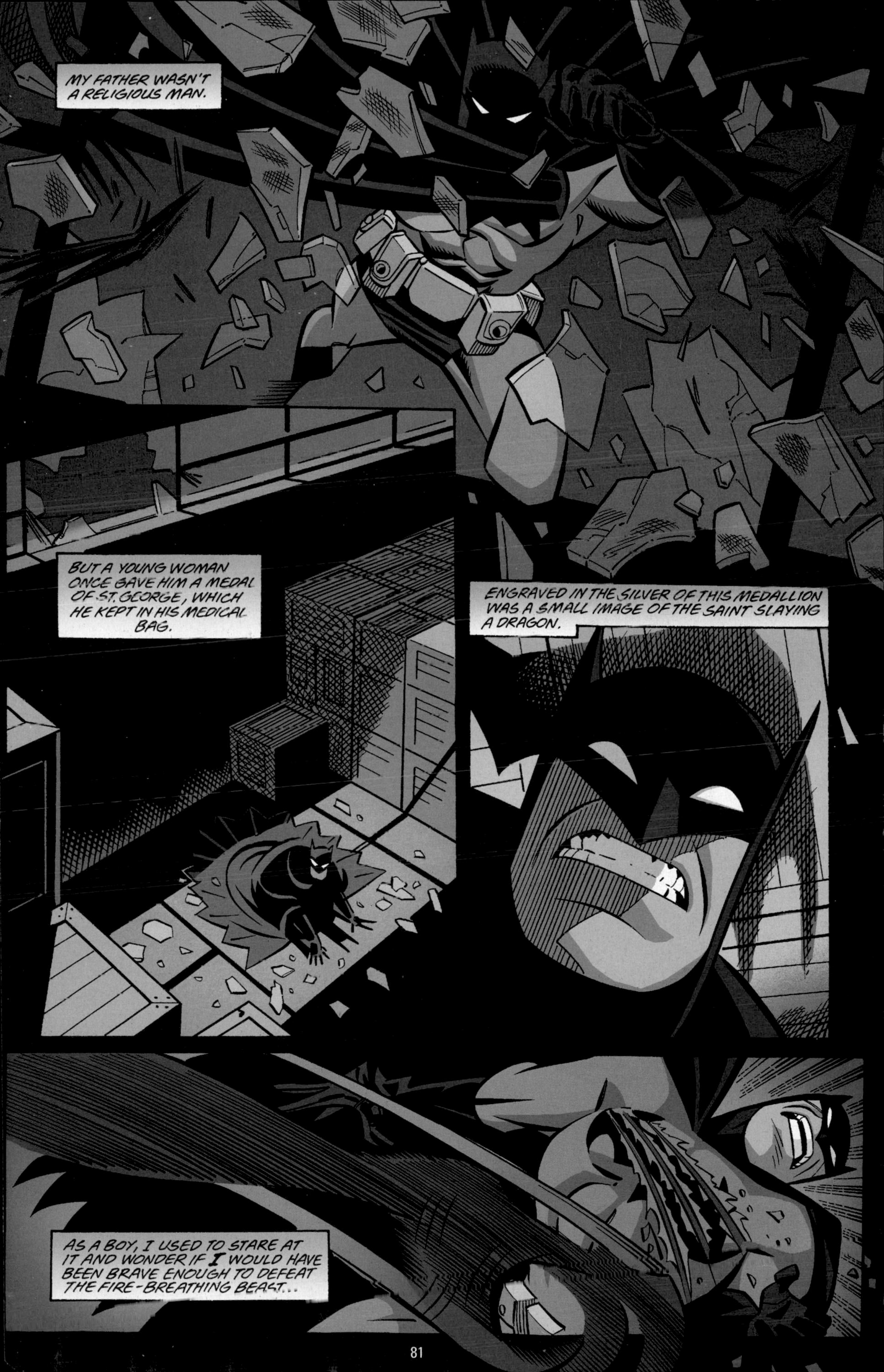
MY FATHER WASN'T A RELIGIOUS MAN.
BUT A YOUNG WOMAN ONCE GAVE HIM A MEDAL OF ST. GEORGE, WHICH HE KEPT IN HIS MEDICAL BAG.
ENGRAVED IN THE SILVER OF THIS MEDALLION WAS A SMALL IMAGE OF THE SAINT SLAYING A DRAGON.
AS A BOY, I USED TO STARE AT IT AND WONDER IF I WOULD HAVE BEEN BRAVE ENOUGH TO DEFEAT THE FIRE-BREATHING BEAST...

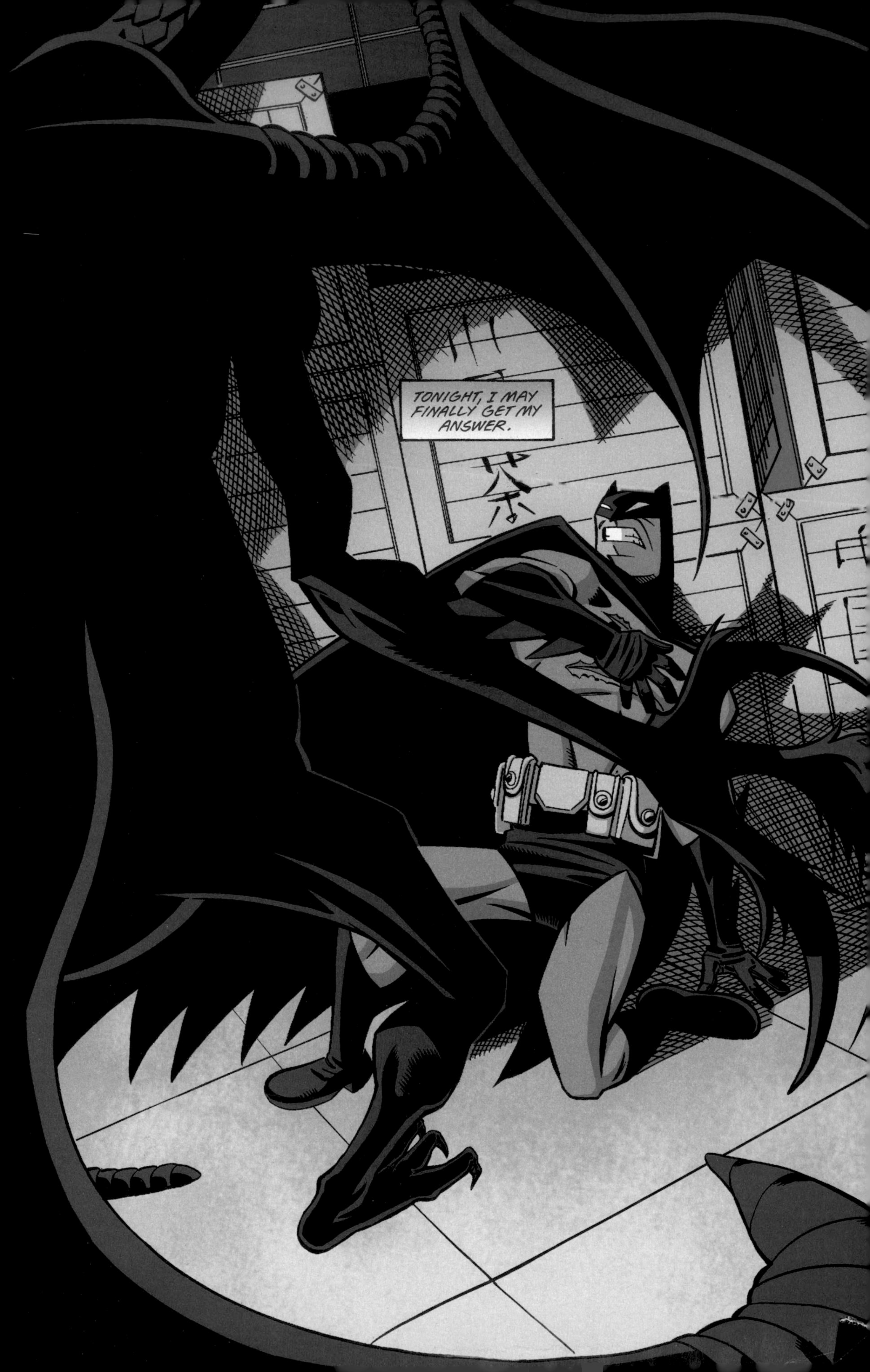
TONIGHT, I MAY FINALLY GET MY ANSWER.

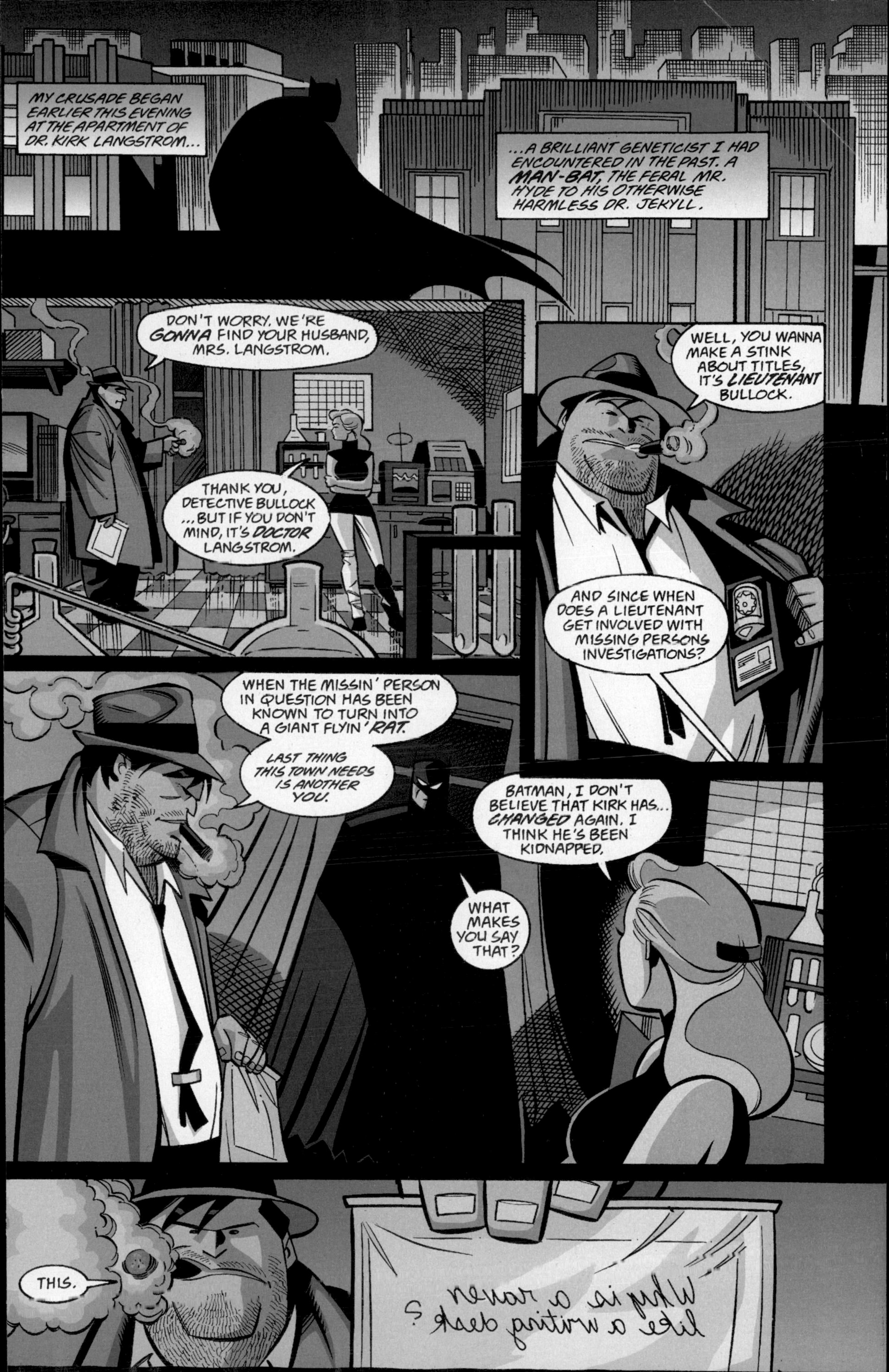
MY CRUSADE BEGAN EARLIER THIS EVENING AT THE APARTMENT OF DR. KIRK LANGSTROM...
...A BRILLIANT GENETICIST I HAD ENCOUNTERED IN THE PAST. A MAN-BAT, THE FERAL MR. HYDE TO HIS OTHERWISE HARMLESS DR. JEKYLL.
DON'T WORRY. WE'RE GONNA FIND YOUR HUSBAND, MRS. LANGSTROM.
THANK YOU, DETECTIVE BULLOCK ...BUT IF YOU DON'T MIND, IT'S DOCTOR LANGSTROM.
WELL, YOU WANNA MAKE A STINK ABOUT TITLES, IT'S LIEUTENANT BULLOCK.
AND SINCE WHEN DOES A LIEUTENANT GET INVOLVED WITH MISSING PERSONS INVESTIGATIONS?
WHEN THE MISSIN' PERSON IN QUESTION HAS BEEN KNOWN TO TURN INTO A GIANT FLYIN' RAT.
LAST THING THIS TOWN NEEDS IS ANOTHER YOU.
BATMAN, I DON'T BELIEVE THAT KIRK HAS... CHANGED AGAIN. I THINK HE'S BEEN KIDNAPPED.
WHAT MAKES YOU SAY THAT?
THIS.
Why is a raven like a writing desk?

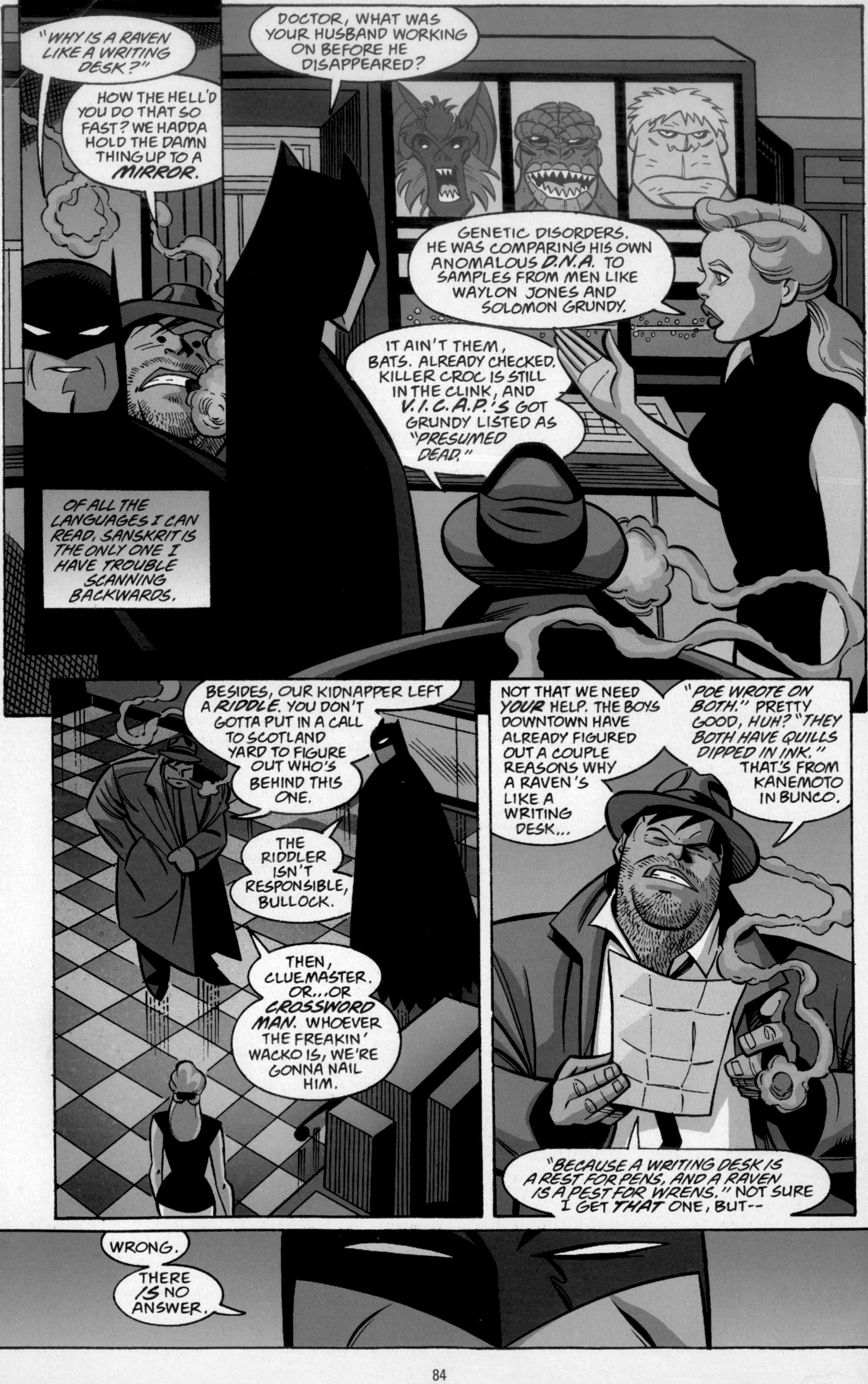
"WHY IS A RAVEN LIKE A WRITING DESK?"
HOW THE HELL'D YOU DO THAT SO FAST? WE HADDA HOLD THE DAMN THING UP TO A MIRROR.
DOCTOR, WHAT WAS YOUR HUSBAND WORKING ON BEFORE HE DISAPPEARED?
GENETIC DISORDERS. HE WAS COMPARING HIS OWN ANOMALOUS D.N.A. TO SAMPLES FROM MEN LIKE WAYLON JONES AND SOLOMON GRUNDY.
IT AIN'T THEM, BATS. ALREADY CHECKED. KILLER CROC IS STILL IN THE CLINK, AND V.I.C.A.P.'S GOT GRUNDY LISTED AS "PRESUMED DEAD."
OF ALL THE LANGUAGES I CAN READ, SANSKRIT IS THE ONLY ONE I HAVE TROUBLE SCANNING BACKWARDS.
BESIDES, OUR KIDNAPPER LEFT A RIDDLE. YOU DON'T GOTTA PUT IN A CALL TO SCOTLAND YARD TO FIGURE OUT WHO'S BEHIND THIS ONE.
THE RIDDLER ISN'T RESPONSIBLE, BULLOCK.
THEN, CLUEMASTER. OR...OR CROSSWORD MAN. WHOEVER THE FREAKIN' WACKO IS, WE'RE GONNA NAIL HIM.
NOT THAT WE NEED YOUR HELP. THE BOYS DOWNTOWN HAVE ALREADY FIGURED OUT A COUPLE REASONS WHY A RAVEN'S LIKE A WRITING DESK...
"POE WROTE ON BOTH." PRETTY GOOD, HUH? "THEY BOTH HAVE QUILLS DIPPED IN INK." THAT'S FROM KANEMOTO IN BUNCO.
"BECAUSE A WRITING DESK IS A REST FOR PENS, AND A RAVEN IS A PEST FOR WRENS." NOT SURE I GET THAT ONE, BUT--
WRONG.
THERE IS NO ANSWER.

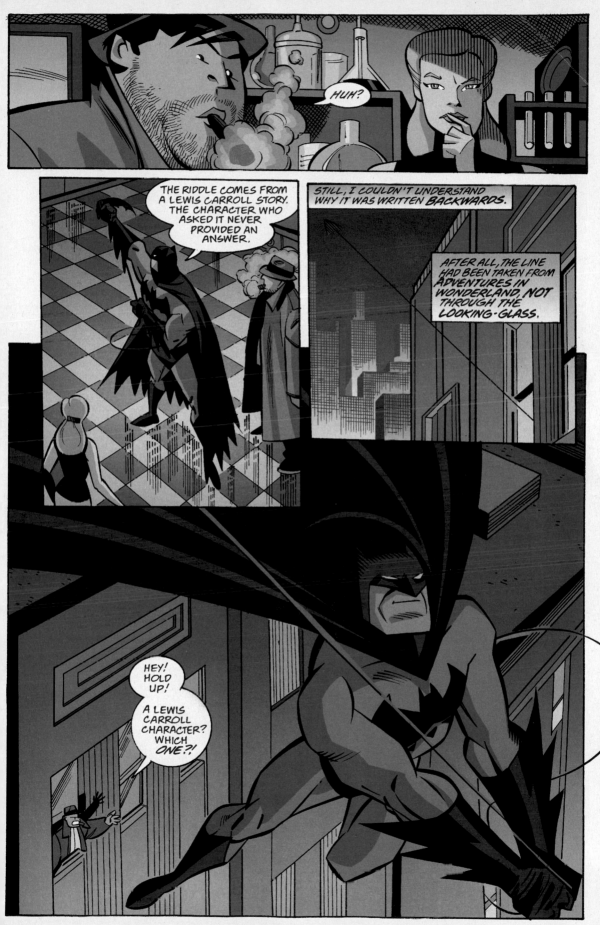

HUH?

THE RIDDLE COMES FROM A LEWIS CARROLL STORY. THE CHARACTER WHO ASKED IT NEVER PROVIDED AN ANSWER.

STILL, I COULDN'T UNDERSTAND WHY IT WAS WRITTEN *BACKWARDS*.

AFTER ALL, THE LINE HAD BEEN TAKEN FROM *ADVENTURES IN WONDERLAND*, *NOT* *THROUGH THE LOOKING-GLASS*.

HEY! HOLD UP!

A LEWIS CARROLL CHARACTER? WHICH *ONE?!*

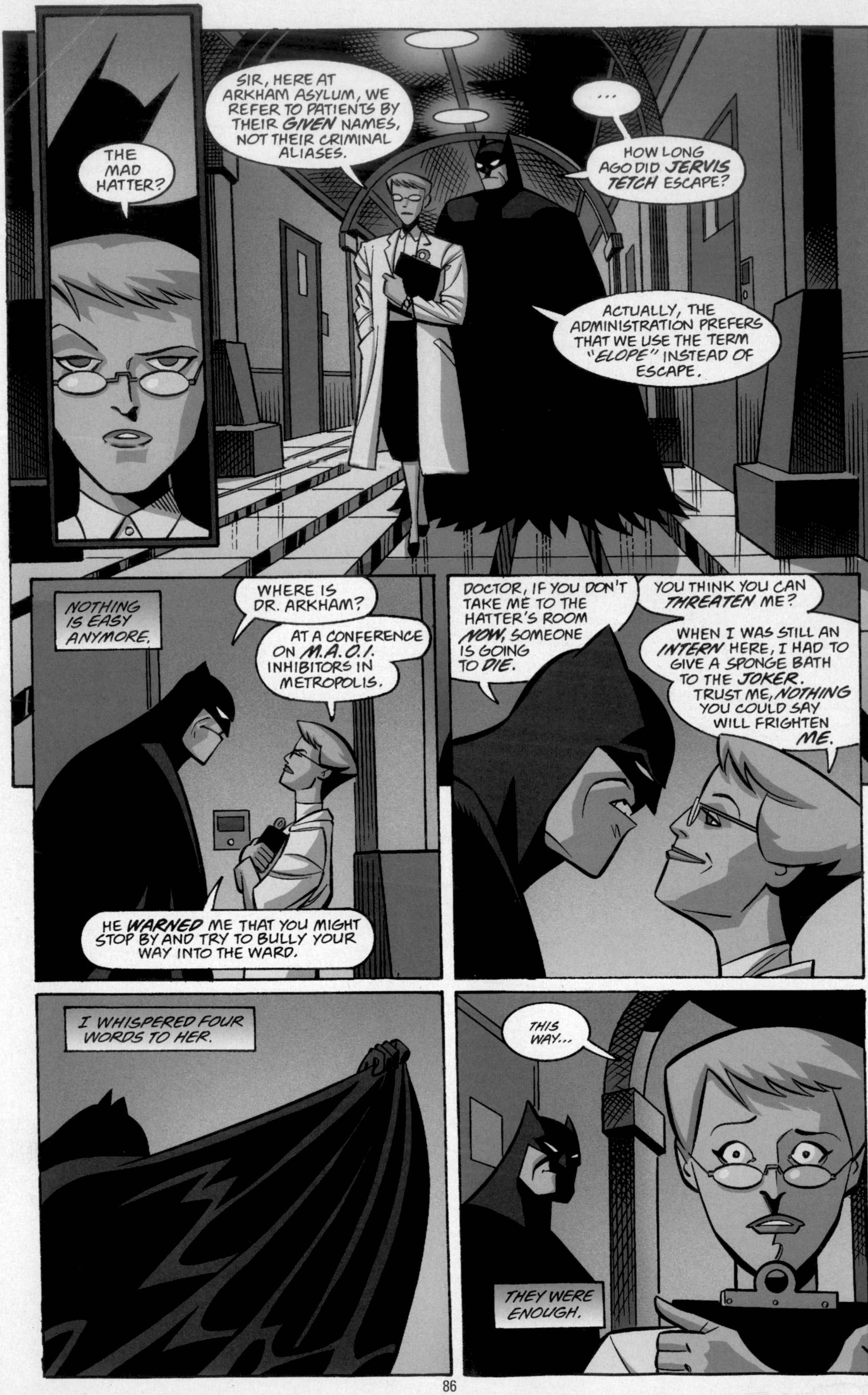

THE MAD HATTER?
SIR, HERE AT ARKHAM ASYLUM, WE REFER TO PATIENTS BY THEIR GIVEN NAMES, NOT THEIR CRIMINAL ALIASES.
...
HOW LONG AGO DID JERVIS TETCH ESCAPE?
ACTUALLY, THE ADMINISTRATION PREFERS THAT WE USE THE TERM "ELOPE" INSTEAD OF ESCAPE.
NOTHING IS EASY ANYMORE.
WHERE IS DR. ARKHAM?
AT A CONFERENCE ON M.A.O.I. INHIBITORS IN METROPOLIS.
HE WARNED ME THAT YOU MIGHT STOP BY AND TRY TO BULLY YOUR WAY INTO THE WARD.
DOCTOR, IF YOU DON'T TAKE ME TO THE HATTER'S ROOM NOW, SOMEONE IS GOING TO DIE.
YOU THINK YOU CAN THREATEN ME?
WHEN I WAS STILL AN INTERN HERE, I HAD TO GIVE A SPONGE BATH TO THE JOKER. TRUST ME, NOTHING YOU COULD SAY WILL FRIGHTEN ME.
I WHISPERED FOUR WORDS TO HER.
THIS WAY...
THEY WERE ENOUGH.

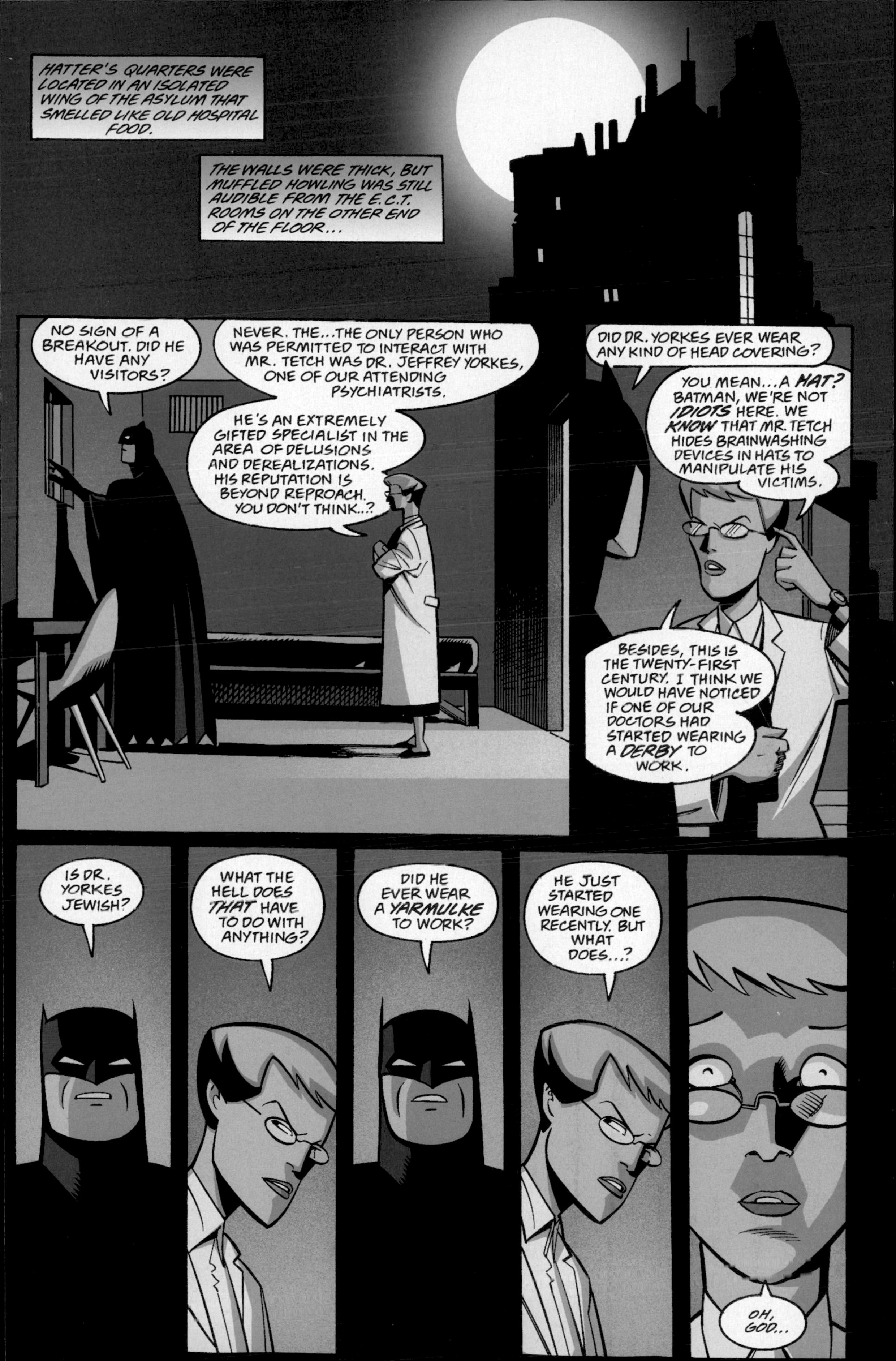
HATTER'S QUARTERS WERE LOCATED IN AN ISOLATED WING OF THE ASYLUM THAT SMELLED LIKE OLD HOSPITAL FOOD.
THE WALLS WERE THICK, BUT MUFFLED HOWLING WAS STILL AUDIBLE FROM THE E.C.T. ROOMS ON THE OTHER END OF THE FLOOR...
NO SIGN OF A BREAKOUT. DID HE HAVE ANY VISITORS?
NEVER. THE...THE ONLY PERSON WHO WAS PERMITTED TO INTERACT WITH MR. TETCH WAS DR. JEFFREY YORKES, ONE OF OUR ATTENDING PSYCHIATRISTS.
HE'S AN EXTREMELY GIFTED SPECIALIST IN THE AREA OF DELUSIONS AND DEREALIZATIONS. HIS REPUTATION IS BEYOND REPROACH. YOU DON'T THINK..?
DID DR. YORKES EVER WEAR ANY KIND OF HEAD COVERING?
YOU MEAN...A HAT? BATMAN, WE'RE NOT IDIOTS HERE. WE KNOW THAT MR. TETCH HIDES BRAINWASHING DEVICES IN HATS TO MANIPULATE HIS VICTIMS.
BESIDES, THIS IS THE TWENTY-FIRST CENTURY. I THINK WE WOULD HAVE NOTICED IF ONE OF OUR DOCTORS HAD STARTED WEARING A DERBY TO WORK.
IS DR. YORKES JEWISH?
WHAT THE HELL DOES THAT HAVE TO DO WITH ANYTHING?
DID HE EVER WEAR A YARMULKE TO WORK?
HE JUST STARTED WEARING ONE RECENTLY. BUT WHAT DOES...?
OH, GOD...

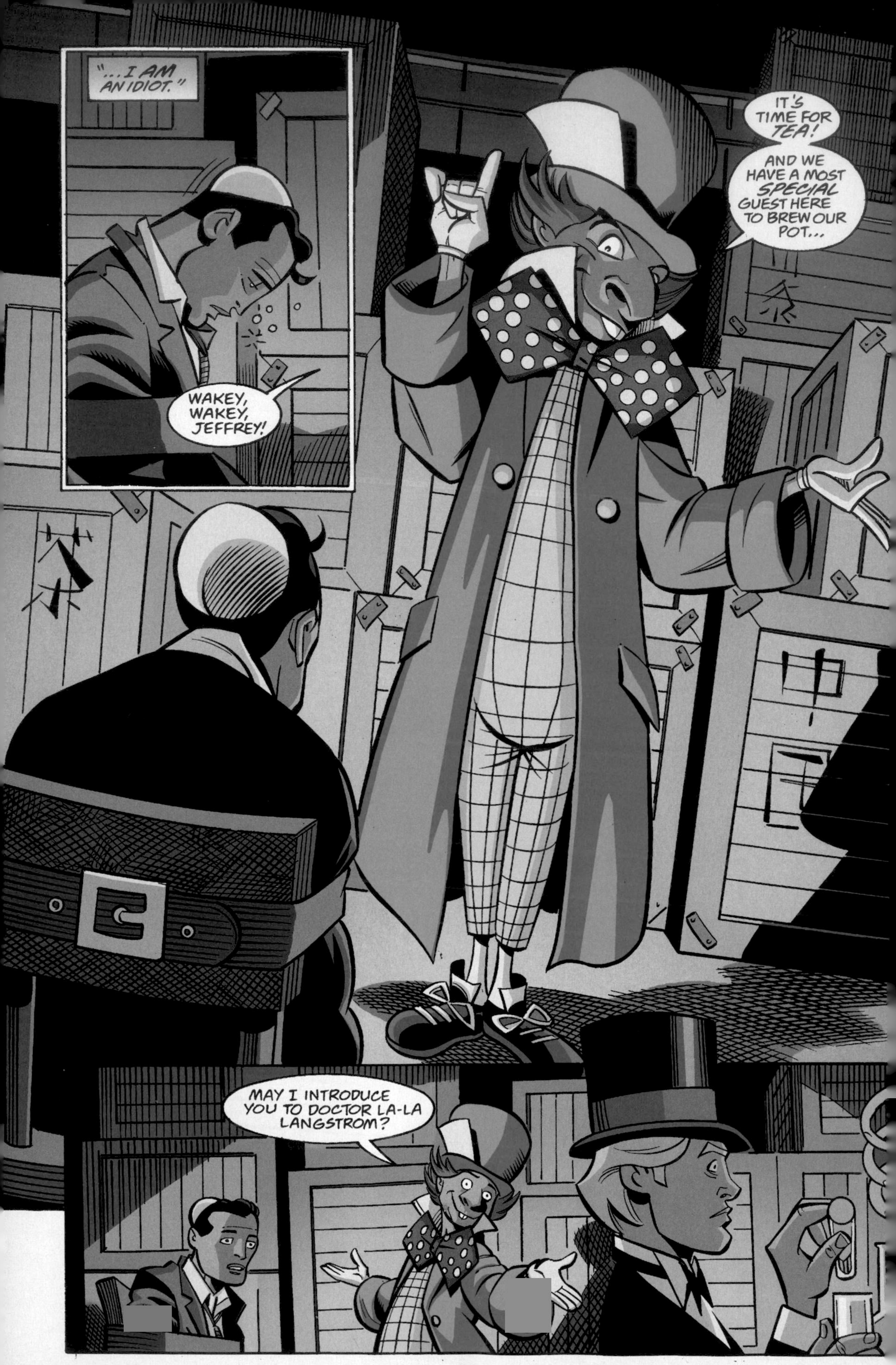
"...I AM AN IDIOT."
WAKEY, WAKEY, JEFFREY!
IT'S TIME FOR TEA!
AND WE HAVE A MOST SPECIAL GUEST HERE TO BREW OUR POT...
MAY I INTRODUCE YOU TO DOCTOR LA-LA LANGSTROM?

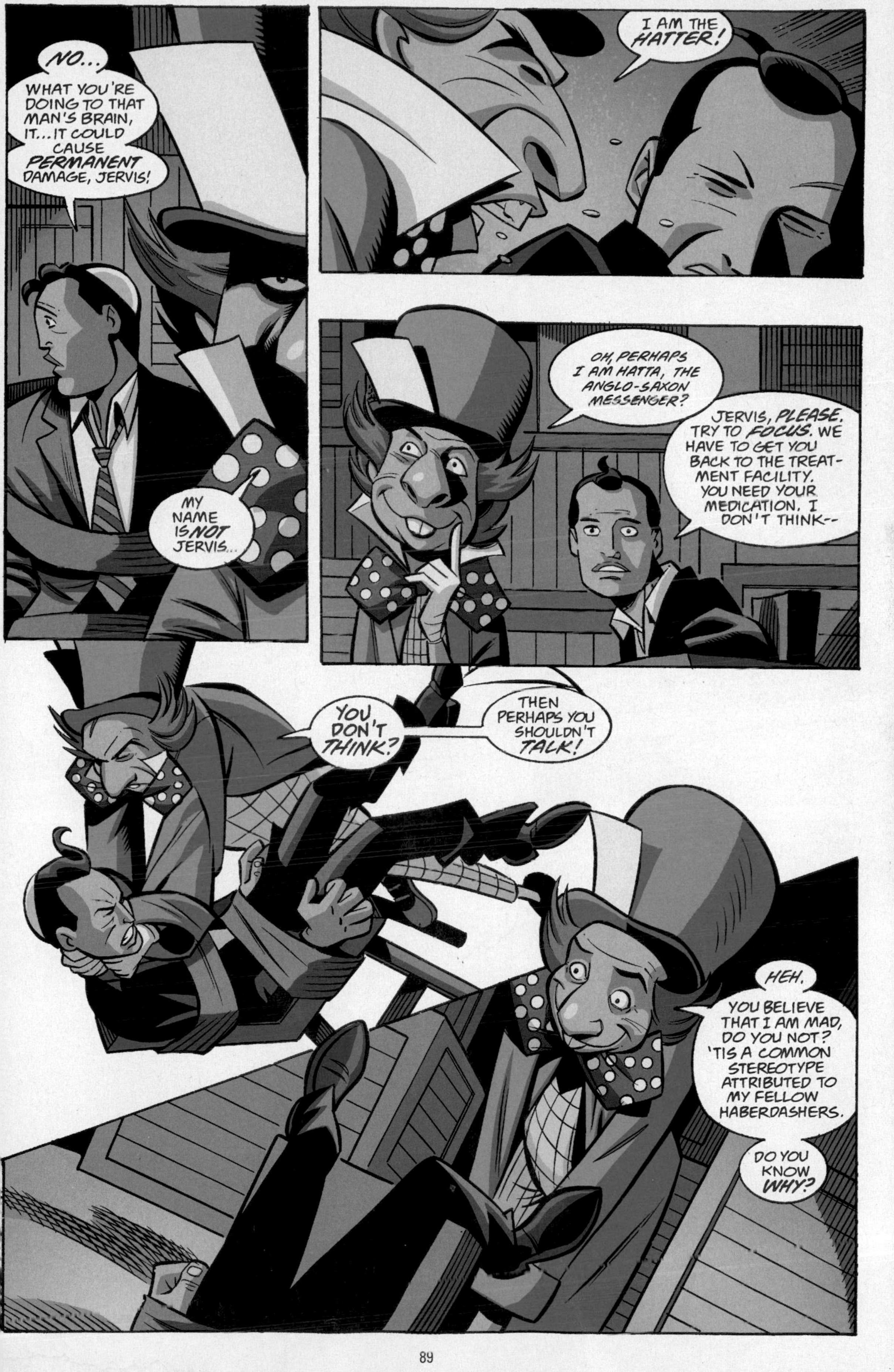
NO...
WHAT YOU'RE DOING TO THAT MAN'S BRAIN, IT...IT COULD CAUSE PERMANENT DAMAGE, JERVIS!
MY NAME IS NOT JERVIS...
I AM THE HATTER!
OH, PERHAPS I AM HATTA, THE ANGLO-SAXON MESSENGER?
JERVIS, PLEASE. TRY TO FOCUS. WE HAVE TO GET YOU BACK TO THE TREATMENT FACILITY. YOU NEED YOUR MEDICATION. I DON'T THINK--
YOU DON'T THINK?
THEN PERHAPS YOU SHOULDN'T TALK!
HEH.
YOU BELIEVE THAT I AM MAD, DO YOU NOT? 'TIS A COMMON STEREOTYPE ATTRIBUTED TO MY FELLOW HABERDASHERS.
DO YOU KNOW WHY?

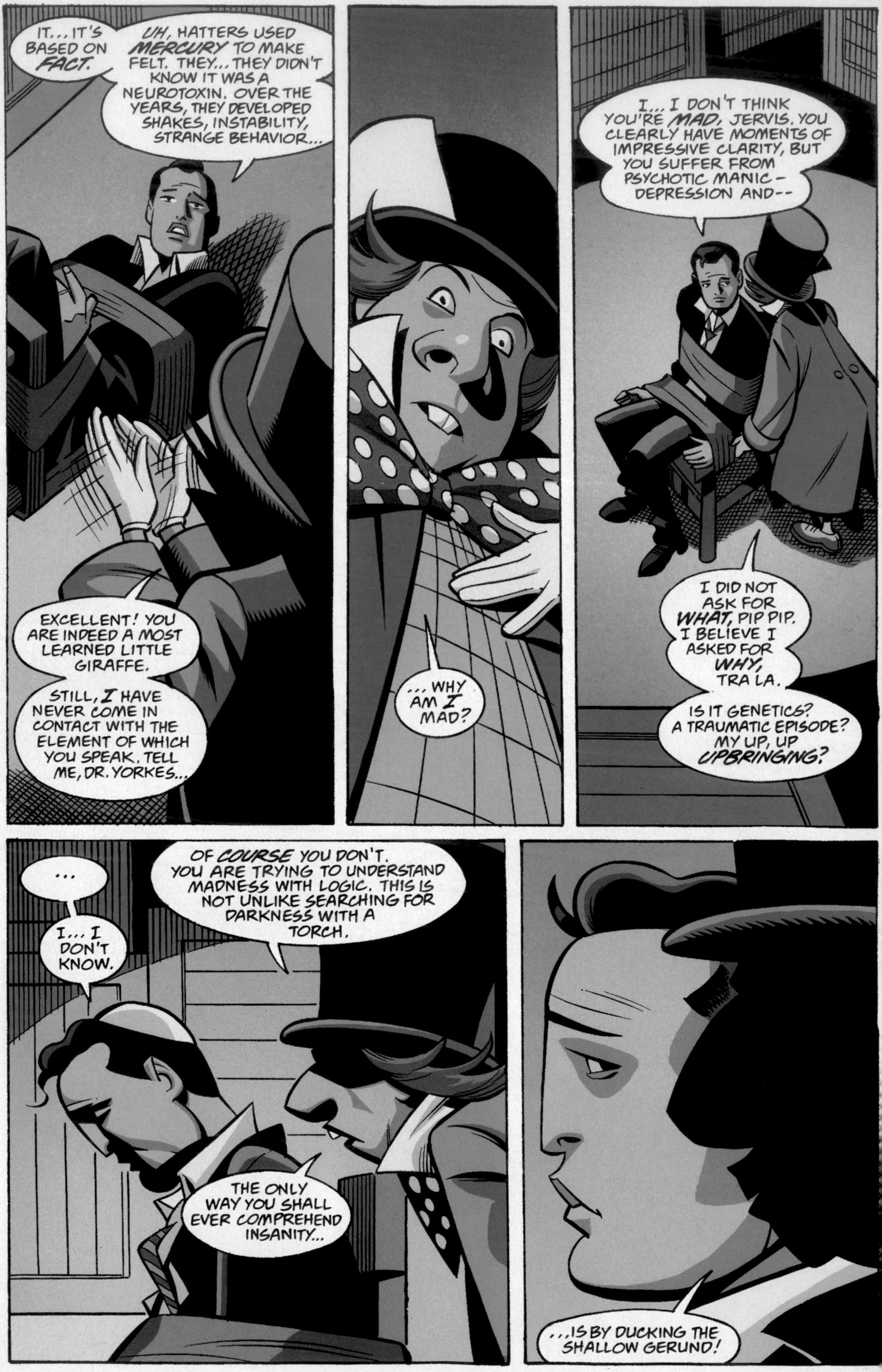
IT... IT'S BASED ON FACT.
UH, HATTERS USED MERCURY TO MAKE FELT. THEY... THEY DIDN'T KNOW IT WAS A NEUROTOXIN. OVER THE YEARS, THEY DEVELOPED SHAKES, INSTABILITY, STRANGE BEHAVIOR...
EXCELLENT! YOU ARE INDEED A MOST LEARNED LITTLE GIRAFFE.
STILL, I HAVE NEVER COME IN CONTACT WITH THE ELEMENT OF WHICH YOU SPEAK. TELL ME, DR. YORKES...
...WHY AM I MAD?
I... I DON'T THINK YOU'RE MAD, JERVIS. YOU CLEARLY HAVE MOMENTS OF IMPRESSIVE CLARITY, BUT YOU SUFFER FROM PSYCHOTIC MANIC-DEPRESSION AND--
I DID NOT ASK FOR WHAT, PIP PIP. I BELIEVE I ASKED FOR WHY, TRA LA.
IS IT GENETICS? A TRAUMATIC EPISODE? MY UP, UP UPBRINGING?
...
I... I DON'T KNOW.
OF COURSE YOU DON'T. YOU ARE TRYING TO UNDERSTAND MADNESS WITH LOGIC. THIS IS NOT UNLIKE SEARCHING FOR DARKNESS WITH A TORCH.
THE ONLY WAY YOU SHALL EVER COMPREHEND INSANITY...
...IS BY DUCKING THE SHALLOW GERUND!

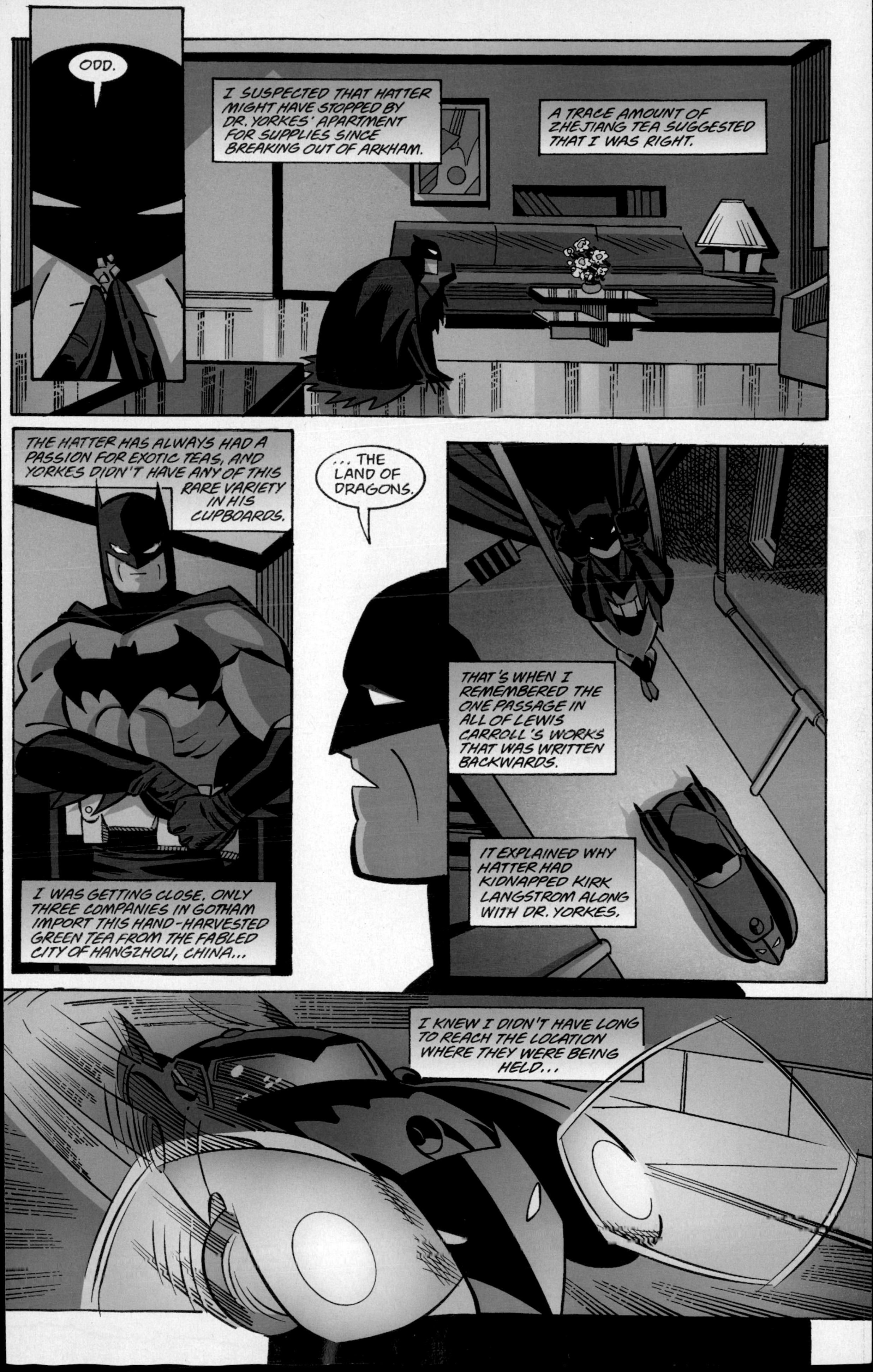
ODD.
I SUSPECTED THAT HATTER MIGHT HAVE STOPPED BY DR. YORKES' APARTMENT FOR SUPPLIES SINCE BREAKING OUT OF ARKHAM.
A TRACE AMOUNT OF ZHEJIANG TEA SUGGESTED THAT I WAS RIGHT.
THE HATTER HAS ALWAYS HAD A PASSION FOR EXOTIC TEAS, AND YORKES DIDN'T HAVE ANY OF THIS RARE VARIETY IN HIS CUPBOARDS.
I WAS GETTING CLOSE. ONLY THREE COMPANIES IN GOTHAM IMPORT THIS HAND-HARVESTED GREEN TEA FROM THE FABLED CITY OF HANGZHOU, CHINA...
...THE LAND OF DRAGONS.
THAT'S WHEN I REMEMBERED THE ONE PASSAGE IN ALL OF LEWIS CARROLL'S WORKS THAT WAS WRITTEN BACKWARDS.
IT EXPLAINED WHY HATTER HAD KIDNAPPED KIRK LANGSTROM ALONG WITH DR. YORKES.
I KNEW I DIDN'T HAVE LONG TO REACH THE LOCATION WHERE THEY WERE BEING HELD...

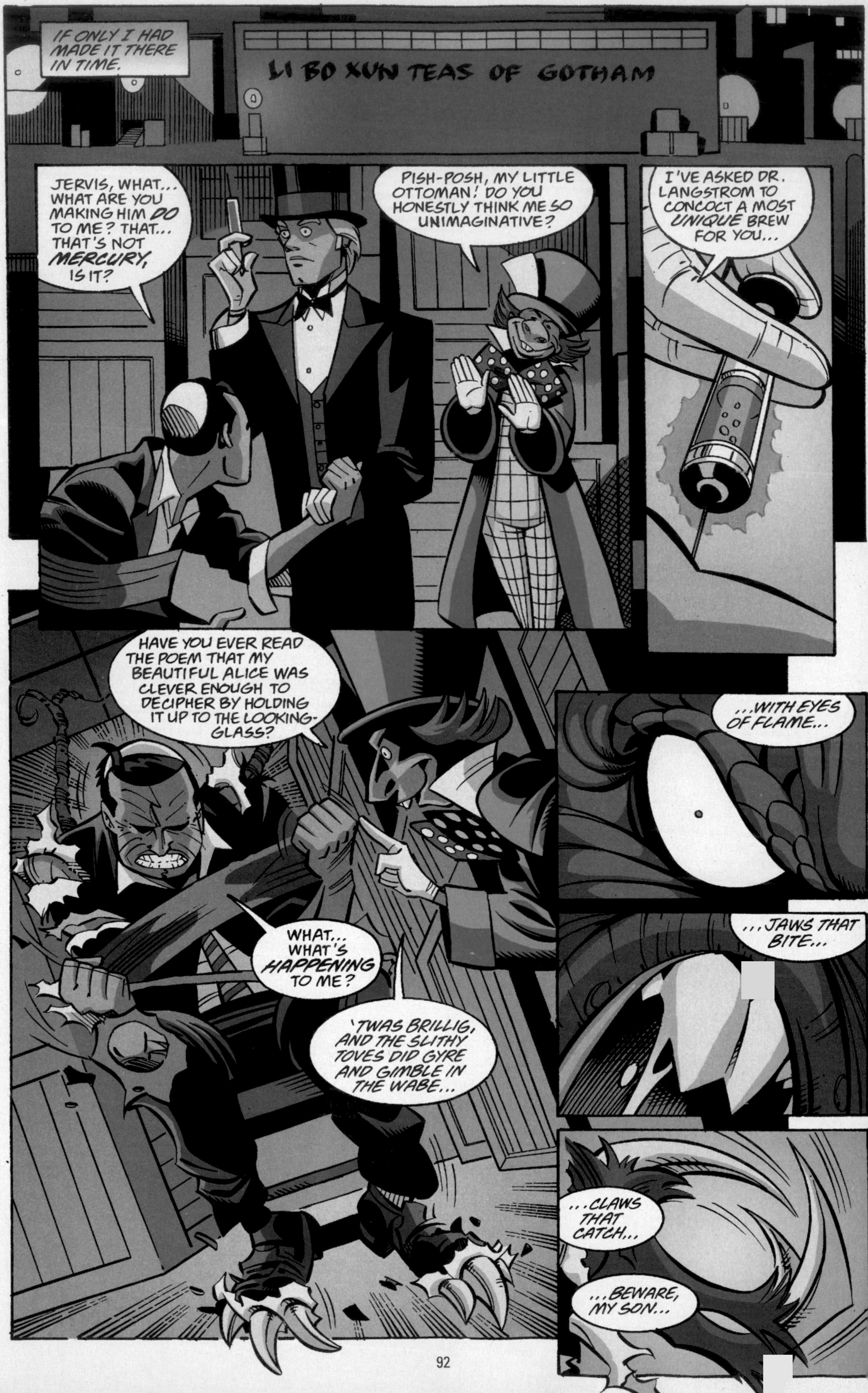

IF ONLY I HAD MADE IT THERE IN TIME.
LI BO XUN TEAS OF GOTHAM
JERVIS, WHAT... WHAT ARE YOU MAKING HIM DO TO ME? THAT... THAT'S NOT MERCURY, IS IT?
PISH-POSH, MY LITTLE OTTOMAN! DO YOU HONESTLY THINK ME SO UNIMAGINATIVE?
I'VE ASKED DR. LANGSTROM TO CONCOCT A MOST UNIQUE BREW FOR YOU...
HAVE YOU EVER READ THE POEM THAT MY BEAUTIFUL ALICE WAS CLEVER ENOUGH TO DECIPHER BY HOLDING IT UP TO THE LOOKING-GLASS?
WHAT... WHAT'S HAPPENING TO ME?
'TWAS BRILLIG, AND THE SLITHY TOVES DID GYRE AND GIMBLE IN THE WABE...
...WITH EYES OF FLAME...
...JAWS THAT BITE...
...CLAWS THAT CATCH...
...BEWARE, MY SON...

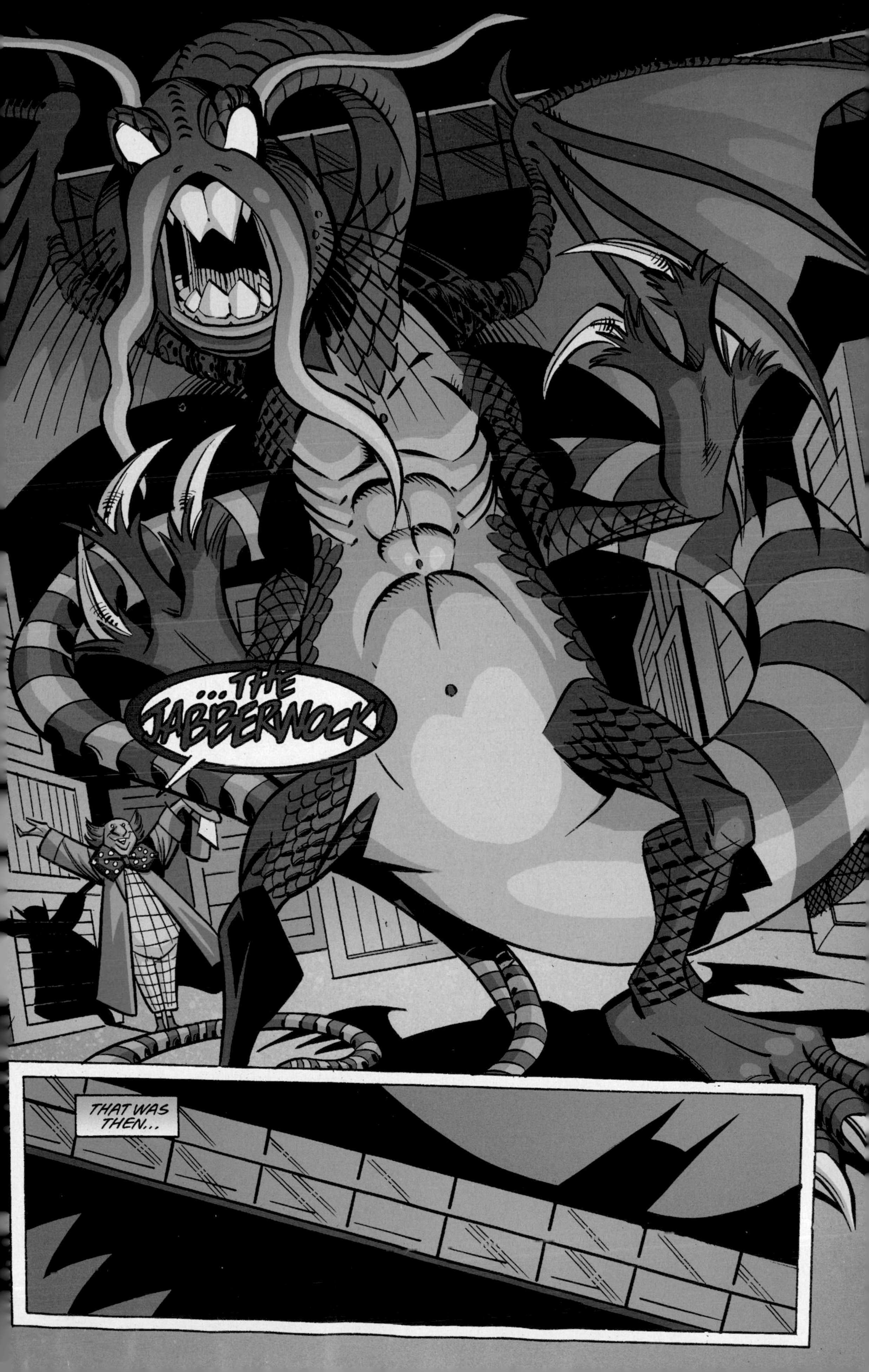
...THE JABBERWOCK!
THAT WAS THEN...

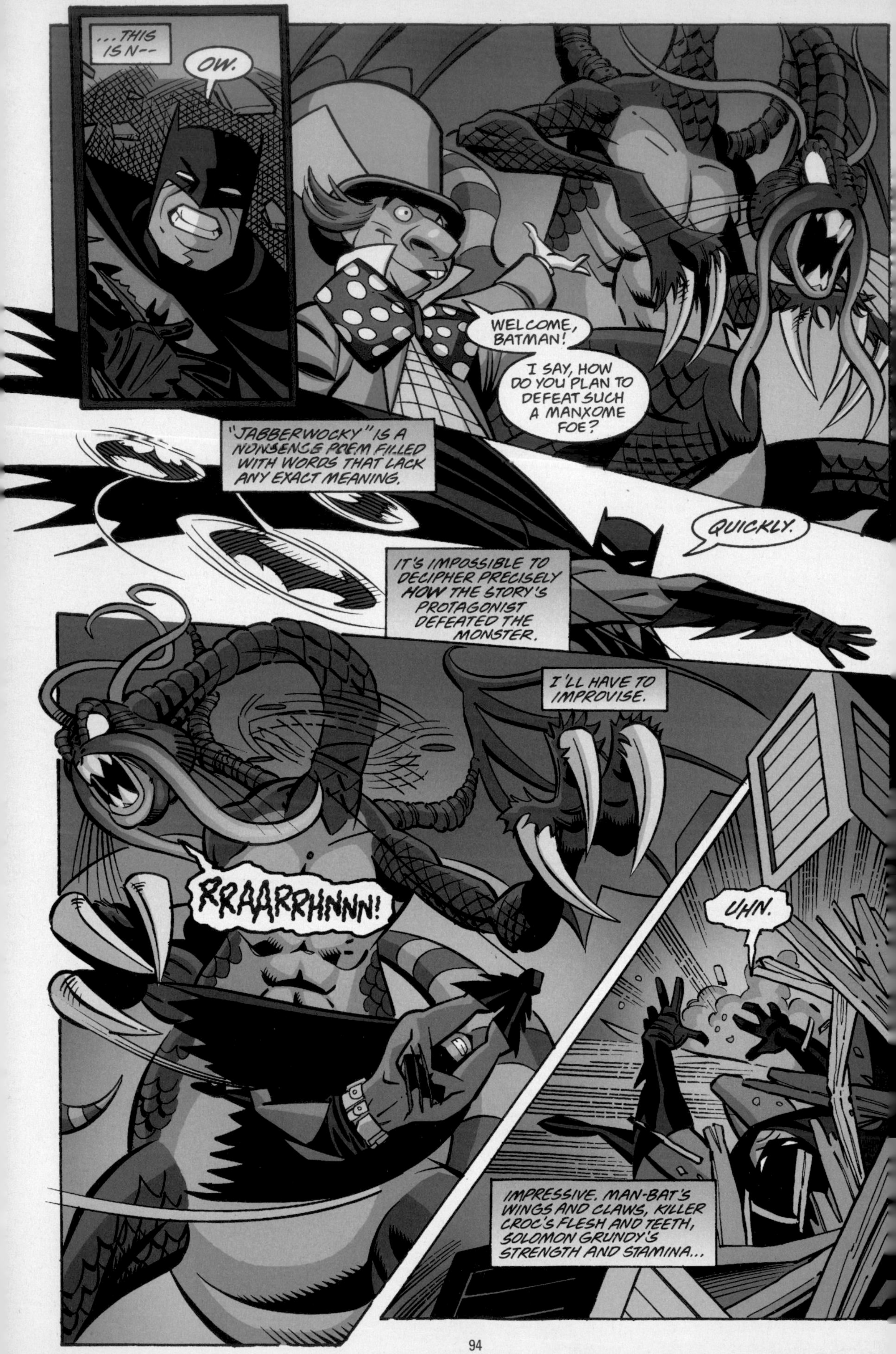
...THIS IS N--
OW.
WELCOME, BATMAN!
I SAY, HOW DO YOU PLAN TO DEFEAT SUCH A MANXOME FOE?
"JABBERWOCKY" IS A NONSENSE POEM FILLED WITH WORDS THAT LACK ANY EXACT MEANING.
QUICKLY.
IT'S IMPOSSIBLE TO DECIPHER PRECISELY HOW THE STORY'S PROTAGONIST DEFEATED THE MONSTER.
I'LL HAVE TO IMPROVISE.
RRAARRHNNN!
UHN.
IMPRESSIVE. MAN-BAT'S WINGS AND CLAWS, KILLER CROC'S FLESH AND TEETH, SOLOMON GRUNDY'S STRENGTH AND STAMINA...

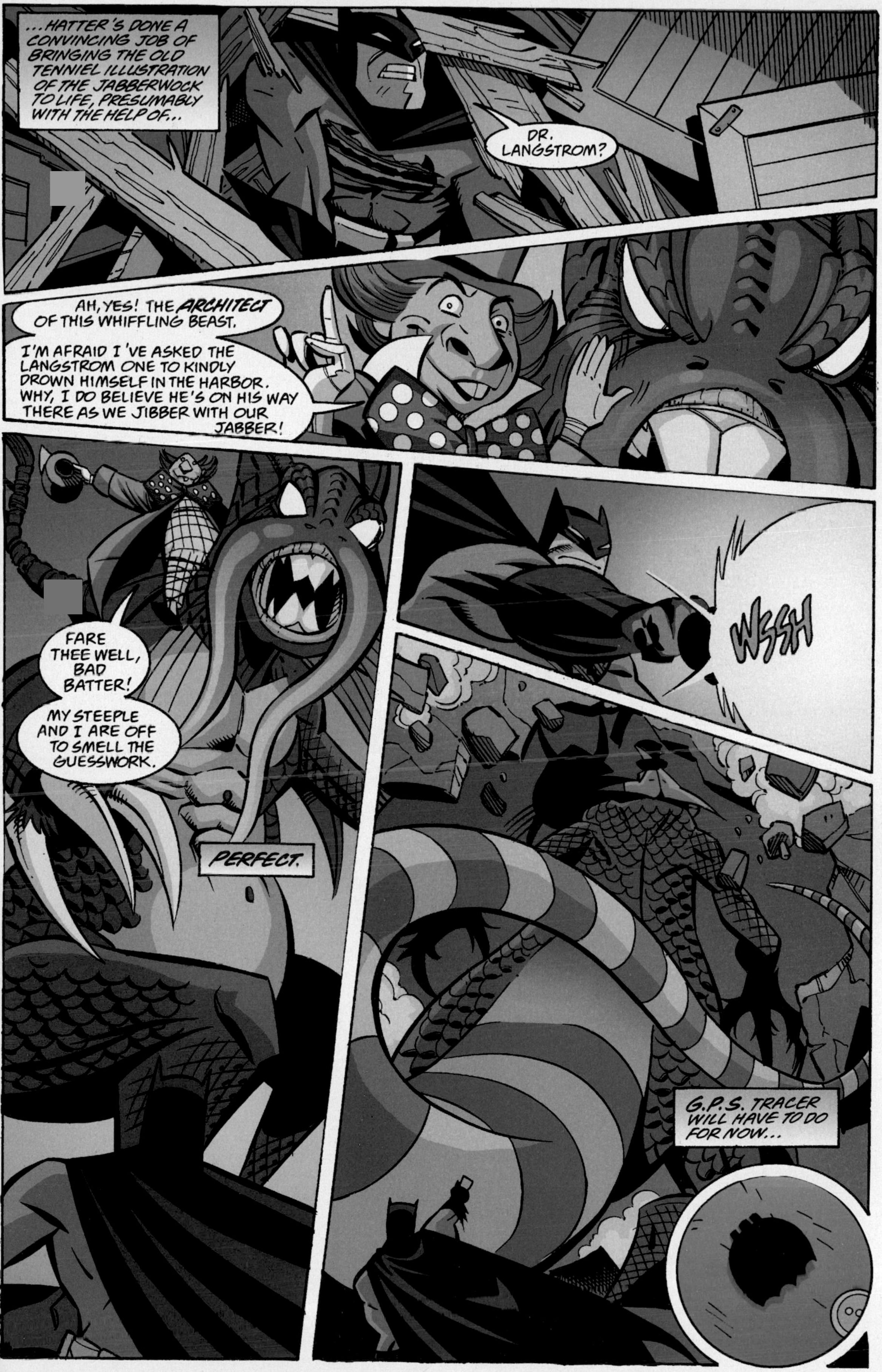

...HATTER'S DONE A CONVINCING JOB OF BRINGING THE OLD TENNIEL ILLUSTRATION OF THE JABBERWOCK TO LIFE, PRESUMABLY WITH THE HELP OF...
DR. LANGSTROM?
AH, YES! THE ARCHITECT OF THIS WHIFFLING BEAST.
I'M AFRAID I'VE ASKED THE LANGSTROM ONE TO KINDLY DROWN HIMSELF IN THE HARBOR. WHY, I DO BELIEVE HE'S ON HIS WAY THERE AS WE JIBBER WITH OUR JABBER!
FARE THEE WELL, BAD BATTER!
MY STEEPLE AND I ARE OFF TO SMELL THE GUESSWORK.
PERFECT.
WSSH
G.P.S. TRACER WILL HAVE TO DO FOR NOW...

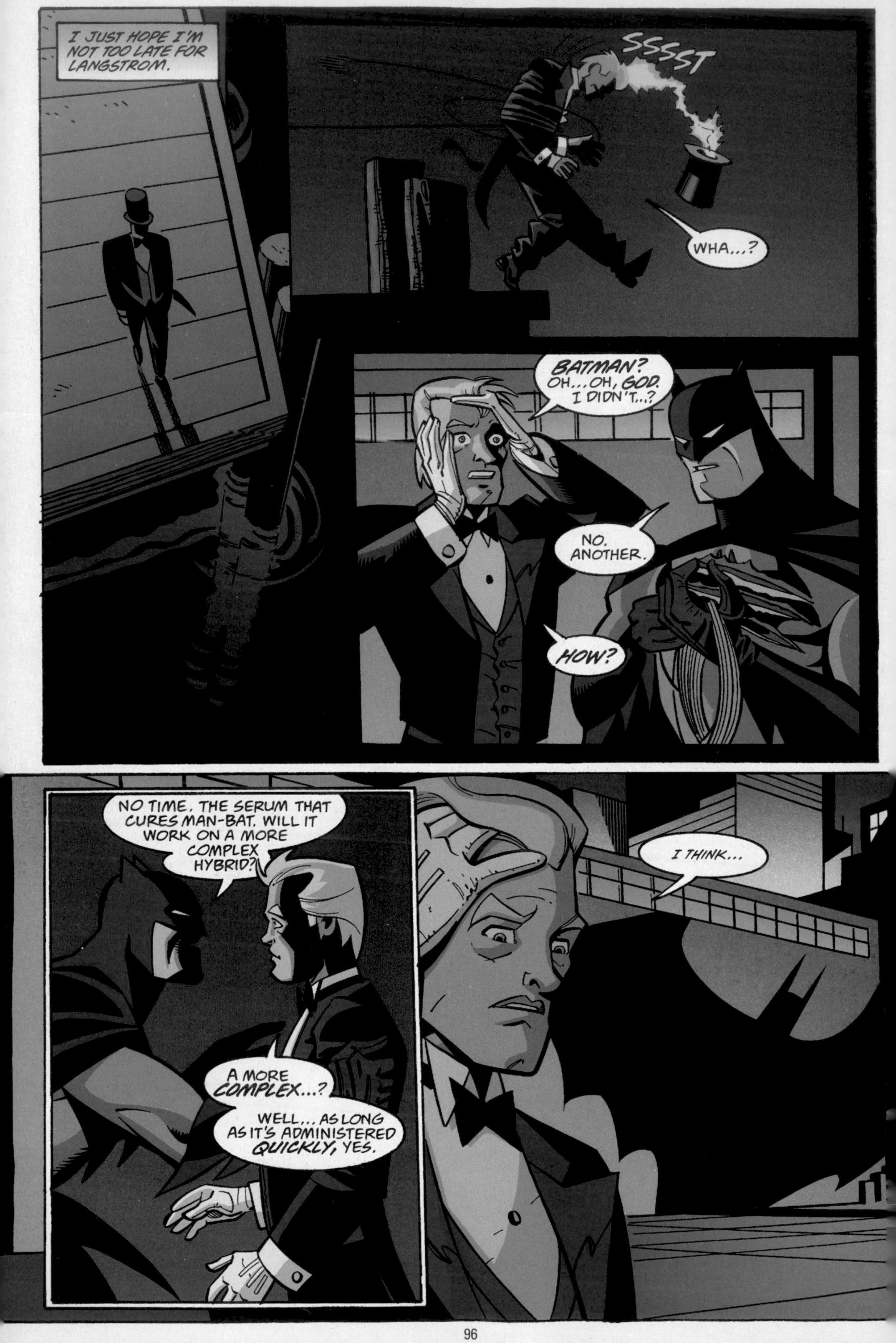
I JUST HOPE I'M NOT TOO LATE FOR LANGSTROM.
SSSSST
WHA...?
BATMAN? OH... OH, GOD. I DIDN'T...?
NO. ANOTHER.
HOW?
NO TIME. THE SERUM THAT CURES MAN-BAT. WILL IT WORK ON A MORE COMPLEX HYBRID?
A MORE COMPLEX...?
WELL... AS LONG AS IT'S ADMINISTERED QUICKLY, YES.
I THINK...

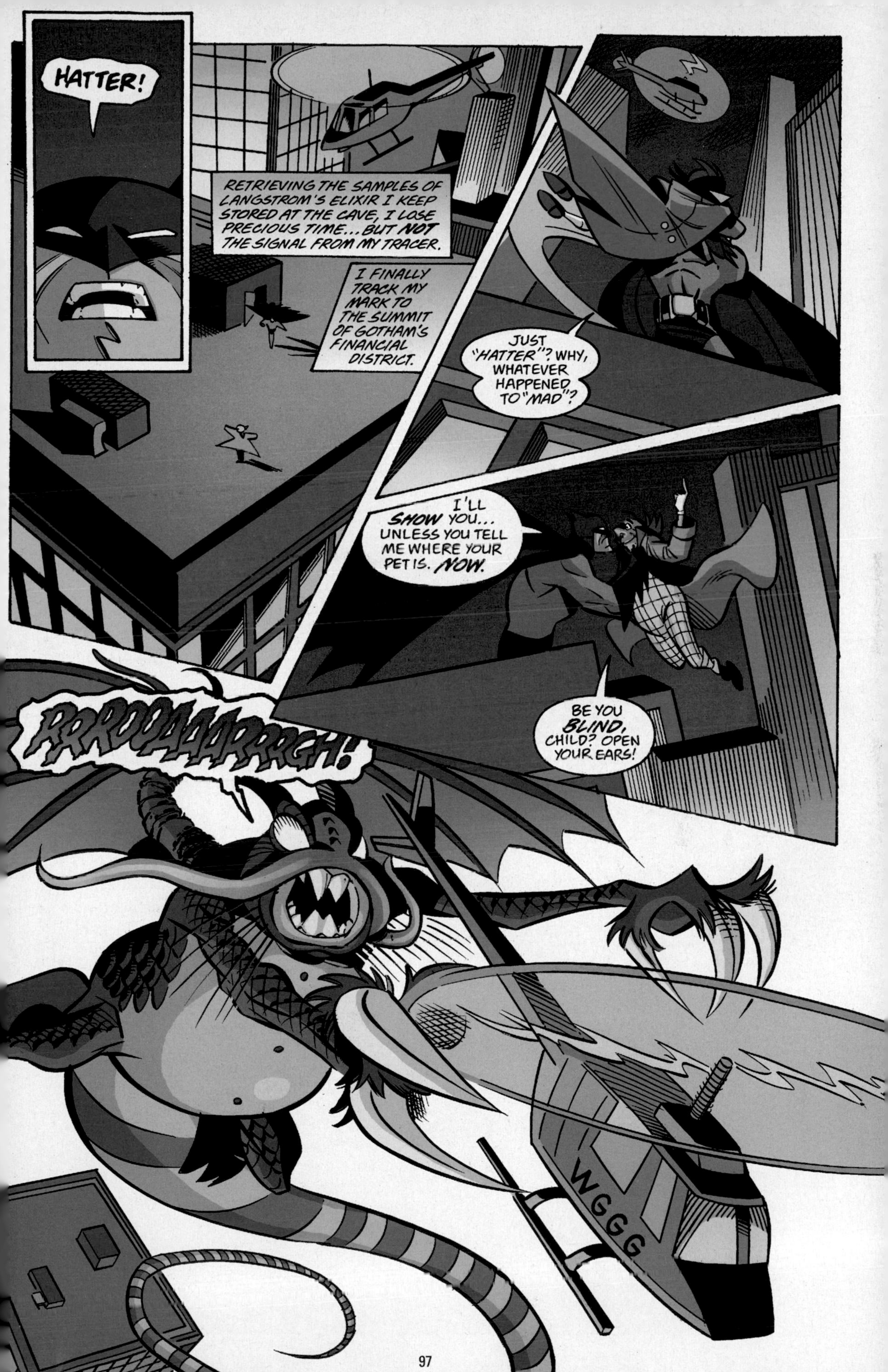
HATTER!
RETRIEVING THE SAMPLES OF LANGSTROM'S ELIXIR I KEEP STORED AT THE CAVE, I LOSE PRECIOUS TIME... BUT NOT THE SIGNAL FROM MY TRACER.
I FINALLY TRACK MY MARK TO THE SUMMIT OF GOTHAM'S FINANCIAL DISTRICT.
JUST "HATTER"? WHY, WHATEVER HAPPENED TO "MAD"?
I'LL SHOW YOU... UNLESS YOU TELL ME WHERE YOUR PET IS. NOW.
BE YOU BLIND, CHILD? OPEN YOUR EARS!
RRROOAAAARRRGH!
WGGG

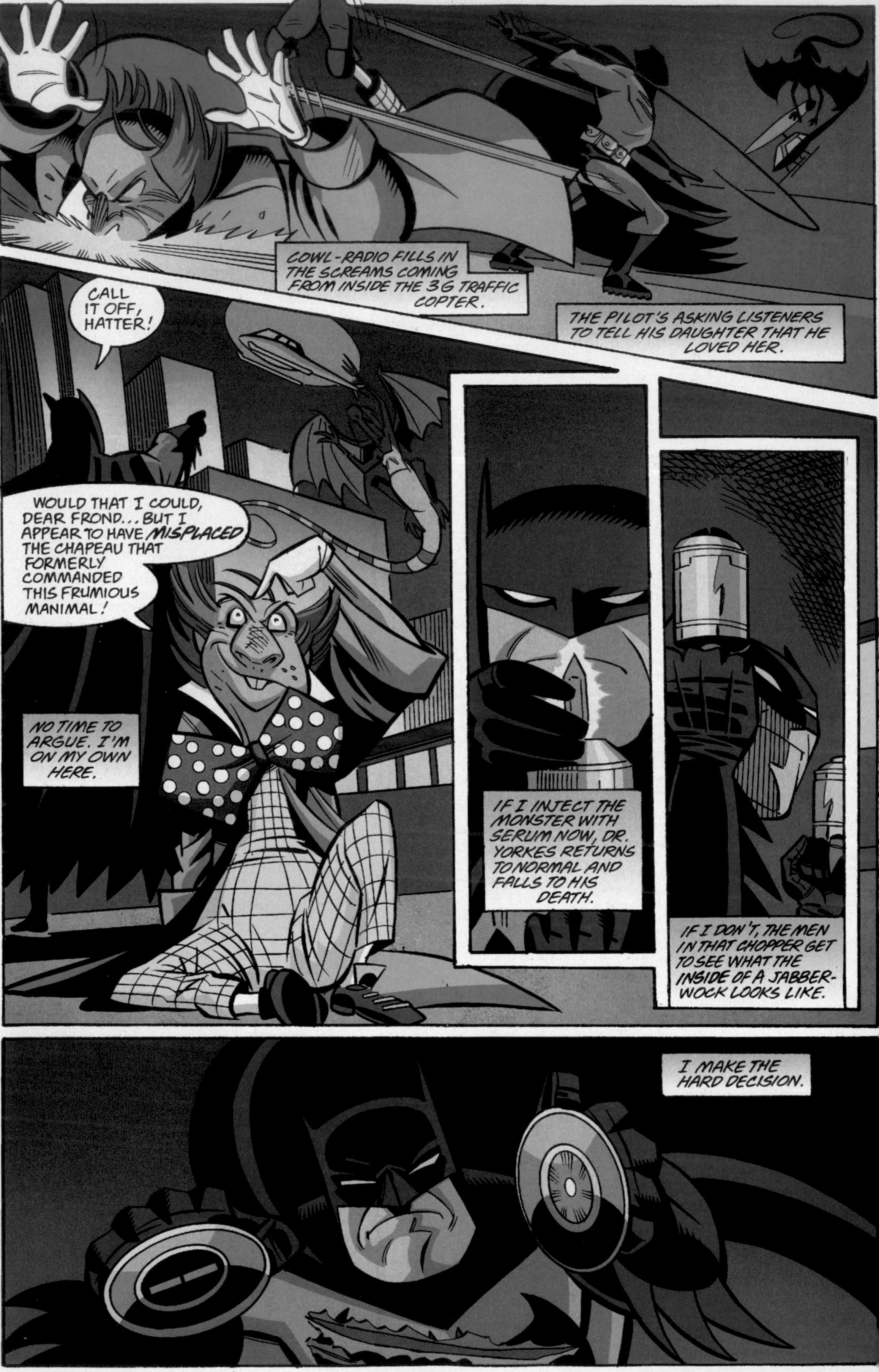
COWL-RADIO FILLS IN THE SCREAMS COMING FROM INSIDE THE 3G TRAFFIC COPTER.
THE PILOT'S ASKING LISTENERS TO TELL HIS DAUGHTER THAT HE LOVED HER.
CALL IT OFF, HATTER!
WOULD THAT I COULD, DEAR FROND... BUT I APPEAR TO HAVE MISPLACED THE CHAPEAU THAT FORMERLY COMMANDED THIS FRUMIOUS MANIMAL!
NO TIME TO ARGUE. I'M ON MY OWN HERE.
IF I INJECT THE MONSTER WITH SERUM NOW, DR. YORKES RETURNS TO NORMAL AND FALLS TO HIS DEATH.
IF I DON'T, THE MEN IN THAT CHOPPER GET TO SEE WHAT THE INSIDE OF A JABBER-WOCK LOOKS LIKE.
I MAKE THE HARD DECISION.

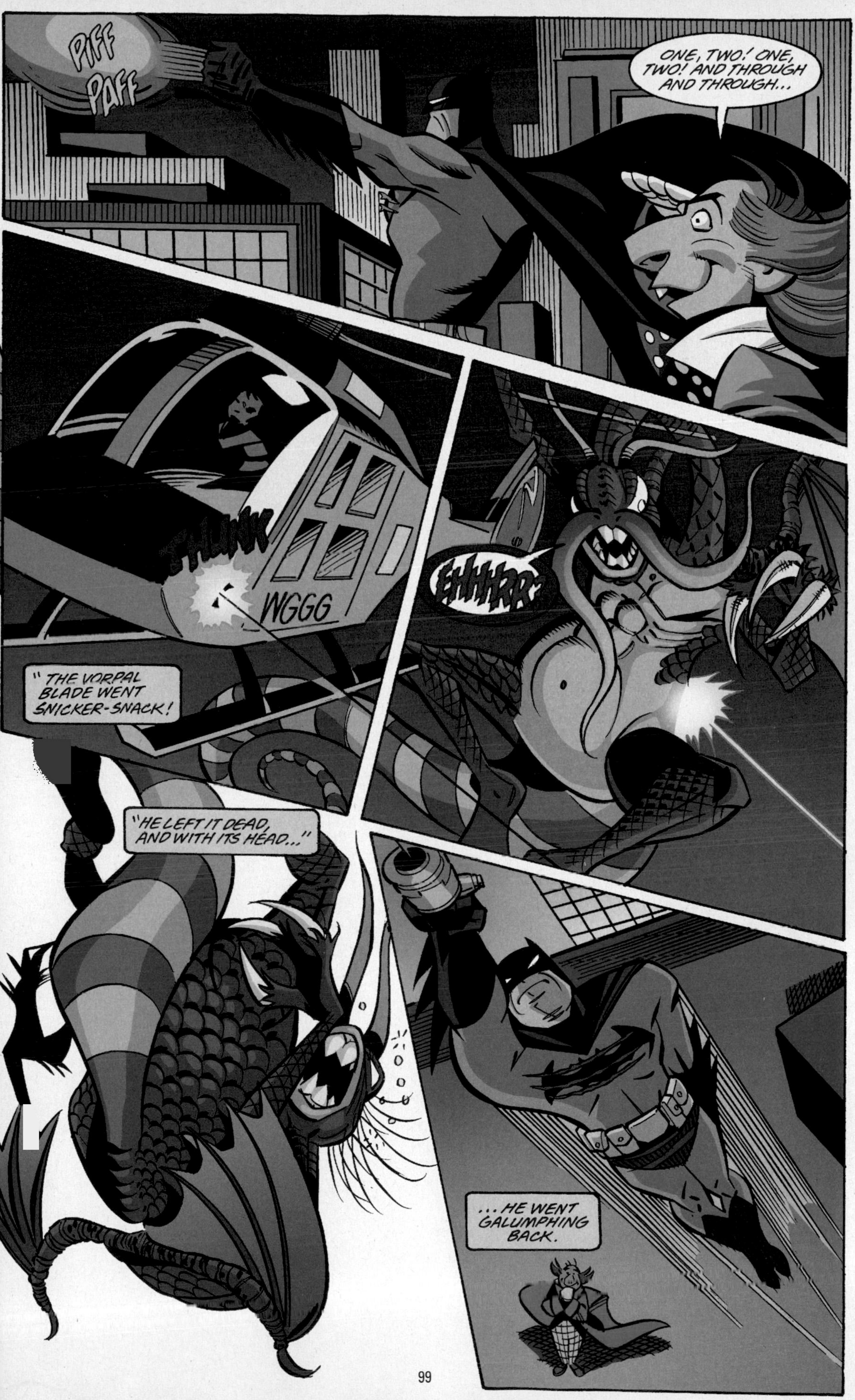
PIFF
PAFF
ONE, TWO! ONE, TWO! AND THROUGH AND THROUGH...
SHUNK
WGGG
"THE VORPAL BLADE WENT SNICKER-SNACK!
EHHRR
"HE LEFT IT DEAD, AND WITH ITS HEAD..."
...HE WENT GALUMPHING BACK.

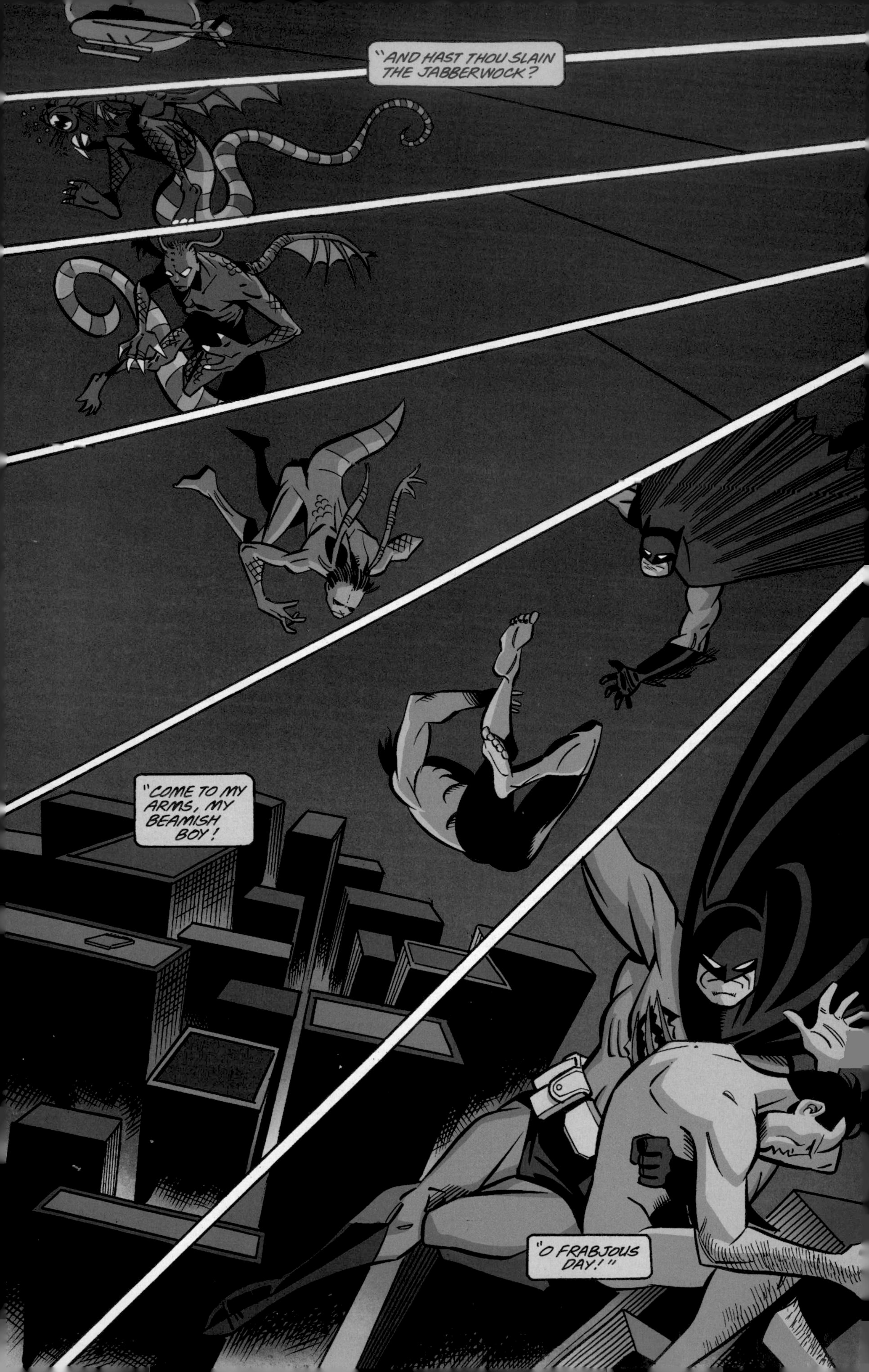
"AND HAST THOU SLAIN THE JABBERWOCK?
"COME TO MY ARMS, MY BEAMISH BOY!
"O FRABJOUS DAY!"

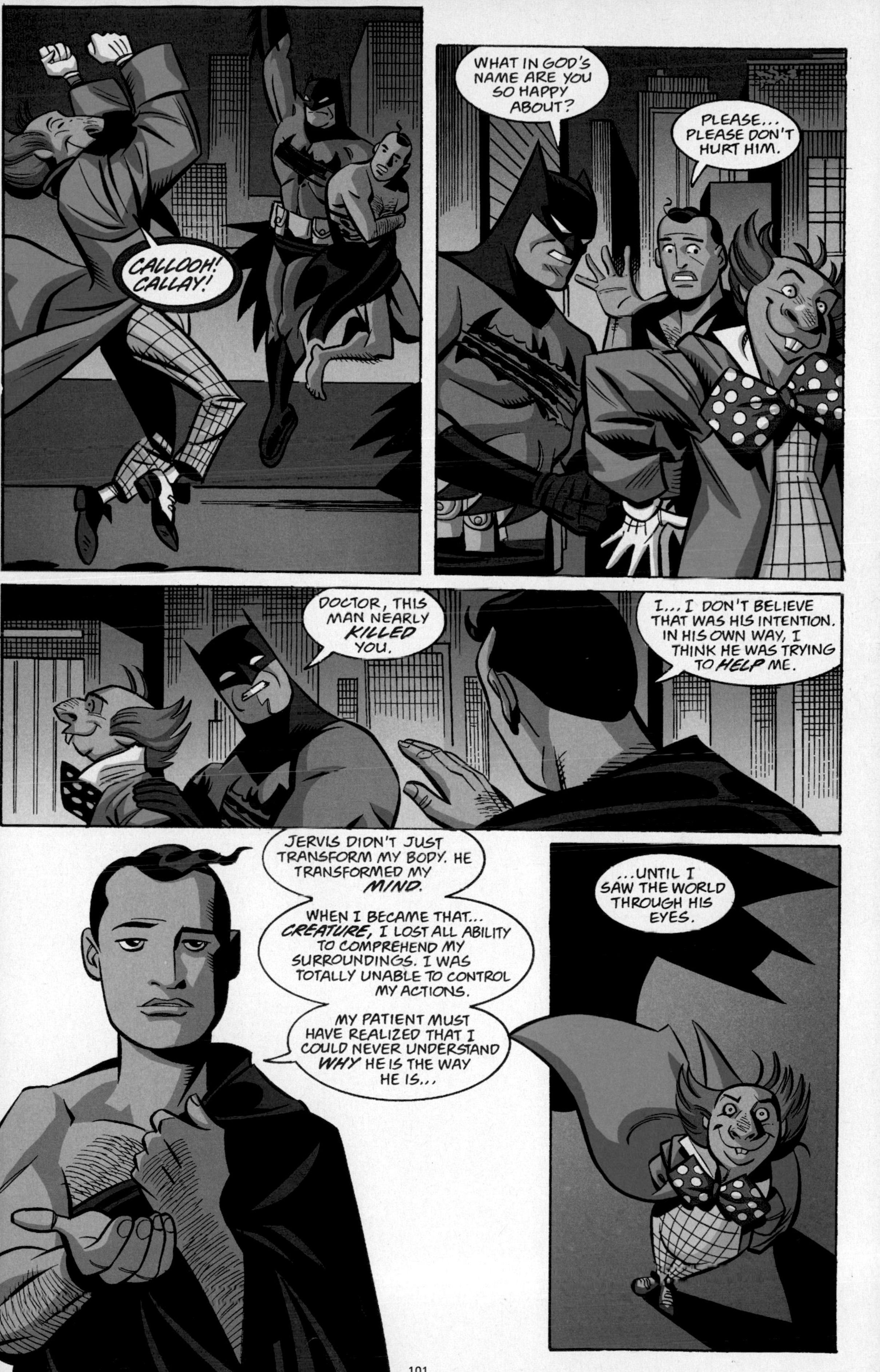
CALLOOH! CALLAY!
WHAT IN GOD'S NAME ARE YOU SO HAPPY ABOUT?
PLEASE... PLEASE DON'T HURT HIM.
DOCTOR, THIS MAN NEARLY KILLED YOU.
I... I DON'T BELIEVE THAT WAS HIS INTENTION. IN HIS OWN WAY, I THINK HE WAS TRYING TO HELP ME.
JERVIS DIDN'T JUST TRANSFORM MY BODY. HE TRANSFORMED MY MIND.
WHEN I BECAME THAT... CREATURE, I LOST ALL ABILITY TO COMPREHEND MY SURROUNDINGS. I WAS TOTALLY UNABLE TO CONTROL MY ACTIONS.
MY PATIENT MUST HAVE REALIZED THAT I COULD NEVER UNDERSTAND WHY HE IS THE WAY HE IS...
...UNTIL I SAW THE WORLD THROUGH HIS EYES.

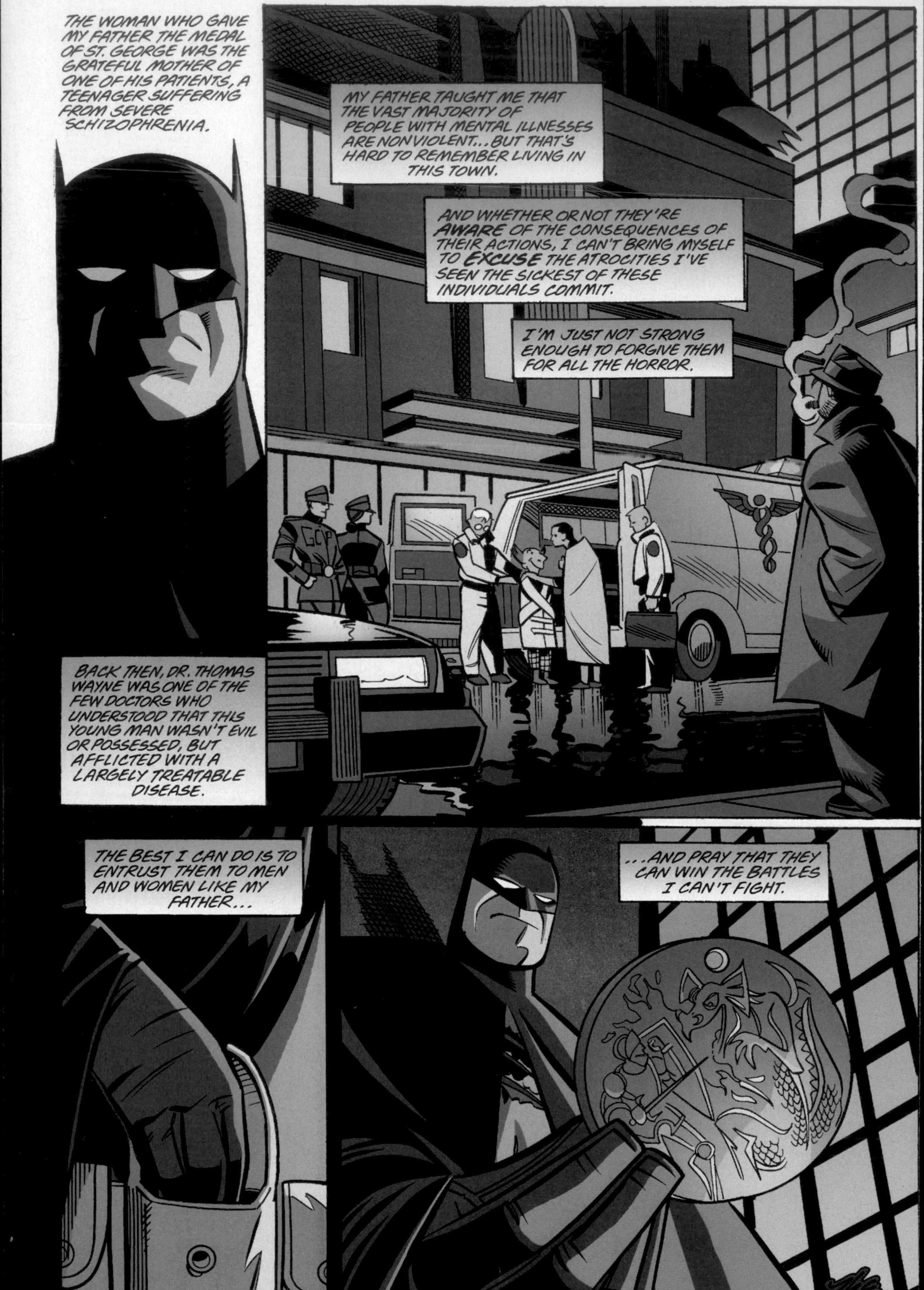
THE WOMAN WHO GAVE MY FATHER THE MEDAL OF ST. GEORGE WAS THE GRATEFUL MOTHER OF ONE OF HIS PATIENTS, A TEENAGER SUFFERING FROM SEVERE SCHIZOPHRENIA.
MY FATHER TAUGHT ME THAT THE VAST MAJORITY OF PEOPLE WITH MENTAL ILLNESSES ARE NONVIOLENT... BUT THAT'S HARD TO REMEMBER LIVING IN THIS TOWN.
AND WHETHER OR NOT THEY'RE AWARE OF THE CONSEQUENCES OF THEIR ACTIONS, I CAN'T BRING MYSELF TO EXCUSE THE ATROCITIES I'VE SEEN THE SICKEST OF THESE INDIVIDUALS COMMIT.
I'M JUST NOT STRONG ENOUGH TO FORGIVE THEM FOR ALL THE HORROR.
GCPD
BACK THEN, DR. THOMAS WAYNE WAS ONE OF THE FEW DOCTORS WHO UNDERSTOOD THAT THIS YOUNG MAN WASN'T EVIL OR POSSESSED, BUT AFFLICTED WITH A LARGELY TREATABLE DISEASE.
THE BEST I CAN DO IS TO ENTRUST THEM TO MEN AND WOMEN LIKE MY FATHER...
...AND PRAY THAT THEY CAN WIN THE BATTLES I CAN'T FIGHT.
THE END

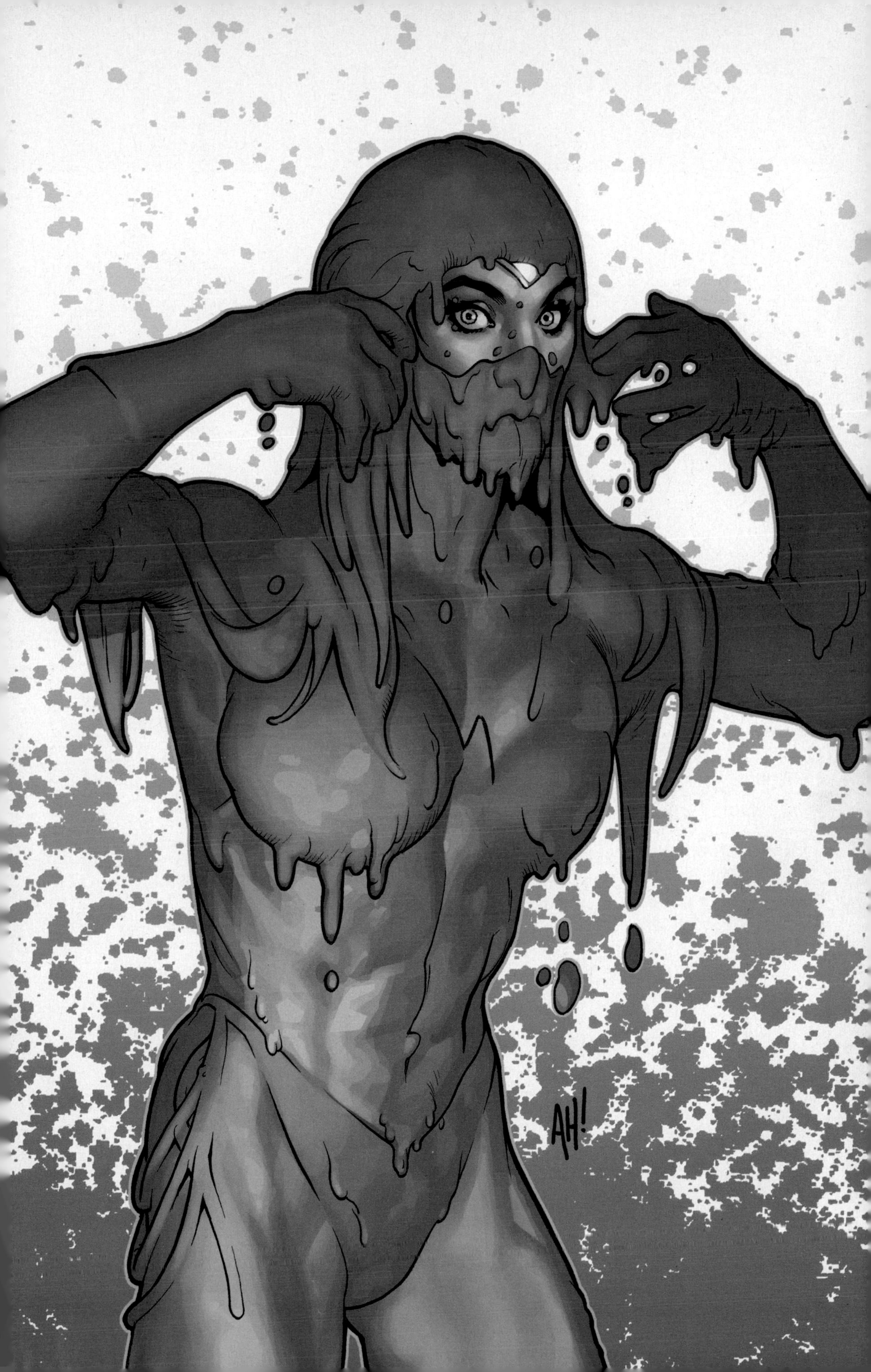
AH!

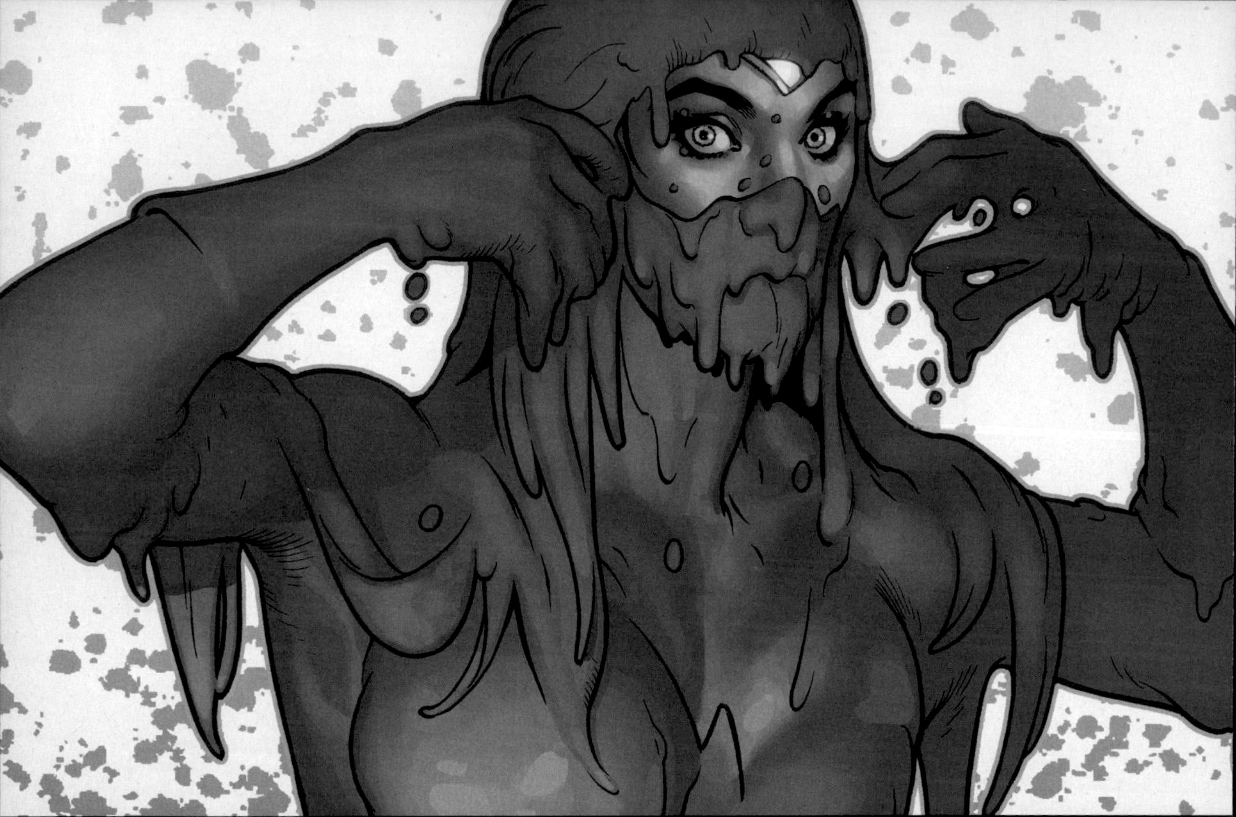

A PIECE OF YOU CHAPTER ONE

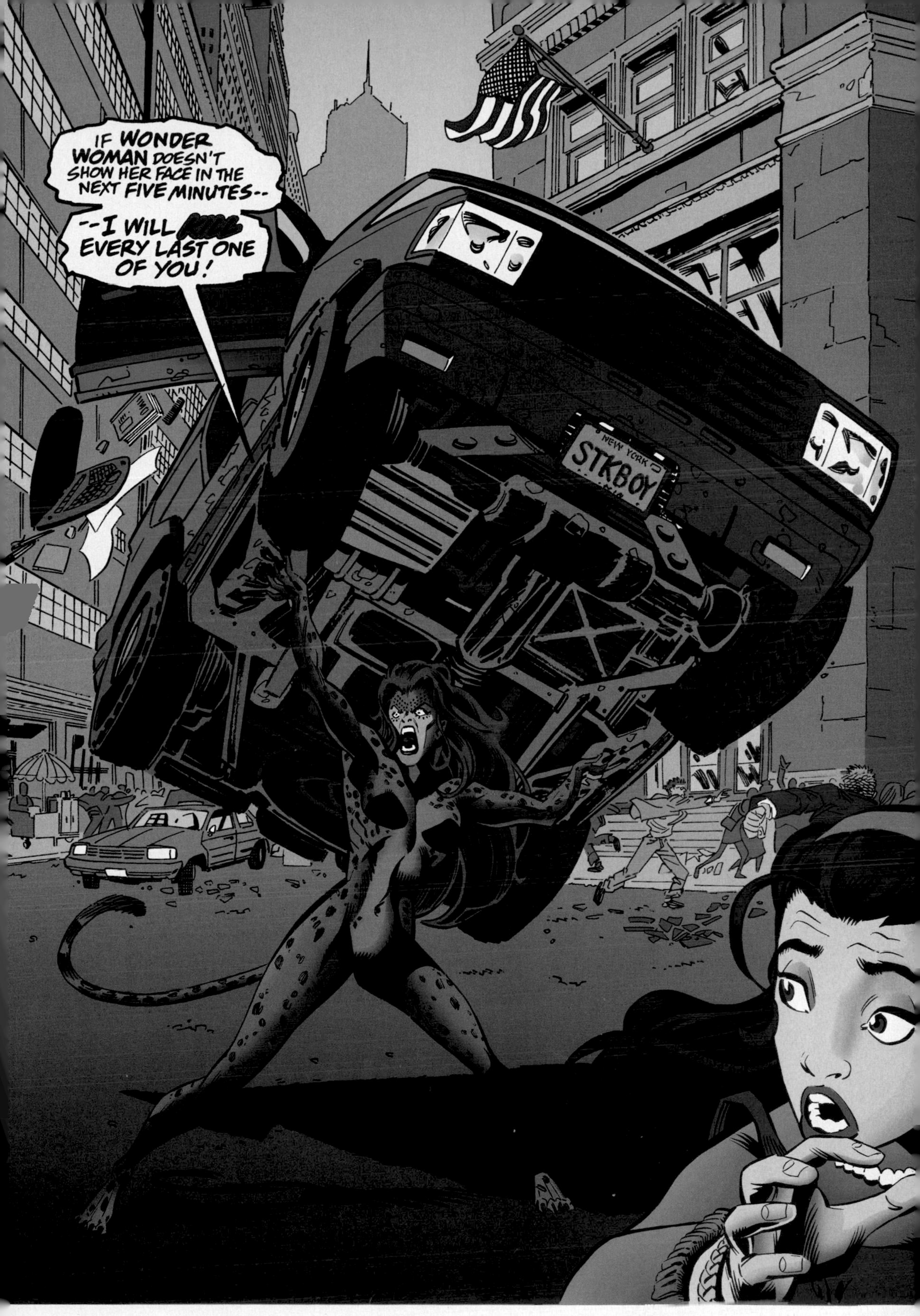
IF WONDER WOMAN DOESN'T SHOW HER FACE IN THE NEXT FIVE MINUTES--
--I WILL [redacted] EVERY LAST ONE OF YOU!
NEW YORK
STKBOY

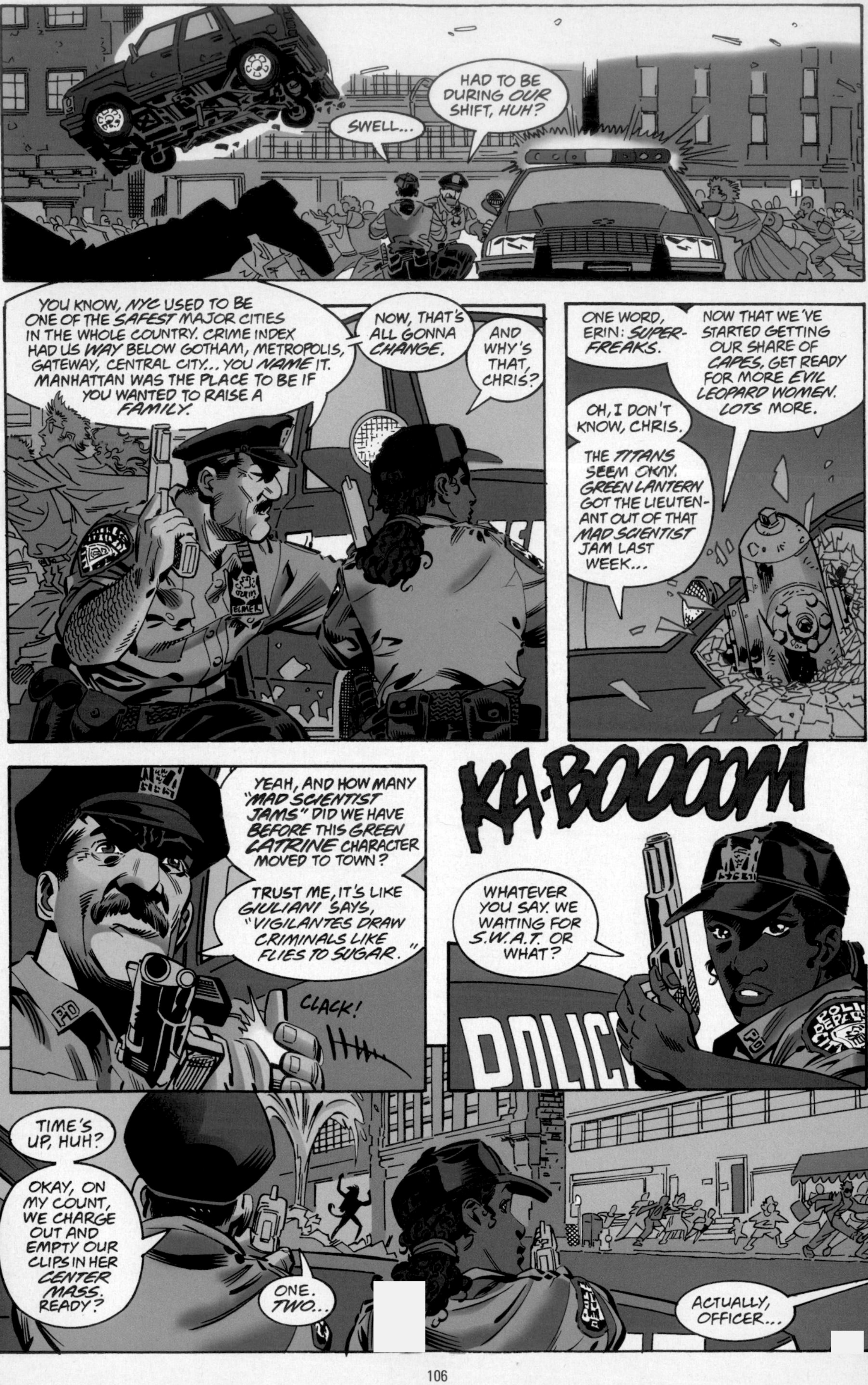

SWELL...
HAD TO BE DURING OUR SHIFT, HUH?
YOU KNOW, NYC USED TO BE ONE OF THE SAFEST MAJOR CITIES IN THE WHOLE COUNTRY. CRIME INDEX HAD US WAY BELOW GOTHAM, METROPOLIS, GATEWAY, CENTRAL CITY... YOU NAME IT. MANHATTAN WAS THE PLACE TO BE IF YOU WANTED TO RAISE A FAMILY.
NOW, THAT'S ALL GONNA CHANGE.
AND WHY'S THAT, CHRIS?
ONE WORD, ERIN: SUPER-FREAKS.
NOW THAT WE'VE STARTED GETTING OUR SHARE OF CAPES, GET READY FOR MORE EVIL LEOPARD WOMEN. LOTS MORE.
OH, I DON'T KNOW, CHRIS.
THE TITANS SEEM OKAY. GREEN LANTERN GOT THE LIEUTEN-ANT OUT OF THAT MAD SCIENTIST JAM LAST WEEK...
YEAH, AND HOW MANY "MAD SCIENTIST JAMS" DID WE HAVE BEFORE THIS GREEN LATRINE CHARACTER MOVED TO TOWN?
TRUST ME, IT'S LIKE GIULIANI SAYS, "VIGILANTES DRAW CRIMINALS LIKE FLIES TO SUGAR."
CLACK!
KA-BOOOOOM
WHATEVER YOU SAY. WE WAITING FOR S.W.A.T. OR WHAT?
POLICE
TIME'S UP, HUH?
OKAY, ON MY COUNT, WE CHARGE OUT AND EMPTY OUR CLIPS IN HER CENTER MASS. READY?
ONE. TWO...
ACTUALLY, OFFICER...

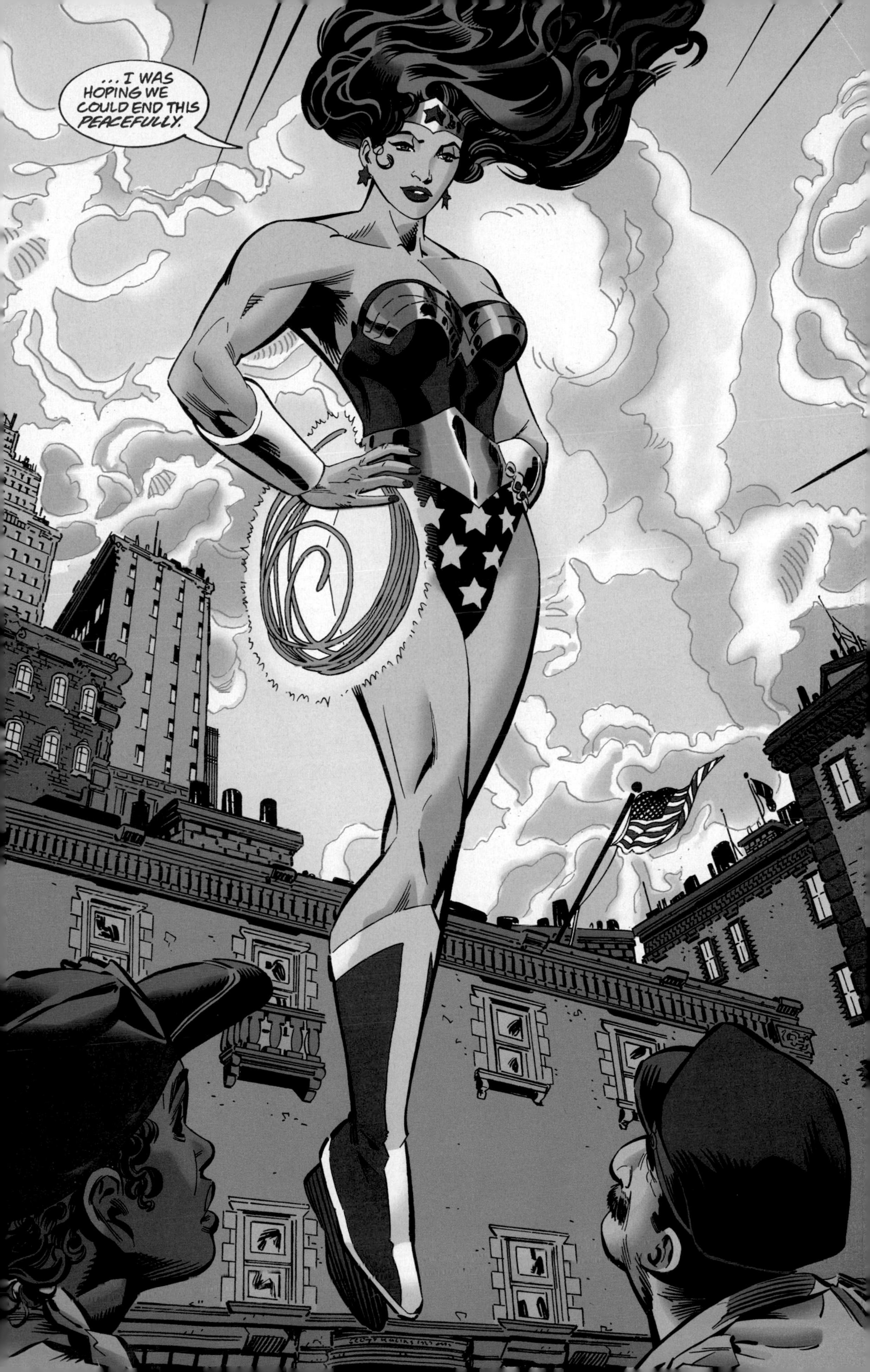
...I WAS HOPING WE COULD END THIS PEACEFULLY.

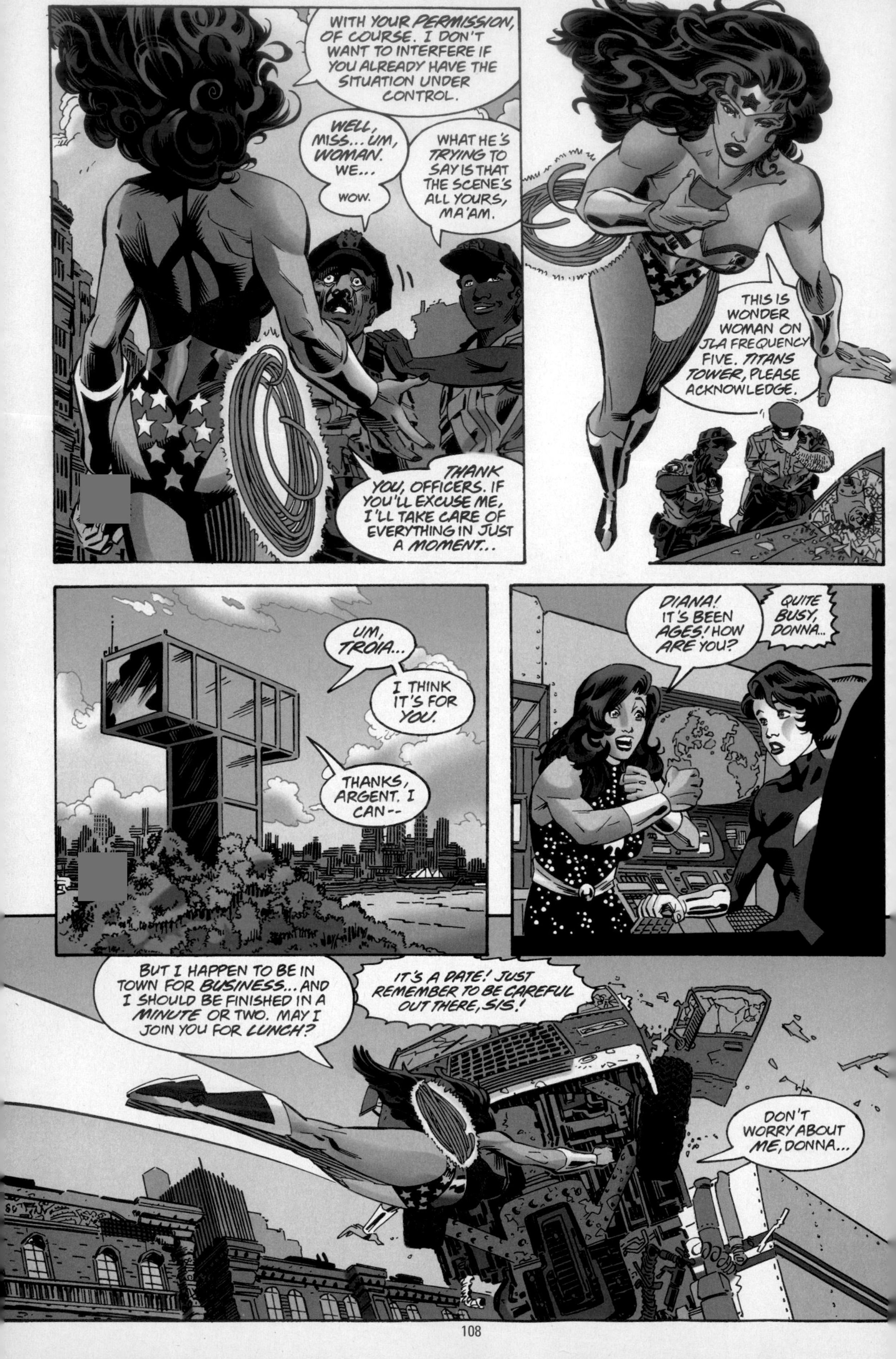
WITH YOUR PERMISSION, OF COURSE. I DON'T WANT TO INTERFERE IF YOU ALREADY HAVE THE SITUATION UNDER CONTROL.
WELL, MISS... UM, WOMAN. WE...
WOW.
WHAT HE'S TRYING TO SAY IS THAT THE SCENE'S ALL YOURS, MA'AM.
THANK YOU, OFFICERS. IF YOU'LL EXCUSE ME, I'LL TAKE CARE OF EVERYTHING IN JUST A MOMENT...
THIS IS WONDER WOMAN ON JLA FREQUENCY FIVE. TITANS TOWER, PLEASE ACKNOWLEDGE.
UM, TROIA...
I THINK IT'S FOR YOU.
THANKS, ARGENT. I CAN--
DIANA! IT'S BEEN AGES! HOW ARE YOU?
QUITE BUSY, DONNA...
BUT I HAPPEN TO BE IN TOWN FOR BUSINESS... AND I SHOULD BE FINISHED IN A MINUTE OR TWO. MAY I JOIN YOU FOR LUNCH?
IT'S A DATE! JUST REMEMBER TO BE CAREFUL OUT THERE, SIS!
DON'T WORRY ABOUT ME, DONNA...

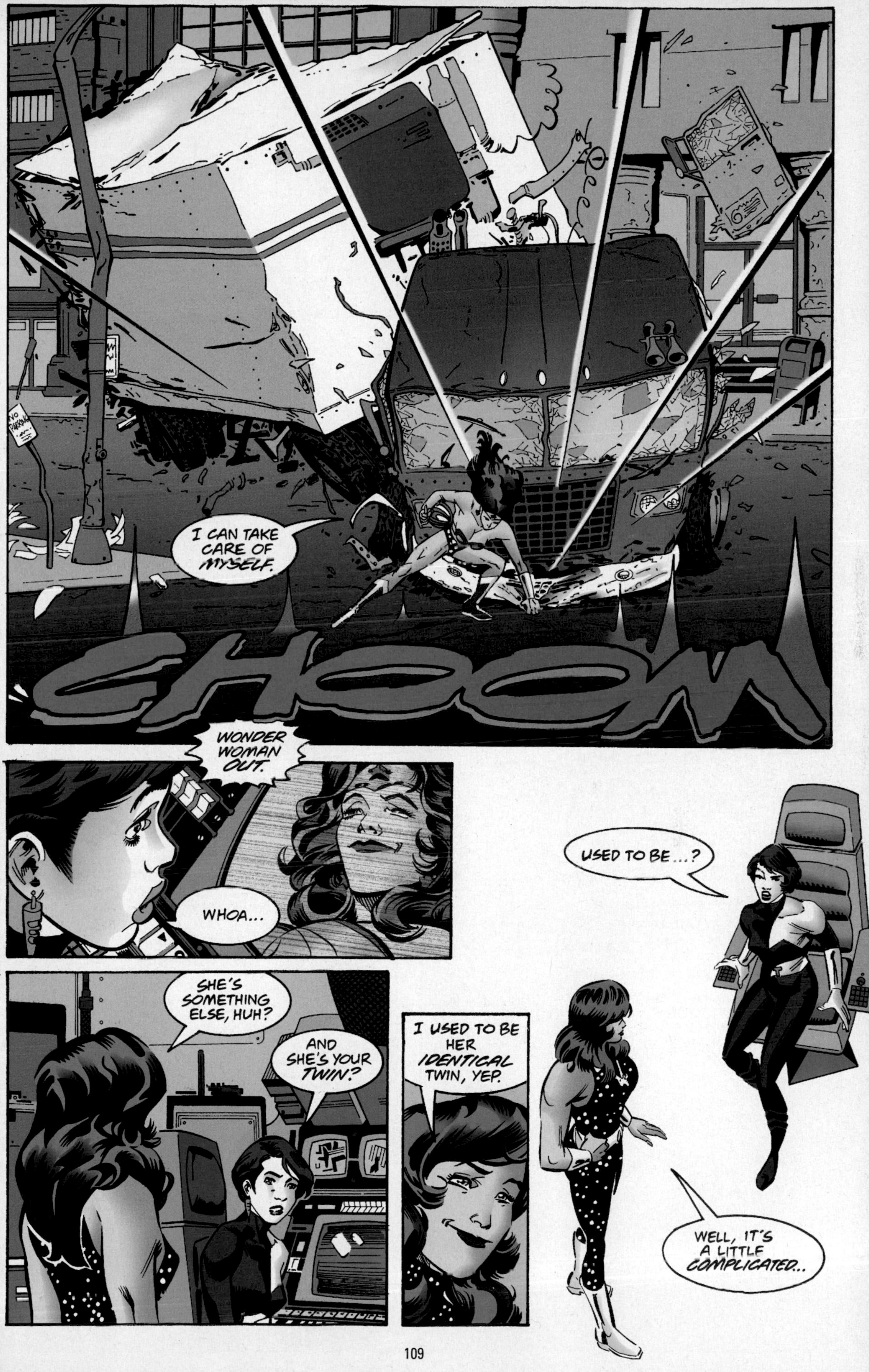
I CAN TAKE CARE OF MYSELF.
CHOOM
WONDER WOMAN OUT.
WHOA...
USED TO BE...?
SHE'S SOMETHING ELSE, HUH?
AND SHE'S YOUR TWIN?
I USED TO BE HER IDENTICAL TWIN, YEP.
WELL, IT'S A LITTLE COMPLICATED...

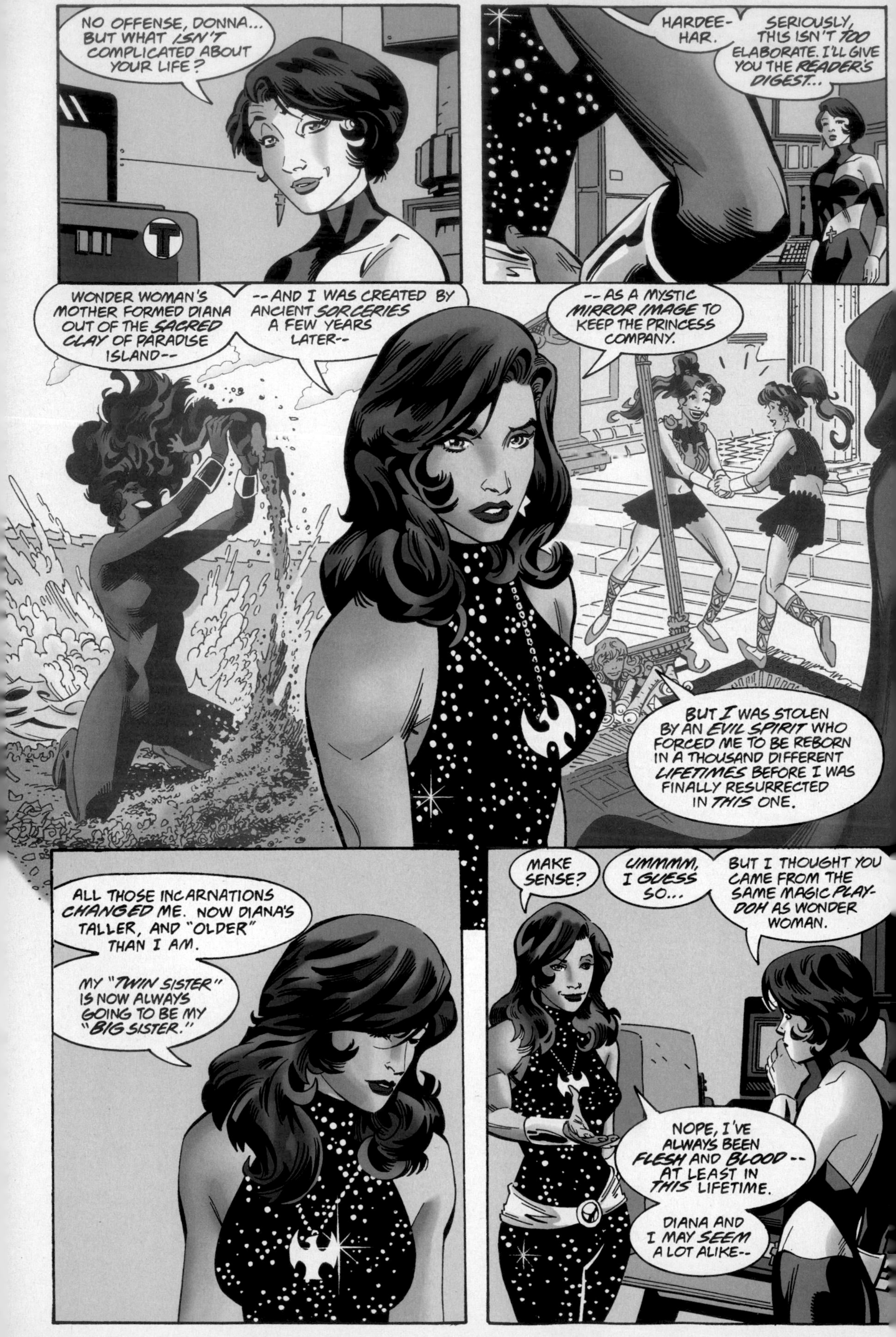
NO OFFENSE, DONNA... BUT WHAT ISN'T COMPLICATED ABOUT YOUR LIFE?
HARDEE-HAR.
SERIOUSLY, THIS ISN'T TOO ELABORATE. I'LL GIVE YOU THE READER'S DIGEST...
WONDER WOMAN'S MOTHER FORMED DIANA OUT OF THE SACRED CLAY OF PARADISE ISLAND--
--AND I WAS CREATED BY ANCIENT SORCERIES A FEW YEARS LATER--
--AS A MYSTIC MIRROR IMAGE TO KEEP THE PRINCESS COMPANY.
BUT I WAS STOLEN BY AN EVIL SPIRIT WHO FORCED ME TO BE REBORN IN A THOUSAND DIFFERENT LIFETIMES BEFORE I WAS FINALLY RESURRECTED IN THIS ONE.
ALL THOSE INCARNATIONS CHANGED ME. NOW DIANA'S TALLER, AND "OLDER" THAN I AM.
MY "TWIN SISTER" IS NOW ALWAYS GOING TO BE MY "BIG SISTER."
MAKE SENSE?
UMMMM, I GUESS SO...
BUT I THOUGHT YOU CAME FROM THE SAME MAGIC PLAY-DOH AS WONDER WOMAN.
NOPE, I'VE ALWAYS BEEN FLESH AND BLOOD-- AT LEAST IN THIS LIFETIME.
DIANA AND I MAY SEEM A LOT ALIKE--

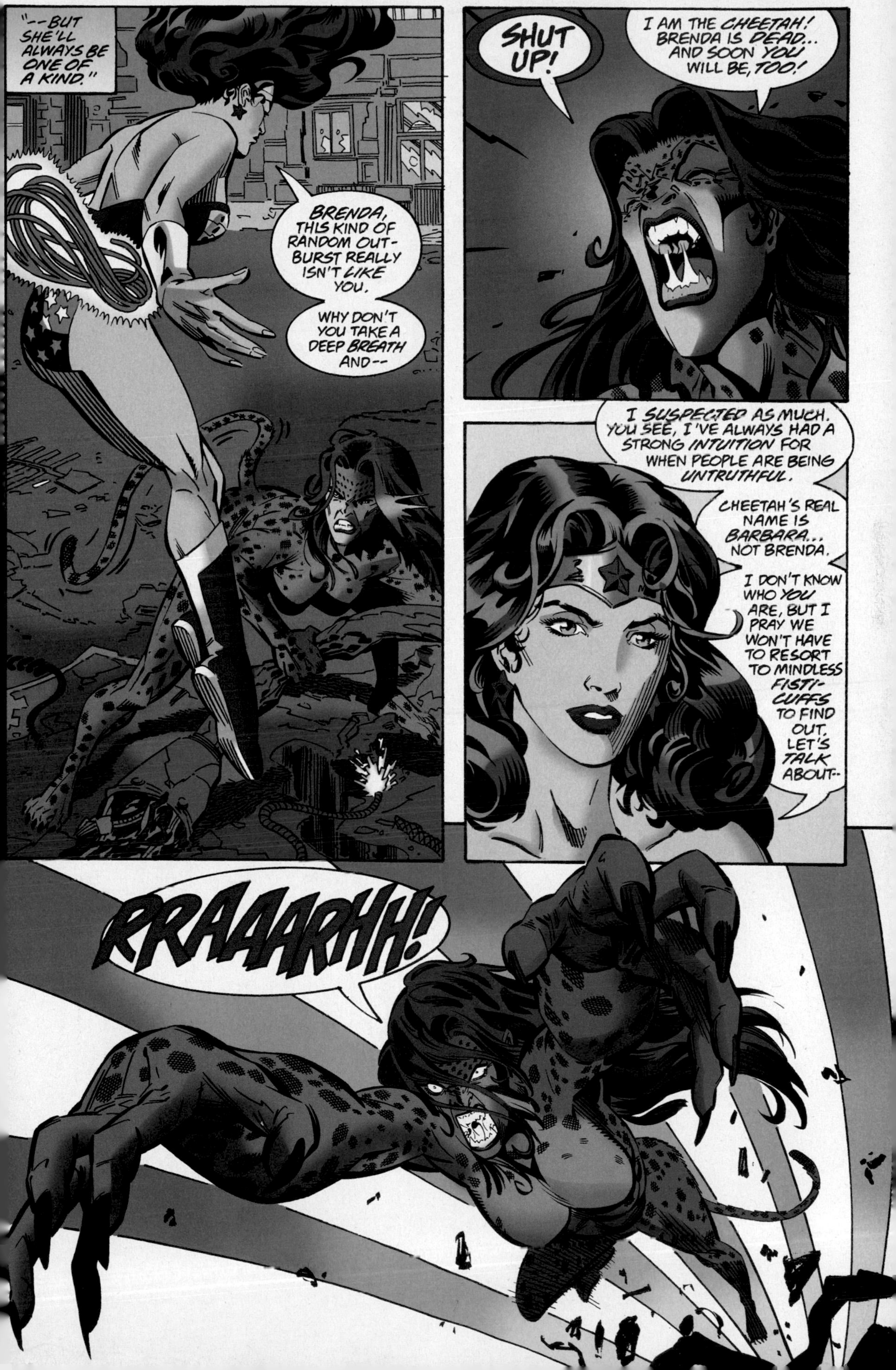
"--BUT SHE'LL ALWAYS BE ONE OF A KIND."
BRENDA, THIS KIND OF RANDOM OUT-BURST REALLY ISN'T LIKE YOU.
WHY DON'T YOU TAKE A DEEP BREATH AND--
SHUT UP!
I AM THE CHEETAH! BRENDA IS DEAD... AND SOON YOU WILL BE, TOO!
I SUSPECTED AS MUCH. YOU SEE, I'VE ALWAYS HAD A STRONG INTUITION FOR WHEN PEOPLE ARE BEING UNTRUTHFUL.
CHEETAH'S REAL NAME IS BARBARA... NOT BRENDA.
I DON'T KNOW WHO YOU ARE, BUT I PRAY WE WON'T HAVE TO RESORT TO MINDLESS FISTI-CUFFS TO FIND OUT. LET'S TALK ABOUT--
RRAAARHH!

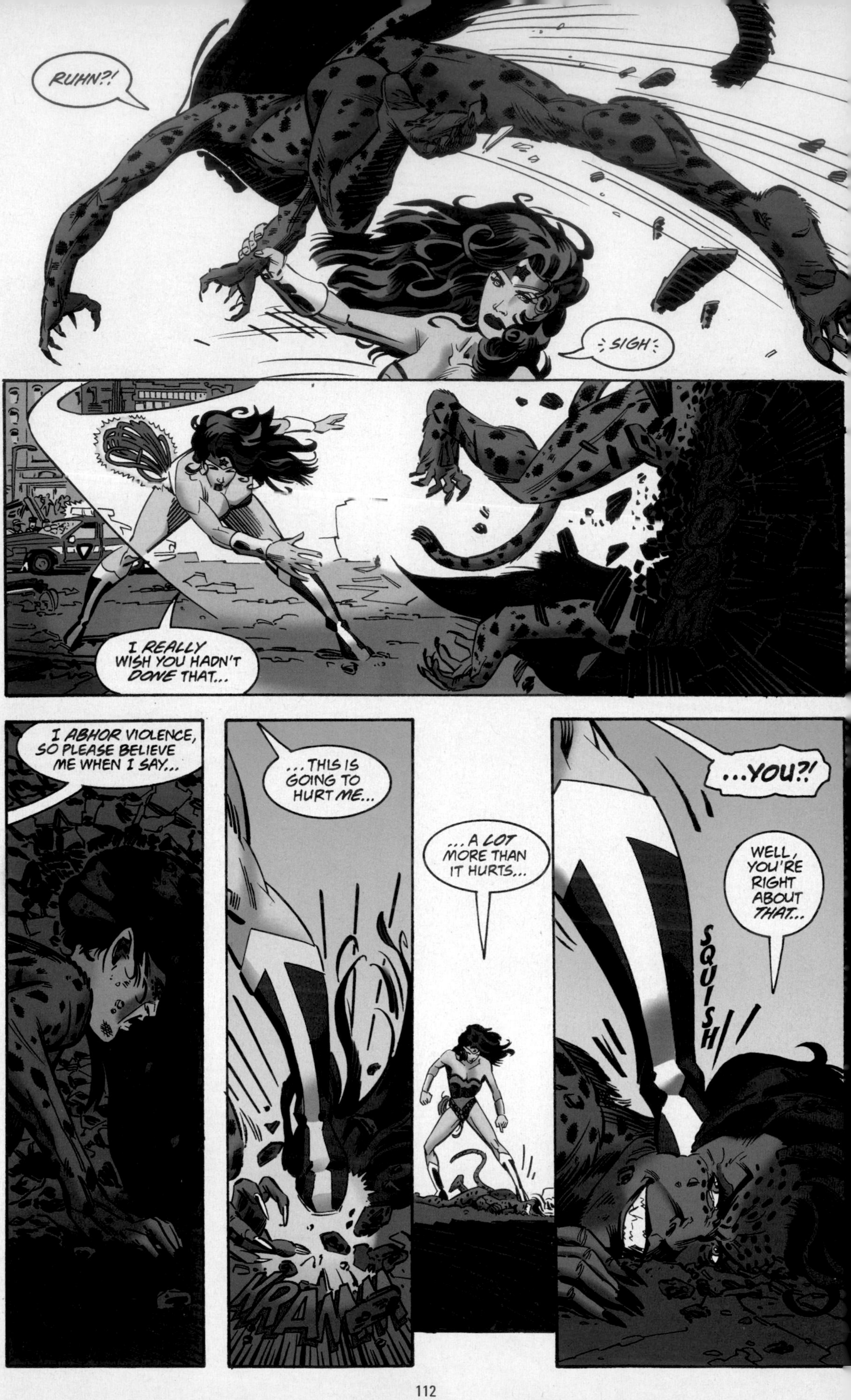
RUHN?!
SIGH
I REALLY WISH YOU HADN'T DONE THAT...
I ABHOR VIOLENCE, SO PLEASE BELIEVE ME WHEN I SAY...
...THIS IS GOING TO HURT ME...
...A LOT MORE THAN IT HURTS...
...YOU?!
WELL, YOU'RE RIGHT ABOUT THAT...
SQUISH

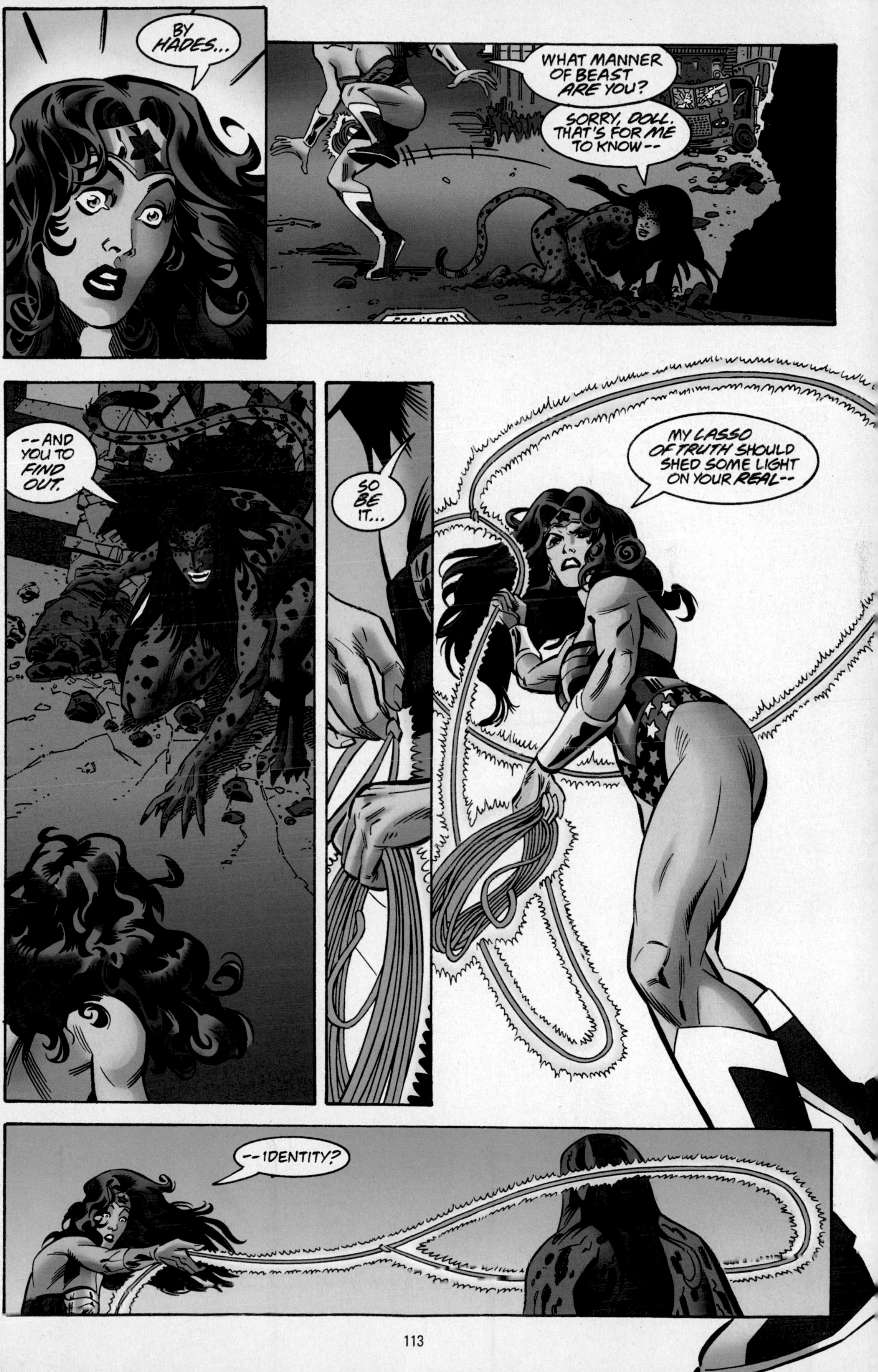
BY HADES...
WHAT MANNER OF BEAST ARE YOU?
SORRY, DOLL. THAT'S FOR ME TO KNOW--
--AND YOU TO FIND OUT.
SO BE IT...
MY LASSO OF TRUTH SHOULD SHED SOME LIGHT ON YOUR REAL--
--IDENTITY?

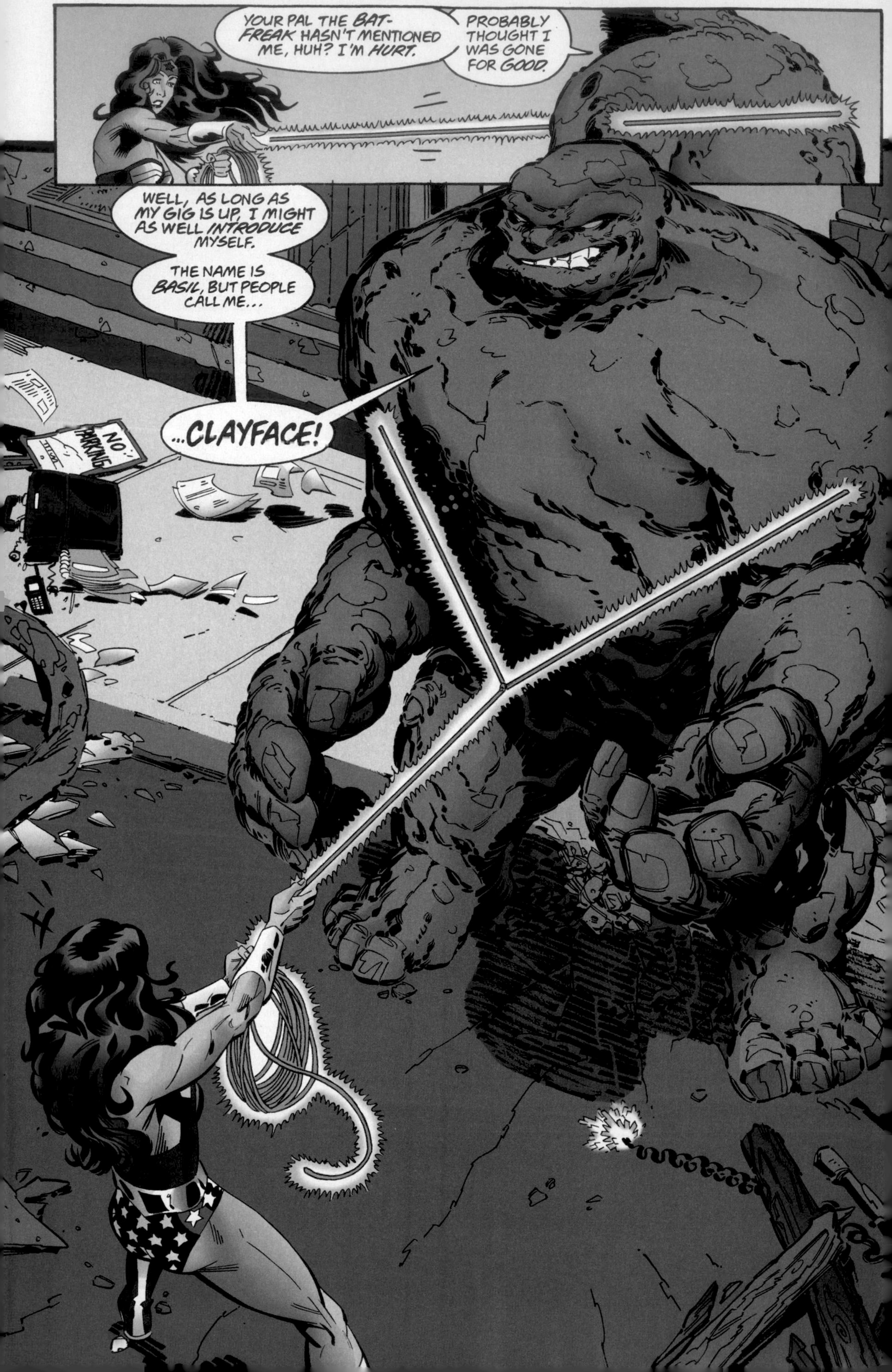
YOUR PAL THE BAT-FREAK HASN'T MENTIONED ME, HUH? I'M HURT.
PROBABLY THOUGHT I WAS GONE FOR GOOD.
WELL, AS LONG AS MY GIG IS UP, I MIGHT AS WELL INTRODUCE MYSELF.
THE NAME IS BASIL, BUT PEOPLE CALL ME...
...CLAYFACE!
NO PARKING

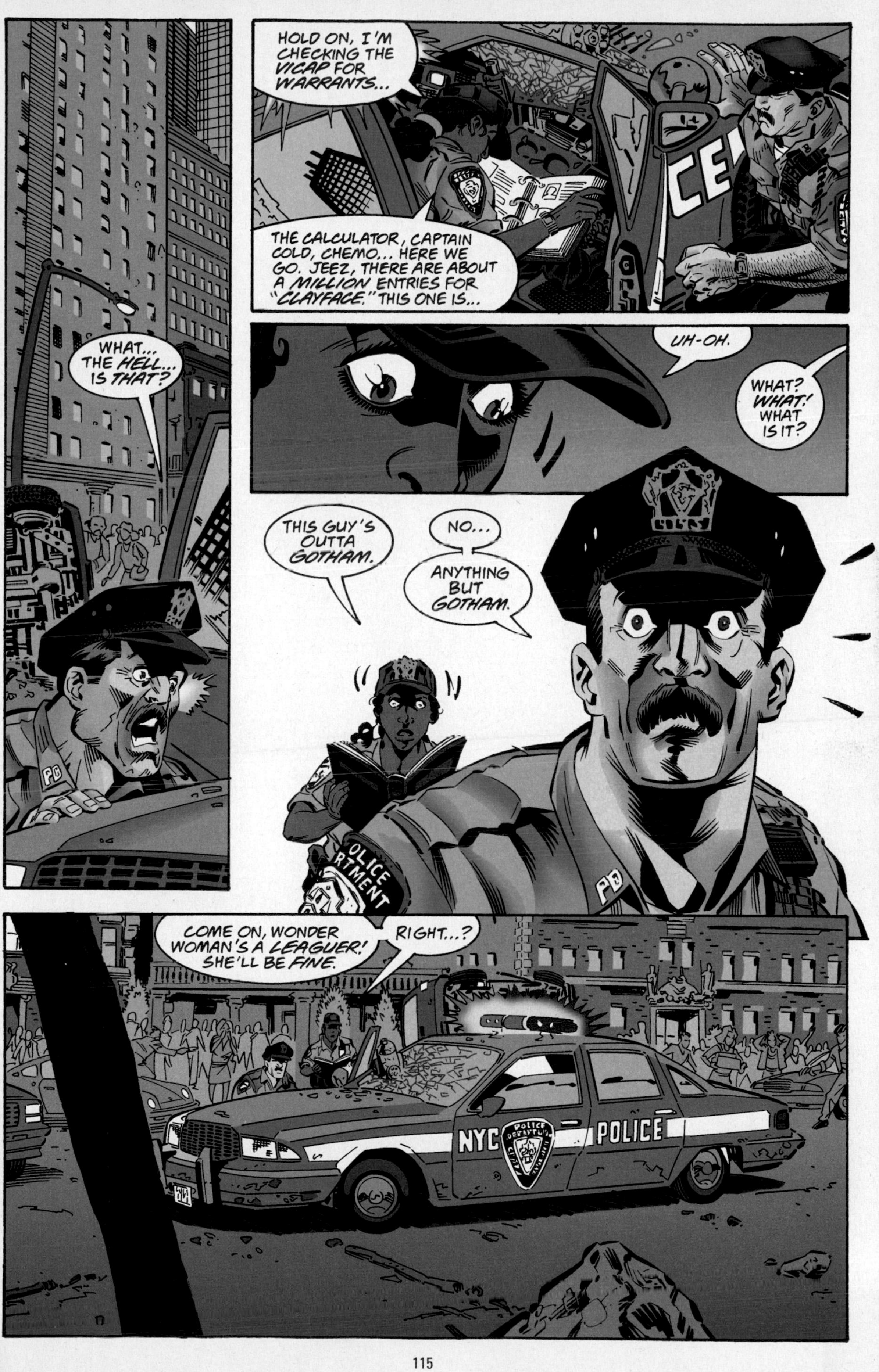
HOLD ON, I'M CHECKING THE VICAP FOR WARRANTS...
THE CALCULATOR, CAPTAIN COLD, CHEMO... HERE WE GO. JEEZ, THERE ARE ABOUT A MILLION ENTRIES FOR "CLAYFACE." THIS ONE IS...
WHAT... THE HELL... IS THAT?
UH-OH.
WHAT? WHAT! WHAT IS IT?
THIS GUY'S OUTTA GOTHAM.
NO...
ANYTHING BUT GOTHAM.
COME ON, WONDER WOMAN'S A LEAGUER! SHE'LL BE FINE.
RIGHT...?
NYC POLICE

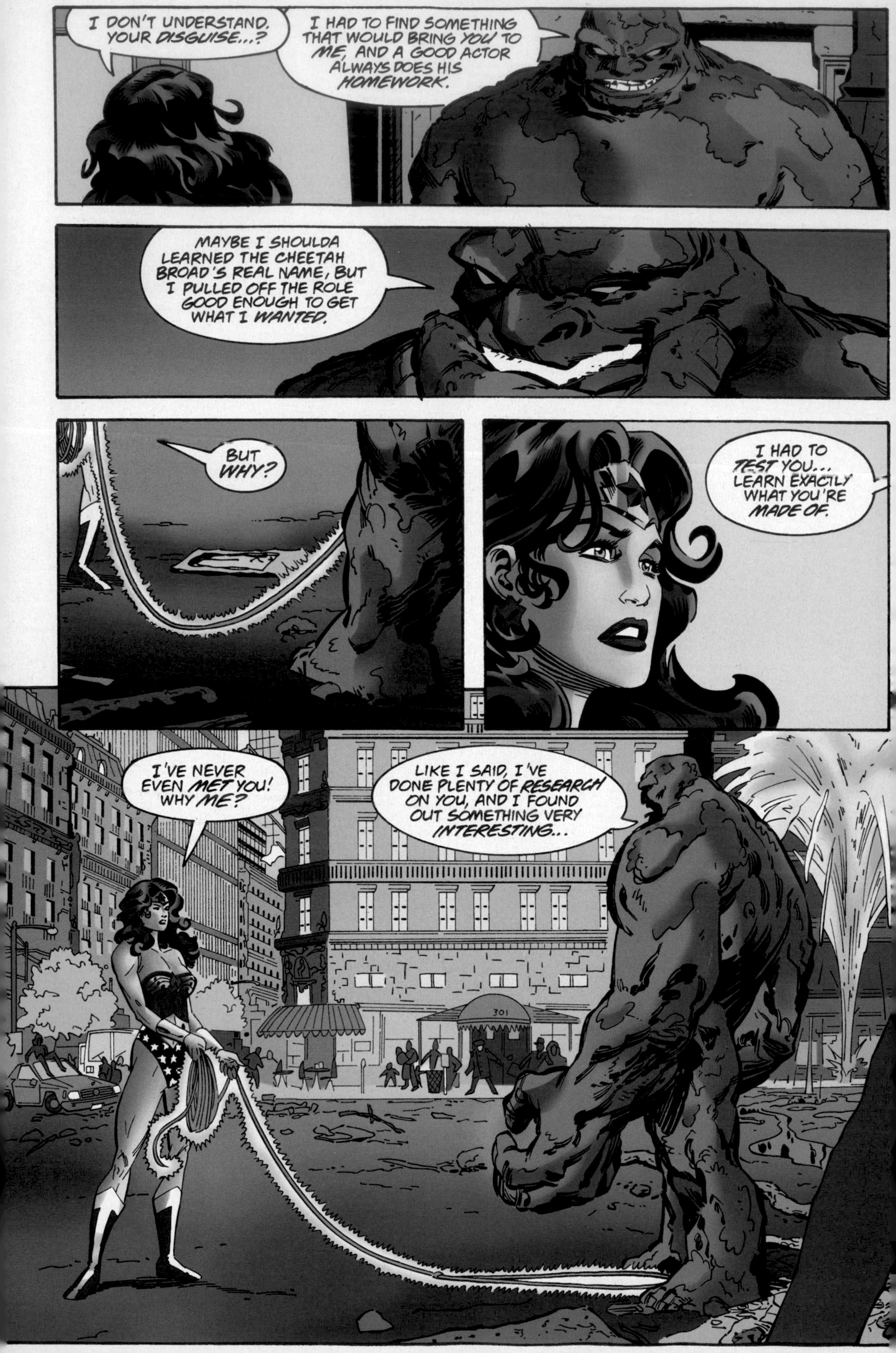
I DON'T UNDERSTAND. YOUR DISGUISE...?
I HAD TO FIND SOMETHING THAT WOULD BRING YOU TO ME, AND A GOOD ACTOR ALWAYS DOES HIS HOMEWORK.
MAYBE I SHOULDA LEARNED THE CHEETAH BROAD'S REAL NAME, BUT I PULLED OFF THE ROLE GOOD ENOUGH TO GET WHAT I WANTED.
BUT WHY?
I HAD TO TEST YOU... LEARN EXACTLY WHAT YOU'RE MADE OF.
I'VE NEVER EVEN MET YOU! WHY ME?
LIKE I SAID, I'VE DONE PLENTY OF RESEARCH ON YOU, AND I FOUND OUT SOMETHING VERY INTERESTING...
301

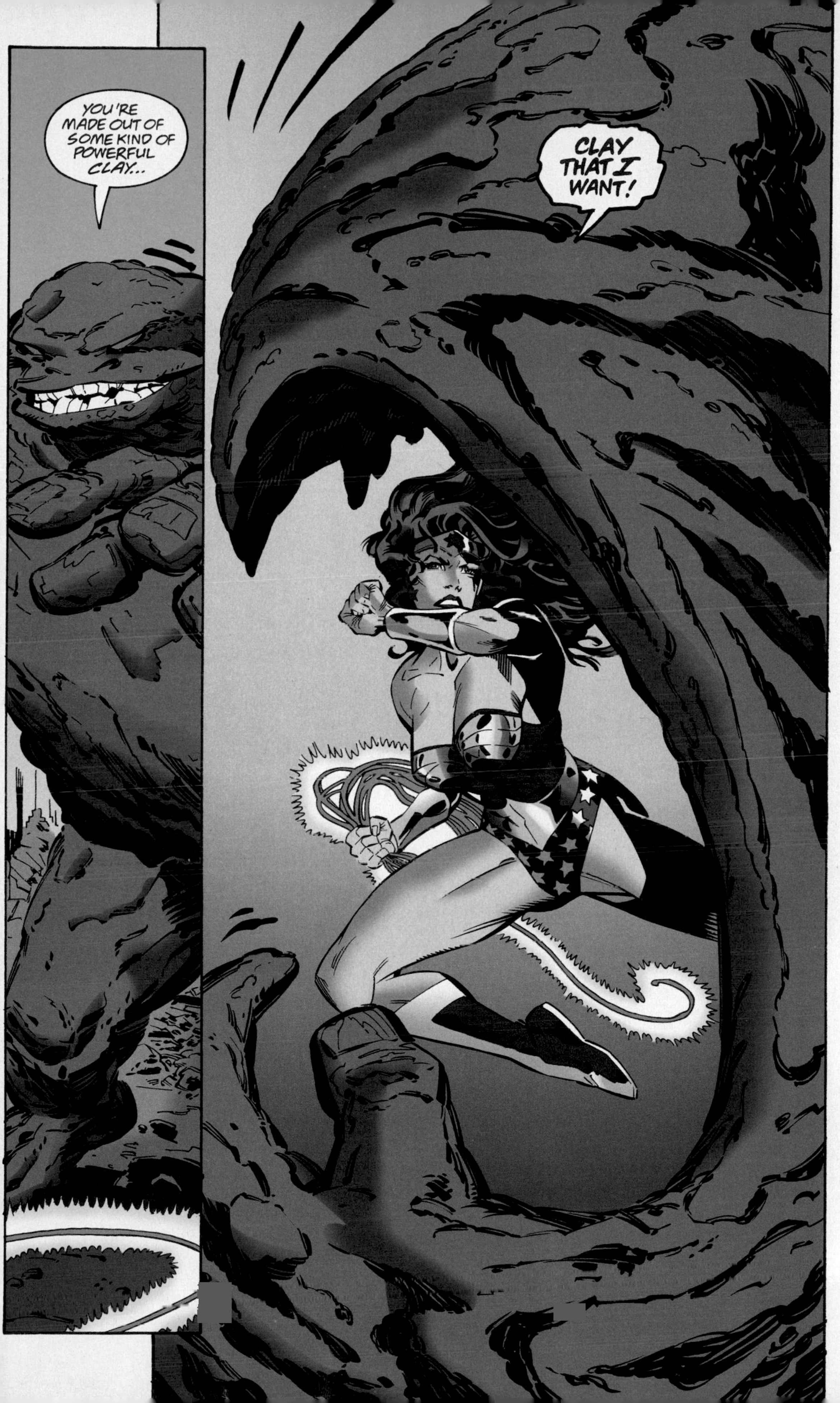
YOU'RE MADE OUT OF SOME KIND OF POWERFUL CLAY...
CLAY THAT I WANT!

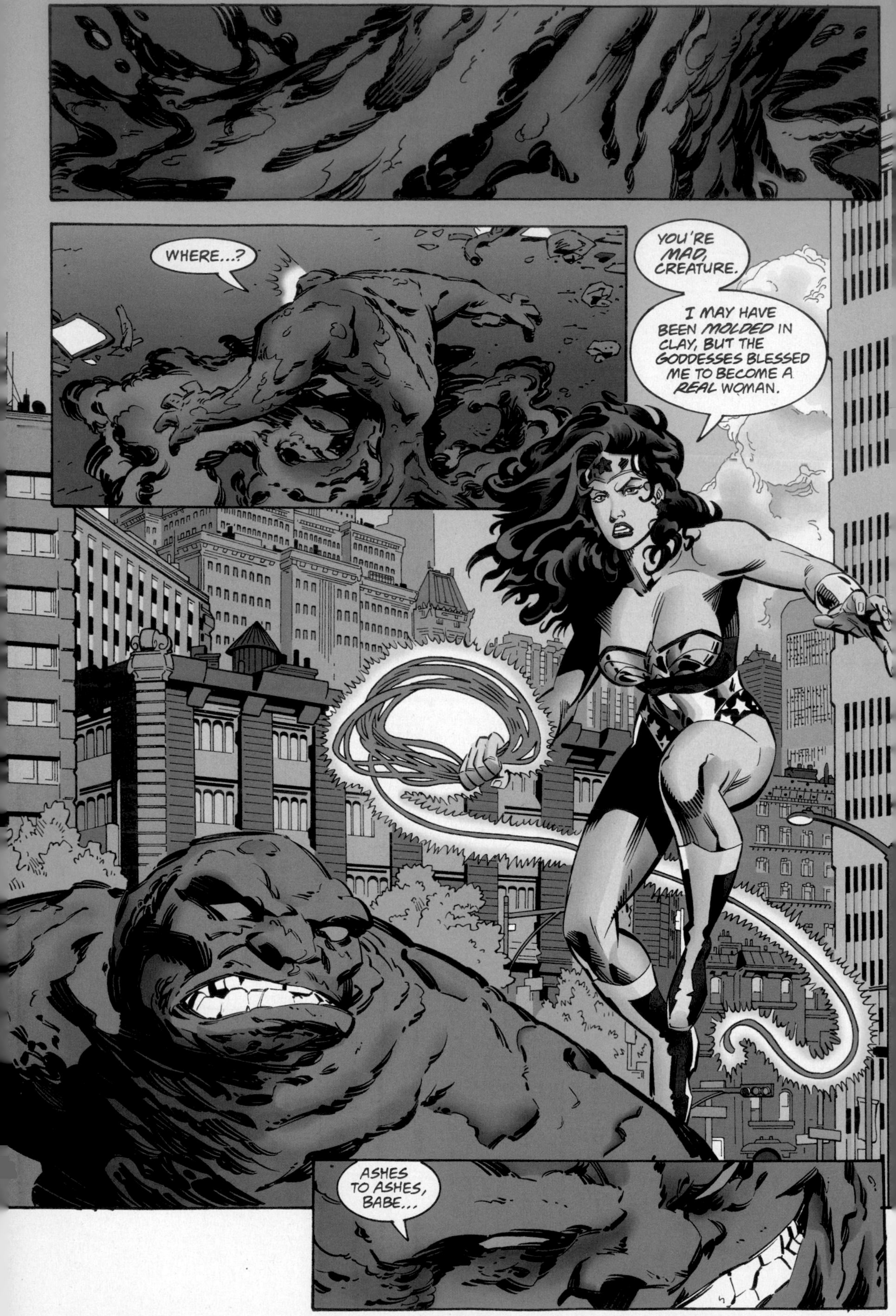
WHERE...?
YOU'RE MAD, CREATURE.
I MAY HAVE BEEN MOLDED IN CLAY, BUT THE GODDESSES BLESSED ME TO BECOME A REAL WOMAN.
ASHES TO ASHES, BABE...

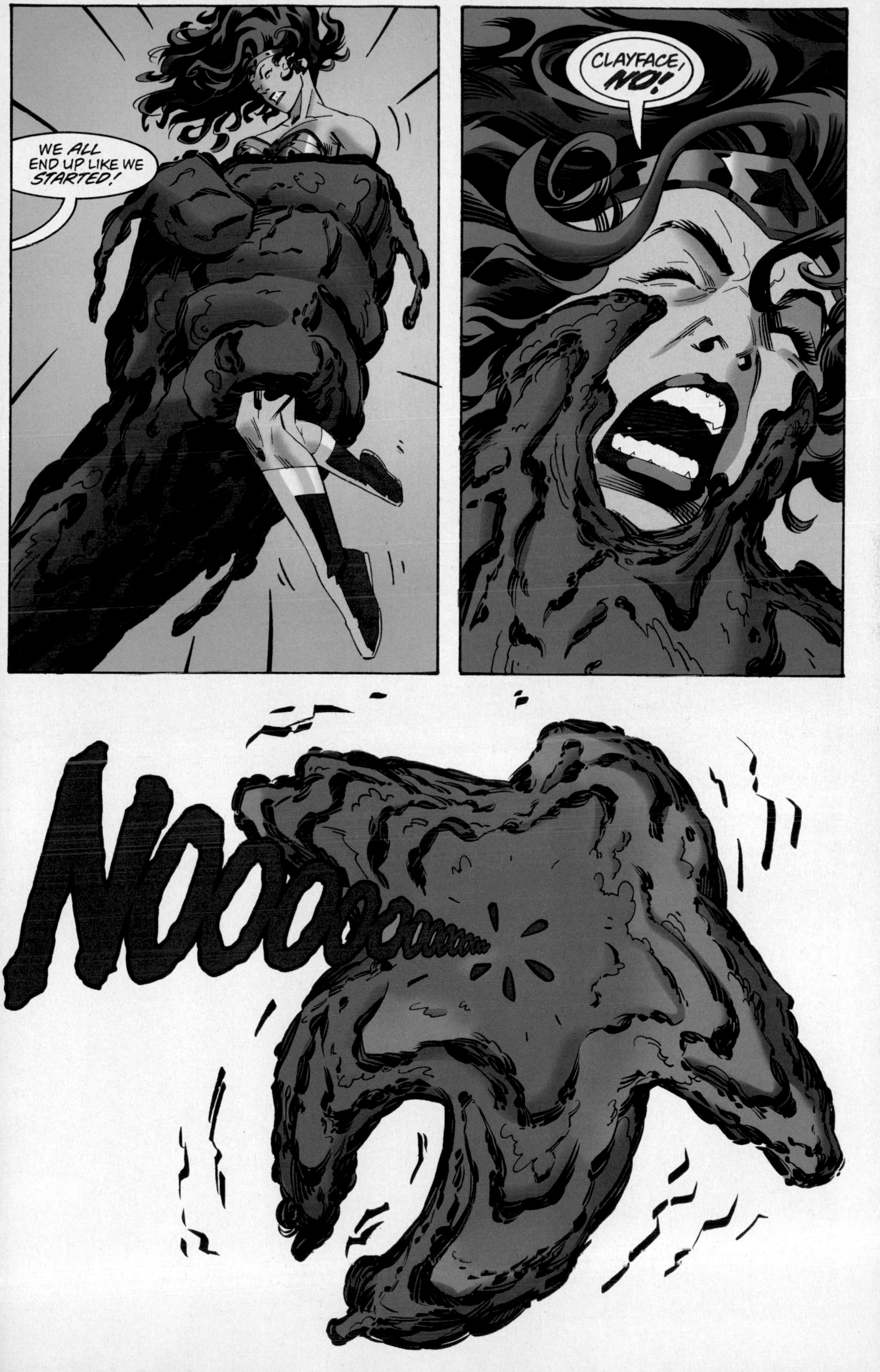
WE ALL END UP LIKE WE STARTED!
CLAYFACE, NO!
NAAAAaaaaa

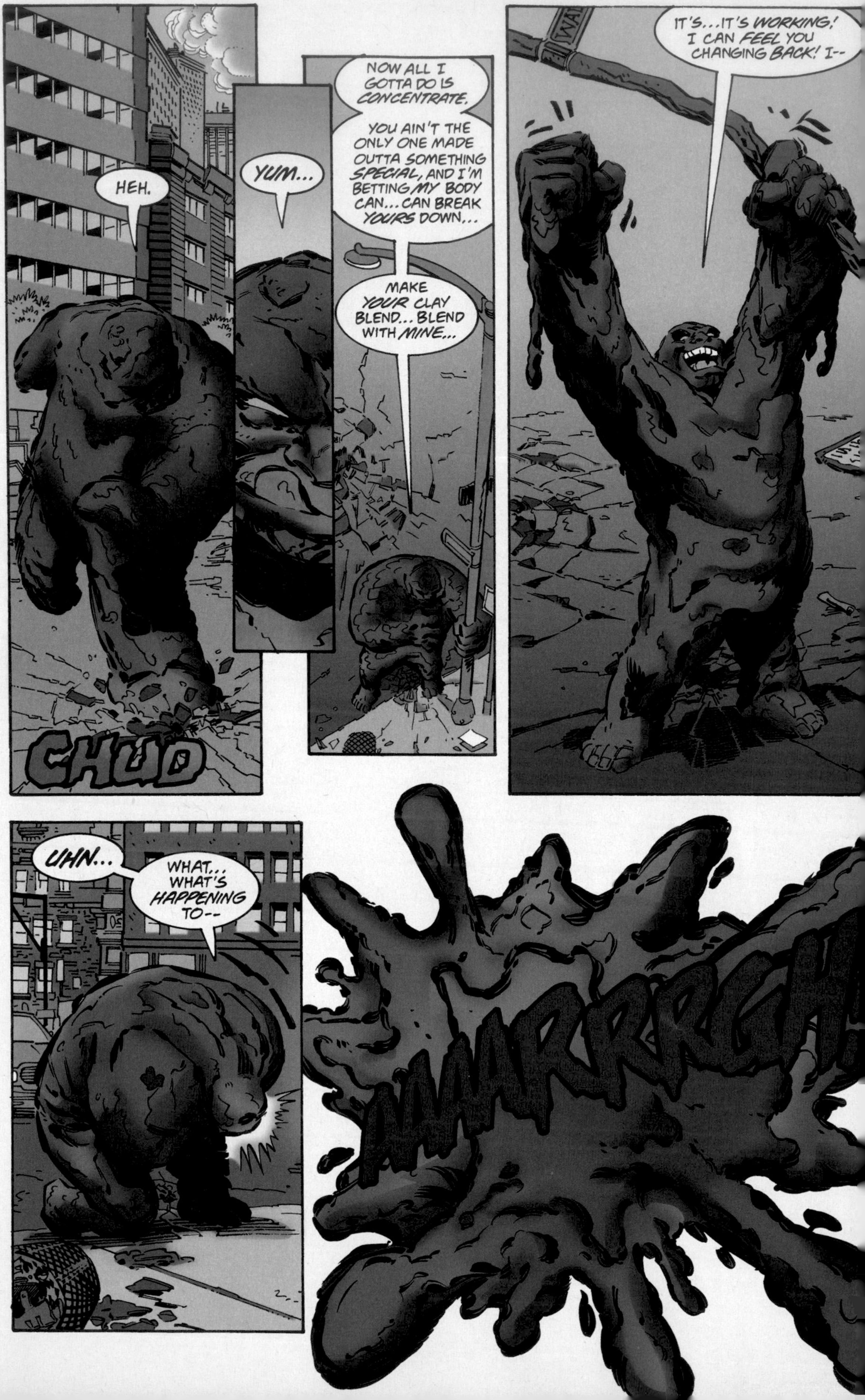
HEH.
CHUD
YUM...
NOW ALL I GOTTA DO IS CONCENTRATE.
YOU AIN'T THE ONLY ONE MADE OUTTA SOMETHING SPECIAL, AND I'M BETTING MY BODY CAN... CAN BREAK YOURS DOWN...
MAKE YOUR CLAY BLEND... BLEND WITH MINE...
IT'S... IT'S WORKING! I CAN FEEL YOU CHANGING BACK! I--
UHN...
WHAT... WHAT'S HAPPENING TO--
WARRRGH

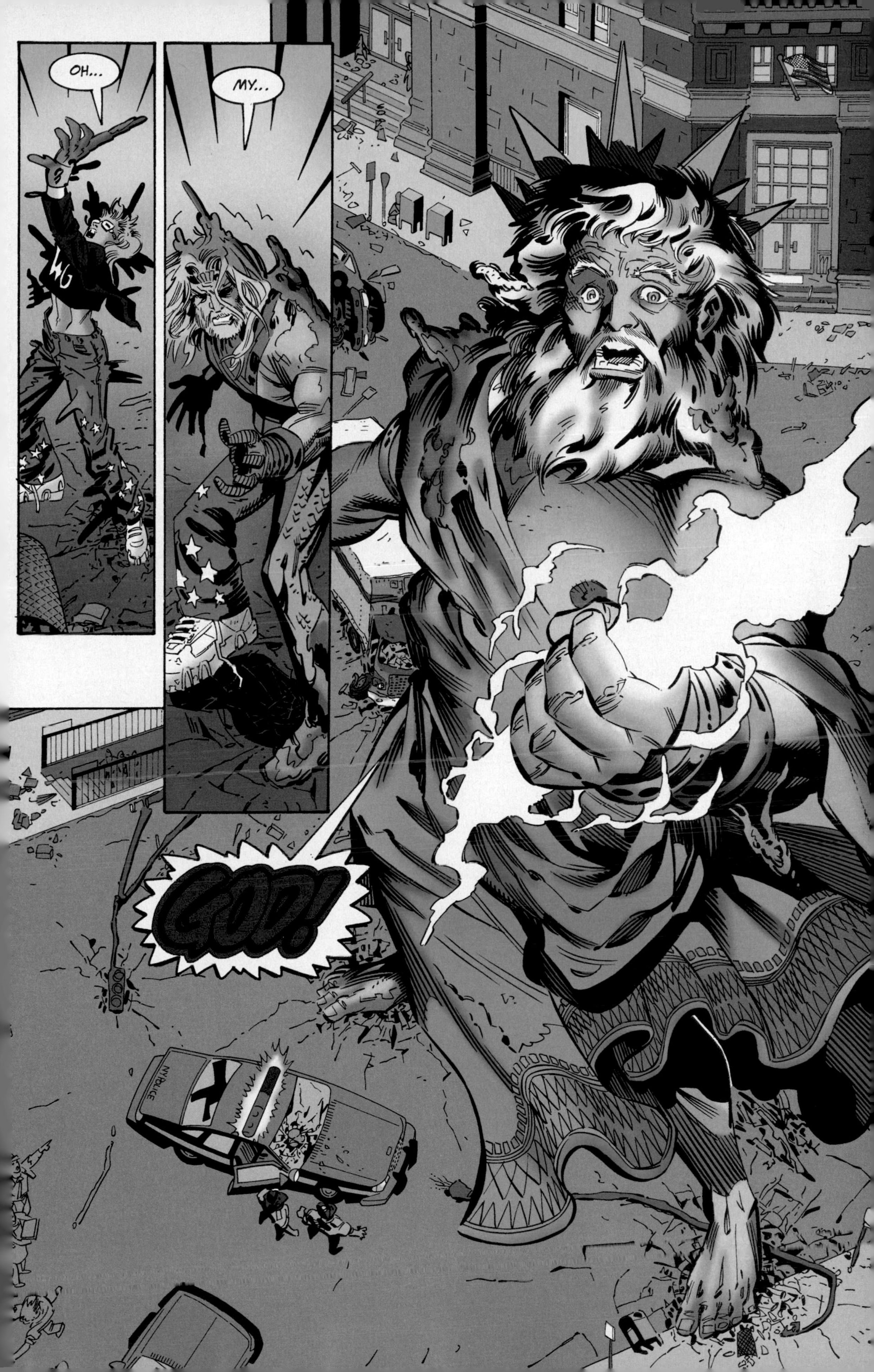
OH...
MY...
GOD!

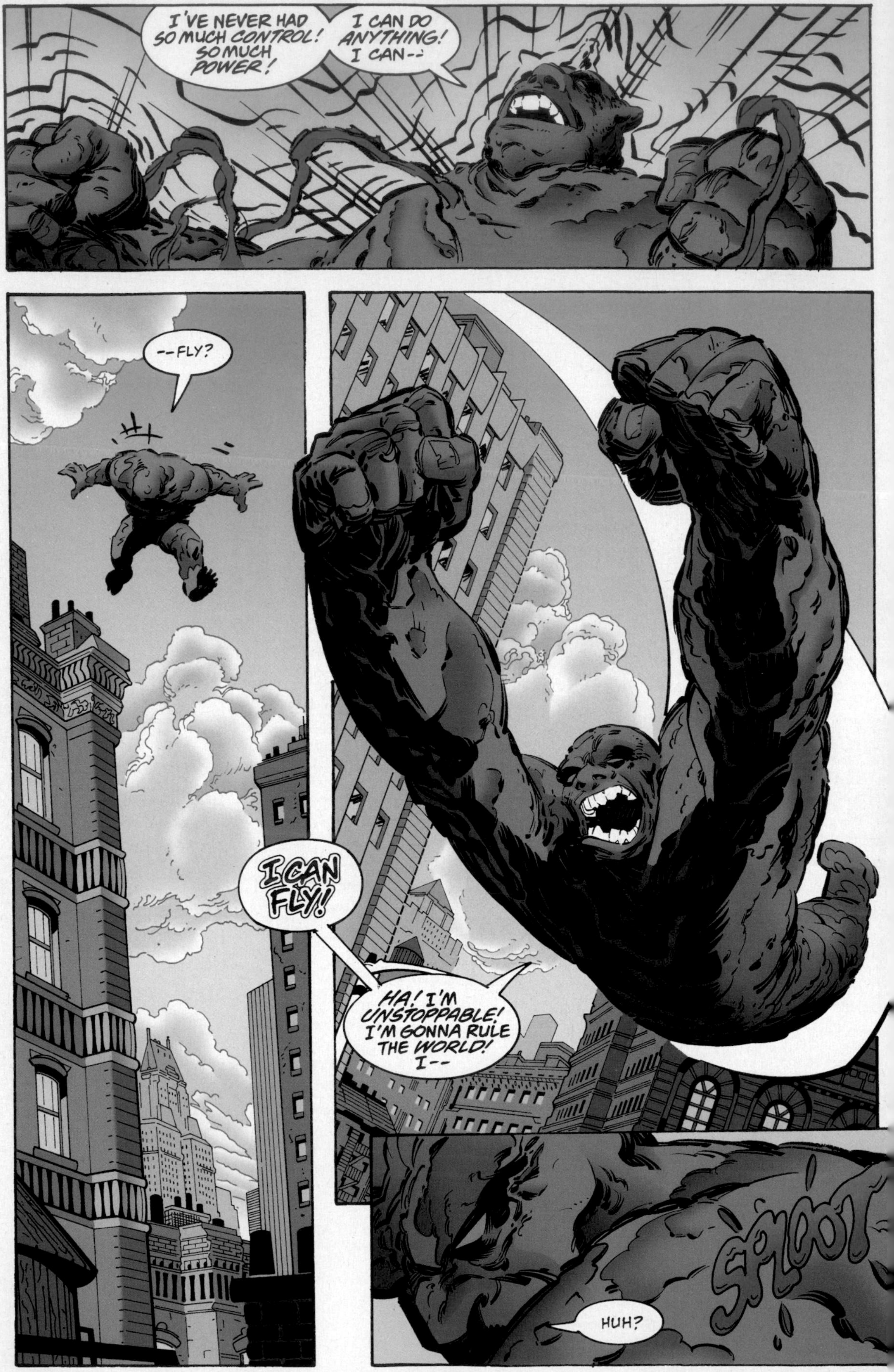
I'VE NEVER HAD SO MUCH CONTROL! SO MUCH POWER!
I CAN DO ANYTHING! I CAN--
--FLY?
I CAN FLY!
HA! I'M UNSTOPPABLE! I'M GONNA RULE THE WORLD! I--
SPLOOT
HUH?

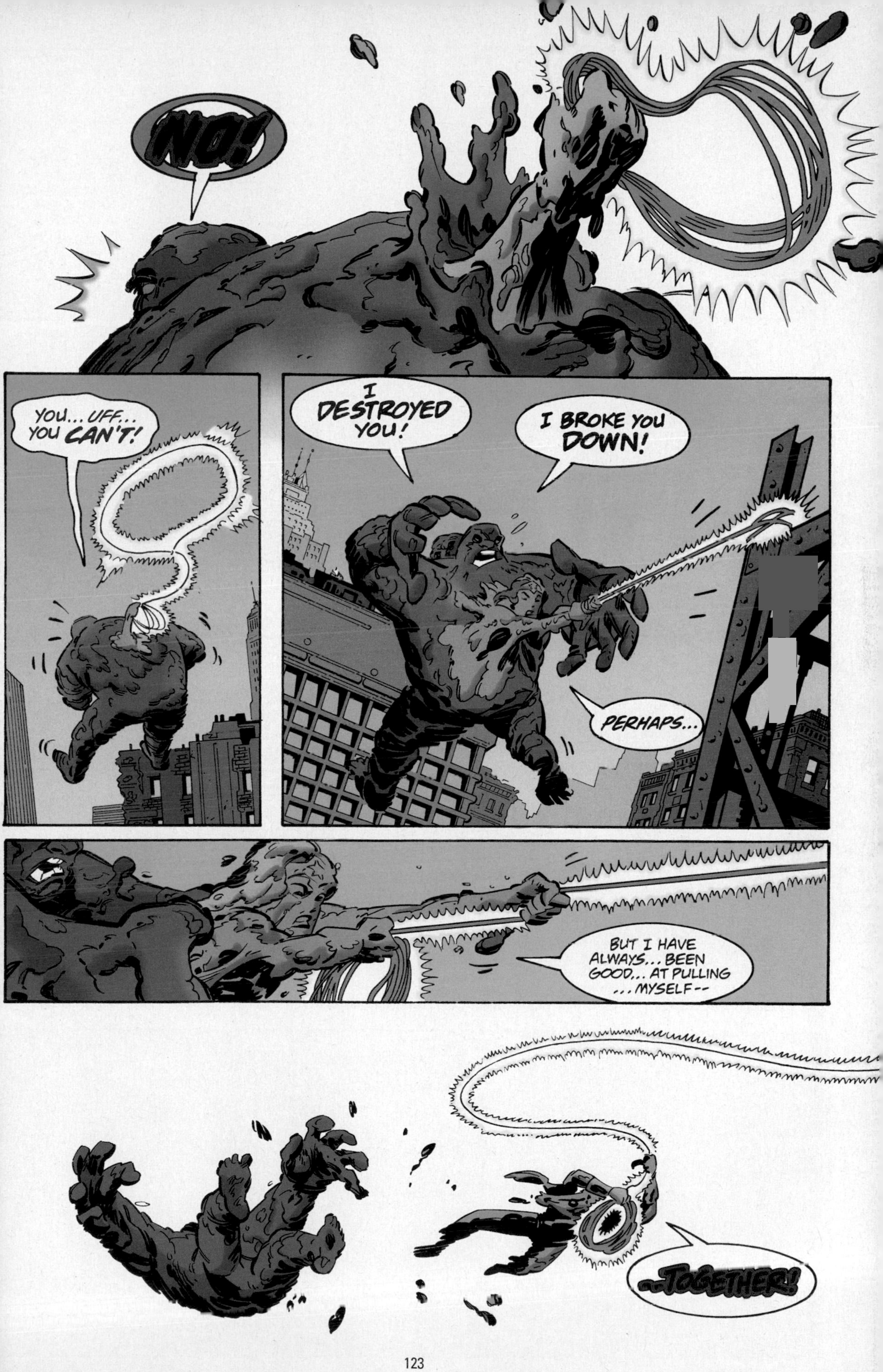
NO!
YOU... UFF... YOU CAN'T!
I DESTROYED YOU!
I BROKE YOU DOWN!
PERHAPS...
BUT I HAVE ALWAYS... BEEN GOOD... AT PULLING ... MYSELF--
--TOGETHER!

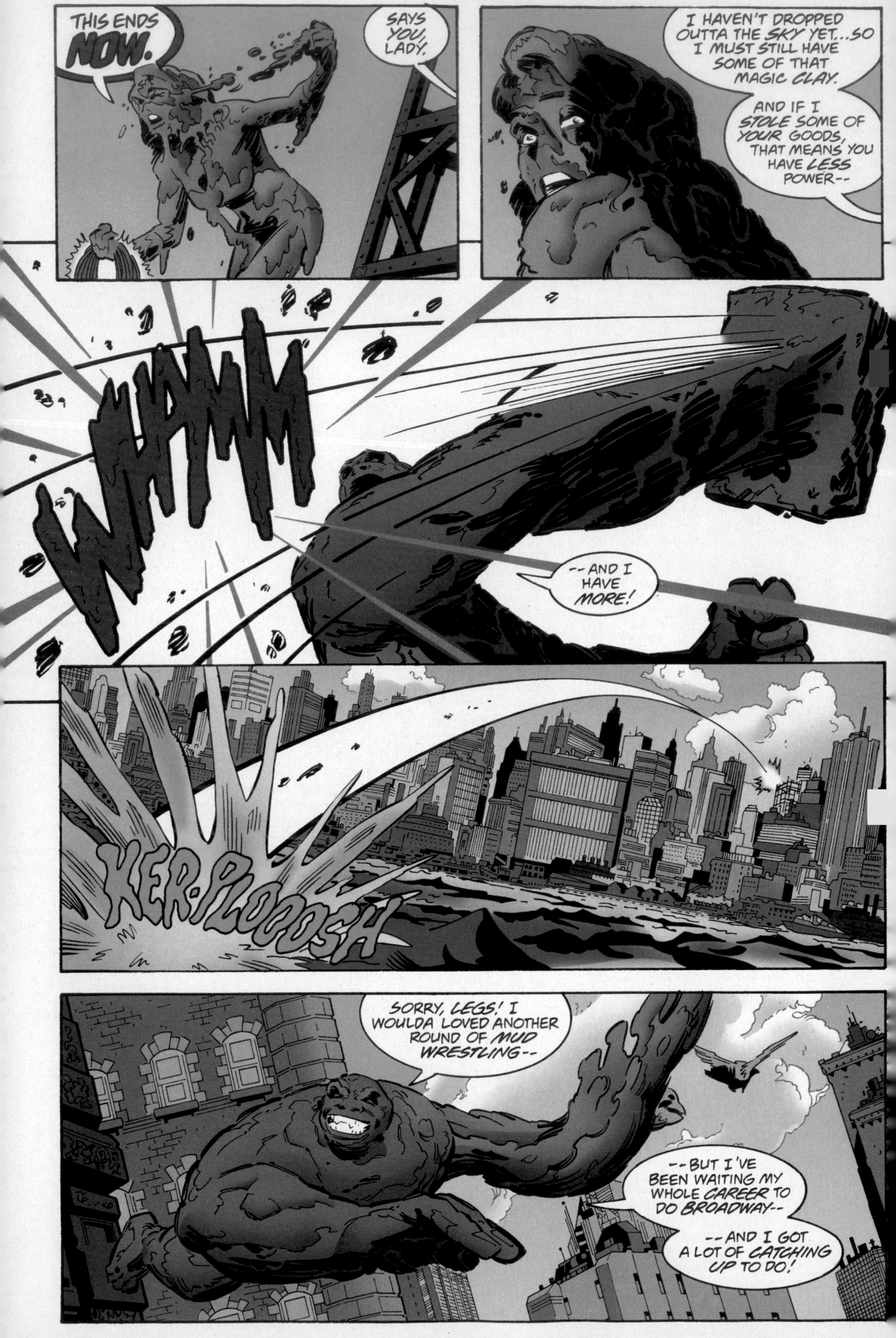
THIS ENDS NOW.
SAYS YOU, LADY.
I HAVEN'T DROPPED OUTTA THE SKY YET...SO I MUST STILL HAVE SOME OF THAT MAGIC CLAY.
AND IF I STOLE SOME OF YOUR GOODS, THAT MEANS YOU HAVE LESS POWER--
WHAMM
--AND I HAVE MORE!
KER-PLOOOSH
SORRY, LEGS! I WOULDA LOVED ANOTHER ROUND OF MUD WRESTLING--
--BUT I'VE BEEN WAITING MY WHOLE CAREER TO DO BROADWAY--
--AND I GOT A LOT OF CATCHING UP TO DO!

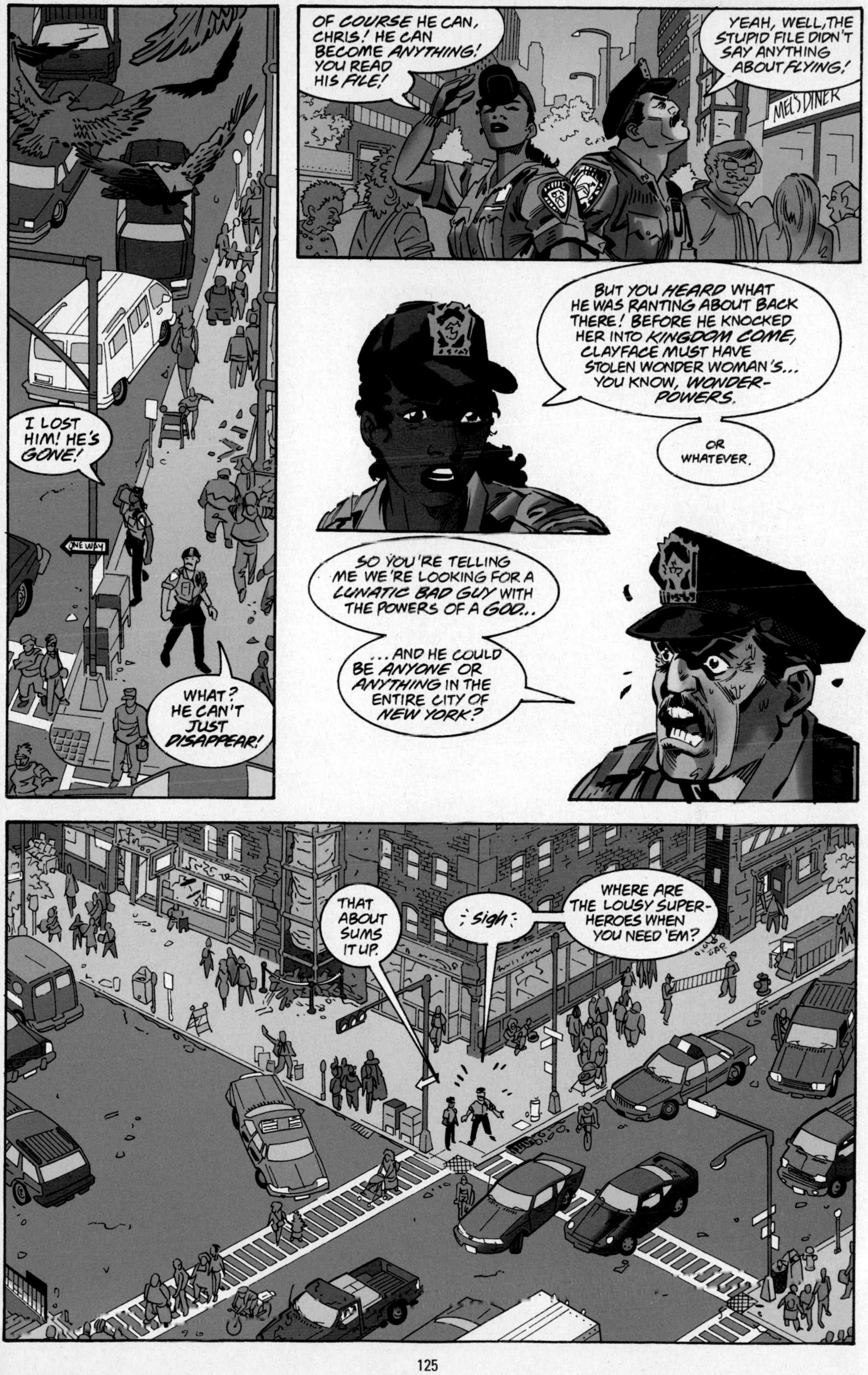
OF COURSE HE CAN, CHRIS! HE CAN BECOME ANYTHING! YOU READ HIS FILE!
YEAH, WELL, THE STUPID FILE DIDN'T SAY ANYTHING ABOUT FLYING!
MEL'S DINER
I LOST HIM! HE'S GONE!
WHAT? HE CAN'T JUST DISAPPEAR!
ONE WAY
BUT YOU HEARD WHAT HE WAS RANTING ABOUT BACK THERE! BEFORE HE KNOCKED HER INTO KINGDOM COME, CLAYFACE MUST HAVE STOLEN WONDER WOMAN'S... YOU KNOW, WONDER-POWERS.
OR WHATEVER.
SO YOU'RE TELLING ME WE'RE LOOKING FOR A LUNATIC BAD GUY WITH THE POWERS OF A GOD...
...AND HE COULD BE ANYONE OR ANYTHING IN THE ENTIRE CITY OF NEW YORK?
THAT ABOUT SUMS IT UP.
sigh
WHERE ARE THE LOUSY SUPER-HEROES WHEN YOU NEED 'EM?

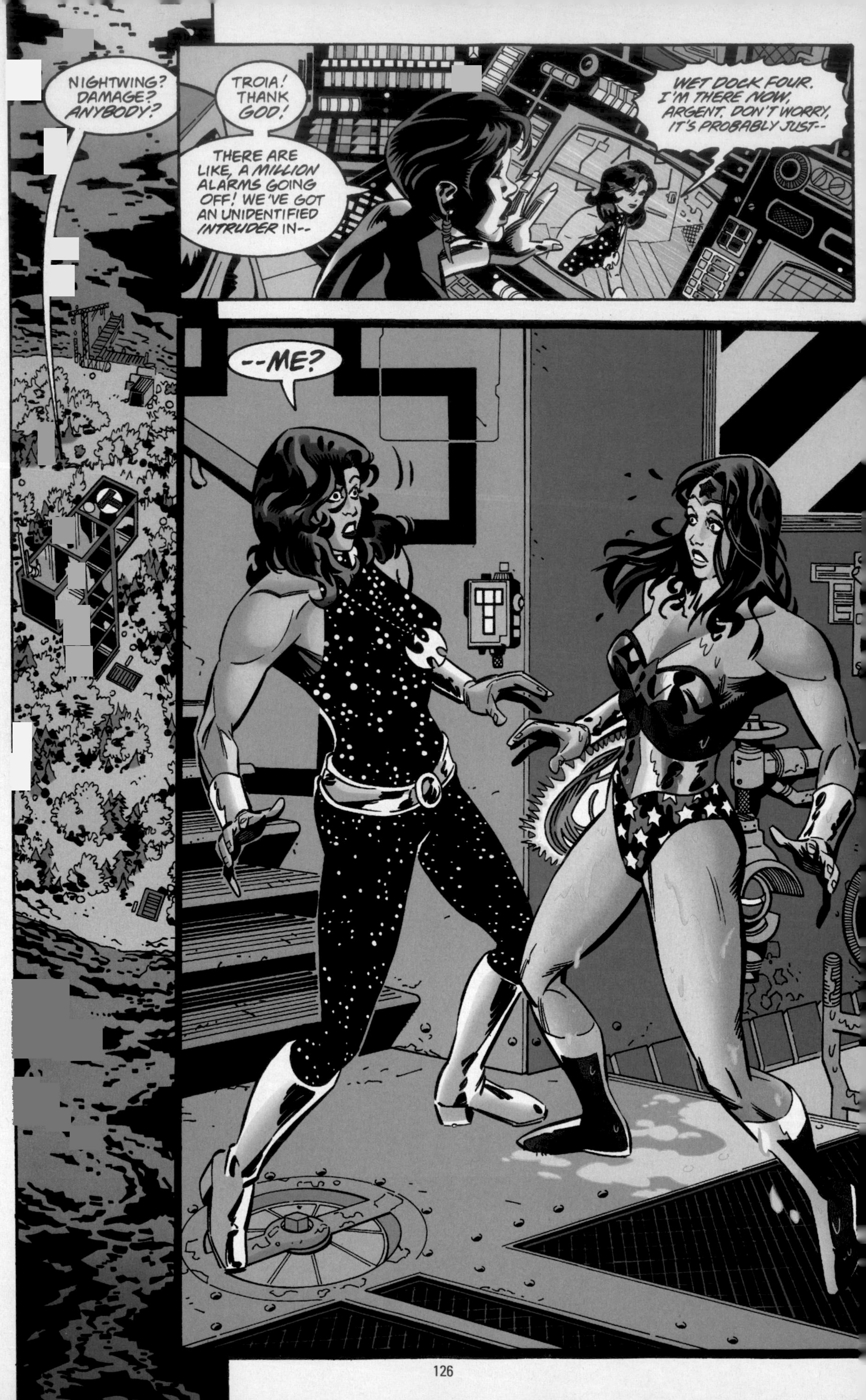
NIGHTWING? DAMAGE? ANYBODY?
TROIA! THANK GOD!
THERE ARE LIKE, A MILLION ALARMS GOING OFF! WE'VE GOT AN UNIDENTIFIED INTRUDER IN--
WET DOCK FOUR. I'M THERE NOW, ARGENT. DON'T WORRY, IT'S PROBABLY JUST--
--ME?

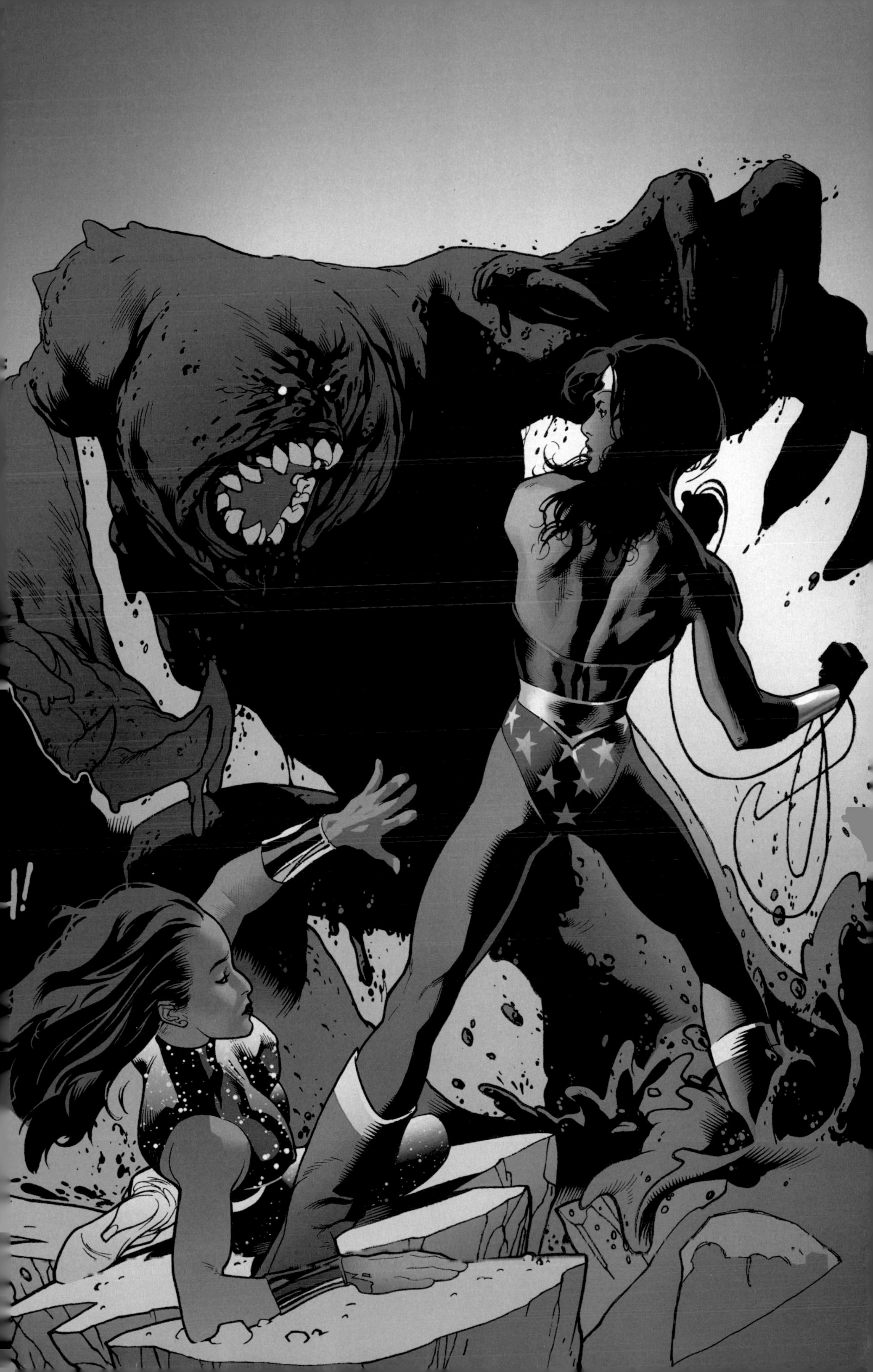

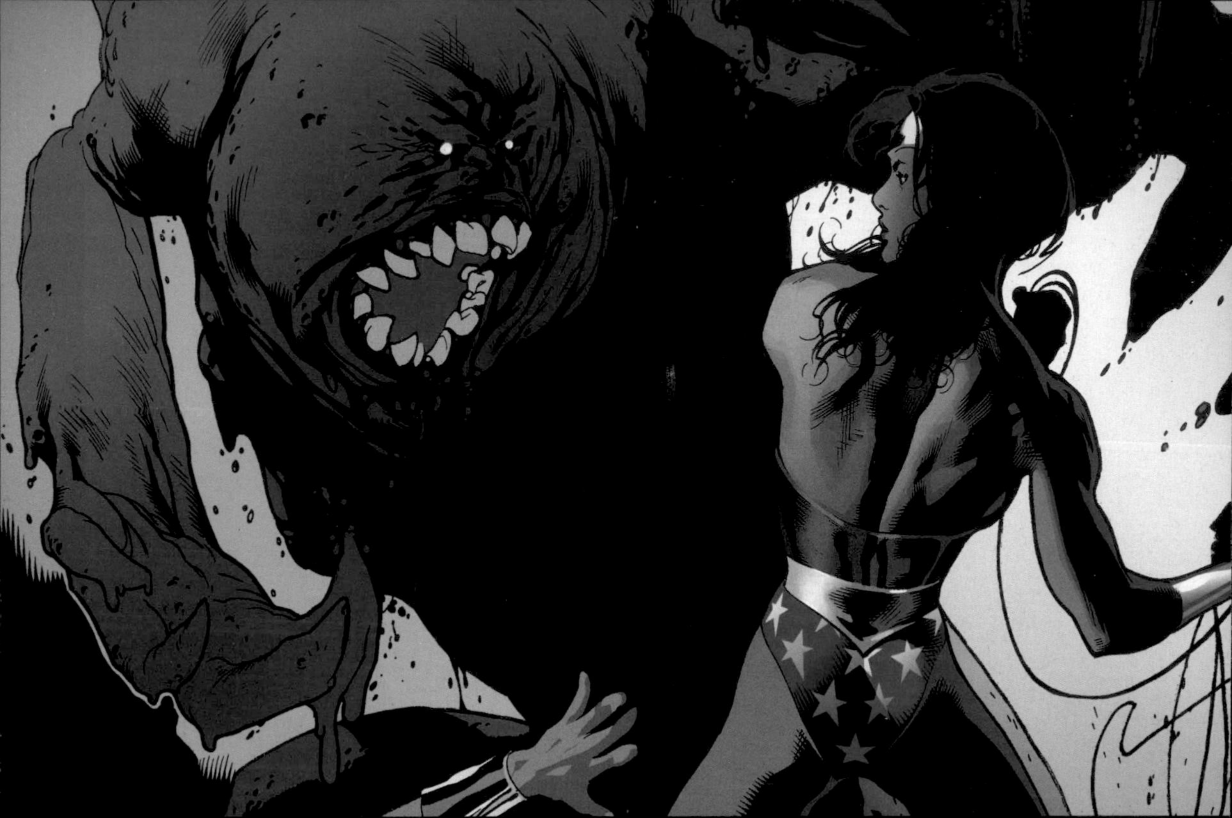

A PIECE OF YOU CHAPTER TWO

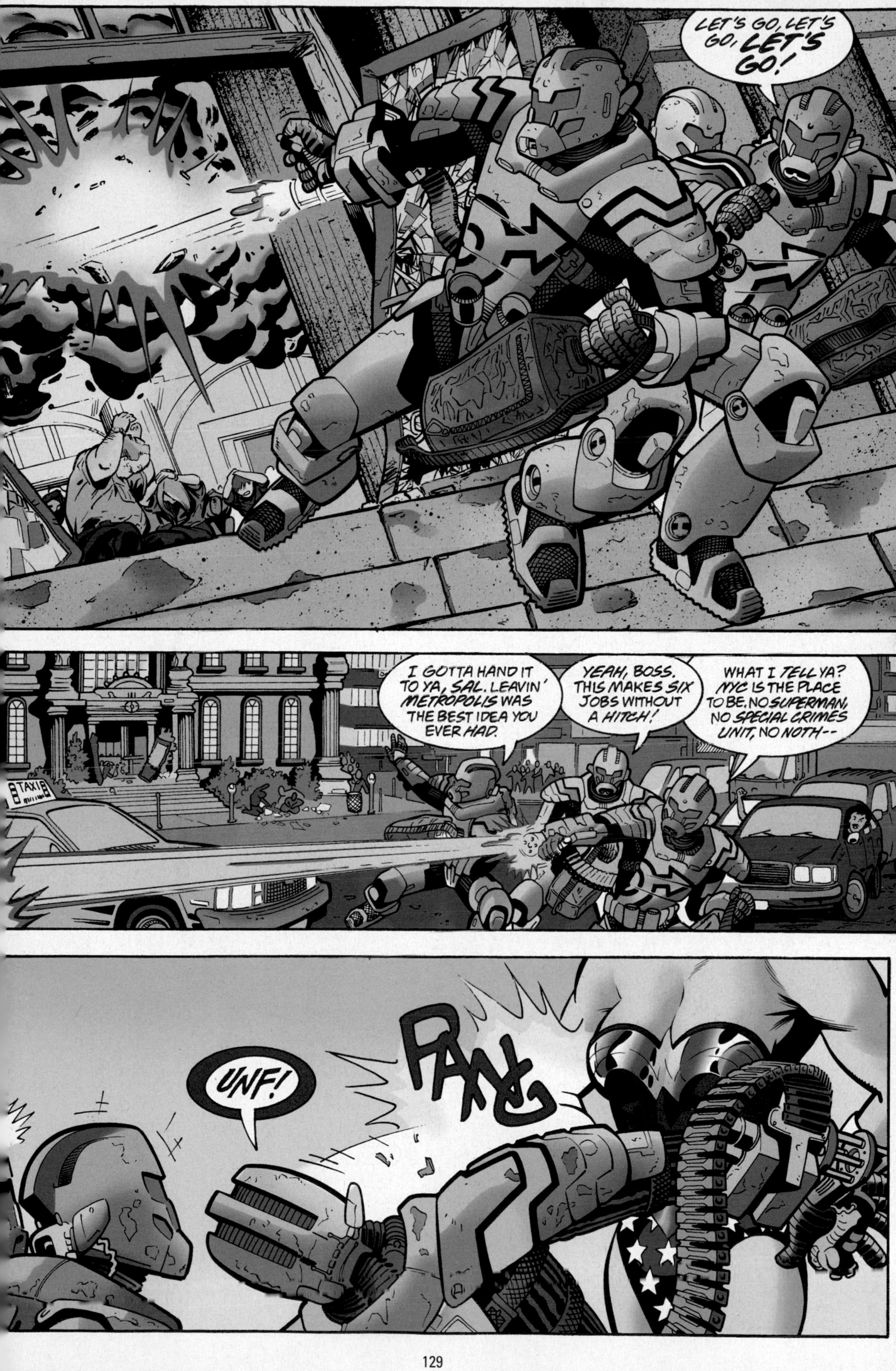
LET'S GO, LET'S GO, LET'S GO!
I GOTTA HAND IT TO YA, SAL. LEAVIN' METROPOLIS WAS THE BEST IDEA YOU EVER HAD.
YEAH, BOSS. THIS MAKES SIX JOBS WITHOUT A HITCH!
WHAT I TELL YA? NYC IS THE PLACE TO BE. NO SUPERMAN, NO SPECIAL CRIMES UNIT, NO NOTH--
TAXI
UNF!
PANG

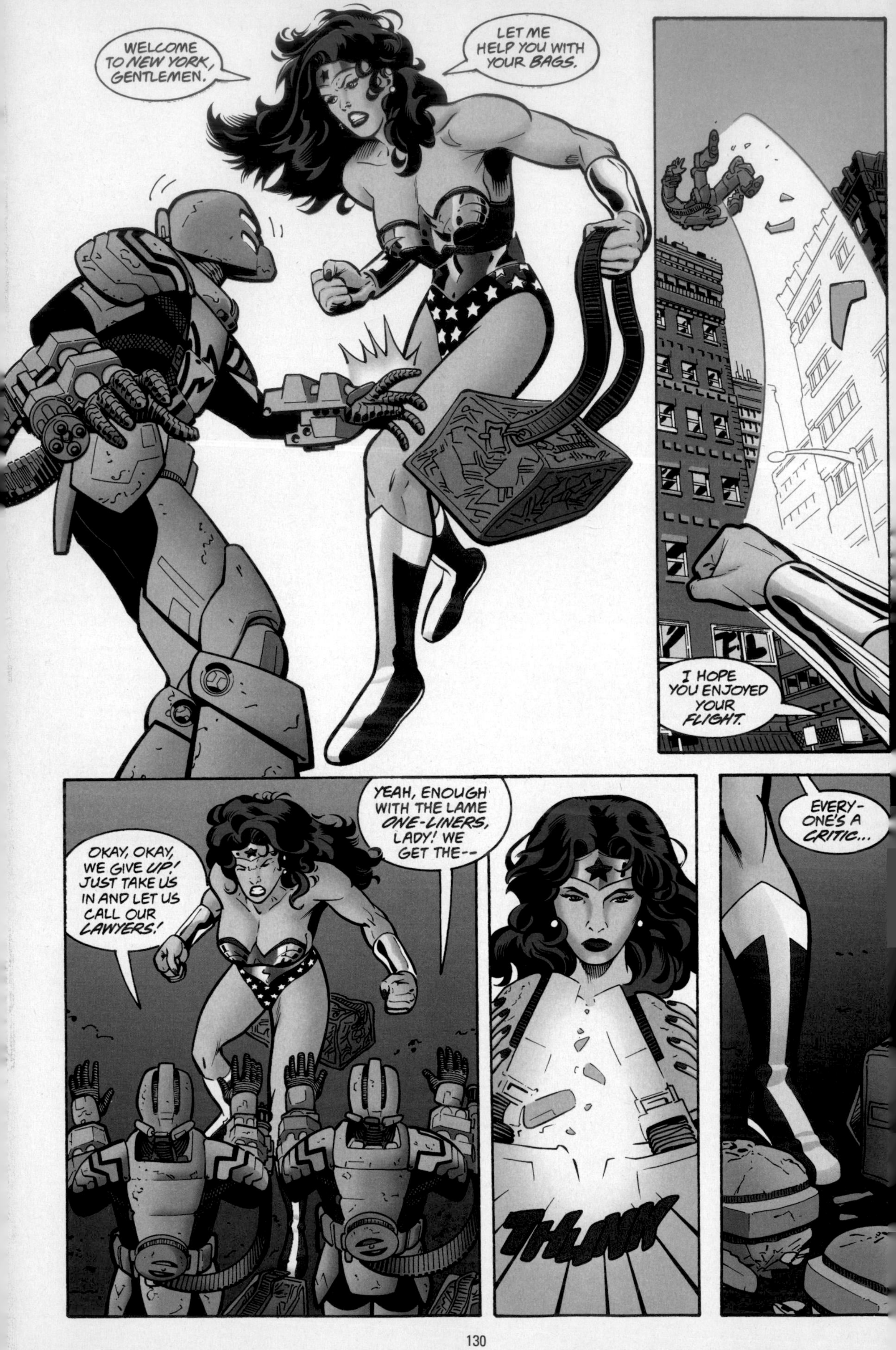
WELCOME TO NEW YORK, GENTLEMEN.
LET ME HELP YOU WITH YOUR BAGS.
I HOPE YOU ENJOYED YOUR FLIGHT.
OKAY, OKAY, WE GIVE UP! JUST TAKE US IN AND LET US CALL OUR LAWYERS!
YEAH, ENOUGH WITH THE LAME ONE-LINERS, LADY! WE GET THE--
THUNK
EVERY-ONE'S A CRITIC...

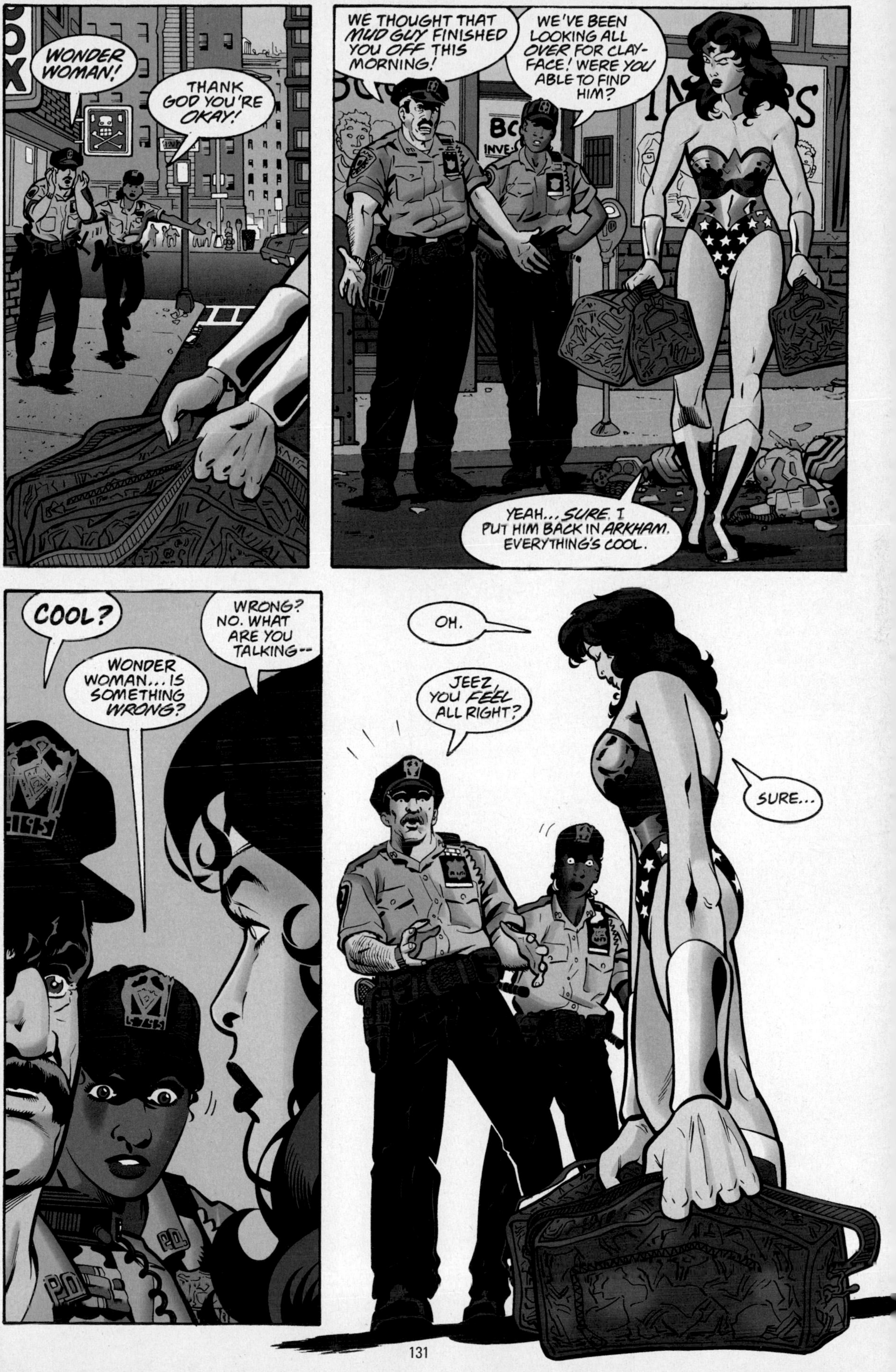
WONDER WOMAN!
THANK GOD YOU'RE OKAY!
WE THOUGHT THAT MUD GUY FINISHED YOU OFF THIS MORNING!
WE'VE BEEN LOOKING ALL OVER FOR CLAY-FACE! WERE YOU ABLE TO FIND HIM?
YEAH... SURE. I PUT HIM BACK IN ARKHAM. EVERYTHING'S COOL.
COOL?
WONDER WOMAN... IS SOMETHING WRONG?
WRONG? NO. WHAT ARE YOU TALKING--
OH.
JEEZ, YOU FEEL ALL RIGHT?
SURE...

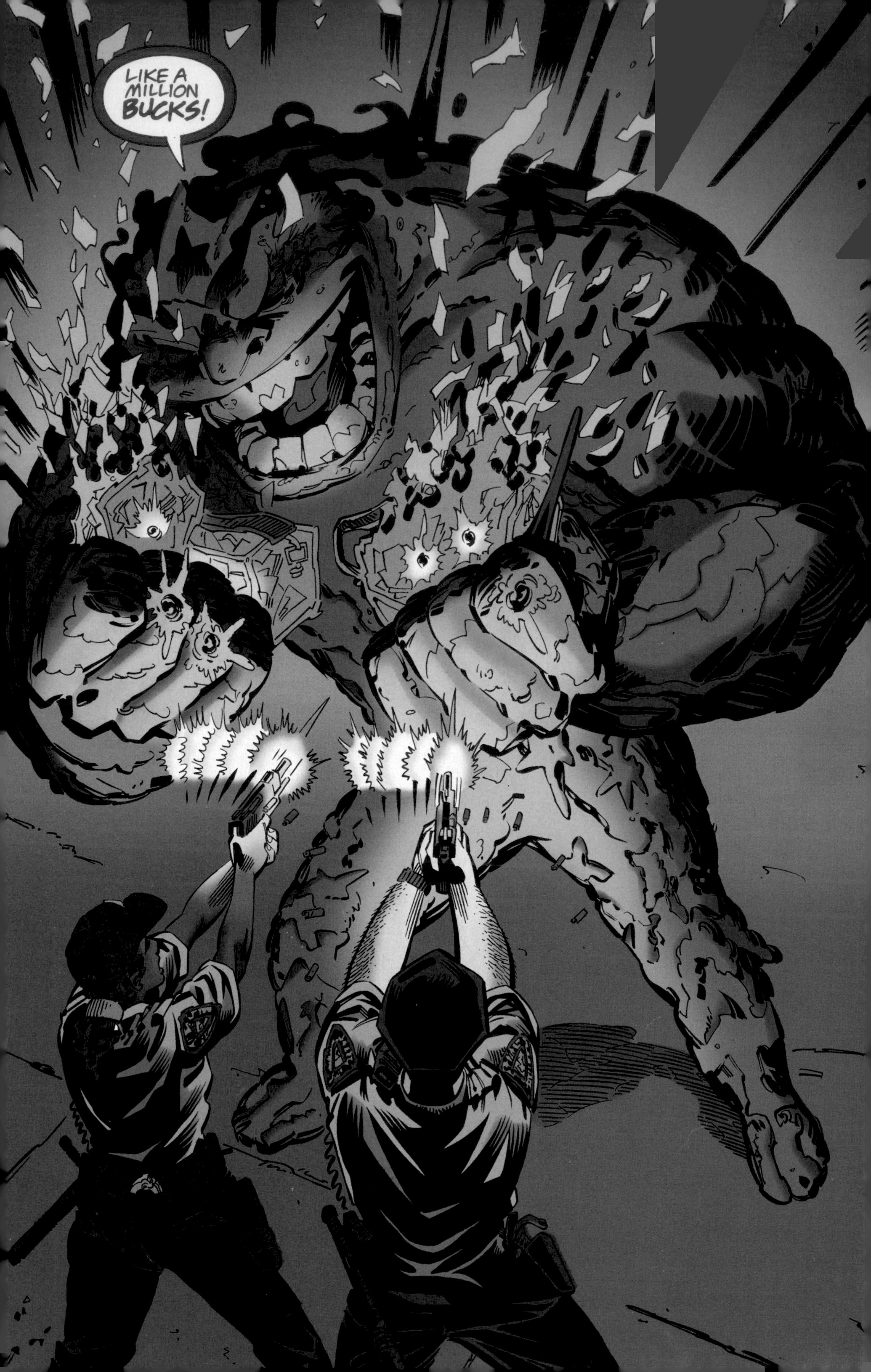
LIKE A MILLION BUCKS!

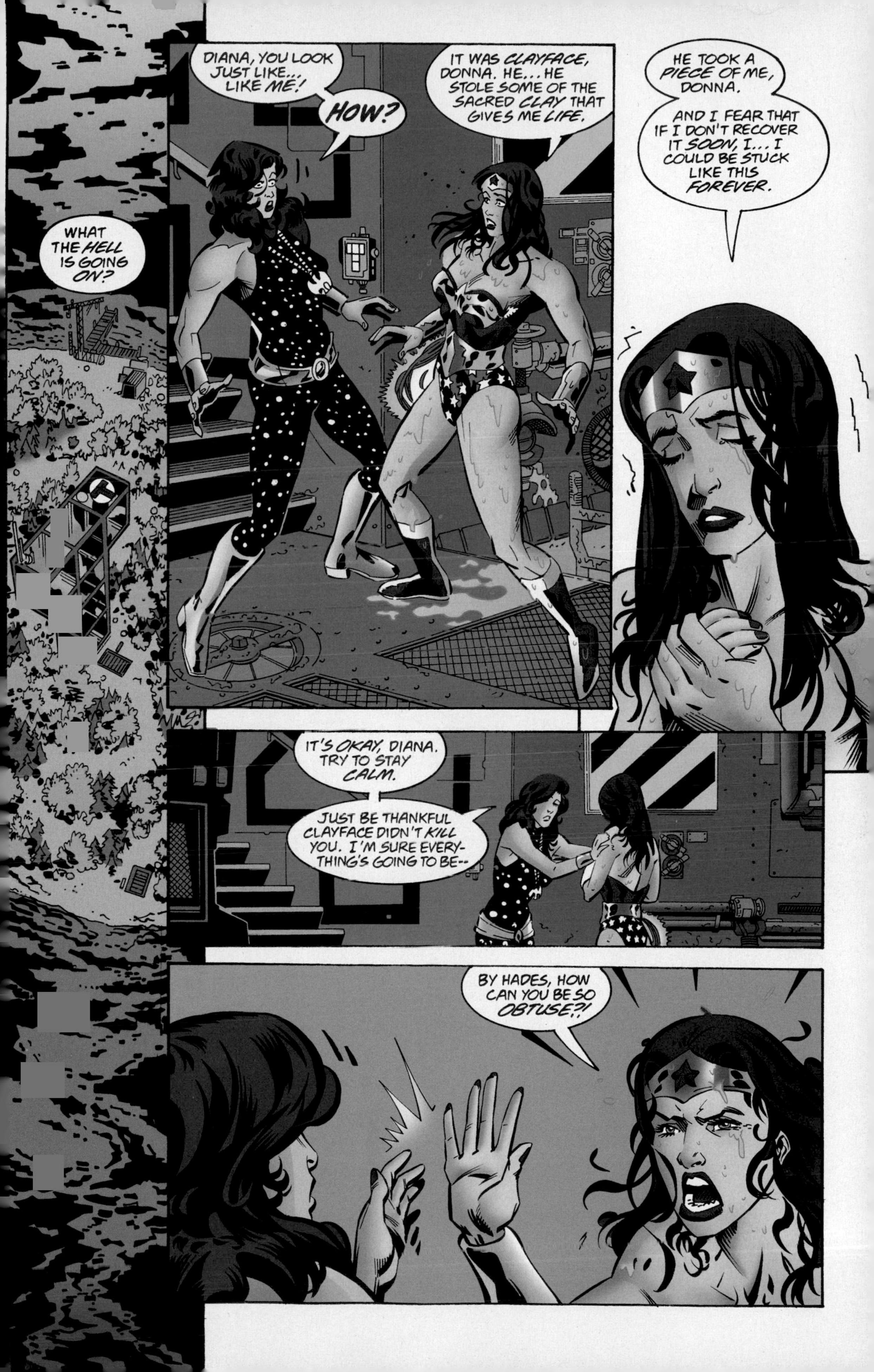
WHAT THE HELL IS GOING ON?
DIANA, YOU LOOK JUST LIKE... LIKE ME!
HOW?
IT WAS CLAYFACE, DONNA. HE... HE STOLE SOME OF THE SACRED CLAY THAT GIVES ME LIFE.
HE TOOK A PIECE OF ME, DONNA.
AND I FEAR THAT IF I DON'T RECOVER IT SOON, I... I COULD BE STUCK LIKE THIS FOREVER.
IT'S OKAY, DIANA. TRY TO STAY CALM.
JUST BE THANKFUL CLAYFACE DIDN'T KILL YOU. I'M SURE EVERYTHING'S GOING TO BE--
BY HADES, HOW CAN YOU BE SO OBTUSE?!

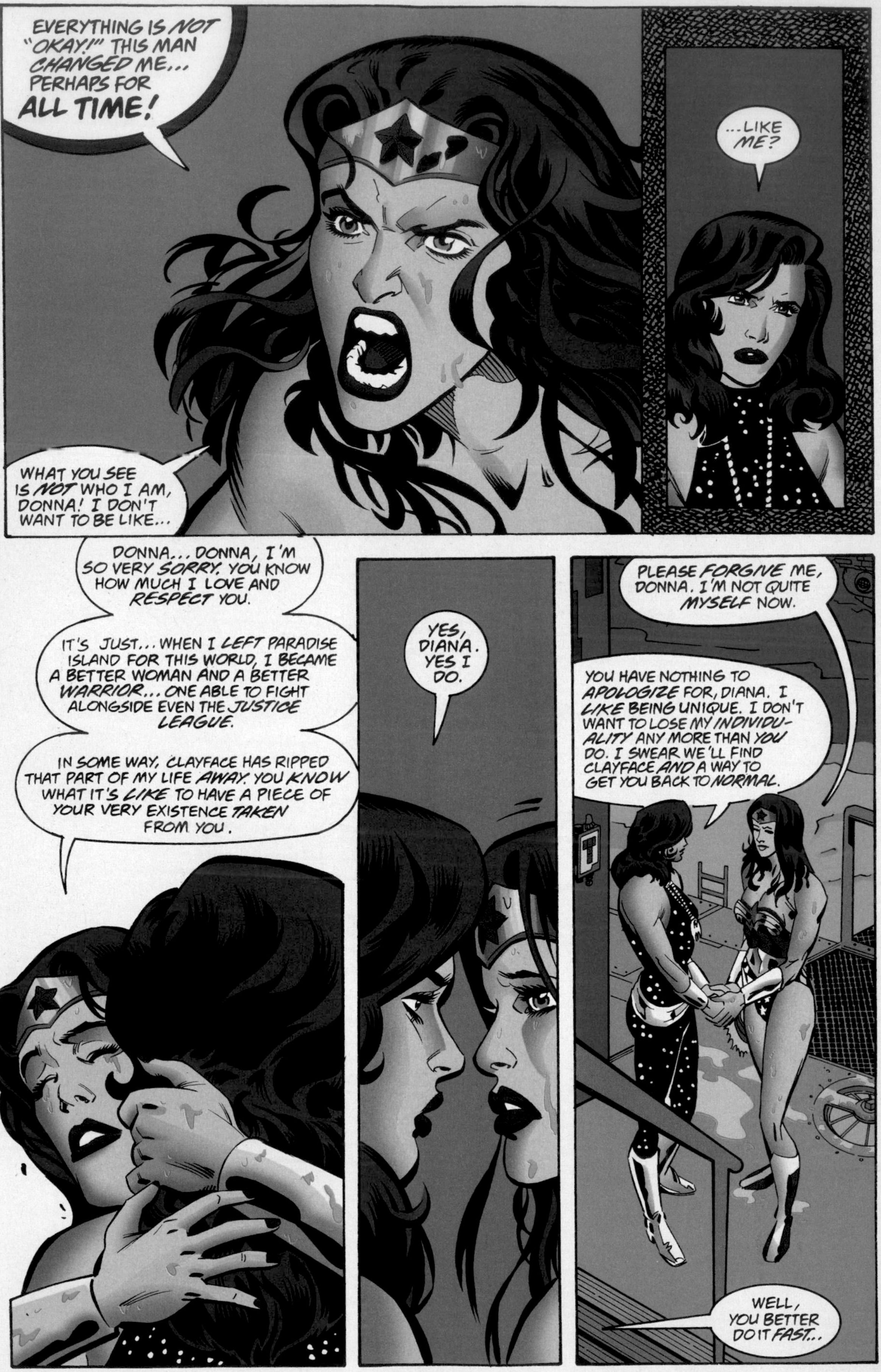
EVERYTHING IS NOT "OKAY!" THIS MAN CHANGED ME... PERHAPS FOR ALL TIME!
WHAT YOU SEE IS NOT WHO I AM, DONNA! I DON'T WANT TO BE LIKE...
...LIKE ME?
DONNA... DONNA, I'M SO VERY SORRY. YOU KNOW HOW MUCH I LOVE AND RESPECT YOU.
IT'S JUST... WHEN I LEFT PARADISE ISLAND FOR THIS WORLD, I BECAME A BETTER WOMAN AND A BETTER WARRIOR... ONE ABLE TO FIGHT ALONGSIDE EVEN THE JUSTICE LEAGUE.
IN SOME WAY, CLAYFACE HAS RIPPED THAT PART OF MY LIFE AWAY. YOU KNOW WHAT IT'S LIKE TO HAVE A PIECE OF YOUR VERY EXISTENCE TAKEN FROM YOU.
YES, DIANA. YES I DO.
PLEASE FORGIVE ME, DONNA. I'M NOT QUITE MYSELF NOW.
YOU HAVE NOTHING TO APOLOGIZE FOR, DIANA. I LIKE BEING UNIQUE. I DON'T WANT TO LOSE MY INDIVIDUALITY ANY MORE THAN YOU DO. I SWEAR WE'LL FIND CLAYFACE AND A WAY TO GET YOU BACK TO NORMAL.
WELL, YOU BETTER DO IT FAST...

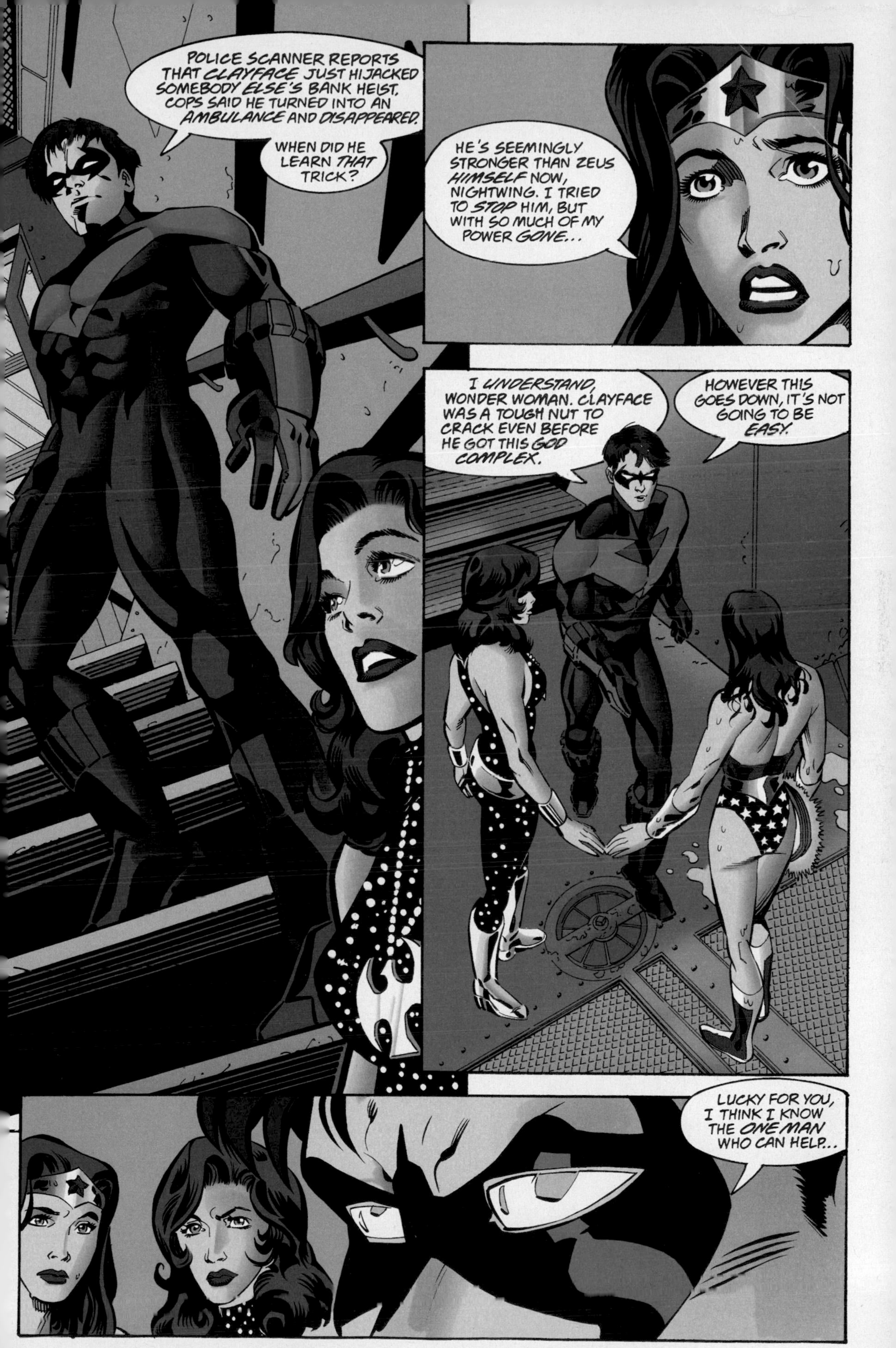
POLICE SCANNER REPORTS THAT CLAYFACE JUST HIJACKED SOMEBODY ELSE'S BANK HEIST. COPS SAID HE TURNED INTO AN AMBULANCE AND DISAPPEARED.
WHEN DID HE LEARN THAT TRICK?
HE'S SEEMINGLY STRONGER THAN ZEUS HIMSELF NOW, NIGHTWING. I TRIED TO STOP HIM, BUT WITH SO MUCH OF MY POWER GONE...
I UNDERSTAND, WONDER WOMAN. CLAYFACE WAS A TOUGH NUT TO CRACK EVEN BEFORE HE GOT THIS GOD COMPLEX.
HOWEVER THIS GOES DOWN, IT'S NOT GOING TO BE EASY.
LUCKY FOR YOU, I THINK I KNOW THE ONE MAN WHO CAN HELP...

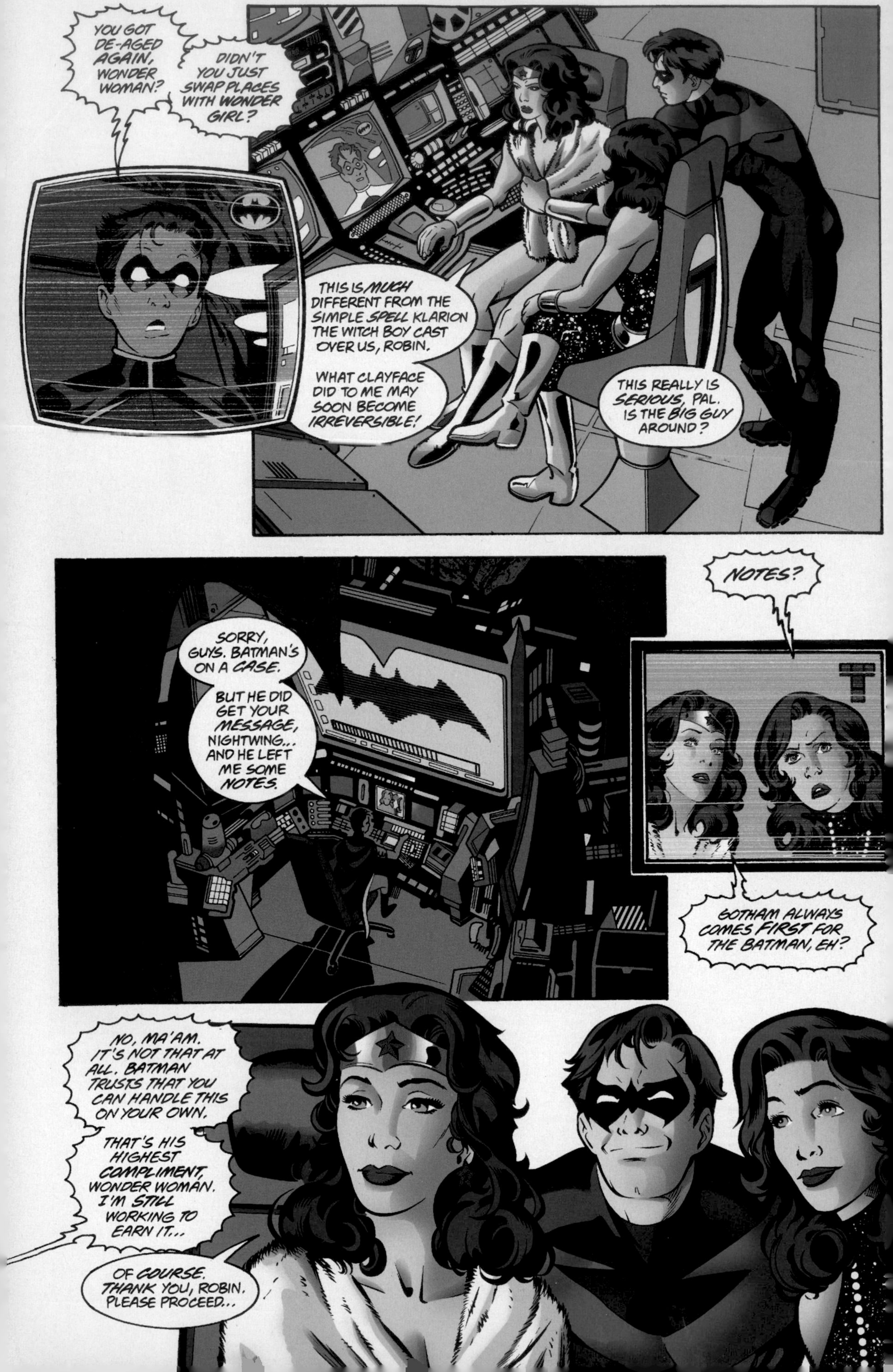
YOU GOT DE-AGED AGAIN, WONDER WOMAN?
DIDN'T YOU JUST SWAP PLACES WITH WONDER GIRL?
THIS IS MUCH DIFFERENT FROM THE SIMPLE SPELL KLARION THE WITCH BOY CAST OVER US, ROBIN.
WHAT CLAYFACE DID TO ME MAY SOON BECOME IRREVERSIBLE!
THIS REALLY IS SERIOUS, PAL. IS THE BIG GUY AROUND?
SORRY, GUYS. BATMAN'S ON A CASE.
BUT HE DID GET YOUR MESSAGE, NIGHTWING... AND HE LEFT ME SOME NOTES.
NOTES?
GOTHAM ALWAYS COMES FIRST FOR THE BATMAN, EH?
NO, MA'AM. IT'S NOT THAT AT ALL. BATMAN TRUSTS THAT YOU CAN HANDLE THIS ON YOUR OWN.
THAT'S HIS HIGHEST COMPLIMENT, WONDER WOMAN. I'M STILL WORKING TO EARN IT...
OF COURSE. THANK YOU, ROBIN. PLEASE PROCEED...

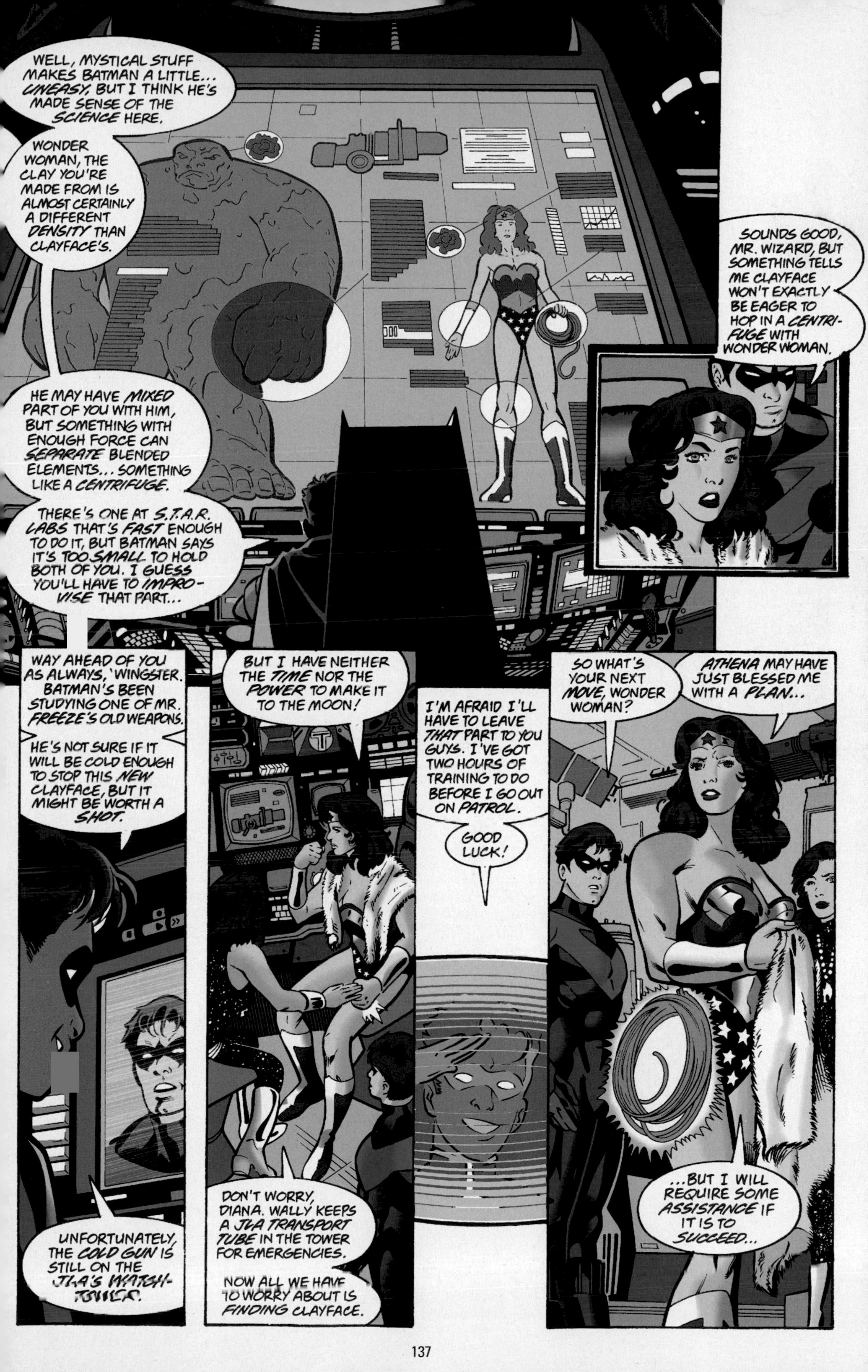
WELL, MYSTICAL STUFF MAKES BATMAN A LITTLE... UNEASY, BUT I THINK HE'S MADE SENSE OF THE SCIENCE HERE.
WONDER WOMAN, THE CLAY YOU'RE MADE FROM IS ALMOST CERTAINLY A DIFFERENT DENSITY THAN CLAYFACE'S.
HE MAY HAVE MIXED PART OF YOU WITH HIM, BUT SOMETHING WITH ENOUGH FORCE CAN SEPARATE BLENDED ELEMENTS... SOMETHING LIKE A CENTRIFUGE.
THERE'S ONE AT S.T.A.R. LABS THAT'S FAST ENOUGH TO DO IT, BUT BATMAN SAYS IT'S TOO SMALL TO HOLD BOTH OF YOU. I GUESS YOU'LL HAVE TO IMPROVISE THAT PART...
SOUNDS GOOD, MR. WIZARD, BUT SOMETHING TELLS ME CLAYFACE WON'T EXACTLY BE EAGER TO HOP IN A CENTRIFUGE WITH WONDER WOMAN.
WAY AHEAD OF YOU AS ALWAYS, 'WINGSTER. BATMAN'S BEEN STUDYING ONE OF MR. FREEZE'S OLD WEAPONS.
HE'S NOT SURE IF IT WILL BE COLD ENOUGH TO STOP THIS NEW CLAYFACE, BUT IT MIGHT BE WORTH A SHOT.
UNFORTUNATELY, THE COLD GUN IS STILL ON THE JLA'S WATCH-TOWER.
BUT I HAVE NEITHER THE TIME NOR THE POWER TO MAKE IT TO THE MOON!
DON'T WORRY, DIANA. WALLY KEEPS A JLA TRANSPORT TUBE IN THE TOWER FOR EMERGENCIES.
NOW ALL WE HAVE TO WORRY ABOUT IS FINDING CLAYFACE.
I'M AFRAID I'LL HAVE TO LEAVE THAT PART TO YOU GUYS. I'VE GOT TWO HOURS OF TRAINING TO DO BEFORE I GO OUT ON PATROL.
GOOD LUCK!
SO WHAT'S YOUR NEXT MOVE, WONDER WOMAN?
ATHENA MAY HAVE JUST BLESSED ME WITH A PLAN...
...BUT I WILL REQUIRE SOME ASSISTANCE IF IT IS TO SUCCEED...

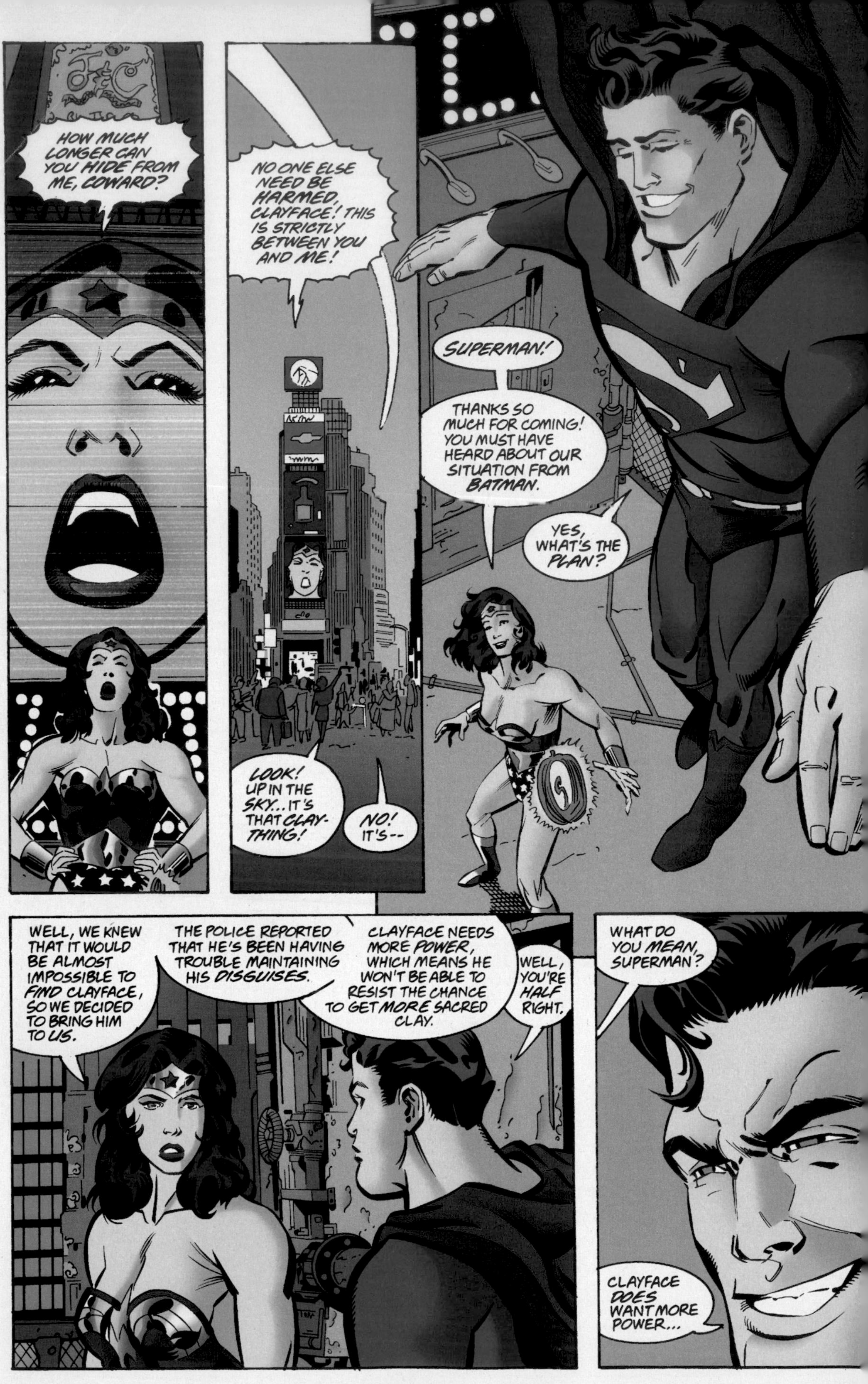

HOW MUCH LONGER CAN YOU HIDE FROM ME, COWARD?
NO ONE ELSE NEED BE HARMED, CLAYFACE! THIS IS STRICTLY BETWEEN YOU AND ME!
LOOK! UP IN THE SKY... IT'S THAT CLAY-THING!
NO! IT'S--
SUPERMAN!
THANKS SO MUCH FOR COMING! YOU MUST HAVE HEARD ABOUT OUR SITUATION FROM BATMAN.
YES, WHAT'S THE PLAN?
WELL, WE KNEW THAT IT WOULD BE ALMOST IMPOSSIBLE TO FIND CLAYFACE, SO WE DECIDED TO BRING HIM TO US.
THE POLICE REPORTED THAT HE'S BEEN HAVING TROUBLE MAINTAINING HIS DISGUISES.
CLAYFACE NEEDS MORE POWER, WHICH MEANS HE WON'T BE ABLE TO RESIST THE CHANCE TO GET MORE SACRED CLAY.
WELL, YOU'RE HALF RIGHT.
WHAT DO YOU MEAN, SUPERMAN?
CLAYFACE DOES WANT MORE POWER...

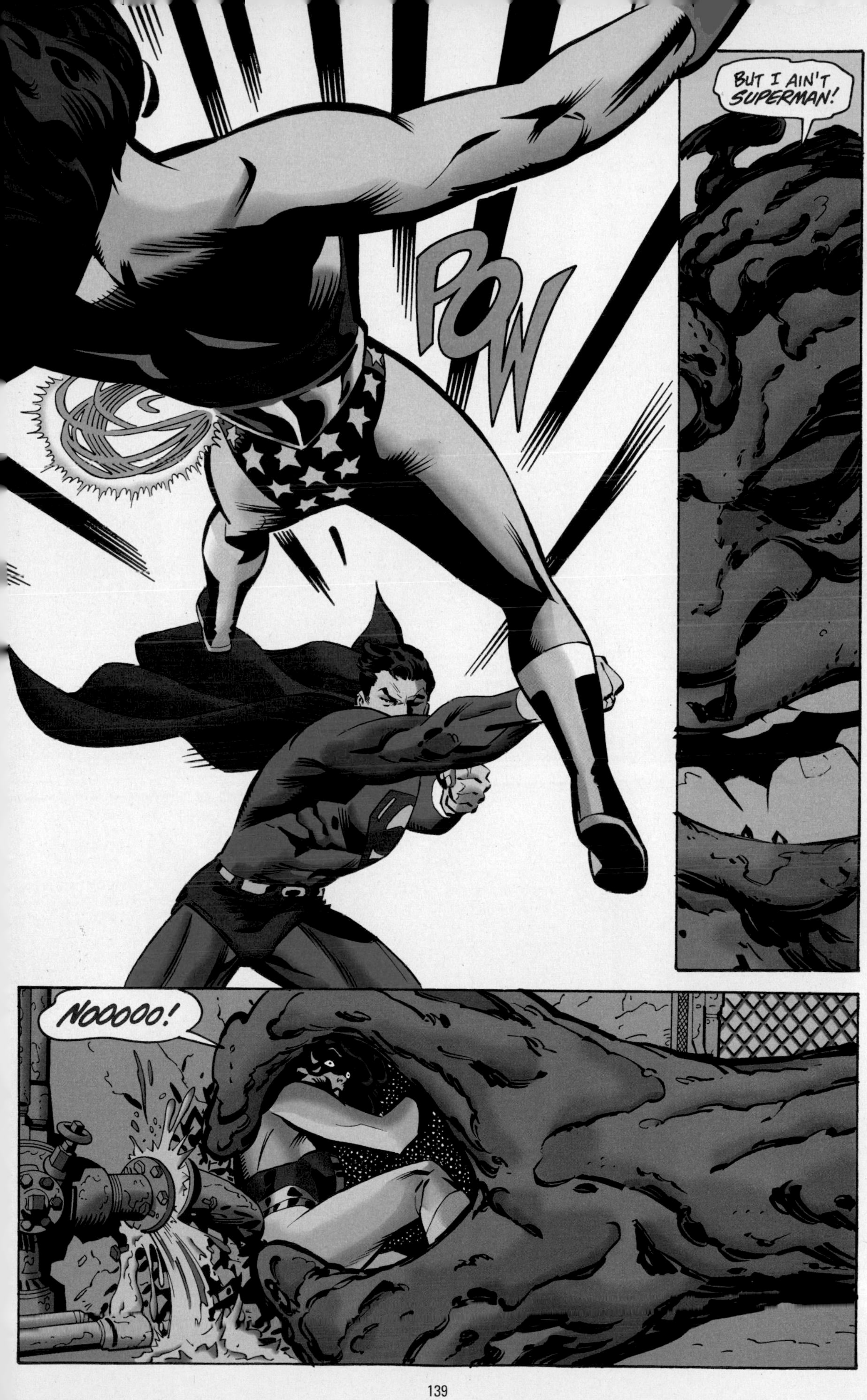
BUT I AIN'T SUPERMAN!
POW
NOOOOO!

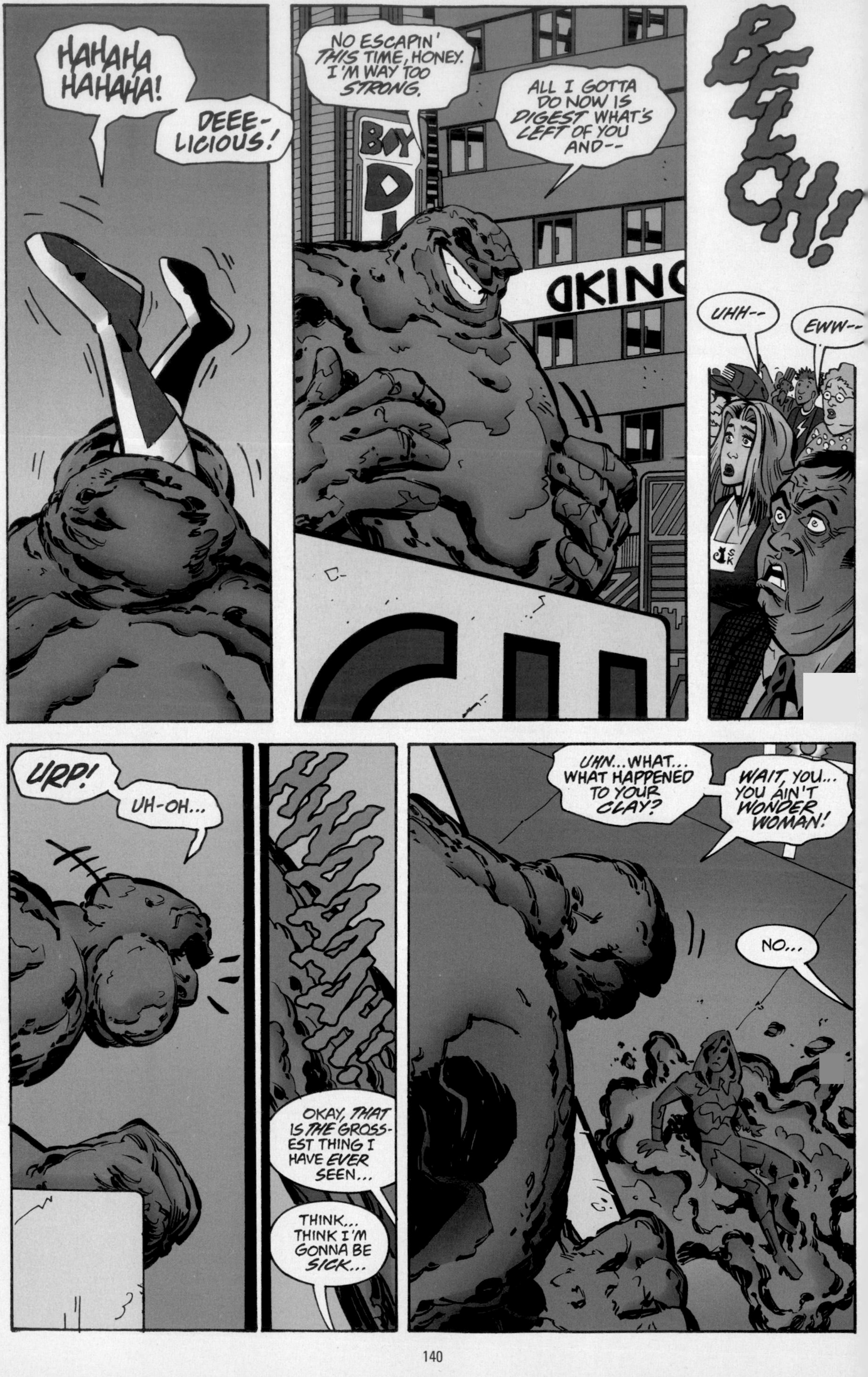
HAHAHA HAHAHA!
DEEE-LICIOUS!
NO ESCAPIN' THIS TIME, HONEY. I'M WAY TOO STRONG.
ALL I GOTTA DO NOW IS DIGEST WHAT'S LEFT OF YOU AND--
BELCH!!
UHH--
EWW--
URP!
UH-OH...
OKAY, THAT IS THE GROSS-EST THING I HAVE EVER SEEN...
THINK... THINK I'M GONNA BE SICK...
UHN... WHAT... WHAT HAPPENED TO YOUR CLAY?
WAIT, YOU... YOU AIN'T WONDER WOMAN!
NO...

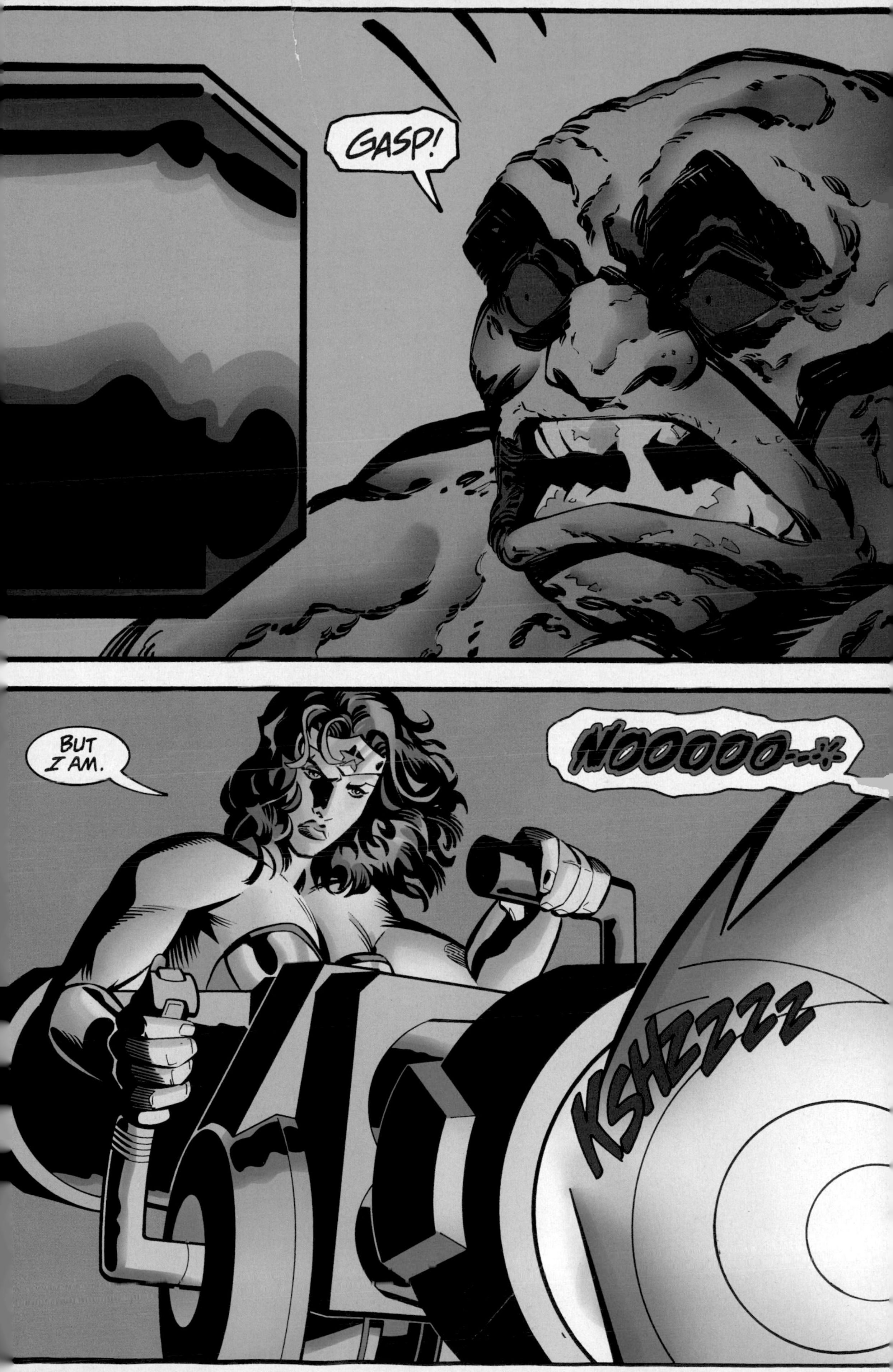
GASP!
BUT I AM.
NOOOOOO--!
KSHZZZZZ

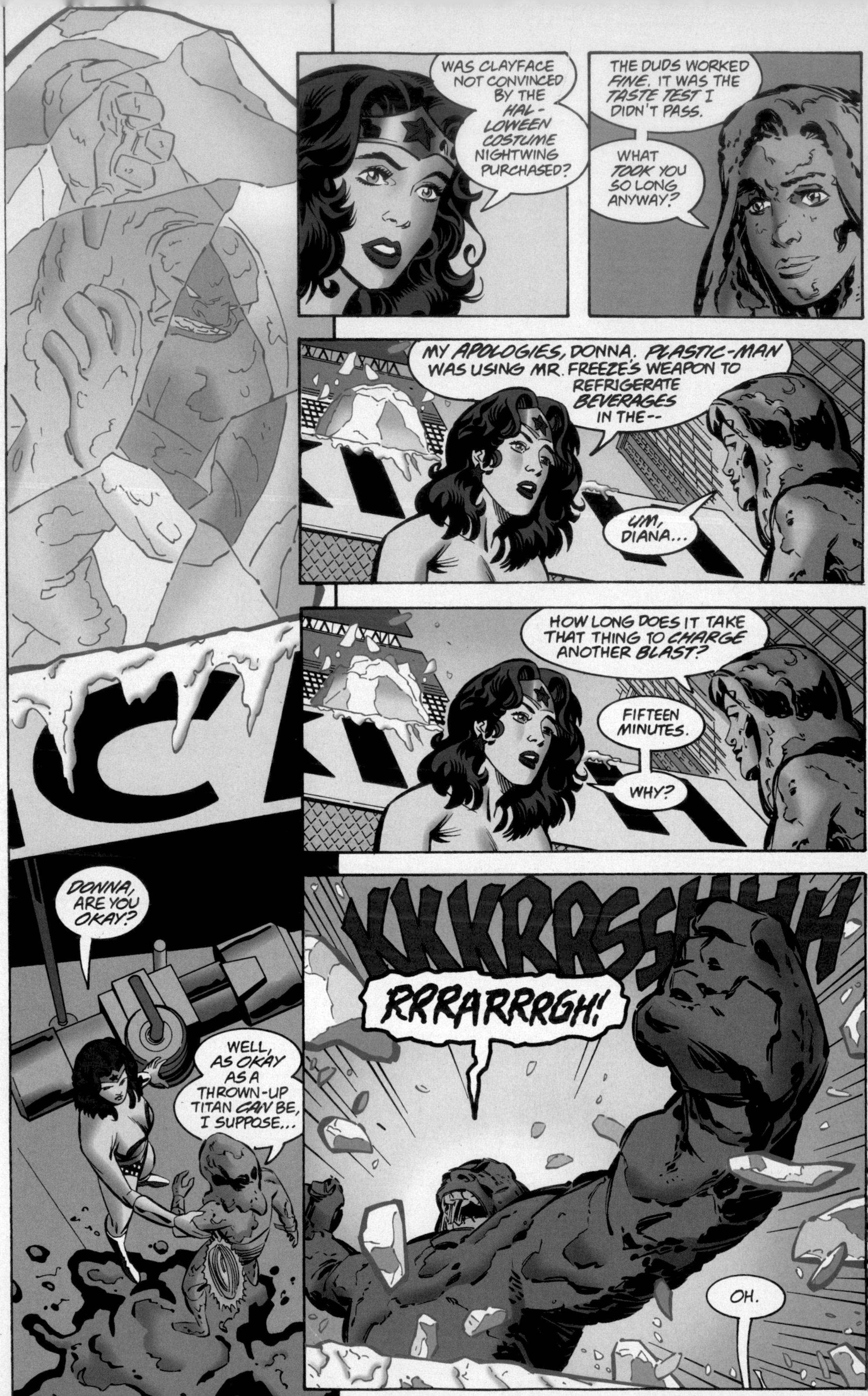
WAS CLAYFACE NOT CONVINCED BY THE HAL-LOWEEN COSTUME NIGHTWING PURCHASED?
THE DUDS WORKED FINE. IT WAS THE TASTE TEST I DIDN'T PASS.
WHAT TOOK YOU SO LONG ANYWAY?
MY APOLOGIES, DONNA. PLASTIC-MAN WAS USING MR. FREEZE'S WEAPON TO REFRIGERATE BEVERAGES IN THE--
UM, DIANA...
HOW LONG DOES IT TAKE THAT THING TO CHARGE ANOTHER BLAST?
FIFTEEN MINUTES.
WHY?
DONNA, ARE YOU OKAY?
WELL, AS OKAY AS A THROWN-UP TITAN CAN BE, I SUPPOSE...
KKKRRSSHHH
RRRARRRGH!
OH.

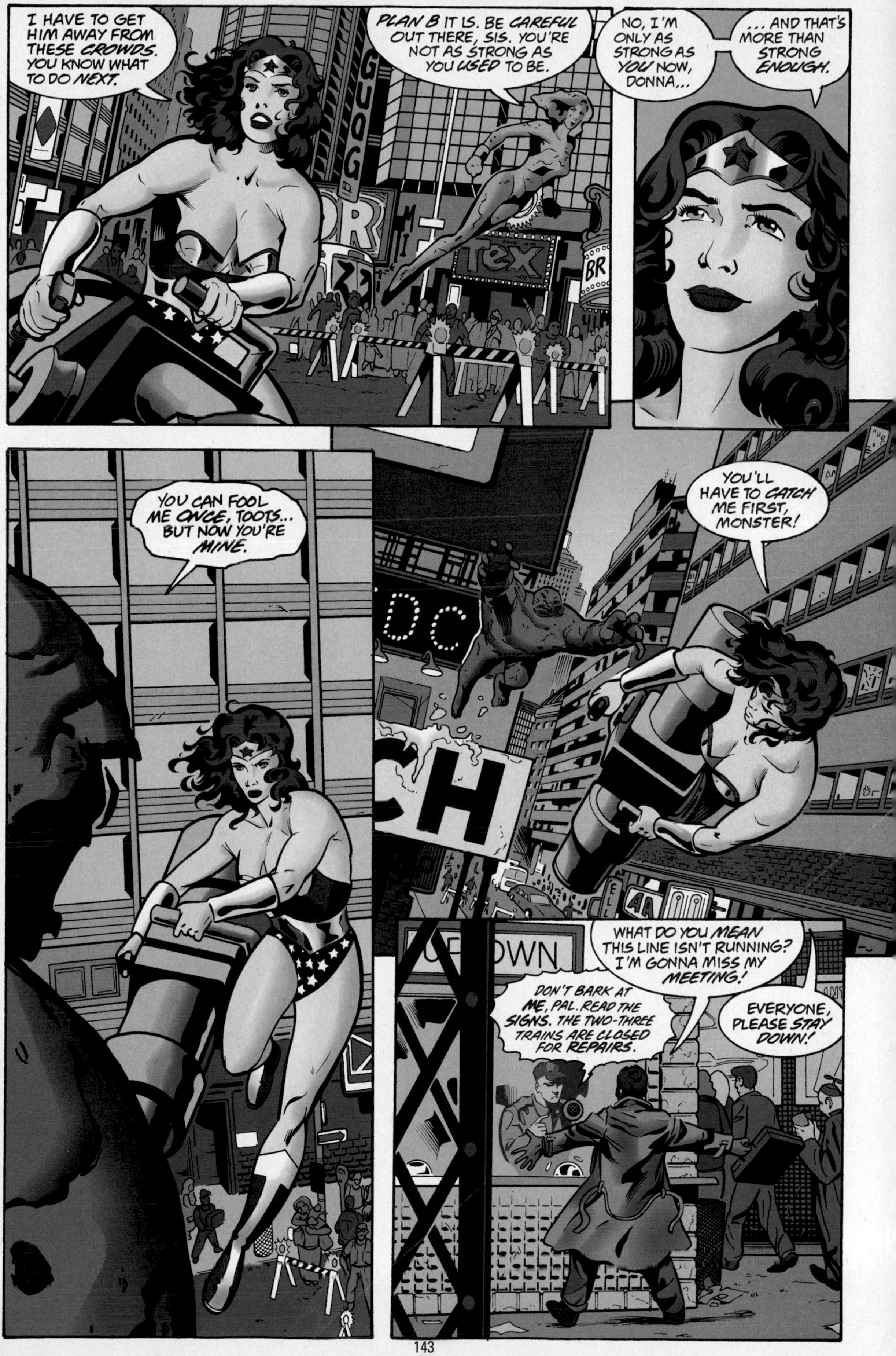
I HAVE TO GET HIM AWAY FROM THESE CROWDS. YOU KNOW WHAT TO DO NEXT.
PLAN B IT IS. BE CAREFUL OUT THERE, SIS. YOU'RE NOT AS STRONG AS YOU USED TO BE.
NO, I'M ONLY AS STRONG AS YOU NOW, DONNA...
... AND THAT'S MORE THAN STRONG ENOUGH.
YOU CAN FOOL ME ONCE, TOOTS... BUT NOW YOU'RE MINE.
YOU'LL HAVE TO CATCH ME FIRST, MONSTER!
WHAT DO YOU MEAN THIS LINE ISN'T RUNNING? I'M GONNA MISS MY MEETING!
DON'T BARK AT ME, PAL. READ THE SIGNS. THE TWO-THREE TRAINS ARE CLOSED FOR REPAIRS.
EVERYONE, PLEASE STAY DOWN!

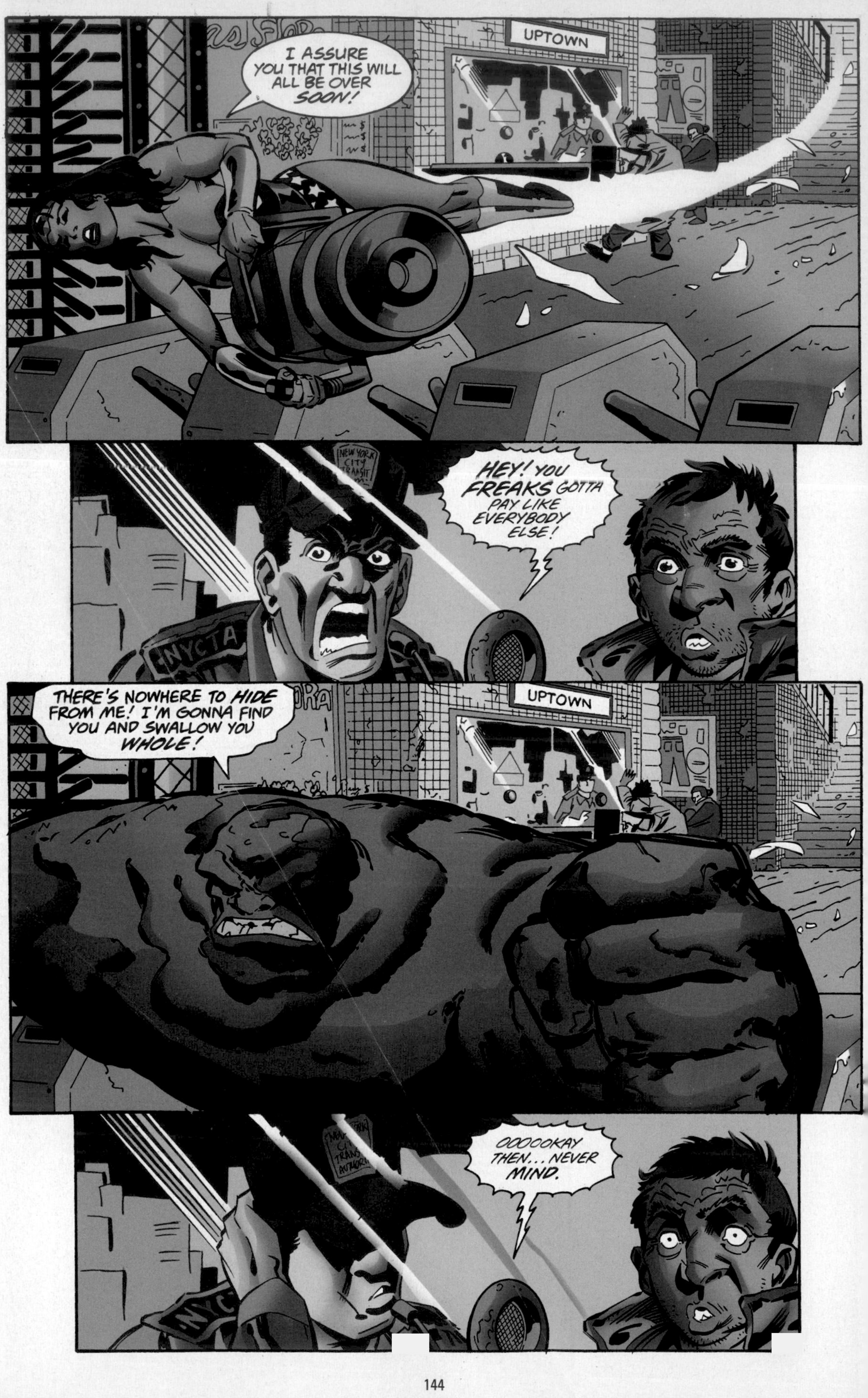
I ASSURE YOU THAT THIS WILL ALL BE OVER SOON!
UPTOWN
NEW YORK CITY TRANSIT
HEY! YOU FREAKS GOTTA PAY LIKE EVERYBODY ELSE!
NYCTA
THERE'S NOWHERE TO HIDE FROM ME! I'M GONNA FIND YOU AND SWALLOW YOU WHOLE!
UPTOWN
OOOOOKAY THEN... NEVER MIND.

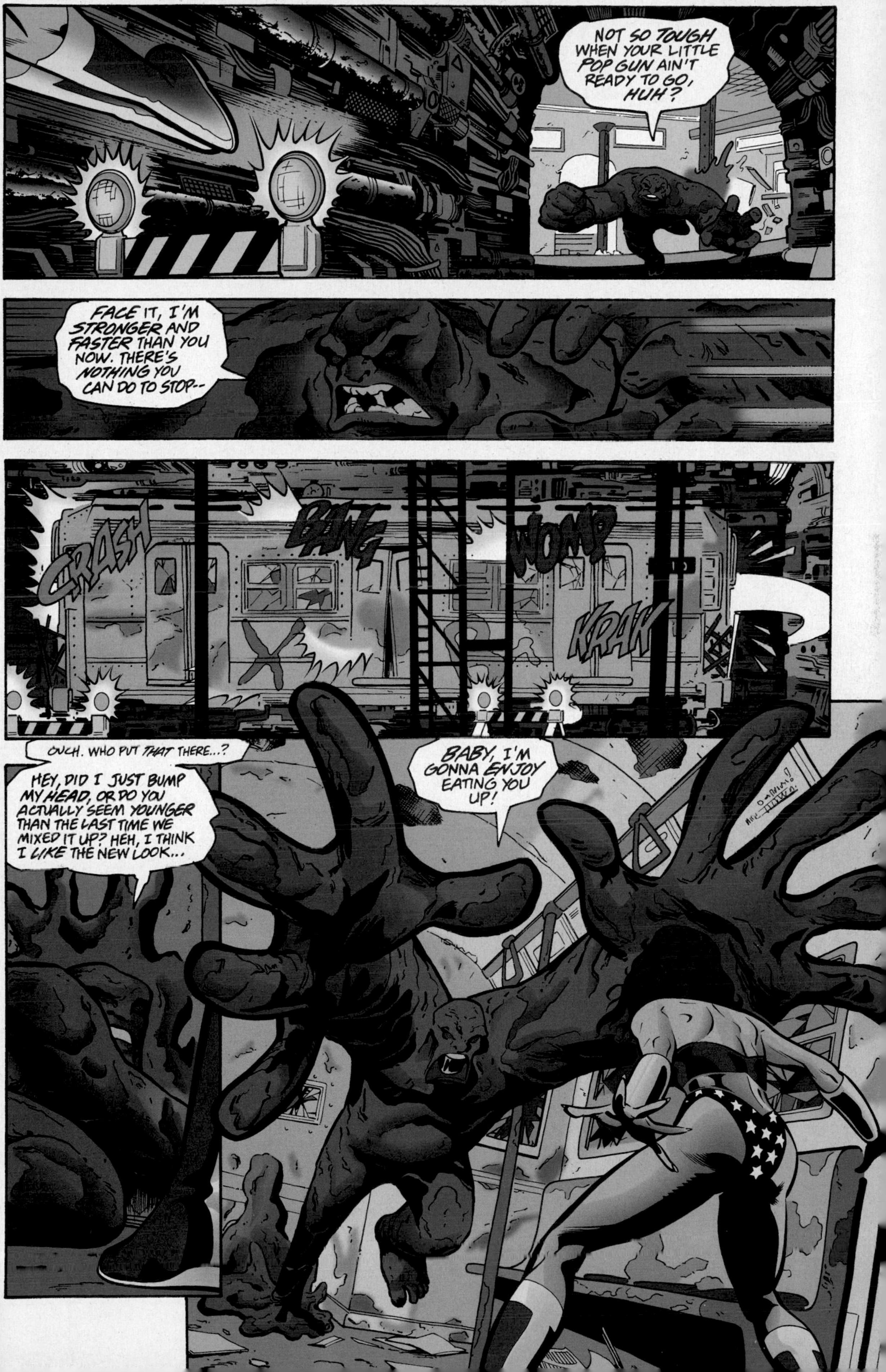

NOT SO TOUGH WHEN YOUR LITTLE POP GUN AIN'T READY TO GO, HUH?
FACE IT, I'M STRONGER AND FASTER THAN YOU NOW. THERE'S NOTHING YOU CAN DO TO STOP--
CRASH
BANG
WOMP
KRAK
OUCH. WHO PUT THAT THERE...?
HEY, DID I JUST BUMP MY HEAD, OR DO YOU ACTUALLY SEEM YOUNGER THAN THE LAST TIME WE MIXED IT UP? HEH, I THINK I LIKE THE NEW LOOK...
BABY, I'M GONNA ENJOY EATING YOU UP!

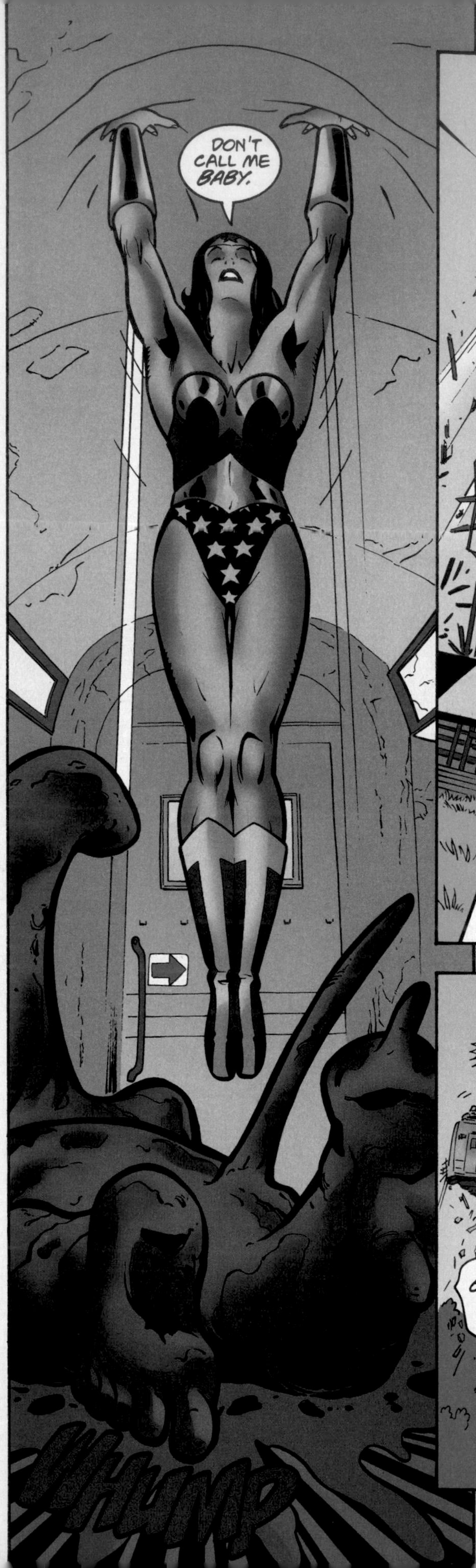
DON'T CALL ME *BABY.*
THUMP

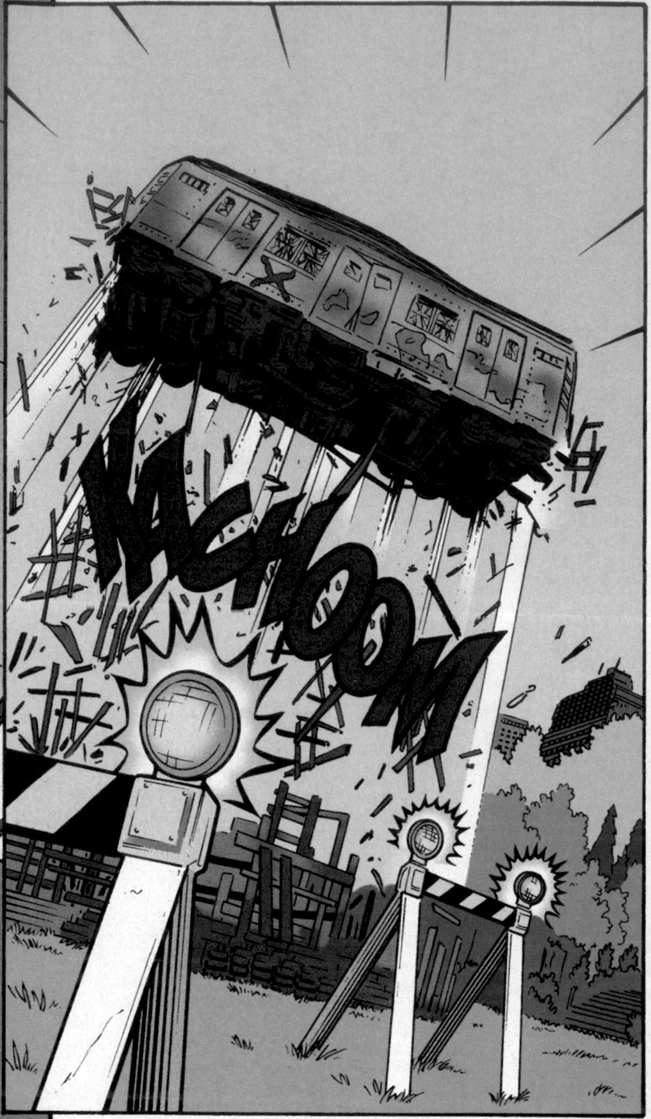
VAHOOM

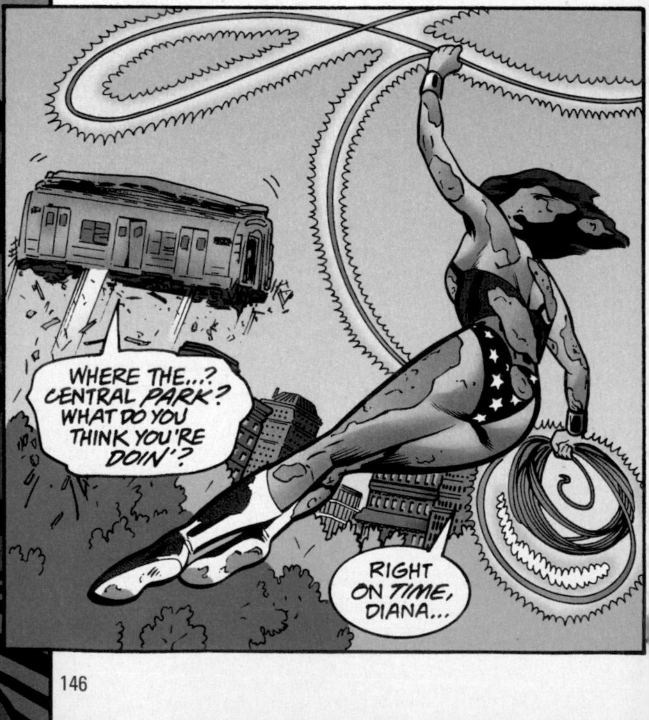
WHERE THE...? CENTRAL *PARK*? WHAT DO YOU THINK YOU'RE *DOIN'*?
RIGHT ON *TIME,* DIANA...

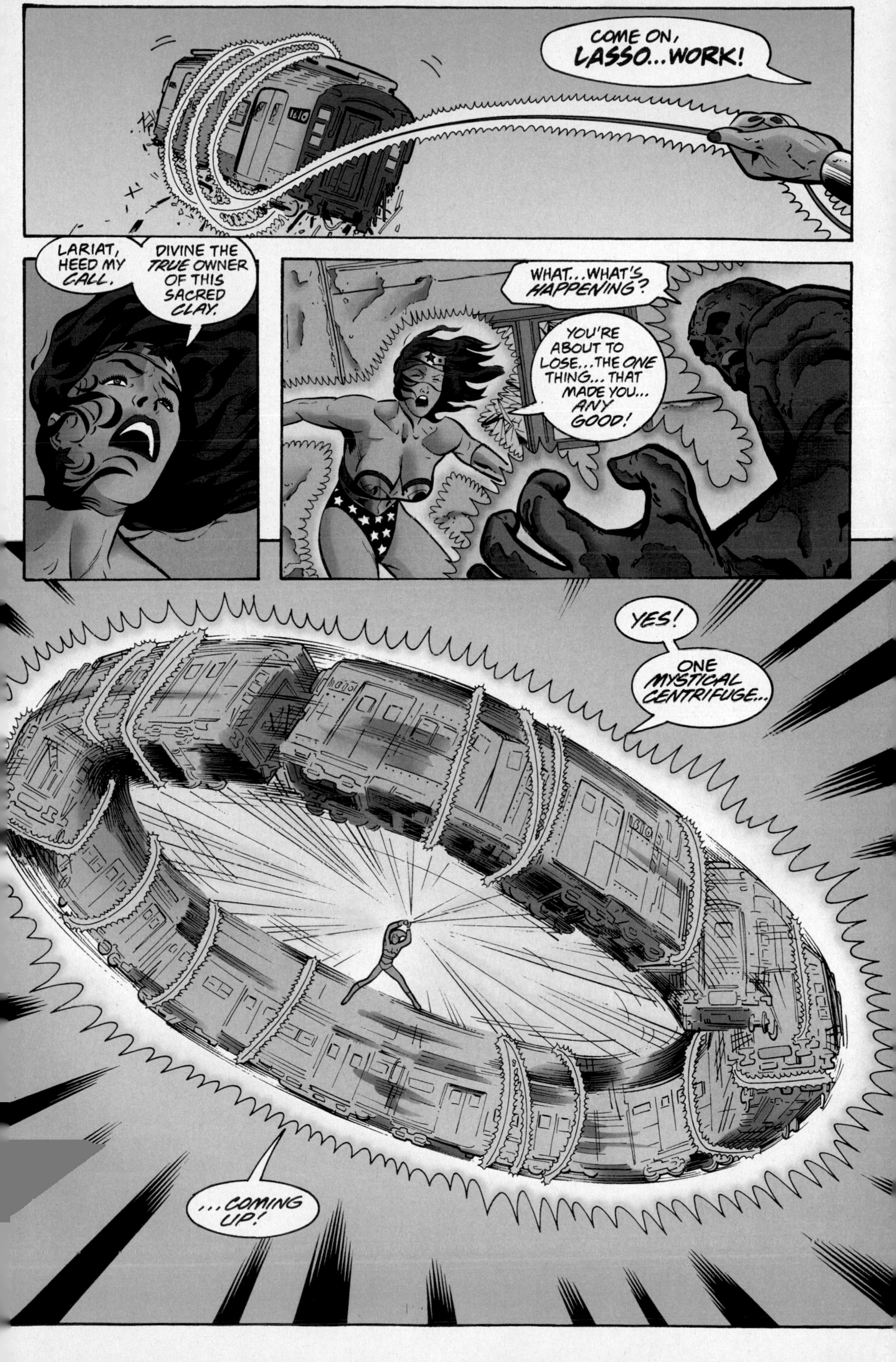
COME ON, LASSO...WORK!
LARIAT, HEED MY CALL.
DIVINE THE TRUE OWNER OF THIS SACRED CLAY.
WHAT...WHAT'S HAPPENING?
YOU'RE ABOUT TO LOSE...THE ONE THING...THAT MADE YOU...ANY GOOD!
YES!
ONE MYSTICAL CENTRIFUGE...
...COMING UP!

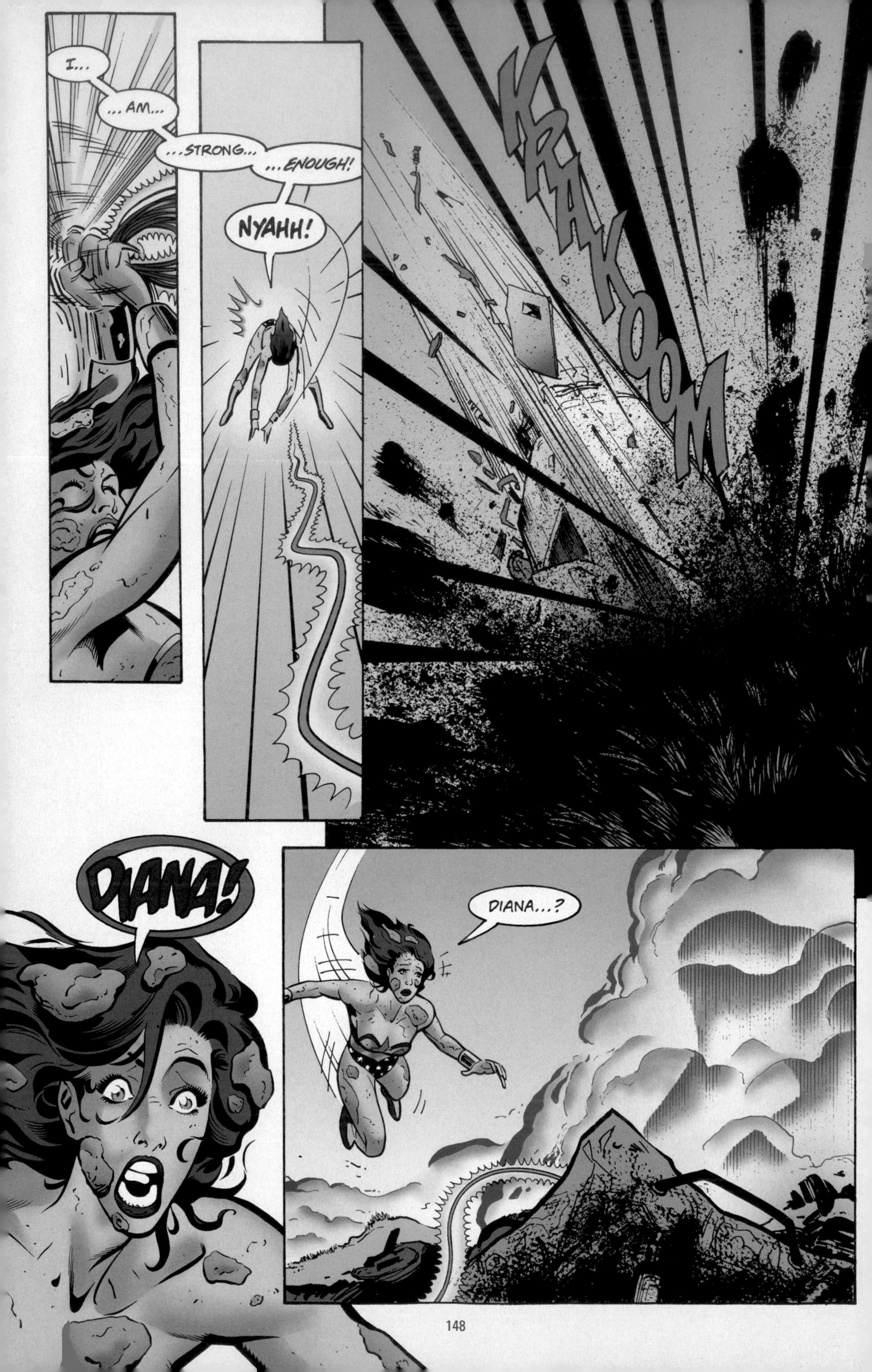
I...
...AM...
...STRONG...
...ENOUGH!
NYAHH!
KRAKOOM
DIANA!
DIANA...?

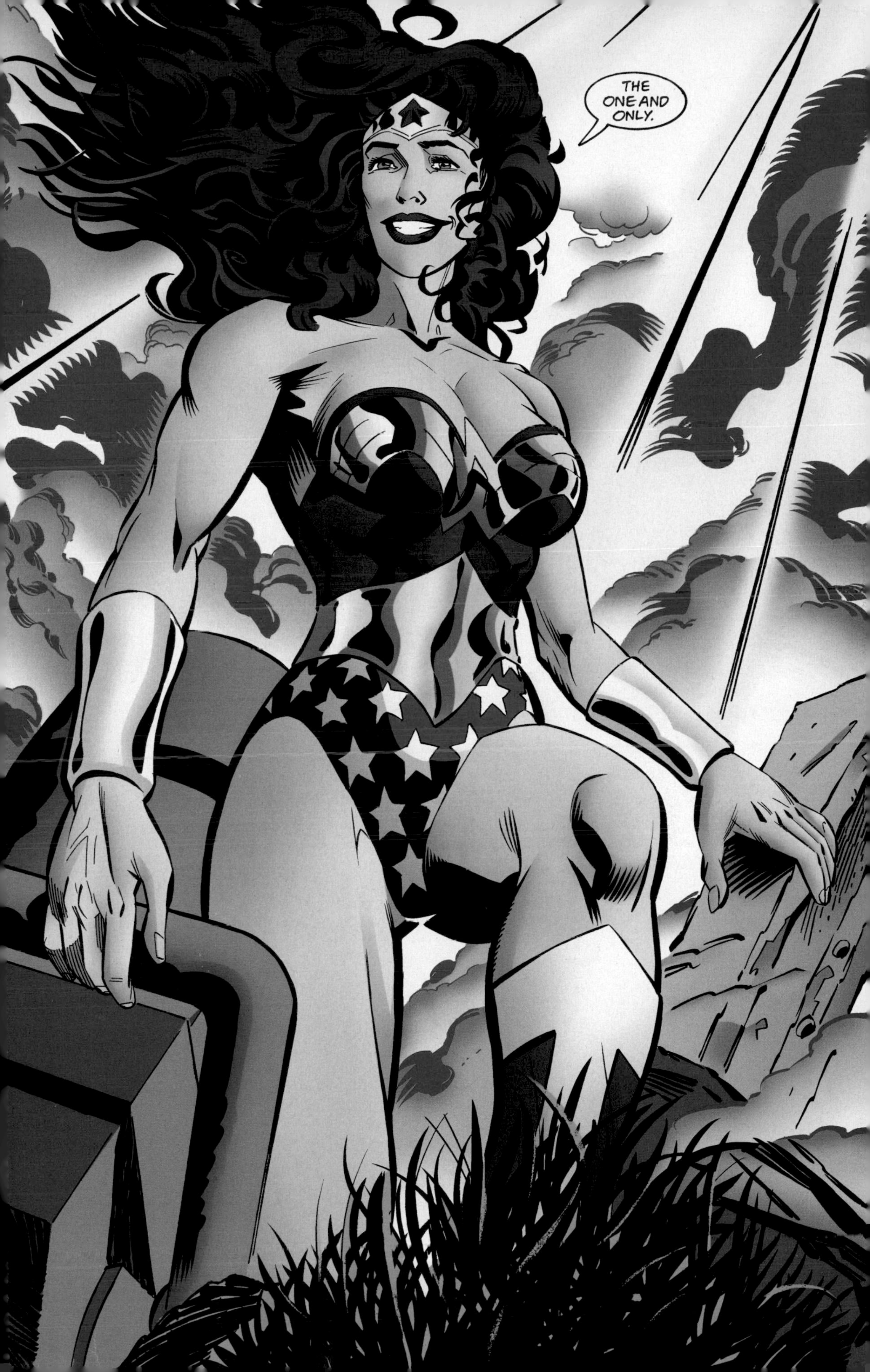
THE ONE AND ONLY.

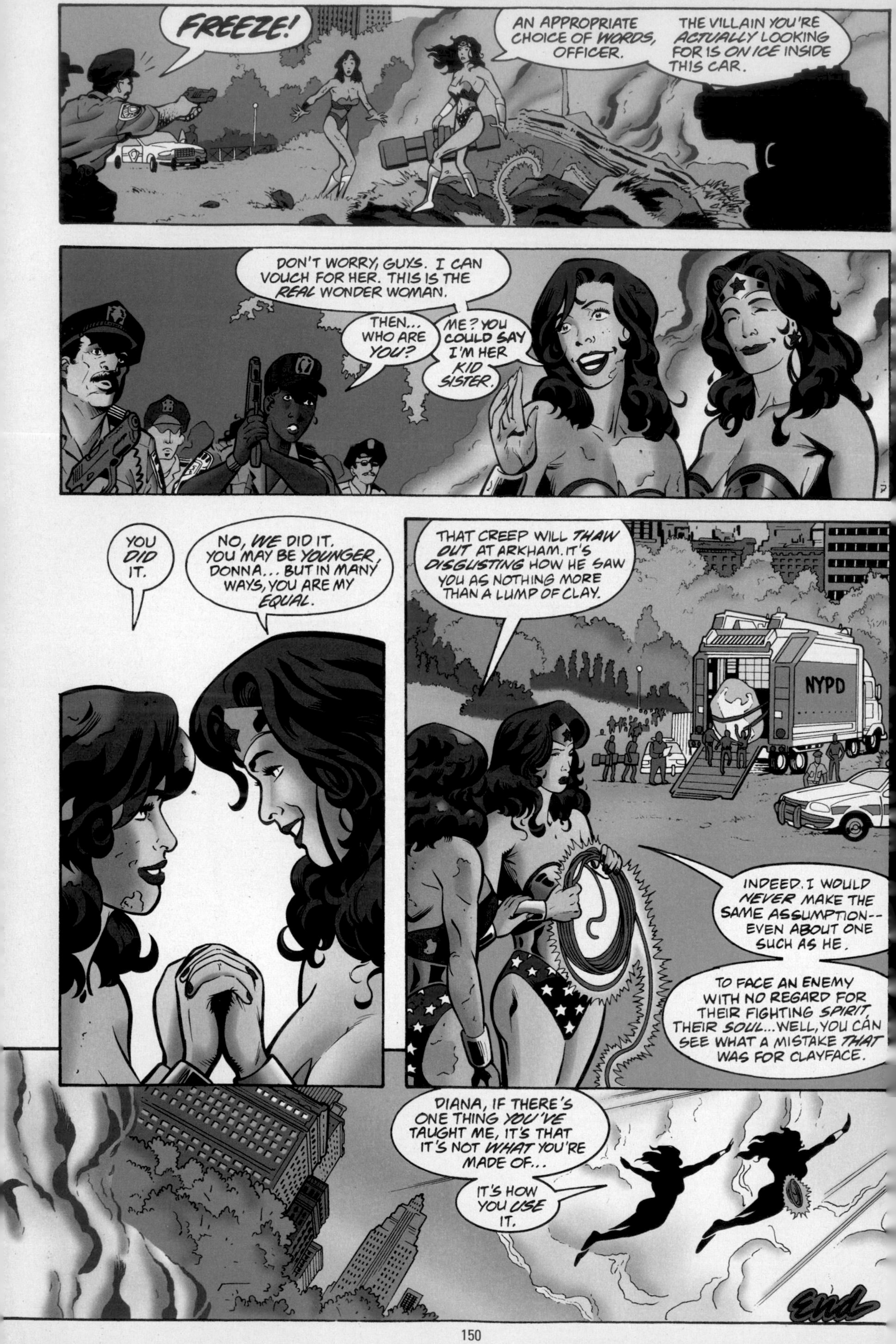
FREEZE!
AN APPROPRIATE CHOICE OF WORDS, OFFICER.
THE VILLAIN YOU'RE ACTUALLY LOOKING FOR IS ON ICE INSIDE THIS CAR.
DON'T WORRY, GUYS. I CAN VOUCH FOR HER. THIS IS THE REAL WONDER WOMAN.
THEN... WHO ARE YOU?
ME? YOU COULD SAY I'M HER KID SISTER.
YOU DID IT.
NO, WE DID IT. YOU MAY BE YOUNGER, DONNA... BUT IN MANY WAYS, YOU ARE MY EQUAL.
THAT CREEP WILL THAW OUT AT ARKHAM. IT'S DISGUSTING HOW HE SAW YOU AS NOTHING MORE THAN A LUMP OF CLAY.
NYPD
INDEED. I WOULD NEVER MAKE THE SAME ASSUMPTION-- EVEN ABOUT ONE SUCH AS HE.
TO FACE AN ENEMY WITH NO REGARD FOR THEIR FIGHTING SPIRIT, THEIR SOUL... WELL, YOU CAN SEE WHAT A MISTAKE THAT WAS FOR CLAYFACE.
DIANA, IF THERE'S ONE THING YOU'VE TAUGHT ME, IT'S THAT IT'S NOT WHAT YOU'RE MADE OF...
IT'S HOW YOU USE IT.
End

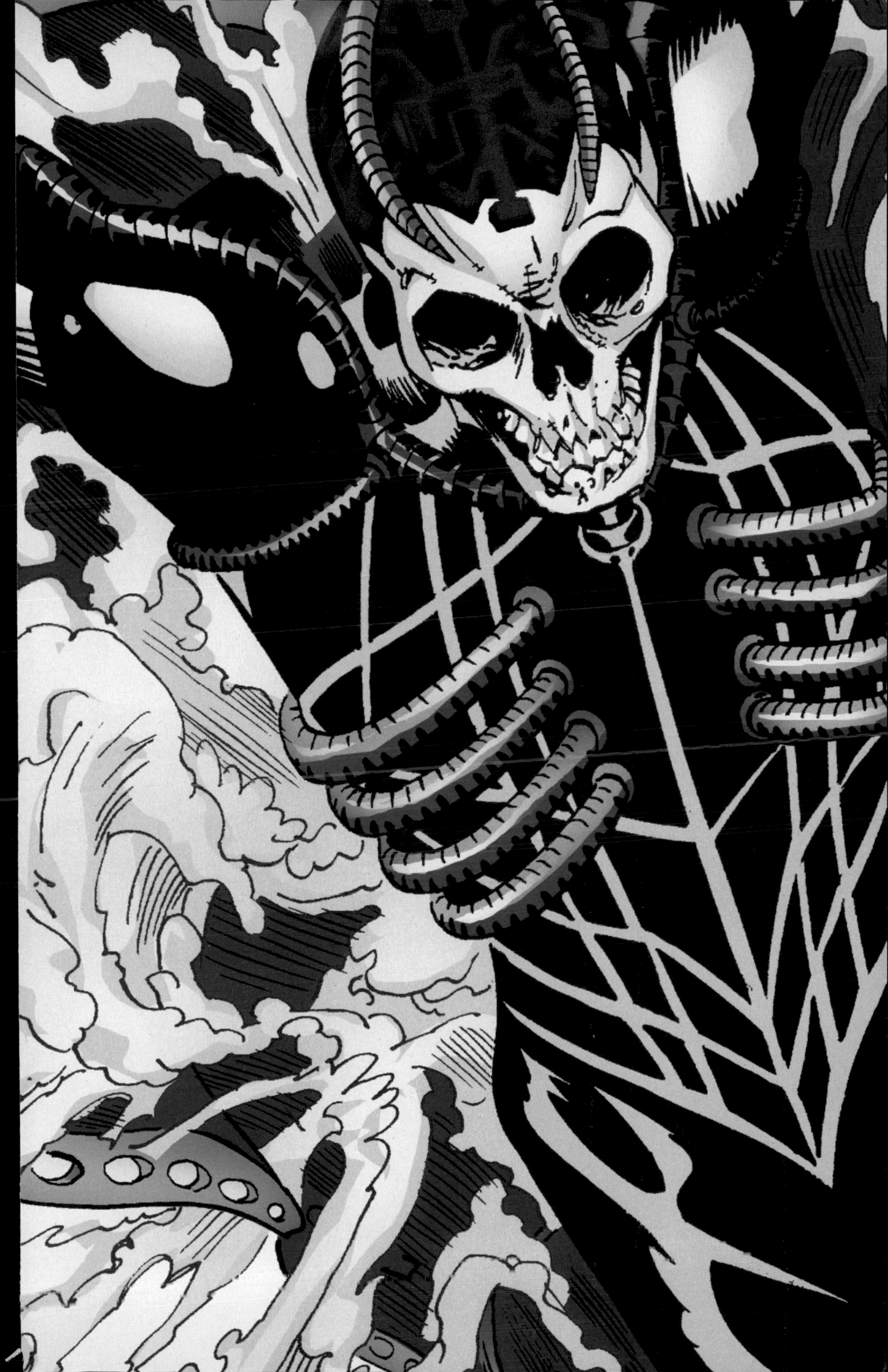

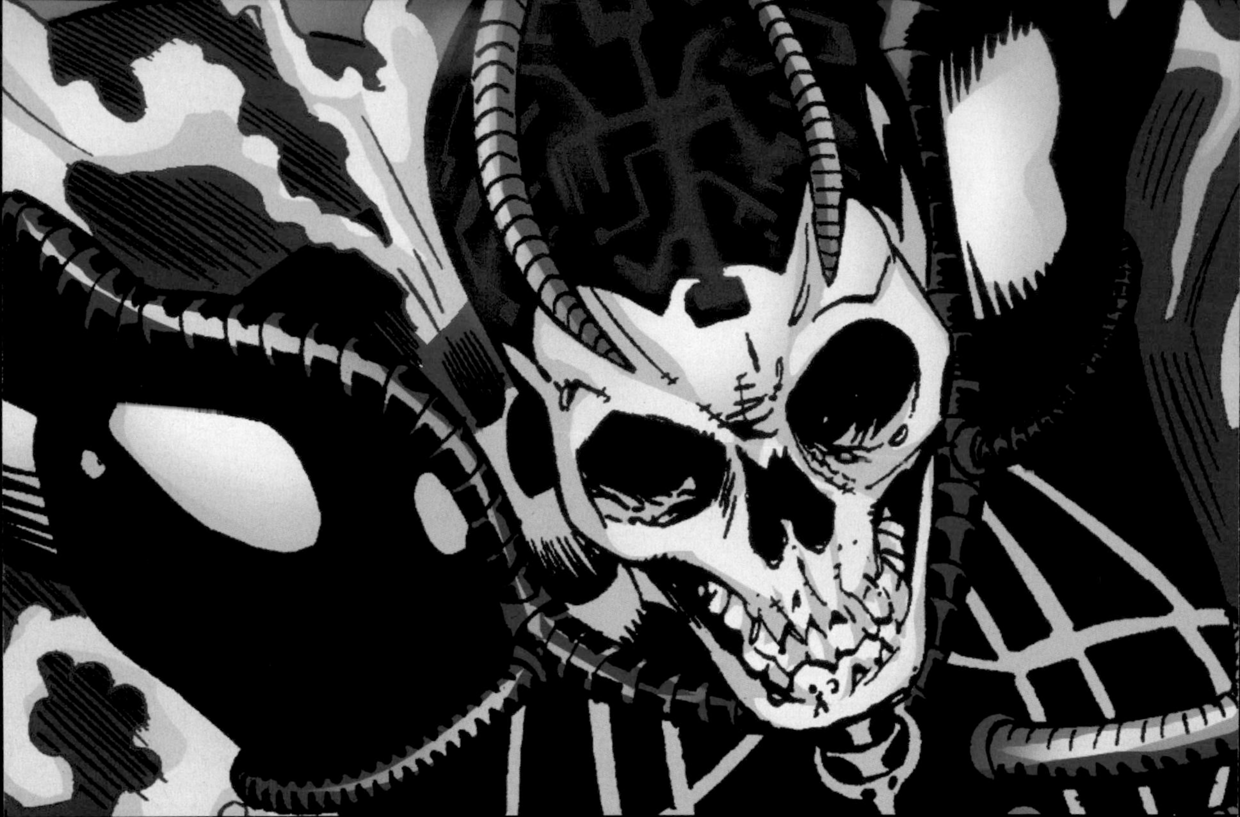

SKULLDUGGERY

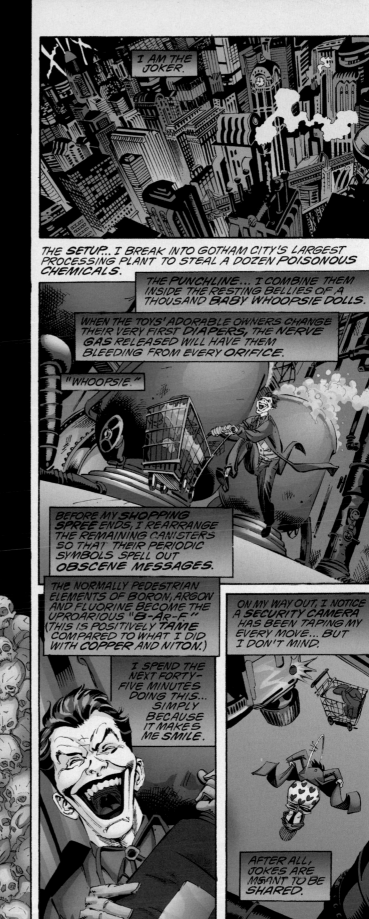

I AM THE JOKER.

THE *SETUP*... I BREAK INTO GOTHAM CITY'S LARGEST PROCESSING PLANT TO STEAL A DOZEN *POISONOUS CHEMICALS.*

THE *PUNCHLINE*... I COMBINE THEM INSIDE THE RESTING BELLIES OF A THOUSAND *BABY WHOOPSIE DOLLS.*

WHEN THE TOYS' *ADORABLE* OWNERS CHANGE THEIR VERY FIRST *DIAPERS*, THE NERVE GAS RELEASED WILL HAVE THEM BLEEDING FROM EVERY *ORIFICE.*

"WHOOPSIE."

BEFORE MY *SHOPPING SPREE* ENDS, I REARRANGE THE REMAINING CANISTERS SO THAT THEIR PERIODIC SYMBOLS SPELL OUT *OBSCENE MESSAGES.*

THE NORMALLY PEDESTRIAN ELEMENTS OF BORON, ARGON AND FLUORINE BECOME THE UPROARIOUS *"B-Ar-F"* (THIS IS POSITIVELY *TAME* COMPARED TO WHAT I DID WITH COPPER AND NITON.)

I SPEND THE NEXT FORTY-FIVE MINUTES DOING THIS... SIMPLY BECAUSE IT MAKES ME SMILE.

ON MY WAY OUT, I NOTICE A *SECURITY CAMERA* HAS BEEN TAPING MY EVERY MOVE... BUT I DON'T MIND.

AFTER ALL, JOKES ARE *MEANT TO BE SHARED.*

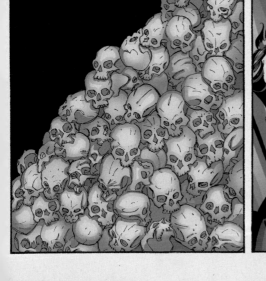

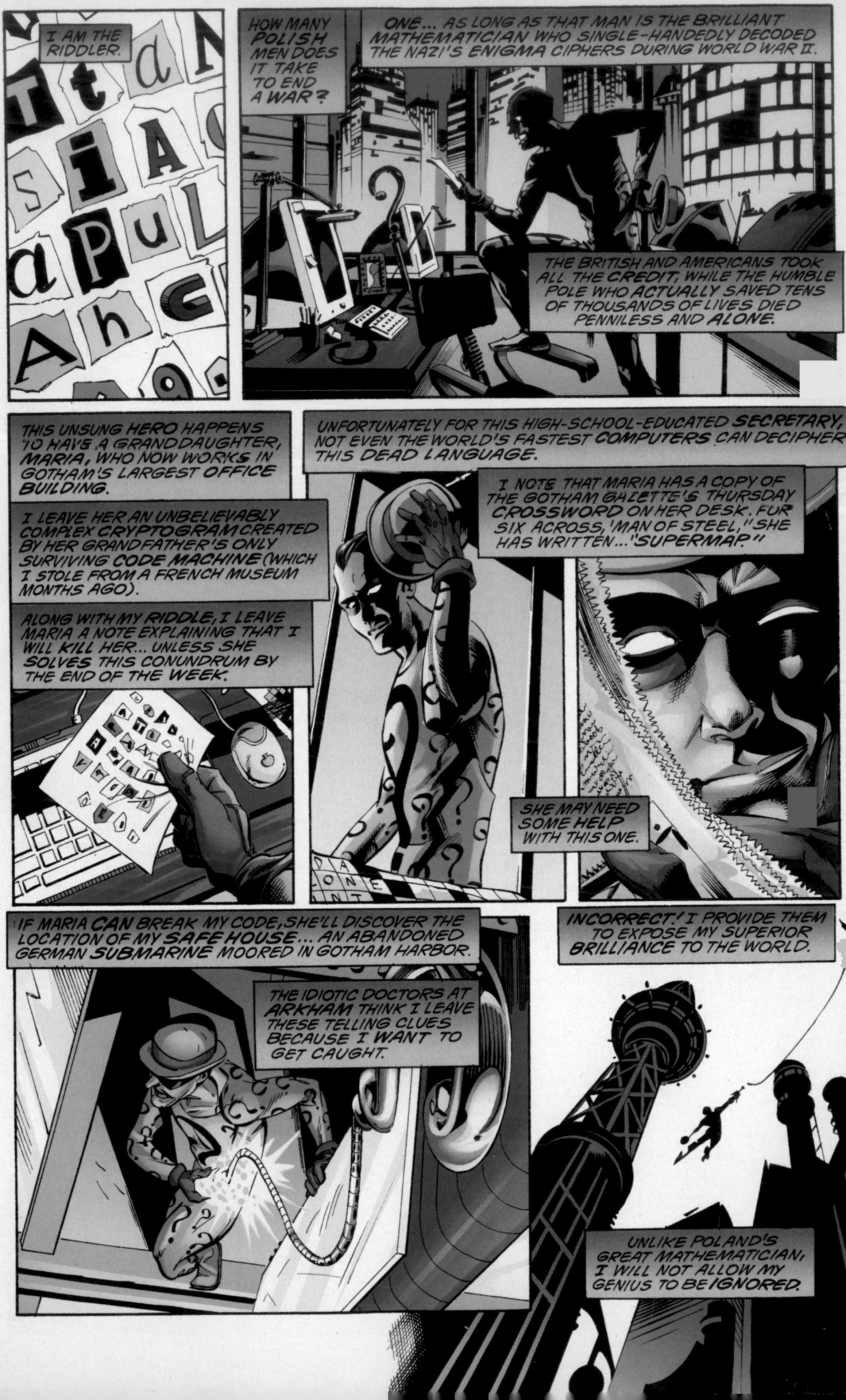

I AM THE RIDDLER.
HOW MANY POLISH MEN DOES IT TAKE TO END A WAR?
ONE... AS LONG AS THAT MAN IS THE BRILLIANT MATHEMATICIAN WHO SINGLE-HANDEDLY DECODED THE NAZI'S ENIGMA CIPHERS DURING WORLD WAR II.
THE BRITISH AND AMERICANS TOOK ALL THE CREDIT, WHILE THE HUMBLE POLE WHO ACTUALLY SAVED TENS OF THOUSANDS OF LIVES DIED PENNILESS AND ALONE.
THIS UNSUNG HERO HAPPENS TO HAVE A GRANDDAUGHTER, MARIA, WHO NOW WORKS IN GOTHAM'S LARGEST OFFICE BUILDING.
I LEAVE HER AN UNBELIEVABLY COMPLEX CRYPTOGRAM CREATED BY HER GRANDFATHER'S ONLY SURVIVING CODE MACHINE (WHICH I STOLE FROM A FRENCH MUSEUM MONTHS AGO).
ALONG WITH MY RIDDLE, I LEAVE MARIA A NOTE EXPLAINING THAT I WILL KILL HER... UNLESS SHE SOLVES THIS CONUNDRUM BY THE END OF THE WEEK.
UNFORTUNATELY FOR THIS HIGH-SCHOOL-EDUCATED SECRETARY, NOT EVEN THE WORLD'S FASTEST COMPUTERS CAN DECIPHER THIS DEAD LANGUAGE.
I NOTE THAT MARIA HAS A COPY OF THE GOTHAM GAZETTE'S THURSDAY CROSSWORD ON HER DESK. FOR SIX ACROSS, "MAN OF STEEL," SHE HAS WRITTEN... "SUPERMAP."
SHE MAY NEED SOME HELP WITH THIS ONE.
IF MARIA CAN BREAK MY CODE, SHE'LL DISCOVER THE LOCATION OF MY SAFE HOUSE... AN ABANDONED GERMAN SUBMARINE MOORED IN GOTHAM HARBOR.
THE IDIOTIC DOCTORS AT ARKHAM THINK I LEAVE THESE TELLING CLUES BECAUSE I WANT TO GET CAUGHT.
INCORRECT! I PROVIDE THEM TO EXPOSE MY SUPERIOR BRILLIANCE TO THE WORLD.
UNLIKE POLAND'S GREAT MATHEMATICIAN, I WILL NOT ALLOW MY GENIUS TO BE IGNORED.

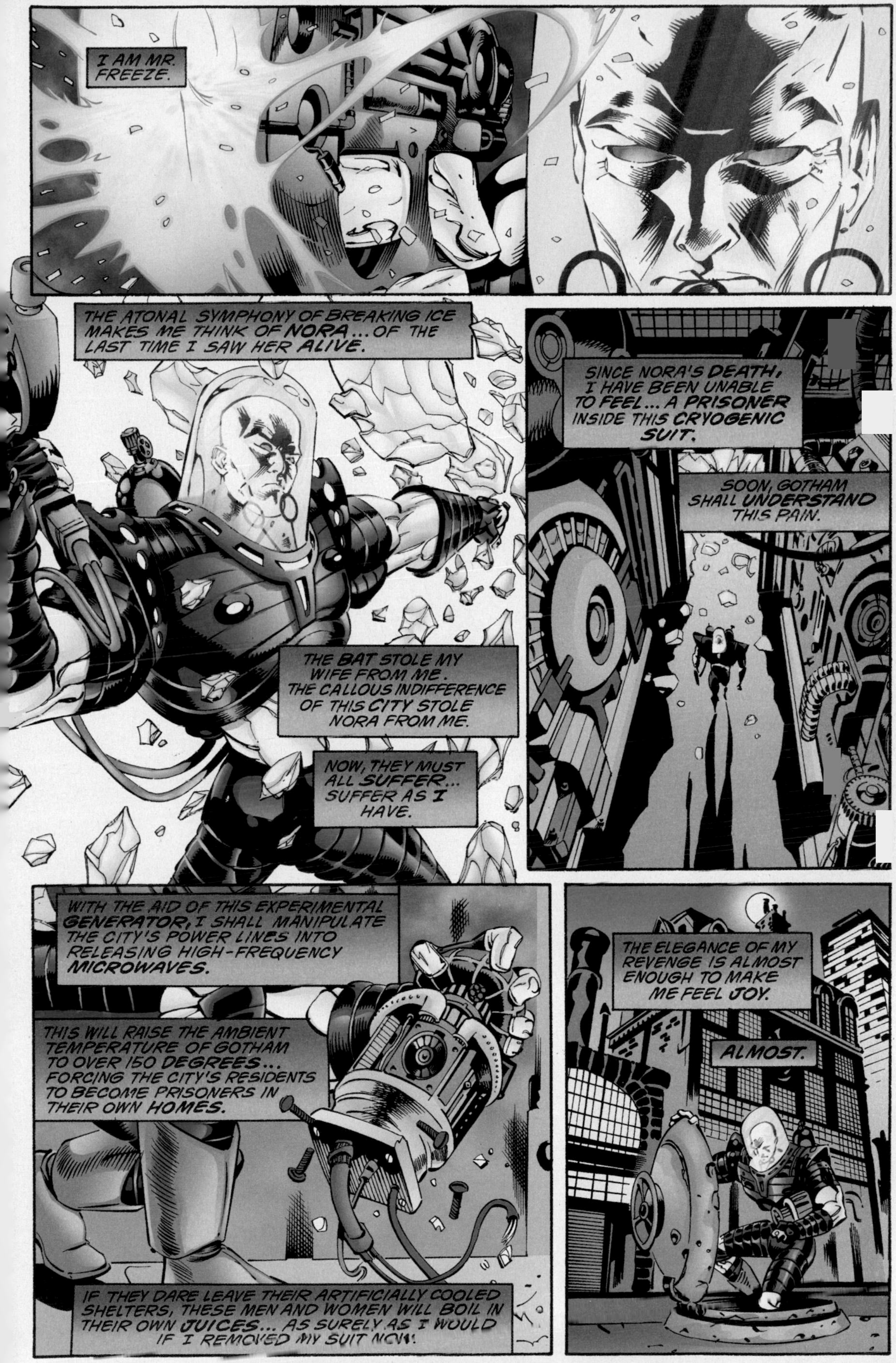

I AM MR. FREEZE.
THE ATONAL SYMPHONY OF BREAKING ICE MAKES ME THINK OF NORA... OF THE LAST TIME I SAW HER ALIVE.
THE BAT STOLE MY WIFE FROM ME. THE CALLOUS INDIFFERENCE OF THIS CITY STOLE NORA FROM ME.
NOW, THEY MUST ALL SUFFER... SUFFER AS I HAVE.
SINCE NORA'S DEATH, I HAVE BEEN UNABLE TO FEEL... A PRISONER INSIDE THIS CRYOGENIC SUIT.
SOON, GOTHAM SHALL UNDERSTAND THIS PAIN.
WITH THE AID OF THIS EXPERIMENTAL GENERATOR, I SHALL MANIPULATE THE CITY'S POWER LINES INTO RELEASING HIGH-FREQUENCY MICROWAVES.
THIS WILL RAISE THE AMBIENT TEMPERATURE OF GOTHAM TO OVER 150 DEGREES... FORCING THE CITY'S RESIDENTS TO BECOME PRISONERS IN THEIR OWN HOMES.
IF THEY DARE LEAVE THEIR ARTIFICIALLY COOLED SHELTERS, THESE MEN AND WOMEN WILL BOIL IN THEIR OWN JUICES... AS SURELY AS I WOULD IF I REMOVED MY SUIT NOW.
THE ELEGANCE OF MY REVENGE IS ALMOST ENOUGH TO MAKE ME FEEL JOY.
ALMOST.

SOON, I RETURN TO MY NOCTURNAL HABITAT... THE SUBTERRANEAN WORLD OF OLD GOTHAM.

AFTER THE QUAKE, THIS DECIMATED SECTION OF TOWN WAS ABANDONED BY EVEN ITS MOST STUBBORN OCCUPANTS, AND A GLISTENING NEW CITY WAS BUILT DIRECTLY OVER THE STILL-WARM CORPSE OF ITS PREDECESSOR.

HERE LIE THE FORGOTTEN BONES OF YESTERDAY... A PERFECT PLACE TO CALL MY HOME.

IT WAS IN THESE RUINS THAT I FOUND THE VACANT SANCTUARIES OF GOTHAM'S MOST HEINOUS CRIMINALS.

I PARADE PAST THE GAUDY COSTUMES I PILFERED FROM THESE HIDEOUTS, AND REST THE EXPERIMENTAL GENERATOR NEXT TO THE DORMANT GAS CANISTERS I STOLE EARLIER.

THERE ARE NO DOLLS, NO SUBMARINES, NO HEAT WAVES. NONE OF THE VILLAINOUS SCHEMES I CONCOCTED WILL EVER BE PUT INTO ACTION.

JOKER. RIDDLER. FREEZE. IT WAS EASY FOR SOMEONE IN MY POSITION TO OBTAIN THEIR PATIENT RECORDS.

SCARECROW

TWO-FACE
DENT, HARVEY

RIDDLER
NIGMA, EDWARD

JOKER
REAL NAME: UN

MR. FREEZE
FRIES, VICTOR

MY EQUIPMENT AIDED IN THE PHYSICAL TRANSFORMATIONS, BUT I HAD TO STUDY THESE KILLERS FOR AGES BEFORE I WAS ABLE TO DUPLICATE THEIR EVERY MOVE, THINK THEIR VERY THOUGHTS.

I AM ALL OF THESE MEN. I AM NONE OF THESE MEN.

I AM THE SKELETON.

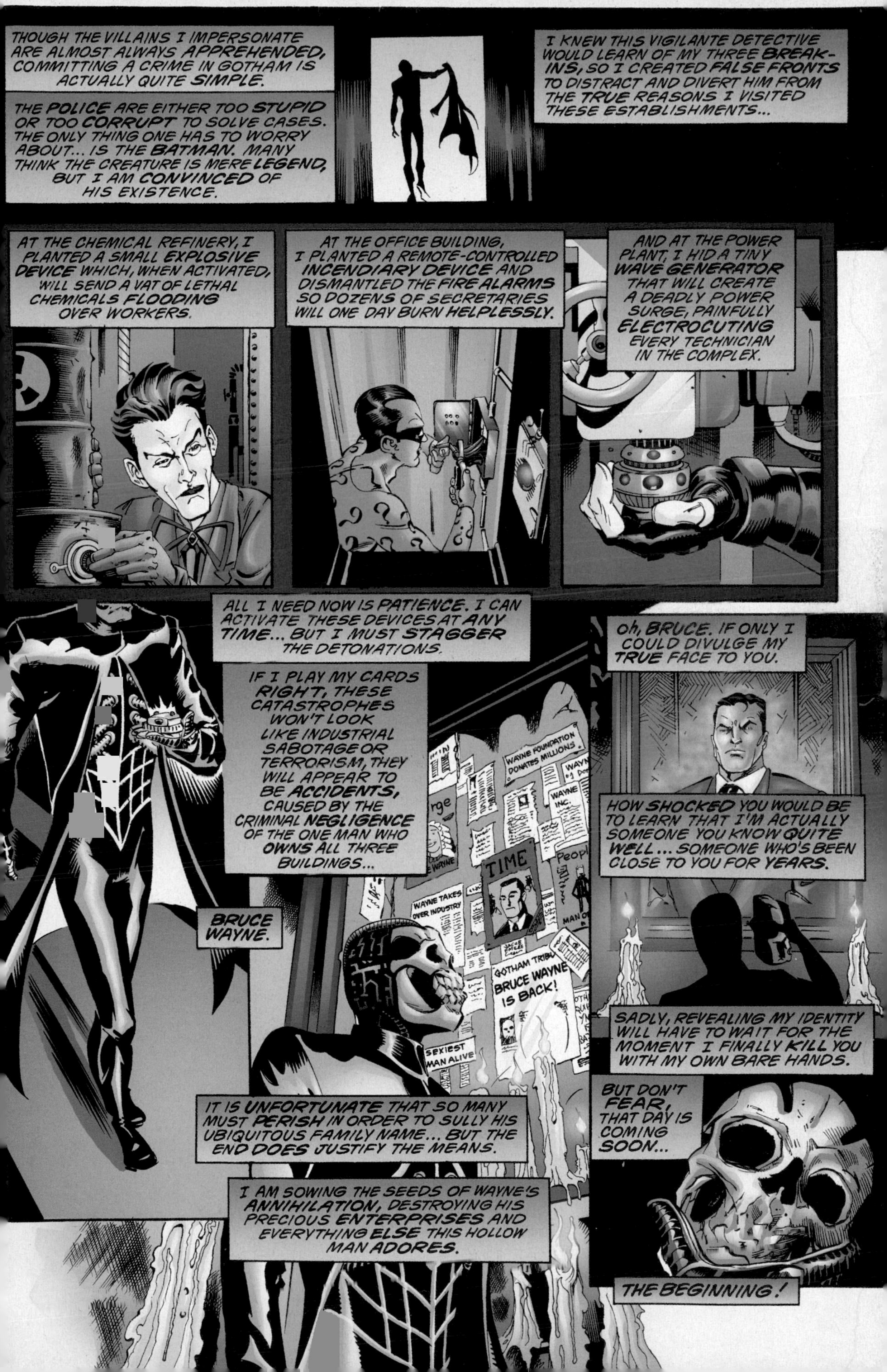
THOUGH THE VILLAINS I IMPERSONATE ARE ALMOST ALWAYS APPREHENDED, COMMITTING A CRIME IN GOTHAM IS ACTUALLY QUITE SIMPLE.
THE POLICE ARE EITHER TOO STUPID OR TOO CORRUPT TO SOLVE CASES. THE ONLY THING ONE HAS TO WORRY ABOUT... IS THE BATMAN. MANY THINK THE CREATURE IS MERE LEGEND, BUT I AM CONVINCED OF HIS EXISTENCE.
I KNEW THIS VIGILANTE DETECTIVE WOULD LEARN OF MY THREE BREAK-INS, SO I CREATED FALSE FRONTS TO DISTRACT AND DIVERT HIM FROM THE TRUE REASONS I VISITED THESE ESTABLISHMENTS...
AT THE CHEMICAL REFINERY, I PLANTED A SMALL EXPLOSIVE DEVICE WHICH, WHEN ACTIVATED, WILL SEND A VAT OF LETHAL CHEMICALS FLOODING OVER WORKERS.
AT THE OFFICE BUILDING, I PLANTED A REMOTE-CONTROLLED INCENDIARY DEVICE AND DISMANTLED THE FIRE ALARMS SO DOZENS OF SECRETARIES WILL ONE DAY BURN HELPLESSLY.
AND AT THE POWER PLANT, I HID A TINY WAVE GENERATOR THAT WILL CREATE A DEADLY POWER SURGE, PAINFULLY ELECTROCUTING EVERY TECHNICIAN IN THE COMPLEX.
ALL I NEED NOW IS PATIENCE. I CAN ACTIVATE THESE DEVICES AT ANY TIME... BUT I MUST STAGGER THE DETONATIONS.
IF I PLAY MY CARDS RIGHT, THESE CATASTROPHES WON'T LOOK LIKE INDUSTRIAL SABOTAGE OR TERRORISM, THEY WILL APPEAR TO BE ACCIDENTS, CAUSED BY THE CRIMINAL NEGLIGENCE OF THE ONE MAN WHO OWNS ALL THREE BUILDINGS...
BRUCE WAYNE.
WAYNE FOUNDATION DONATES MILLIONS
WAYNE INC.
TIME
WAYNE TAKES OVER INDUSTRY
GOTHAM TRIBU
BRUCE WAYNE IS BACK!
SEXIEST MAN ALIVE
IT IS UNFORTUNATE THAT SO MANY MUST PERISH IN ORDER TO SULLY HIS UBIQUITOUS FAMILY NAME... BUT THE END DOES JUSTIFY THE MEANS.
I AM SOWING THE SEEDS OF WAYNE'S ANNIHILATION, DESTROYING HIS PRECIOUS ENTERPRISES AND EVERYTHING ELSE THIS HOLLOW MAN ADORES.
oh, BRUCE. IF ONLY I COULD DIVULGE MY TRUE FACE TO YOU.
HOW SHOCKED YOU WOULD BE TO LEARN THAT I'M ACTUALLY SOMEONE YOU KNOW QUITE WELL... SOMEONE WHO'S BEEN CLOSE TO YOU FOR YEARS.
SADLY, REVEALING MY IDENTITY WILL HAVE TO WAIT FOR THE MOMENT I FINALLY KILL YOU WITH MY OWN BARE HANDS.
BUT DON'T FEAR, THAT DAY IS COMING SOON...
THE BEGINNING!

READ MORE OF THE DARK KNIGHT DETECTIVE'S ADVENTURES IN THESE COLLECTIONS FROM DC COMICS:

BATMAN

BATMAN
HUSH
JEPH LOEB
JIM LEE
SCOTT WILLIAMS
VOLUME ONE

BATMAN: HUSH VOLUME 1

Jeph Loeb, Jim Lee and **Scott Williams** tell an epic tale of friendship, trust and betrayal, in the first volume of a tale that spans a lifetime of the Dark Knight.

"THE ACTION IS EXCITING AND THE DETAIL IS METICULOUS."
— CRITIQUES ON INFINITE EARTHS

BATMAN:
THE DARK KNIGHT RETURNS

BATMAN: THE DARK KNIGHT RETURNS
FRANK MILLER
with KLAUS JANSON and LYNN VARLEY

FRANK MILLER
KLAUS JANSON
LYNN VARLEY

BATMAN:
THE LONG HALLOWEEN

From the Eisner Award-winning creators
JEPH LOEB TIM SALE
BATMAN
THE LONG HALLOWEEN

JEPH LOEB
TIM SALE

BATMAN:
YEAR ONE

YEAR ONE
FRANK MILLER
DAVID MAZZUCCHELLI

FRANK MILLER
DAVID MAZZUCCHELLI

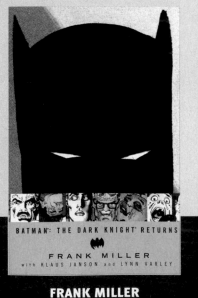

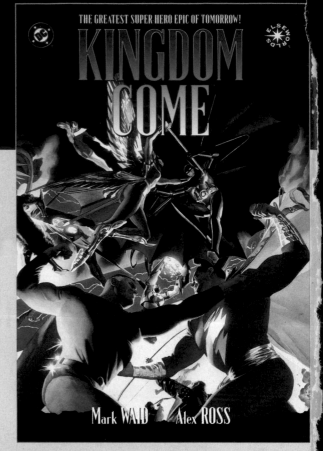